Master Data Management and Customer Data Integration for a Global Enterprise

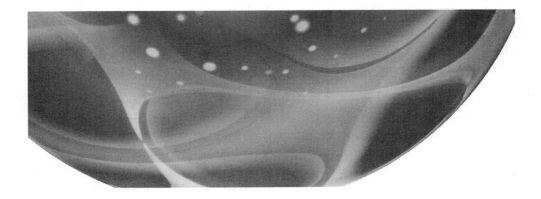

About the Authors

Alex Berson is an internationally recognized expert, author, and educator in various areas of information technologies. Throughout his professional career, Alex Berson has held key technology and management positions in several major corporations including BearingPoint Inc., Merrill Lynch, Entrust, enCommerce, Dun & Bradstreet, PricewaterhouseCoopers, Solomon Smith Barney, and others.

Mr. Berson holds graduate and postgraduate degrees in Computer Sciences and Applied Math, and focuses his professional activities on Identity Management; Information Security, Risk and Compliance; Master Data Management (MDM), Customer Data Integration (CDI), and Customer Relationship Management (CRM); data warehousing and data mining; Web Services, service-oriented architectures; and middleware and enterprise application integration.

Mr. Berson is a member of Standard & Poor's Vista Research Society of Industrial Leaders (SIL). He is also an active member of professional associations in the industry, such as the IEEE Computer Society, ACM, and Aberdeen Group's Technology Forecasting Consortium; standards organizations including OASIS, OMG, and Open Group; and various industry consortia including Securities Industry Middleware Council (SIMC) and the Data Warehousing Institute. Alex Berson sits on the advisory boards of several technology and financial services companies. He has published numerous technical articles and direction-setting white papers in trade magazines. He is the author of a number of best-selling professional books including *Building Data Mining Applications for CRM, Data Warehousing, Data Mining and OLAP*; *Client/Server Architecture*; *SYBASE and Client/Server Computing*; and *APPC: Introduction to LU6.2*.

Larry Dubov is a recognized expert and thought leader in the implementation of complex business-driven technology solutions for financial services, banking and pharmaceutical verticals with the primary focus on Customer Data Integration (CDI), Master Data Management (MDM), Customer Relationship Management (CRM), data warehousing, and operational data stores. He has gained both depth and breadth of technical knowledge in multiple areas of Customer Data Integration and Master Data Management including data and solution architecture, customer recognition, customer-centric data transformations, data stewardship, and information quality. He has developed a strong holistic vision of the CDI problem domain and CDI implementation methodology based on practical experience gained through successful project implementations. He is a recognized speaker on the topic of Master Data Management and has participated in a number of MDM-CDI conferences.

Larry has held senior technology and management positions with consulting companies BearingPoint and FutureNext ZYGA. Larry formerly worked as an independent consultant for a number of companies across various industry verticals.

The list of Larry's clients includes Fortune 1000 companies and established mid-size organizations: Merrill Lynch, Bessemer Trust, Washington Mutual, Cenlar Bank, Merck, Johnson & Johnson, Hoffmann La Roche, Aventis, Estée Lauder, AT&T, and Daimler-Benz.

Larry spent two years at Princeton University as a visiting research scientist working on mathematical models for optimal control of molecular processes. Earlier, during his career in Russia he gained a strong scientific background with Ph.D. and Dr.Sci. degrees in Mathematical Physics. Larry is the author of over 70 publications.

A combination of multiple backgrounds—science (physics, chemistry, and advanced math), deep knowledge of Information Technology, and understanding of business processes—helps Larry see unique approaches to complex business problems and offer their solutions.

About the Technical Editors

Joe Bower has over 30 years experience in business management and systems development. As a seasoned line manager, Joe was responsible for managing various operational units. In most instances, each position found Joe involved in application development.

As both a manager and a consultant, Joe works in regulated industries that include telecommunications, pharmaceutical, and finance. For various employers and client companies, Joe has authored over 400 business manuals.

Joe's background in information security spans 14 years. He routinely manages security policies and standards, information security programs, information security project management, selective vendor relationships, compliance, and reporting. Joe obtained the Certified Information Security Manager (CISM) certification in 2005.

Bernard K. Plagman is cofounder and Chairman of TechPar Group (TPG), a technology advisory services company that consults on all facets of the Information Technology (IT) industry. TPG focuses on delivering strategic and tactical advisory services to technology investors, technology vendors, and technology users.

Charles Popper is cofounder and CEO of TechPar Group (TPG), a technology advisory services company that consults on all facets of the Information Technology (IT) industry. TPG focuses on delivering strategic and tactical advisory services to technology investors, technology vendors, and technology users. In its first four-plus years, TPG has grown from three partners to a team of more than 50 consultants, delivering services to 100 clients.

Prior to founding TPG, Dr. Popper was Vice Chairman and Chief Technologist for Orama Partners, a boutique investment bank servicing and investing in high-tech start-ups, with a strong focus on Israeli companies. Previously, he was

Vice President of Corporate Computer Resources and CIO at Merck & Co., Inc. from October, 1991 until January, 1999. He was responsible for all areas of computer and telecommunications technology at Merck, including application development, technical support, and operations. The scope of his responsibility was worldwide and included support for all segments of the company: research, manufacturing, marketing, and corporate administration. He was responsible for an annual operating budget of about $400M, in addition to a capital budget of about $100M. Dr. Popper served as a member of a number of business leadership groups, such as the Manufacturing Management Council, the HR Strategy Team, and the Worldwide Cholesterol Business Management Team; he was a regular participant in other senior leadership councils.

Before joining Merck in October, 1991, Dr. Popper was a partner in the management consulting practice of Deloitte & Touche. He has worked as a mathematician for the National Security Agency, a research scientist at Bell Laboratories, Director of Advanced Technology for American Express, and Vice President of Advanced Technology at Lehman Brothers Kuhn Loeb.

Dr. Popper received his B.A. (Magna Cum Laude, Phi Beta Kappa) and Ph.D. degrees from Harvard in Applied Mathematics and Computer Science. Two of his papers have been published by the Harvard Program on Information Resource Policy: "A Holistic Framework for IT Governance," and "Achieving Software System Quality Via a Comprehensive Approach to Testing and Validation."

Paul Raskas has 30+ years of Fortune 500 consulting experience, including working as a senior executive at IBM and working as an independent consultant. His work addresses applications solutions across a number of industries, such as financial services, pharmaceutical, telecom, and utilities, focusing on data architecture, integration, and quality and business intelligence solutions.

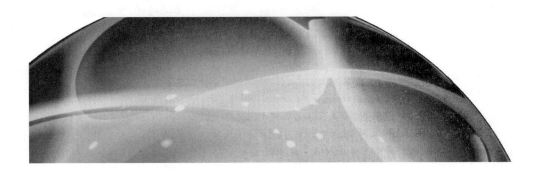

Master Data Management and Customer Data Integration for a Global Enterprise

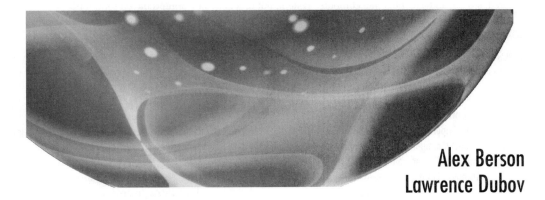

Alex Berson
Lawrence Dubov

New York   Chicago   San Francisco
Lisbon   London   Madrid   Mexico City Milan
New Delhi   San Juan Seoul   Singapore   Sydney   Toronto

The McGraw·Hill Companies

Library of Congress Cataloging-in-Publication Data

Berson, Alex.
    Master data management and customer data integration for a global
enterprise / Alex Berson, Lawrence Dubov.
       p.   cm.
    ISBN 0-07-226349-0 (alk. paper)
    1. Customer relations—Data processing.   2. Data warehousing.
I. Dubov, Lawrence.   II. Title.
HF5415.5.B4835   2007
658.8'120285574—dc22

                        2007017816

Master Data Management and Customer Data Integration for a Global Enterprise

234567890 DOC DOC 01987

ISBN-13: 978-0-07-226349-7
ISBN-10: 0-07-226349-0

Sponsoring Editor	Lisa McClain	**Indexer**	Kevin Broccoli
Editorial Supervisor	Patty Mon	**Production Supervisor**	Jean Bodeaux
Project Manager	Madhu Bhardwaj	**Composition**	International
Acquisitions Coordinator	Mandy Canales		Typesetting and
Technical Editors	Joe Bower		Composition
	Charles Popper	**Illustration**	International
	Bernard K. Plagman		Typesetting and
	Paul Raskas		Composition
Copy Editor	Margaret Berson	**Art Director, Cover**	Jeff Weeks
Proofreader	Upendra Prasad	**Cover Designer**	Pattie Lee

To Irina, Vlad, Michelle, Tara, and Colin Alexander
—Alex Berson

To Irene, Anthony, Stacy, and my mother and father
—Larry Dubov

Contents

Foreword . . . . *xvii*

Acknowledgments . . . . *xix*

Introduction . . . . *xxi*

Part I **Introduction to Master Data Management and Customer Data Integration**

Chapter 1 **Overview of Master Data Management and Customer Data Integration** **5**

Master Data Management (MDM) 6

    Why Master Data Management Now? 6

    Challenges of Creating and Managing Master Data 8

    Defining Master Data Management 11

Customer Data Integration (CDI) 13

    Evolution of CDI 16

Key Benefits of Master Data Management and Customer Data Integration 18

Chapter 2 **CDI: Overview of Market Drivers and Key Challenges** **21**

The Business View 22

    CDI as a Vehicle for Competitive Advantage 22

Industry Views of CDI 29

    What Most CDI Implementation Approaches Have in Common 29

    Commercial Marketplace: Domain-Specific CDI Features 31

    Public Sector: Domain-Specific CDI Features 35

Geographic Views: CDI Goes Global 36

Chapter 3 **Challenges, Concerns, and Risks of Moving Toward Customer Centricity** **39**

Business Challenges in Moving Toward Customer Centricity 40

    Senior Management Commitment and Value Proposition 40

    Business Drivers 41

Customer Centricity and a 360-Degree View of a Customer 43
Challenges of Selling CDI Inside the Enterprise 44
Technical Challenges in Moving Toward Customer Centricity 47
Implementation Costs and Time-to-Market Concerns 48
Data Quality, Data Synchronization, and Integration Challenges 50
Data Visibility, Security, and Regulatory Compliance 52

Part II **Architectural Considerations**

Chapter 4 **CDI Architecture and Data Hub Components** **59**
Architectural Definition of Master Data Management and Customer Data Integration 60
Evolution of Customer Data Integration Architecture 61
CDI Architectural Philosophy 65
Enterprise Architecture Framework: A Brief Introduction 66
CDI Architecture Viewpoints 69
Services Architecture View 70
Consumption and Reconciliation Viewpoint 76
Reference Architecture Viewpoint 79

Chapter 5 **Architecting for Customer Data Integration** **83**
Emerging Architecture Concerns of MDM-CDI Solutions 84
CDI and Customer Relationships 84
CDI and Party Data Model 88
What Is Required to Create and Maintain the MDM-CDI Platform? 90
CDI Solution as Service-Oriented Architecture Platform 92
Identity Recognition, Matching, and Generation of Unique Party Identifiers 95
Matching and Linking Services 95
Aggregating Customer Information 100
Data Hub Keys and Management Services 101
Key Management and Key Generation Service 102
Record Locator Services 104

Chapter 6 **Data Management Concerns of MDM-CDI Architecture** **107**
Data Strategy 108
Data Governance 109
Data Quality 112

Managing Data in the Data Hub   115
    Data Zone Architecture Approach   116
    Loading Data into the Data Hub   121
    Data Synchronization   123
    Data Delivery and Metadata Concerns   127
    Enterprise Information Integration and Integrated Data Views   130

Part III   **Data Security, Privacy, and Regulatory Compliance**

Chapter 7   **Overview of Risk Management**
                for Integrated Customer Information **135**
Risk Taxonomy   136
Regulatory Compliance Landscape   139
    Integrated Risk Management: Benefits and Challenges   140
Emerging Regulatory Compliance Requirements
    and Their Impact on MDM IT Infrastructure   142
    The Sarbanes-Oxley Act   144
    Gramm-Leach-Bliley Act Data Protection Provisions   146
    Other Regulatory/Compliance Requirements   148
Key Information Security Risks and Regulatory Concerns   153
    Identity Theft   153
    GLBA, FCRA, Privacy, and Opt-Out   154
Key Technical Implications of Data Security and Privacy Regulations
    on MDM Architecture   155

Chapter 8   **Introduction to Information Security and Identity Management** **157**
Traditional and Emerging Concerns of Information Security   158
    What Do We Need to Secure?   158
    End-to-End Security Framework   161
    Traditional Security Requirements   162
    Emerging Security Requirements   164
Overview of Security Technologies   169
    Confidentiality and Integrity   169
    Network and Perimeter Security Technologies   172
    Application, Data, and User Security   175
Integrating Authentication and Authorization   178
    SSO Technologies   179

Web Services Security Concerns 179
    Authentication 179
    Data Integrity and Confidentiality 179
    Attacks 180
    WS-Security Standard 180
Putting It All Together 181

Chapter 9   **Protecting Content for Secure Master Data Management** **183**
Data Security Evolution 184
    Emerging Information Security Threats 185
    Regulatory Drivers for Data Protection 187
    Risks of Data Compromise 188
Data Security Overview 189
    Layered Security Framework 190
    Data-In-Transit Security Considerations 192
    Data-at-Rest Protection 193
Enterprise Rights Management 196
    ERM Processes and MDM Technical Requirements 199
    ERM Examples 200

Chapter 10   **Enterprise Security and Data Visibility in Master**
               Data Management Environments **203**
Access Control Basics 204
    Groups and Roles 205
    Roles-Based Access Control (RBAC) 207
Policies and Entitlements 210
    Entitlements Taxonomy 211
    Transactional Entitlements 213
Entitlements and Visibility 214
    Customer Data Integration Visibility Scenario 214
    Policies, Entitlements, and Standards 216
Integrating CDI Solutions with Enterprise Information Security 219
    Overview of Key Architecture Components for Policy Decision and Enforcement 220
    Integrated Conceptual Security and Visibility Architecture 221

Part IV   **Implementing Customer Data Integration for the Enterprise**

Chapter 11   **Project Initiation** **231**
Implementation Begins 232

Scope Definition 237
    Business Processes 238
    Lines of Business and Functions 238
    Customer Touch Points, Product Types, and Account Types 239
    Levels of Aggregation and Relationship Types 239
    Entities and Attributes 240
    Systems and Applications in Scope 241
Customer Data Hub Solution Architecture 241
    Data Hub Architecture Styles 241
    Phased Implementation of Customer Data Hub 246
    Artifacts That Should Be Produced in the Project Initiation Phase 246
Project Work Streams 247

Chapter 12   **Customer Identification** **249**
A 360-Degree View of a Customer: Frequently Used Terms and Definitions 251
    Reasons for False Positives 252
    Reasons for False Negatives 253
Attributes and Attribute Categories Commonly Used for Matching
   and Customer Identification 254
    Identity Attributes 254
    Discrimination Attributes 256
    Record Qualification Attributes 258
Customer Identification, Matching Process, and Models 261
    Minimum Data Requirements 261
    Matching Modes 261
    Defining Matching Rules for Customer Records 263
    Effect of Chaining 266
    Break Groups and Performance Considerations 268
    Similarity Libraries and Fuzzy Logic for Attribute Comparisons 270
Summary of Data-Matching Requirements and Solutions 271

Chapter 13   **Beyond Party Match: Merge, Split, Party Groups,**
               and Relationships **275**
Merge and Split 276
    Merge 276
    Split 278
Relationships and Groups 279
    Direct Business Relationships with an Individual 280
    Households and Family Groups 282

Customer Groups 283
Relationships Between Institutional Customers and Individuals 284
Relationships Between Institutional Customers 285
Need for Persistent Match Group Identifier 287
Additional Considerations for Customer Identifiers 288

Chapter 14   Data Governance, Standards, Information Quality, and Validation **291**
Overview of Data Governance, Standards, and Information Quality 292
Information Quality 297
Information Quality in Master Data Management vs. Data Warehousing 297
Information Quality Loop and Interaction with the Match Process 299
Data Validation 302

Chapter 15   Data Synchronization **309**
Goals of Data Synchronization 310
Technology Approach to Use Case Realization 310
Identity Hub with Multiple Points of Entry for Customer Information 311
Considerations for the Transaction Hub Master Model 315
Batch Processing 319
Other Considerations 323

Chapter 16   Additional Implementation Considerations **327**
Considerations on the CDI Presentation Layer 328
Customer-Centric Applications 328
Reporting 329
Administrative Applications 329
Testing Considerations 330
Testing of CDI Data and Services 330
Match Group Testing 336
Creation and Protection of Test Data 337
Additional Technical and Operational Concerns 339
Environment and Infrastructure Considerations 339
Deployment 341
Considerations for the CDI Data Hub Data Model and Services 342

Part V   **Master Data Management: Markets, Trends, and Directions**

Chapter 17   **MDM-CDI Vendors and Products Landscape** **347**

Data Hub Products   350
     IBM WCC   350
     Siperian   351
     Initiate Systems   352
     Siebel/Oracle   352
     Oracle   353
     Purisma   353
     Sun Microsystems   354
     GoldenSource   354
     SAP   355
     DataFlux Data Hub Product   355
     VisionWare MultiVue   356
     ObjectRiver   356

Information Quality Products   357
     Business Objects (First Logic)   357
     Trillium   358
     DataFlux Information Quality Product   358
     IBM Product Suite   359
     Group 1 Software   359
     Informatica   360
     Innovative Systems   361

Data Providers   361
     Acxiom   361
     Dun and Bradstreet   362
     Experian   363

Delivery Accelerators   364
     DataDelta   364
     Netrics   364
     Identity Systems   365
     Exeros   365

Chapter 18   **Where Do We Go from Here?** **367**

Master Data Management and Customer Data Integration Today   368

Main Reasons CDI Projects Fail   370

Master Data Management and Customer Data Integration: Trends and Directions   373

Appendix A   **List of Acronyms** **377**

Appendix B   **Glossary** **381**

Appendix C   **Regulations and Compliance Rules Impacting Master Data Management and Customer Data Integration Projects** **389**

Regulations and Guidelines   390

Representative Regulatory Bodies   392

Index **393**

Foreword

Finally we have the book! One that is from seasoned practitioners who are destined to stay on the cutting edge of deploying enterprise Master Data Management (MDM) solutions.

While the web has greatly enabled our intergalactic research capabilities (in addition to the SOHO restructuring of corporate America, globally distributed workforces, etc.), at the same time it has destroyed our abilities to gather information for making savvy business decisions because it has flooded us with data. In this new state of "data affluenza," we all need navigators to assist us in collecting, compiling, and correlating relevant information that will enable us to create a competitive advantage in the new global economy.

As chief research officer of The CDI-MDM Institute, I am directly involved with Global 5000 companies and their race to gain a leading edge via MDM and its siblings, customer data integration and data governance. Clearly, enterprise MDM will redefine competitive advantage via a new acme of customer loyalty as the main driver for customer profitability. For example, numerous financial services providers and telcos still tragically suffer from their myopic focus on accounts or product lines, which results in an inability to have a panoramic customer view.

The corporate evolution from account- or product-centricity to customer-centricity opens up a new IT solutions market[1] for not only a next-generation software platform and requisite systems integration services but also a completely new level of process analysis consultation regarding relationship hierarchies, data governance, etc.

Although established in the Global 5000-size enterprises to some degree, enterprise MDM solutions are still an emerging area. Clearly, Master Data Management, especially customer MDM, is not easy. When the seasoned veterans and true thought leaders at last take up the pen, we know that the market has gone mainstream and is no longer an early adopter.

At this point, the potential reader should not need any more encouragement to read this book by two of the most experienced practitioners I know of. Alex Berson and Larry Dubov started working on CDI engagements before our industry had yet

---

[1] US \$2 billion in software and services by 2010 per the CDI-MDM Institute annual MarketPulse report.

rallied around the term "customer data integration." Not only is such early-adopter experience and knowledge extremely valuable to others undertaking such MDM journeys, but it also puts tremendous pressure on such thought leaders to keep pace with the volatile technology mix that comprises an MDM ecosystem (we are already looking forward to the next edition). Fortunately, as such thought leaders, they are called upon repeatedly to sharpen their insight into the "why" and "how" of these initiatives. My team of research analysts and their Global 5000 IT clients dearly value the knowledge and skills that experienced systems integrators such as Alex and Larry bring to any CDI or MDM endeavor.

—Aaron Zornes,
Chief Research Officer,
The CDI-MDM Institute,
San Francisco,
and Conference Chairman,
CDI-MDM SUMMIT

Acknowledgments

First, I want to thank my coauthor Larry Dubov for his knowledge, persistence, and dedication, without which this book would not have happened. I also want to thank Aaron Zornes, Founder and Chief Research Officer of The CDI-MDM Institute, for his support and help.

Very special thanks to my many friends and colleagues at BearingPoint including Ramesh Nair, Chris Format, Christopher Hamilton, Hyong Kim, Kris Bryant, Paul Dunay, Manuel Barbero, Peter Horowitz, Scott Claus, and many others for their continuous support and for giving me an opportunity to learn and work in a very stimulating and challenging environment on the leading edge of information technology.

I truly appreciate the opportunity to work with my friends and colleagues Bernie Plagman and Charles Popper at TechPar Group, and to learn from their wisdom and lifelong experiences.

I also would like to express gratitude and appreciation to my numerous friends and colleagues at IBM, Merrill Lynch, Entrust, CitiGroup, The CDI-MDM Institute, and many other organizations who inspired me to write this book and helped with their knowledge, vision, optimism, perseverance, and invaluable insights. I want to specifically thank Guy Pujol, Gafar Lawal, Harish Ragavan, Mark Albin, Alberto Yepez, Peter Meekin, David Ketsdever, Kurt Gilman, Shanker Ramamurthy, Joe Hollander, George Anderson, Larry Caminiti, and Anatoly Kissen.

I would like to thank all those who have helped me with clarifications, criticism, and valuable information during the writing of this book, and were patient enough to read the entire manuscript and make many useful suggestions. Special thanks and gratitude go to Bernie Plagman, Charles Popper, Paul Raskas, and Joe Bower for their insightful edits.

And, of course, we would have never finished this book without the invaluable assistance and thoroughness of McGraw-Hill's Lisa McClain, Mandy Canales, Patty Mon, and Margaret Berson, and the great team from International Typesetting and Composition led by Madhu Bhardwaj.

Finally, the key reason for writing this book is my family. My very special thanks to my wife, Irina, my son Vlad and his wife Tara, my daughter Michelle, my new grandson Colin Alexander (who became an added inspiration for writing this book), my mother, and my mother- and father-in-law for giving me time to complete the book and never-ending optimism, support and love, and for understanding the book's importance.

—Alex Berson

I am grateful to my coauthor Alex Berson for the idea of writing this book and bringing me on board. It was a great pleasure working with Alex on summarizing our experiences, formulating the ideas, and reconciling our views. The views, sometimes different on the surface, were usually very similar when discussions were taken to the right depth. This work and discussions with Alex helped me a lot in deepening, summarizing, and systematizing my knowledge in Customer Data Integration and Master Data Management.

I am thankful to Aaron Zornes, the Founder and Chief Research Officer of The CDI-MDM Institute, for his support and discussions.

I highly appreciate the work done by the technical editors of this book, Paul Raskas, Charles Popper, Bernard Plagman, and Joe Bower, for their great comments and suggestions, which helped us improve the readability and overall quality of this book. I would like to express my special gratitude to my friend and colleague Paul Raskas for helpful discussions on CDI-related topics and for partnership on a number of projects.

My knowledge of the Master Data Management and Customer Data Integration space comes mainly from practical project implementations. Therefore, many people who worked on CDI projects with me contributed indirectly to this book. I am thankful to my colleagues and friends at BearingPoint, particularly Ramesh Nair, Peter Horowitz, Manuel Barbero, Hyong Kim, Ari Marcus, Ajay Nayar, Sandy Grigsby, Greg Sarafin, Bill Sommers, Kathy Garrett, Pete Anuchitworawong, Balu Ramachandran, Amar Talamanchi, Arun Sarathy, Bill Wysocki, Sridhar Dronamraju, Frank Bakka, William Poon; colleagues I used to work with at Merrill Lynch: Guy Pujol, Gafar Lawal, Helen Stein, Pushkar Bapat, Jim McGovern, John Stevens, Dan Magno, Harish Ragavan, and Sankara Mutnuru; and Bessemer Trust: Hugh Bagatelle, Peter Packard, Rich Toomey, Anna Aronov, and Hoshi Merchant.

I highly appreciate the work performed by the teams that helped us with book edits and bringing the book to production, McGraw-Hill: Lisa McClain, Mandy Canales, Patty Mon, David Zielonka, and Margaret Berson; International Typesetting and Composition: Madhu Bhardwaj.

I am very thankful to my wife Irene, my son Anthony, and my daughter Anastasia for their encouragement and patience since this book took a lot of my time from the family. Indeed the book was written over the weekends and on vacation. I am also grateful to my mother and mother-in-law, and my sister Julia and her family for encouragement and their interest in this book.

—Larry Dubov

Introduction

About This Book

This book is about interesting and exciting new developments in the area of information management. These developments are focused on new ways of structuring, choosing, understanding, and integrating information that is needed to run a business, service customers, and comply with numerous regulatory requirements.

To paraphrase Claude Shannon, the "father" of information theory and the concepts of information entropy, information is that which resolves uncertainty. Our entire existence is a process of gathering, analyzing, understanding, and acting on information. Progressive resolution of uncertainty is the key to the way we make business and personal decisions. The need to sustain new regulatory pressures and achieve competitive advantages by managing customer-level profitability and risk-adjusted return on investment drives profound changes in the way business and government organizations operate. Traditional account-centric and application-specific silos of business processes restrict organizations' ability to meet the aforementioned challenge. Therefore, in order to succeed in today's highly competitive global and dynamic markets, businesses are making serious investments in the new customer-centric processes and technical capabilities. These new capabilities should allow organizations to effectively select, acquire, understand, and manage accurate and relevant information about customers, products, partners, patients, inventories, prices, and other areas of business concerns.

In doing so, enterprises are collecting and processing ever-increasing volumes of information, especially as business conditions change, markets shrink or expand, companies grow organically or by acquisitions, and customer retention becomes one of the key business metrics.

As we entered the digital age, this accumulation of data has been accelerating. Now we have access to the ocean of information that was created by or stored in computer systems and networks over the last several years. In addition, we also brought with us data that previously existed only in nondigital form, such as books and paper documents. We have learned to digitize that data quickly and efficiently, and thus created even more computer files and databases, all the time hoping that all this "stuff" will be managed transparently and effectively by our reliable, trusted computer systems and applications. The reasons for engaging in this data collection are obvious: We live in the new age of digital information where the Internet and the World Wide Web have made enterprise boundaries porous or fuzzy in order to attract a large number of customers and to enhance their experience. In this new digital age, an agile enterprise can become competitive only when it has access to more relevant, accurate, timely, and complete data about business conditions and performance metrics, enterprise customers, prospects and partners, products and markets, and a myriad of other things. Having the right data at the right time is even more imperative if you consider the challenges and the revolutionary nature of transforming a traditional account-centric business into a customer-centric, global, agile, and intelligent enterprise.

Given the ever-growing amount of data that is collected and managed by the business units of global enterprises today, we are facing the difficult challenge of creating, finding, selecting, and managing data that is complete, accurate, relevant, and secure, and that is uniformly available to all businesses and users who need this data to run the business. This challenge of creating and managing a new authoritative system of record is the focus of Master Data Management (MDM). The issues, approaches, concerns, and applications of Master Data Management and its customer-focused version known as Customer Data Integration (CDI) are the subject of this book.

Who Should Read This Book

The topics of Master Data Management and Customer Data Integration have very broad applicability across all industries. Indeed, the notion of transforming business from account-centric to customer-centric enterprise applies equally well to any industry segment that deals with customers, including financial services, health care, pharmaceutical, telecommunications, retail, etc. We can make similar arguments for areas that need an authoritative source of product information, pricing and market data, and reference data in general. The same logic applies to government entities that need to have a complete and accurate view of individuals for a variety of legitimate purposes, not the least of which are law enforcement and national security.

To discuss major issues related to Master Data Management and Customer Data Integration, the book covers a broad set of topics including the areas of business transformations, data management, information security, regulatory compliance, and business process redesign. Therefore, this book is a must-read for a variety of business and technology professionals across all industry segments and the public sector. The audience for this book includes business unit managers; business process analysts and designers; technology project managers; infrastructure and operations staff; data analysts, data stewards, data quality managers, and database administrators; application developers; corporate strategists; information security specialists; corporate risk and regulatory compliance officers; and members of the offices of the CFO, CSO, CRO, and CIO.

Due to the complexity of the MDM-CDI problem space, many Master Data Management and Customer Data Integration initiatives happen to be multiyear, multimillion dollar projects that involve large teams of employees, external consultants, system integrators, and vendor-supplied professional services organizations. All these professionals will benefit from reading this book.

Finally, the topics of MDM and CDI are getting "hot" and attracting significant attention from the general and specialized industry analysts. All major industry research and analyst organizations including the Gartner Group and Forrester Research have initiated appropriate coverage or created research services focusing on Master Data Management and Customer Data Integration. Many vendors that have or plan to have MDM-CDI solutions in their portfolios are organizing user groups and vendor-sponsored conferences. Dedicated organizations such as The CDI-MDM Institute have leaped into existence and are aggressively organizing industry-wide forums and conferences. Technical and business professionals who plan to attend these types of conferences would find this book very useful.

The Style of This Book

This book is different from research and analysts' reports on the subject of MDM and CDI in that it does not base its discussion strictly on industry-wide surveys and published statistics. Rather, the book is based on the actual professional experience of the authors who continue to be involved in some of the more advanced and large-scale implementations of MDM and CDI in the commercial sector, especially in financial services and pharmaceuticals. The book has been structured as a self-teaching guide that includes an introduction to the business problem domain related to MDM and CDI, and a discussion on the core architecture principles and concerns that should be interesting to those readers looking to learn not just the "how" but also the "why" of the MDM and CDI architecture choices.

The book includes a rather detailed discussion of the issues related to information security and data protection in MDM and CDI environments. The authors feel very strongly that MDM and CDI designers and implementers should address these topics at the inception of every MDM-CDI initiative, whether or not a chosen vendor solution provides these capabilities directly or indirectly.

In addition to being an architectural primer for MDM and CDI, the book is also a practical implementation guide that can help MDM-CDI practitioners to avoid costly technical, business process, and organizational mistakes. To that end, the book includes several chapters that provide a step-by-step discussion of the practical issues and concerns relating to the implementation approaches of MDM and CDI projects.

And for those readers who are looking to select a vendor solution, the book offers a brief overview of the state of the art in the vendor solution marketplace for MDM and CDI.

The book concludes with a few thoughts about the trends and directions in the area of Master Data Management and Customer Data Integration.

The book includes a fair amount of diagrams, figures, examples, and illustrations in an attempt to present a lot of rather complicated material in as simple form as possible. Due to the high degree of complexity of MDM-CDI, wherever possible, the book combines theoretical and architectural discussion of a specific subject with some practical examples of how these issues could be addressed in real-life implementations.

The book is about a "hot" new but very dynamic subject. All material included in the book was current at the time the book was written. The authors realize that as Master Data Management and Customer Data Integration continue to evolve, and as the MDM-CDI vendor solutions mature, changes to the material covered in the book will be necessary. The authors intend to revise the book if and when significant developments in the areas of Master Data Management and Customer Data Integration warrant changes.

What This Book Includes

The book contains five parts and three appendixes. Part I of the book defines the business imperative, drivers, and benefits of Master Data Management and Customer Data Integration. It also discusses the challenges and risks associated with transforming an account-centric business to a customer-centric enterprise.

Part II of the book continues the MDM-CDI discussion by taking a closer look at the architecture and design concerns of MDM-CDI solutions, with a strong emphasis on the design issues of CDI Data Hub platforms. Part II offers an architecture backgrounder that introduces readers to several key concepts including the enterprise architecture framework and service-oriented architecture.

Part III deals with major regulations, compliance requirements, and risks associated with implementing MDM-CDI solutions. This part offers detailed discussion on general information security goals, techniques, and approaches. It concentrates on several important themes including general data protection, intellectual property, and content protection using Enterprise Rights Management. This part of the book also provides an in-depth look at authentication, authorization, access control, policies, entitlements, and data visibility issues that have to be addressed in practically every MDM-CDI implementation.

Part IV of the book discusses a broad set of issues, concerns, and practical approaches to implement an MDM-CDI solution. Part IV specifically talks about how to start a successful CDI project. It provides an in-depth discussion on the implementation aspects of customer identification and processes designed to discover and leverage the totality of customer relationships with the enterprise. This part of the book also discusses implementation concerns related to data synchronization, data quality, data governance, and data management standards.

Part V of the book concludes with a brief discussion of the market landscape and an overview of the relevant vendor solutions that were available on the market at the time of this writing. It also provides a brief discussion on future trends and directions for Master Data Management and Customer Data Integration.

The appendixes include a list of common abbreviations, a glossary, and a summary of relevant regulatory and compliance rules.

PART

I

Introduction to Master Data Management and Customer Data Integration

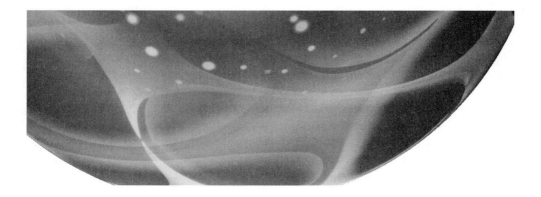

Our civilization has evolved into a modern society by continuously acquiring and developing new knowledge and creating innovative ways to improve personal and business conditions. This evolution in large part is based on our ability and ever-growing need to collect and understand data in order to run businesses, predict the weather, analyze market performance, manage personal finances, define medical diagnoses in order to prescribe proper medication, and in general, to do both mundane and new, exciting things.

Over the course of history, we have collected a huge amount of data, learned how to interpret it and transform it into useful, meaningful information, and even created a number of extremely sophisticated information theories and branches of information science. One interesting observation about the way we collect and use data is our reluctance to discard data that is either old or no longer relevant. For example, you may have a collection of old professional books and most of them have some value. You have to decide which books are redundant and need to be discarded and which books should still be retained because some chapters or sections are still valuable. You might also be thinking that it is a good idea to create a catalog of books with pointers to their locations. Otherwise you will not be able to find the book you want promptly when you need it. Other examples of data that we tend to collect and keep include items of family history and sentimental value such as photographs, letters from parents and grandparents, certificates of awards you received in school—things you want to keep for a variety of reasons, all of which make the data more valuable as time goes on. Of course, there are other types of information you may have to keep in order to comply with the law (such as income tax returns) or for personal protection (paid promissory notes or signed legal papers). Finally, some of us like to keep documents that are no longer valid and are replaced by newer, more accurate versions, for example, old resumes or outdated wills. Keeping this old "stuff" eventually becomes a storage problem, and this is when people move the boxes with old documents into their attics and basements. As the amount of data stored this way grows, the task of finding the right document stored somewhere in the attic becomes a challenge. This can become more than just an inconvenience: Storing outdated or inaccurate documents may have some interesting and even unpleasant consequences. For example, if there are two significantly different versions of a Last Will and Testament document, using the wrong version during the settlement may have drastically different consequences from those intended by the owner of the will. And of course, data is different from other "stuff"—you cannot have a garage sale to get rid of data you no longer need!

The business world has certainly experienced this dramatic data growth phenomenon as well. And this trend has become even more pronounced as we entered the digital age and now have access not only to the ocean of data naturally created by or stored in the computer systems, but also to data that previously existed only in a paper form but has been digitized to be managed by computer systems and applications. This data proliferation in the business world has not been driven only by traditional organizational structures and processes where various application areas and lines of business created and managed their own versions or view of the data. The Internet and the World Wide Web have made enterprise boundaries porous or fuzzy in order to attract large numbers of customers and to enhance the customers' experience. In this new digital age, an agile enterprise can become competitive only when it has access to more relevant, accurate, and complete information about business conditions and performance metrics, enterprise customers, prospects and partners, products and markets, and a myriad of other things. Given the ever-growing amount of data that is collected and managed by the business units of global enterprises today, we can draw an analogy similar to searching for old files in the attics and basements. Enterprises have a hard time creating, finding, and managing data that is complete, accurate, relevant, and is uniformly available to all businesses and users that need this data to run the business. In addition to the technical challenges of creating a master data facility, there are several organizational and political obstacles to cleaning existing data stores. A common example would be the individual business unit's desire to hold on to its version of data because it is deemed unique to the business unit's goals, or because it helps eliminate dependencies of data management across business units. Some of these reasons are perfectly valid, but they do not eliminate the need to have enterprise-wide, accurate, and complete business and customer information.

Master Data Management

The need to clean up the "old stuff" and create an accurate, timely, and complete set of data needed to manage and grow the business is the focus of Master Data Management (MDM).

The issues, approaches, concerns, and applications of Master Data Management (MDM) and its customer-data-focused variant, known as Customer Data Integration (CDI), are the subject of this book.

Overview of Master Data Management and Customer Data Integration

IN THIS CHAPTER

Master Data Management (MDM)

Customer Data Integration (CDI)

Key Benefits of Master Data Management and Customer Data Integration

Master Data Management (MDM)

It is often said that Master Data Management enables an enterprise to create and use a "single version of the truth." As such, Master Data Management applies to almost all industries and covers a broad category of corporate data. Banks, insurance companies and brokerage houses, service companies, hotels, airlines, car manufacturers, publishing houses, health care providers, telecommunication companies, retail businesses, high-technology organizations, manufacturing, energy providers, and law firms have at least one common need—the need to have access to complete, accurate, timely, and secure information about their respective businesses' financial and market performance, partners, customers, prospects, products, competitors, and other important business attributes. Similarly, this need to create and use accurate and complete information about individuals and organizational entities applies equally well to the government agencies. To put it another way, the scope of Master Data Management is very broad and may cover customer data, product data, supplier data, employee data, reference data, and other key types of data that should be used to consistently manage the entire enterprise in an integrated fashion. And the primary vehicle by which Master Data Management enables this consistent and integrated management of the business is the ability to create and maintain an accurate and timely authoritative "system of record" for a given subject domain. In the case of customer data, for example, Master Data Management can support various aspects of customer, partner, and prospect information, including customer profiles, accounts, buying preferences, service requests and complaints, contact information, and other important attributes. MDM strategy, architecture, and enabling technologies dealing with various aspects of customer data constitute what is known as Customer Data Integration (CDI). As a special type of MDM, Customer Data Integration enables enterprises to reach the often-elusive goal of creating a "single version of the truth about their customers." This single version of the truth is one of the requirements to support the fundamental transformation of an enterprise from an account-centric business to a new, effective, and agile customer-centric business—a transformation that has a profound impact on the way companies conduct business and interact with their customers.

Why Master Data Management Now?

Although the aspirations of MDM are not new, the interest in developing MDM solutions has recently become real enough to start major MDM-related initiatives across the wide spectrum of industries. This timing is not accidental, and is among several key reasons why implementing Master Data Management has become such a universal requirement for almost any business and any industry. Some of these reasons are driven by recently adapted and emerging regulations:

▶ **Regulatory compliance**   A number of well-publicized corporate scandals and class action shareholder lawsuits gave rise to new pieces of legislation and regulations such as the Sarbanes-Oxley Act, the Basel II Capital Accord, and numerous Securities and Exchange Commission (SEC) rulings, all of which were focused on companies' need and requirement to provide, use, and report accurate, verifiable, and relevant data about their financial performance and significant material events that could impact company valuations and the shareholder value.

▶ **Privacy and data protection**   In addition to the overarching reporting regulations such as the Sarbanes-Oxley Act, companies have to comply with a multitude of local, state, federal, and international regulations focused on various aspects related to protecting enterprise data from unauthorized access, use, and compromise; on capturing and enforcing customer privacy preferences; and on protecting customer data from the malicious use and fastest-growing white collar crime—identity theft. Regulations such as the Gramm-Leach-Bliley Act, the Health Insurance Portability and Accountability Act (HIPAA), and state regulations such as California's SB1386 require that companies implement effective and verifiable security controls designed to protect data, ensure data integrity, and provide appropriate notification in case of the security breach resulting in data privacy and integrity compromise.

▶ **Safety and security**   The increased volume and global reach of money-laundering activity, the events of September 11, 2001, and growing appreciation of the terrorist threats gave rise to regulations such as USA Patriot Act with its Anti-Money Laundering (AML) and Know Your Customer (KYC) provisions. These regulations not only require an enterprise to maintain accurate and timely data on its customers and their financial transactions, but also to manage this data in such a way that it can be analyzed to detect and prevent money-laundering or other fraudulent activities before these transactions can take place.

These regulations require that an organization maintain integrity, security, accuracy, timeliness, and proper controls over the content and usage of corporate and customer data—in effect, this is the requirement to implement Master Data Management for any data subject area that needs to be in compliance with key oversight tenets of Sarbanes-Oxley, Basel II, Gramm-Leach-Bliley, and others.

In addition to the nondiscretionary requirements of regulatory compliance, the need for Master Data Management can be easily traced to more traditional drivers such as Customer Service and Customer Experience Management, in particular:

▶ Having an accurate "single version of the truth" allows an organization to understand the factors and trends that may affect the business.

▶ Having a single master data set allows an organization to reduce costs by sunsetting and discontinuing old application systems that create and use various "local" versions of the data.

▶ Having accurate and complete data about customers and their interactions with the enterprise allows an organization to gain better insight into the customer's goals, demands, ability, and propensity to request additional products and services, thus increasing the cross-sell and up-sell revenue opportunities

▶ Having a complete picture of the customer allows an enterprise to offer a rich set of personalized services and appropriate treatments—the factors leading to improved customer experience and reduced customer attrition.

These traditional drivers apply to several types of Master Data Management but are especially relevant to Customer Data Integration, discussed later in the chapter.

Challenges of Creating and Managing Master Data

Understanding the reasons for embarking on a Master Data Management initiative does not make it easier to accomplish the goals of MDM. There are some significant challenges that have to be overcome in order to make Master Data Management a reality. As the term "Master Data Management" implies, one of these challenges is centered on how to make data under management a "golden," authoritative version known as the "master."

Master Data

Master data can be defined as the data that has been cleansed, rationalized, and integrated into an enterprise-wide "system of record" for core business activities.

For example, in the case of building Customer Relationship Management (CRM) solutions across sales, marketing, and customer service channels, master data may consist of customer personal information (e.g., name, address, tax identification number), their assets and account numbers, service/warranty records, and history of service or product complaints. In the health care industry, master data may include not only customer personal information but also some diagnostic and prescription data, data on health care providers such as doctors and hospitals, health insurance information, and similar data points. In the consumer retail business master data may include information on products, product codes, suppliers, contracts, stores, sales, inventory levels, current and planned sales promotions, etc. Even within the organization, master data varies from one business unit to another. For example, the scope of the master data subset for the accounting department within a retail enterprise may include information on budgets, cost centers, department codes, company hierarchies, invoices, accounts payable, and accounts receivables. Of course, in this case, the goal of Master Data Management would be to eventually integrate various subsets of department-level master data into an integrated enterprise-wide master data superset.

Whether it is about customers, products, partners, or invoices, having relevant information in the form of master data allows businesses to capture key performance indicators, analyze all business transactions, and measure results to increase business effectiveness and competitiveness.

In order to create this domain-specific, complete, accurate, and integrated master data, an organization needs to develop and institutionalize processes that help discover and resolve inconsistencies, incompleteness, and other data quality issues caused in significant part by the way the established enterprises collect, store, and process data. Typically, the data that should be used to build the enterprise master is collected, stored, and processed by different business units, departments, and subsidiaries using different application systems, different definitions for the same data attributes, and different technologies, processes, formats, and transformation rules. The result is disjoined islands of data that manifest data quality issues in a number of ways:

▶ Semantic inconsistencies at the data attribute level include the following symptoms:

   ▶ Different business units often use the same data attributes to describe different entities. For example, a customer identifier for CRM master data may point to a social security number, but could be a Dun & Bradstreet DUNS number for a supply chain business area.

   ▶ Data attributes that describe business entities (e.g., product names, total revenue, etc.) often contain different values for the same attributes across different applications and lines of business. For example, a product name in one application may mean a product type in the other, and a product code in a third one.

   ▶ Business entities may be identified differently across the enterprise because different applications systems may use different reference data sources.

▶ Inconsistencies in attribute-level data often go hand in hand with the inconsistencies across data-related business rules that define the way the data has to be formatted, translated, and used; these rules often vary from one business unit and application system to another.

▶ Data relationship inconsistencies impact the ability to identify explicit and/or inferred relationships between business entities (e.g., accounts and payments, customers and households, products and suppliers). These relationships are often defined differently in different applications and across lines of business. This is not a pure technology issue, although it is not unusual to find an organization that over time created various data stores designed strictly to support business requirements of an individual business unit. This "stovepipe" design approach often results in situations that by definition create inconsistencies in data definitions, content, and structures such as expressions of how various entities are related to one another.

► Business entities such as products, partners, and suppliers are sometimes inherently organized into hierarchies. For example, the corporate structure of a large supplier may contain a parent company and several levels of subsidiaries. Traversing these hierarchies is one of the requirements for applications that, for example, need to understand and manage intercompany relationships and to measure total value of the transactions conducted with all business entities of a given corporate structure. Depending on the scope and design of an individual application, these hierarchies may be represented differently across system domains.

And the list can go on and on…

This discussion of data quality may appear to be of a more traditional nature and only slightly related to the goals of Master Data Management. In fact, the issues of data quality raised here are the primary factors, making the MDM goal of data integration across the enterprise much harder.

To put it another way, MDM is much more than traditional data quality initiatives: While most of the data quality initiatives are concerned with improving data quality within the scope of a particular application area or at a level of the specific line of business, MDM is focused on solving data-quality concerns in the integrated fashion across the entire enterprise.

The reason for this differentiation is a direct consequence of the MDM goal of achieving a "single version of the truth." The way Master Data Management approaches this goal of delivering an integrated data view is by matching all data across different application systems, lines of business, and enterprise entities in order to identify and link similar data records into uniquely identified groups of records, sometimes called affinity clusters. For example, a Customer Data Integration solution for a financial institution would attempt to find all records about a individual customer from all available data sources that come from various lines of business such as banking, credit cards, insurance, and others, and link them into a group of all individuals that comprise that customer's household. Fundamentally, this matching and linking activity is infeasible or at least unreliable if the data that is being matched displays the properties of inconsistency, inaccuracy, incompleteness, and other data quality issues discussed earlier in this section.

To sum up, one of the goals and challenges of Master Data Management is to allow organizations to create, manage, and deliver a master data platform that can demonstrate acceptable and measurable levels of data quality and enables consistent and effective integration of various data entities into cohesive and complete data views.

Defining Master Data Management

We have now reached the point where we can formally define Master Data Management. Although there are a number of MDM definitions available, we need to define MDM in a way that is agnostic of the particular data subject area and provides sufficiently complete description representing both the business and technology view.

Defining MDM

Master Data Management (MDM) is the framework of processes and technologies aimed at creating and maintaining an authoritative, reliable, sustainable, accurate, and secure data environment that represents a "single version of truth," an accepted system of record used both intra- and interenterprise across a diverse set of application systems, lines of business, and user communities.

This need to achieve a "single version of truth" is not a particular property of one industry. In the next chapter we will show that MDM has extremely broad applicability not only across industries but also across various types of organizations, including private and public companies as well as government organizations.

In achieving this ambitious goal of creating a "single version of the truth," Master Data Management helps any organization that has disparate data sources and data stores, various applications, and multiple lines of business. In doing so, MDM can be viewed as an evolutionary, next-generation data management discipline, and we'll show some components of that evolution in the example of Customer Data Integration later in this chapter. At the same time, given the breadth, depth, and profound consequences of implementing Master Data Management, we can see it as a revolutionary, disruptive approach to data management, and we'll show later in the book that the impact of MDM is reaching deep into the core of many established business processes. These revolutionary properties of MDM require significant financial, time, and organizational commitment across the entire enterprise, including participation from both business and technology sides of the company. Indeed, Master Data Management is an enterprise-wide data and system integration activity that requires a multidisciplinary, extremely well-planned and executed program that involves business process analysis; data analysis and mapping; data cleaning, enrichment and rationalization; data matching, linking and integration; data synchronization and reconciliation; data security, and data delivery.

In addition, we'll show in Part II of the book that an enterprise-class MDM solution should be implemented as an instance of a service-oriented architecture (SOA), and thus the program would include design, development, testing, and deployment of both business and technical services that enable an MDM platform to function and continuously manage the new "system of records." While this is far from a complete list of activities required to implement an MDM solution, many of these activities have to be planned, managed, and executed in a holistic fashion whether an MDM initiative is focused on a small or large organization as well as whether its focus is on customer data as in Customer Data Integration (CDI), product or reference data management, or other data domains. Moreover, MDM applies not only within an enterprise but also across enterprises when new efficiencies, standards, or regulations demand that two or more companies need to share data across enterprise boundaries, for example, when various government agencies need to share data about potential threats to national security, or when financial services companies need to support global industry initiatives such as Straight Through Processing (STP) and next-day settlement (T+1). On the one hand, when we look at the wide open field of MDM opportunities it is hard to imagine any enterprise, large or small, that has only a single source of data that it uses to manage the business. However, when we talk about initiatives of the scale and impact of MDM, size does matter, and many small-to-midsize companies have to limit the scope and investment of the MDM initiatives to avoid the challenges of justifying this level of commitment and investment.

Master Data Management and Reference Data

As we have stated, one of the key activities required to implement an MDM solution is focused on matching and linking of data records in order to find and integrate similar records. The natural question of what is similar is the subject of extensive research and its answer apparently depends on the domain of data that is being matched. For example, matching records about individuals is a relatively well-known problem, and there are a large number of matching techniques and solutions that use a variety of attributes of the individual (e.g., name, address, date of birth, social security number, work affiliation, and even physical attributes if they are known) to deliver a high-confidence matching result. We discuss matching and linking in more in Part II and Part IV of this book.

The situation changes when we move to other domains, such as product reference data and company hierarchies.

Current published research shows that product matching, for example, can be much more complex than name and/or address matching. This complexity is driven by the fact that while product attributes may represent a standard set for each product category (e.g., consider a TV set as a product whose features and technical characteristics are well known), different manufacturers or suppliers may use different expressions including abbreviations and attribute values to describe the same feature. From a consumer perspective, if you try to review a technical description of a plasma TV set from a variety of product and store catalogs, you may find that a feature described one way in a manufacturer's catalog is described differently or simply is missing in a store catalog.

A similar problem exists and is magnified at a business level when you have to deal with a variety of suppliers. That is why there are a number of industry initiatives under way to develop a library of common standards that describe entities for Business-to-Business (B2B) commerce in general (e.g., ebXML, Radio Frequency Identification [RFID]), or for a given domain (e.g., RosettaNet for various vertical industries such as electronic components manufacturing and supply chain automation, HL7 for the pharmaceutical industry, ACORD for the insurance industry, FpML and FixML for the financial services industry, etc.).

But while the standards are being developed and ratified, an MDM solution may have to deal with complex, sometimes unstructured data such as documents describing investment instruments, features and functions of High Definition TV sets, specifications of "smart" mobile phones and Personal Digital Assistants (PDAs), or home/office décor supplies, to name just a few. In many cases of these types of product information, the relevant data is presented in different formats and the data attributes used for matching are intermingled and ordered differently as we move from source to source, thus making it difficult to match records even using statistical pattern-matching techniques.

In general, cleaning, standardizing, rationalizing, matching, and linking records are some of the key challenges and key differentiation of Master Data Management solutions.

Customer Data Integration (CDI)

As previously mentioned, situations where Master Data Management is focused on creating and managing an authoritative system of records about customers is the subject of the MDM variant known as Customer Data Integration (CDI). This term, however, may be misleading in that it may create an impression that CDI only deals with customer information where customers are individuals who have predefined, known, usually account-based relationships with the enterprise.

In fact, even though CDI stands for Customer Data Integration, the word "Customer" is used as a generic term that can be replaced by industry or line-of-business–specific terms such as: Client, Contact, Party, Counterparty, Patient, Subscriber, Supplier, Prospect, Service Provider, Citizen, Guest, Legal Entity, Trust, Business Entity, and other terms. We will use terms like Customer and Party as primary descriptors of the CDI customer entities interchangeably throughout the book.

Once we clearly define the data domain as the one dealing with a generic term "customer," we can provide a working definition of Customer Data Integration. This definition builds on the definition of MDM presented in the preceding section.

Defining CDI

Customer Data Integration (CDI) is a comprehensive set of technology components, services, and business processes that create, maintain, and make available an accurate, timely, integrated, and complete view of a customer across lines of business, channels, and business partners.

To state it slightly differently, a CDI solution takes customer data from a variety of data sources, discards redundant data, cleanses the data, and then rationalizes and aggregates it together. We can graphically depict a CDI system as a hub-and-spokes environment. The spokes are information sources that are connected to the central Hub as a new "home" for the accurate, aggregated, and timely customer data (see Figure 1-1). This description also helps explain why we often use the term "Data Hub" when discussing CDI and MDM solution space.

CDI is a special, customer-data-focused type of Master Data Management, with the same goals, objectives, and benefits. However, since CDI deals with customer information that it collects, cleanses, rationalizes, and aggregates into a holistic

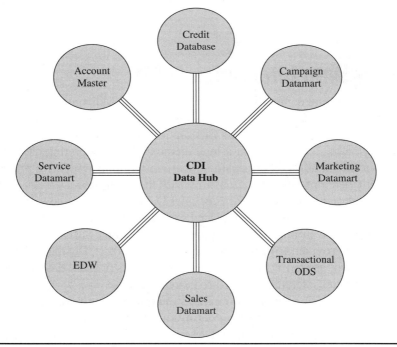

Figure 1-1   *CDI as a Data Hub*

customer view, a comprehensive CDI initiative can have a profound impact on the way any enterprise conducts its business and interacts with its customers.

Specifically, a CDI solution can allow the enterprise to discover various relationships that the customers may have with one another, relationships that can allow the enterprise to understand and take advantage of potential opportunities offered by customer groups that define households, communities of interest, and professional affiliations. For example, a CDI solution implemented by a financial services firm can indicate that a group of its customers have created a private investment club, and that club could present a very attractive opportunity for the new services and product offerings.

The benefits of discovering and understanding relationships among individuals apply not just to commercial businesses. Understanding the relationships between individuals has direct and profound implications on various government activities including law enforcement, risk management for global financial transactions, and national security. Indeed, if the CDI capabilities of individual recognition, identification, and relationships discovery had been available globally, the tragic events of September 11, 2001 might not have happened since we now know that there was a sufficient amount of information available about the hijackers and their relationships. Unfortunately, this information was collected and analyzed by different government services but never integrated and delivered to the right people at the right time.

While discovering and managing the relationships is a very useful capability, CDI benefits don't stop there. A CDI solution (often referred to as a Data Hub) can allow an enterprise to drastically change its business model from a traditional, account-centric approach to a new, more effective and rewarding customer-centric model that can significantly improve customer experience, reduce customer attrition, strengthen customer relationships with the enterprise, and even increase the customer's share of the wallet for the enterprise.

CDI and Customer-Centric Enterprise Transformation

CDI-enabled transformation from the account-centric to the customer-centric model is revolutionary, and it can drastically impact the established business processes and change the way the enterprise treats its customers, competes in the market, and grows its core customer-driven revenue.

We'll discuss account-centric to customer-centric transformations in more details in Chapter 3.

Combined with the fact that CDI enables a near-real-time accurate and complete "single version of the truth" about the customer, the properties and benefits of CDI described in this chapter make it abundantly clear that CDI solutions are much more than simply another customer database or a new enterprise CRM platform, even though we can find the genesis of CDI in these and similar customer management technologies.

Evolution of CDI

Business and government entities have historically striven to create and maintain authoritative and timely information sources. This natural enterprise requirement has been further emphasized by a number of regulatory requirements that include the Sarbanes-Oxley Act and the Basel II Capital Accord (see discussion on these regulations in Part III of the book).

In the case of Customer Data Integration, organizations had been working on creating customer-centric business models, applications, and enabling infrastructure for a long time. However, as the business complexity, number of customers, number of lines of business, and number of sales and service channels continue to grow, and as this growth often proceeded in a tactical, nonintegrated fashion, many organizations evolved into a state with a wide variety of customer information stores and applications that manage customer data.

The customer data in those "legacy" environments was often incomplete and inconsistent across various data stores, applications, and lines of business. Although in many cases individual applications and lines of business were reasonably satisfied with the quality and scope of customer data that they managed, the lack of completeness, accuracy, and consistency of data across lines of business (LOB) prevented organizations from creating a complete, accurate, and up-to-date view of customers and their relationships.

Recognizing this customer data challenge and the resulting inability to transform the business from an account-centric to a customer-centric business model, organizations have persisted in developing a variety of strategies and solutions designed to achieve this transformation. They offered new customer insights, new ways to improve customer service, and increased cross-selling and up-selling. Yet they were limited to being deployed within the boundaries of the existing organizational units and lines of business and were not positioned to become true enterprise-wide, cross-LOB global solutions.

The continual cross-industry opportunities they offered to realize customer centricity have helped define Master Data Management in general and Customer Data Integration strategies and architecture in particular. CDI has emerged to become not just a vehicle for creating the authoritative system of customer information but also an enabler of achieving customer centricity.

Let's briefly look at what has been done and what, if any, elements can be and should be leveraged in implementing a CDI solution. These CDI predecessors include Customer Information File (CIF); Extract, Transform, and Load Technologies (ETL); Enterprise Data Warehouse (EDW); an Operational Data Store (ODS); Data

Quality Technologies (DQ); Enterprise Information Integration (EII); and Customer Relationship Management systems (CRM):

▶ **Customer Information File (CIF)** is typically a legacy environment that represents some basic static information about the customers. CIF systems have a number of constraints including limited flexibility and extensibility; they are not well suited to capturing and maintaining real-time customer data, customer privacy preferences, customer behavior traits, and customer relationships. CIF systems are often used to feed the company's Customer Relationship Management systems.

▶ **Extract, Transform, and Load (ETL) tools** are designed to extract data from multiple data sources, perform complex transformations from source formats to the target formats, and efficiently load the transformed and formatted data into a target database such as CDI Data Hub. Contemporary ETL tools include components that perform data consistency and data quality analysis as well as providing the ability to generate and use metadata definitions for data elements and entities. While not pure CDI solutions, ETL tools have been a part of other CDI predecessors and represent an important functionality required to build a CDI Data Hub platform.

▶ **Enterprise Data Warehouse (EDW)** is an information system that provides its users with current and historical decision support information that is hard to access or present in traditional operational data stores. An enterprise-wide data warehouse of customer information was considered to be an integration point where most of the customer data can be stored for the purpose of supporting business intelligence applications and customer relationship management systems. Classical Data Warehouses provide historical data views and do not support operational applications that need to access real-time transactional data associated with a given customer, and thus are falling short of delivering on the CDI promise of accurate and timely system of record for customer information.

▶ **Operational Data Store (ODS)** is a data technology that allows transaction-level detail data records to be stored in a nonsummarized form suitable for analysis and reporting. Typical ODS does not maintain summarized data nor does it manage historical information. Similar to the EDW, an ODS of customer data can and should be considered a valuable source of information for building a CDI data Hub.

▶ **Data Quality Technologies (DQ)**, strictly speaking, are not customer data platforms, but they play an important role in making these platforms useful and useable whether they are built as data warehouses, operational data stores, or customer information files. Given the importance of data quality as one of the key requirements to match and link customer data as well as to build an authoritative source of accurate, consistent, and complete customer information, data quality technologies are often considered not just as predecessors of the CDI but as key CDI enablers.

▶ **Enterprise Information Integration (EII)** tools are designed to aggregate distributed data in memory or nonpersistent storage, thus potentially delivering a "just-in-time" customer data view. Depending on data sources, data quality, and data availability, these EII solutions could be used as components of a full-function CDI Data Hub.

▶ **Customer Relationship Management (CRM)** is a set of technologies and business processes designed to understand customers, improve customer experience, and optimize customer-facing business processes across marketing, sales, and servicing channels. As such, CRM solutions are probably the closest to what a CDI Data Hub can offer to its consumers. CRM has been adopted by many enterprises as a strategy to integrate information across various customer data stores and to deliver appropriate analytics and improve customer interactions with the enterprise across primary channels of marketing, sales, and services. Unfortunately, experience shows that CRM systems that were positioned for enterprise-wide deployment could not scale well as an integrated system of complete and timely customer information.

Each of these predecessor technologies has its advantages and shortcomings. A detailed discussion of these technologies is beyond the scope of this book, but we offer some additional considerations regarding these technologies in Chapter 4.

Key Benefits of Master Data Management and Customer Data Integration

A discussion of Master Data Management and Customer Data Integration cannot be complete unless we look at the benefits these types of solutions bring to the enterprise. Companies embark on major MDM and CDI initiatives because of their natural need to establish a single, authoritative, accurate, timely, and secured master data system. In turn, they can create more accurate and timely key performance metrics, measure and manage risks, and develop competitive winning strategies. Furthermore, MDM allows enterprises to be compliant with appropriate regulatory requirements including those defined by the Gramm-Leach-Bliley Act, the Sarbanes-Oxley Act, the Basel II Accord, and many others (discussion on these regulations can be found in Chapters 3 and 7). This compliance allows organizations to avoid costly penalties and bad publicity. Having a single authoritative system of record positions an enterprise to gradually sunset a number of legacy systems and applications and therefore realize significant cost savings.

In addition to potential cost savings and gaining compliance, Master Data Management offers a number of critical capabilities to the enterprise and government agencies alike, including the ability to detect and prevent illegal money-laundering activities and other fraudulent financial transactions in accordance with regulations such as AML and the KYC provisions of the USA Patriot Act. Moreover, the ability of MDM and CDI to discover and expose previously unknown relationships between individuals can be extremely useful in the global fight against terrorist organizations.

However, Master Data Management and Customer Data Integration are not just about cost savings and compliance. MDM and CDI create new opportunities and ways to drastically improve customer experience and increase top-line revenue. Indeed, many new and established enterprises are looking to differentiate themselves from the competition by significantly increasing customer satisfaction and improving customer experience. Having an accurate and complete system of record for customer information allows enterprises to gain new and more actionable intelligence into the customer's buying behavior and thus allows companies to create and offer better and more accurate personalized products and services. Master Data Management and Customer Data Integration solutions allow enterprises to capture and enforce the customer's privacy preferences and ensure protection of the customer's confidential data—actions that result in the enterprise's ability to establish and strengthen trusted relationships with their customer, thus creating additional competitive advantage.

MDM and CDI not only help retain profitable customers but also address the challenge of any enterprise to grow its customer base. This customer base growth opportunity comes from several different directions:

▶ Accurate and complete customer data allows the enterprise to better leverage various cross-sell and up-sell opportunities.

▶ Master data that contains information about prospects allows enterprises to increase prospect-to-customer conversion ratio, thus increasing the customer base.

▶ CDI ability to discover and understand the complete picture of current and potential relationships allows an enterprise to create a targeted set of marketing campaigns and product and services offers that may prove to be more cost-effective and demonstrate higher lift than traditional mass marketing.

Finally, any discussion about the benefits of Customer Data Integration would not be complete without mentioning the disruptive, transformational nature of CDI, which allows an enterprise to change its core business model and customer-facing products and services by transforming itself from an account-centric to a customer-centric enterprise. This new, transformed enterprise no longer views, recognizes, and services customers by their account number.

That old account-centric model does not enable an enterprise to easily and reliably identify individuals who are associated with the account. Moreover, the old model does not enable an enterprise to discover associations and relationships between individuals owning the accounts and other individuals and businesses that own other accounts. For example, an individual may have several accounts with a bank, and some of these accounts may have designated an individual in the role of a beneficiary or a power-of-attorney who may own another set of accounts, some of which may be managed by another business unit. Ideally, the enterprise would gain a significant competitive advantage if these intra- and inter-LOB relationships were discovered and leveraged, to increase the customer base and corresponding share of customer wallet.

Discovering these relationships may have an extremely high impact on the way the enterprise should treat the individual. Indeed, recognizing the total lifetime value of the customer would allow the enterprise to provide an appropriate set of products, services, and special treatments that are commeasurable with the total value of the relationships that the customer may have with the enterprise. For example, an individual who opens a low-value savings account may be treated differently by the bank if it is known that this individual is also a high-net-worth customer of the bank's wealth management business, or if the customer is also a president of a medium-size company, or if the customer's spouse has a separate high value account or if this customer's child who does not yet have an account with the bank has inherited a multimillion dollar trust fund, etc.

In short, CDI-enabled transformation from the account-centric to the customer-centric model is revolutionary, and it can drastically impact established business processes and change the way the enterprise treats its customers, competes in the market, and grows its core customer-driven revenue.

CHAPTER
2

CDI: Overview of Market Drivers and Key Challenges

IN THIS CHAPTER
The Business View
Industry Views of CDI
Geographic Views: CDI Goes Globel

The Business View

In the first chapter of this book we discussed the reasons for and the evolution of Master Data Management and Customer Data Integration. We also offered a working definition of both MDM and CDI. Specifically, we defined Master Data Management as the framework of processes and technologies aimed at creating and maintaining an authoritative, reliable, sustainable, accurate, and secure data environment that represents a "single version of truth," an accepted system of record used both intra- and interenterprise across a diverse set of application systems, lines of business, and user communities.

Using this definition as a guide we showed that Master Data Management is a horizontal technology that applies equally well to all industries and markets, and is global in nature. The latter point has two equally important aspects:

▶ MDM and its customer-centric version known as Customer Data Integration are especially effective in modernizing a global enterprise.

▶ The need for an authoritative, accurate, timely, and secure "single version of the truth" is pervasive and is not particular to a specific country or geography.

We also mentioned that Customer Data Integration, while evolutionary from the pure technological point of view, is revolutionary in its potential business impact and represents a particularly interesting opportunity to any Business-to-Consumer (B2C) and even Government-to-Consumer/Citizen (G2C) entity.

Using all these factors as background we are now ready to focus on a business view of CDI and discuss the reasons for its rapid proliferation, the challenges that its adopters have to overcome in order to succeed in implementing CDI initiatives, and the way the market has been growing and reacting to the demands and opportunities of CDI.

This chapter will concentrate on three key CDI subjects:

▶ Competitive advantage
▶ Industry views
▶ Geographic views

Chapter 3 will focus on the ability of CDI solutions to help transform an enterprise from an account-centric to a customer-centric, agile business model.

CDI as a Vehicle for Competitive Advantage

According to the survey data published by the CDI Institute (www.the-cdi-institute .com), 68 percent of Global 2000 companies are actively evaluating or building

CDI solutions. The evaluation activities are focused on both business and technical aspects of the CDI, and try to weigh the potential benefits of implementing a CDI platform against the cost, implementation, and operational risk of new technologies, potential shortage of qualified resources, and the impact on established business processes. Of course, many organizations that subscribe to the "buy before build" principle are also evaluating CDI vendors and system integrators as potential technology partners. The survey has also found that many CDI initiatives that may have started as small pilots that were developed in-house are rapidly growing in size and visibility and have been repositioned to use best-in-class commercially available solutions.

While this trend is encouraging and indicates CDI market expansion, we need to recognize that embarking on a CDI journey is not a small or easy task. From a business perspective, building or buying a CDI solution is a significant undertaking that has to be supported by a comprehensive and compelling business case. Indeed, considering the high degree of risks, significant software licenses and implementation costs, long duration, and very high level of visibility and organizational commitment required to implement a full-fledged Customer Data Integration initiative, a CDI project should only be considered if it can provide an enterprise with a well-defined and measurable set of benefits and a positive return on investment (ROI) in a reasonable time. In short, a completed and deployed CDI solution should provide the enterprise with a tangible competitive advantage.

One way for a customer-facing enterprise to achieve competitive advantage is to know their best and largest customers, and be able to organize them into groups based on explicit or implied relationships including corporate and household hierarchies. Knowing customers and their relationships allows an enterprise to assess and manage customer lifetime value, increase effectiveness of marketing campaigns, improve customer service, and therefore reduce attrition rates. While it may appear that the same can be accomplished using a more traditional CRM system, a full-function CDI solution can extend the scope of already familiar CRM sales-services-marketing channels by integrating additional information sources that may contain customer-related data including back-office systems, finance and accounting departments, product master references, or supply chain applications. This broad and far-reaching scope of CDI data coverage provides a number of opportunities for a CDI-empowered enterprise to achieve a sustainable competitive advantage. Let's look at some prominent components of this competitive advantage.

Improving Customer Experience

Customer experience is rapidly emerging as a clear competitive differentiator. In the Internet-enabled e-Business world, customer experience is viewed as one of the key factors that can strengthen or destroy trusted relationships that a customer may have with the enterprise. Customer experience includes a variety of tangible and intangible factors that collectively can make a customer a willing and eager participant or a dissatisfied party looking to take his or her business to a competitor as soon as possible. And in the era of e-Banking, e-Sales, and other Internet-enabled businesses, customers can terminate their relationship with the enterprise literally at a click of the mouse.

As a master customer data facility that manages all available information about the customer, CDI allows an enterprise to recognize a customer at any "point of entry" into the enterprise and to provide an appropriate level of customer service and personalized treatment—some of the factors driving customer experience. Let's illustrate this point with the example of a financial services company.

This company has created a wealth management organization that deals with affluent customers each of whom gets services from a dedicated personal financial advisor (PFA). When such an affluent customer calls his or her financial advisor, it is extremely important for the advisor to be able to access all the required information promptly, should it be information about a new product or service, a question about the investment options, or a concern about tax consequences of a particular transaction. Unfortunately in many cases lack of customer data integration does not allow companies to provide an adequate level of service.

For example, it is customary in wealth management to have a variable fee structure, with the amount of service fees inversely proportional to the amount of money under management (in other words, it is not unusual to waive fees for a customer who has total balances across all accounts that exceed a certain company-defined threshold). Of course, such service would work only if the enterprise can readily and accurately recognize a customer not as an individual account holder but as an entity that owns all her or his accounts. What if a high-net-worth client calls because his fees were calculated incorrectly? The advisor could not obtain necessary information during the call, and thus would not be able to provide an explanation to the customer and would ask for extra time and possibly an additional phone call to discuss the results of the investigation. This is likely to upset the customer who, as an affluent individual, has become used to quick and effective service. This situation can deteriorate rapidly if, for example, the investigation shows that the fee system interpreted the customer's accounts as belonging to multiple individuals. The corrective action may take some time, several transactions, and in extreme cases, a number of management approvals, all of which can extend the time required to fix the problem, and thus make the customer even more unhappy.

This is a typical symptom indicating that a sound CDI solution is required. If the situation is not resolved and occurs frequently, this may hamper client relationships and eventually cause increased attrition rates.

Improving Customer Retention and Reducing Attrition Rates

To achieve sustainable growth a company needs to focus on the customer segments with the highest growth potential in the area in which the company specializes—and build high loyalty by helping the customer to realize his or her growth opportunities. Conceptually, these segments can be classified into *new high-revenue-potential* customers and *existing customers whose total revenue potential has not yet been realized.*

In the case of new customer segments, every customer-facing enterprise has to solve the challenge of finding and acquiring new customers at lower acquisition cost. However, whether it is a new or an existing customer, enterprises have to find ways to improve customer retention rates at lower costs. This last point is very important: experience and market studies show that the cost of new customer acquisition could be many times the cost of retaining the existing customer, so the enterprise needs to understand the reasons that cause an existing customer to leave and go to a competitor. As mentioned in the preceding section, among the reasons for attrition are cumbersome or inconvenient ways to do business (for example, an inefficient or aesthetically unappealing web portal, few retail bank branches, inconvenient locations or working hours), poor customer service, lack of personalized or specific product and services offerings, lack of trust caused by violation of the customer's privacy and confidentiality, overly aggressive sales and marketing, and other factors that individually or collectively comprise customer experience. The cause of many of these factors is the lack of accurate business intelligence about the customer. Business intelligence has always been a valuable competitive differentiator, and best-in-class BI solutions such as customer analytics and customer data mining are critical to achieve a competitive advantage. The accuracy of business intelligence, in turn, depends on the availability, quality, and completeness of customer information. And it is a CDI solution that is designed to acquire and deliver such customer information to appropriate users including business intelligence applications.

Growing Revenue by Leveraging Customer Relationships

Enterprises have come to realize that customer loyalty is eroding and with shortening product life cycles, most markets are facing intense competition and commoditization. In addition, and especially in financial services, the institutions have made a significant effort to acquire what is known as "most profitable customers." However, since the total population of "best customers" is finite (i.e., there are only so many customers that are worth doing business with), the financial institutions have realized that the new sources of revenue may come not from new customers but from the ability to understand and leverage the totality of the relationships a given customer may have with the financial institution. Therefore, the companies have to manage the life cycle of their customers beyond the acquisition. To state it differently, the strategy involves the notion of acquiring, understanding, and servicing the customer *in the context* of his or her relationships with the enterprise. This is different from the commonly used segmentation approach of CRM systems, which is based on the history of customer transactions.

Understanding and leveraging the relationships is one of the ways CDI can help grow the business through increasing the "share of the wallet" by extending additional services to the existing customers individually and as part of various customer groups. This goal can be accomplished if the enterprise has developed and maintains accurate, complete, and insightful customer intelligence—a set of analytical insights and predictive traits indicating the best customers and the types of services and products that need to be offered in order to gain an increased share of the wallet. This customer intelligence is especially effective if it is gathered in the context of customer relationships with the enterprise and other customers. Examples of the relationship include a household, family, business partners, or any other group of customers that can be viewed as a single group from the service perspective. This relationship-based intelligence allows the enterprise to service individual customers based not only on their requirements and propensity to buy products and services, but also on the added opportunity of leveraging customer relationships for increased revenue as a percent of the entire relationship group's share of the wallet. Needless to say, the ability to discover the relationships across a variety of customer data files is one of the key benefits of a full-function CDI solution.

In addition to the increased "share of the wallet" from the existing customers and relationship groups, a CDI solution can help grow the customer base by identifying opportunities for acquiring new customers through actionable referrals. These CDI-enabled revenue growth opportunities drive market demand for CDI data integration products and services.

Improving Customer Service Time: Just-in-Time Information Availability

As mentioned in Chapter 1, one of the drivers behind Master Data Management and Customer Data Integration is the need to make accurate data available to the users and applications more quickly. In many cases the latency of information has a significant negative impact on customer service and the resulting customer experience. Indeed, imagine a customer contacting a service center with a question or complaint only to hear that the customer service representative cannot get to the right information because "our system is slow" or "this information is in our marketing systems and we don't have access to it." Listening to these excuses during the phone call does not improve the customer's confidence in the way the enterprise manages the business.

Timely data access is clearly a requirement for any customer-facing enterprise, especially those that support a variety of online channels. This data availability and timeliness has two key components:

▶ Physical near-real-time access to data is a function of operational online systems, applications, and databases. Practically every organization has deployed these systems and the underlying technical infrastructures to enable near-real-time execution of online transactions.

▶ Accurate and timely data content is created by aggregating and integrating relevant information from a variety of data sources, and this integration is the job for a CDI solution.

The latter point is one of the reasons enterprises seriously consider significant investment into CDI initiatives. Having just-in-time accurate and complete customer information can not only improve customer service, but it can also enable the enterprise to create near-real-time cross-sell and up-sell opportunities across various online channels. Successful cross-sell and up-sell activities have a significant positive impact on cost of sales and result in increased sales revenue.

A typical overnight batch-cycle data latency provided by traditional data warehouses is no longer sufficient. Enterprises are looking for ways to cross-sell or up-sell immediately when a customer is still in the store or shopping online on the company's web site. Today, sophisticated customer analytics and fraud detection systems can recognize a fraudulent transaction as it occurs. CDI-enabled data integration allows an enterprise to build sophisticated behavior models that provide real-time recommendations or interactive scripts that a salesperson could use to entice the customer to buy additional products or services.

For instance, you have just relocated and purchased a new home. You need to buy a number of goods. The store should be able to recognize you as a new customer in the area and impress you with prompt offering of the right products that fit your family needs. In order to do this efficiently, a CDI system would find and integrate the customer profile, household information, and buying pattern into one holistic customer view. Using this integrated data approach, the advanced sales management system would be able to recognize the individual as a high-potential-value customer regardless of the channel the customer is using at any given time.

Improving Marketing Effectiveness

Marketing organizations develop CDI solutions to improve the effectiveness of their marketing campaigns and enable up-sell and cross-sell activities across the lines of business. It is not unusual for a CDI solution to increase the effectiveness of marketing campaigns by an order of magnitude. According to Michael Lowenstein, in "CDI: The CRM Dance Every Marketer Must Learn" (*CRM News*, February 2, 2002), Royal Bank reduced the number of marketing mailings from 300,000 to 20,000 by making marketing campaigns more intelligent, targeted and event-driven (see http://searchcrm .techtarget.com/originalContent/0,289142,sid11_gci799952,00.html).

At a high level marketing campaigns are similar across industries. There are some industry-specific marketing areas, though, e.g. Communities of Practice. This marketing solution is well known in the pharmaceutical industry. The Communities of Practice solution is based on a methodology aimed at identifying medical professionals considered to be thought leaders by their professional communities within a given geography and specialization area (specific infectious diseases, certain inflammatory diseases, areas of oncology, etc). As soon as the thought leaders are identified, the pharmaceutical company can launch a highly selective marketing campaign targeting the thought leaders who are expected to influence their colleagues on the merits of the drug or product. One of the key challenges in implementing the Communities of Practice approach is to recognize medical professionals and maintain the required profile information and information about their professional relationships and organizations.

Reducing Administrative Process Costs and Inefficiencies

A significant CDI driver recognized by the enterprise management is its ability to help reduce the administrative time spent on account administration, maintenance, and processing. It is not unusual that every time a new account for an existing customer needs to be opened, the customer profile information is entered redundantly again and again. Many current processes do not support reuse of the data that has been already entered into the account profile opened at a different time or by a different line of business. One of the reasons for not reusing the data is the complexity associated with finding other account or profile data for the customer across various application silos.

A CDI solution capable of maintaining the client profile and relationships information centrally can significantly reduce the overhead of account opening and maintenance.

In addition, a comprehensive CDI solution can help improve data quality and reduce the probability of errors in books and records of the film. This improved accuracy not only helps maintain a high level of customer satisfaction but also enables an enterprise to be in a better position to comply with the requirements of government and industry regulations such as the Sarbanes-Oxley Act for the verifiable accuracy and integrity of financial reporting. Some financial service organizations invest in CDI with the goal of reducing the administration time spent by the sales force by 50 percent.

Reducing Information Technology Maintenance Costs

In addition to the business drivers described in the preceding section, enterprise-wide CDI initiatives focused on creation of a new authoritative, complete, and accurate system of customer records are often driven by the objective to reduce the cost of ongoing maintenance of IT infrastructure, applications, and operations. Lack of common system architecture, lack of systemic controls, and data inconsistencies cause data processing errors and increase the cost of IT maintenance and operations. In addition, from the information technology perspective, absence of a holistic authoritative system of records results in the limited ability of the enterprise to adapt to the ever-changing business requirements and processes, such as those driven by new and emerging regulatory and compliance demands. The need for system and application agility to support business and regulatory demands is a powerful CDI-MDM driver. Properly implemented CDI-MDM solutions enable application development and reduce system implementation costs and risks. Many enterprise-wide initiatives, such as CRM or Enterprise Data Warehouse, often failed because in the pre-CDI days the issues of data accuracy, timeliness, and completeness had not been resolved proactively or in some cases, successfully.

Industry Views of CDI

As we have mentioned before, Master Data Management and Customer Data Integration are horizontal in nature, and apply equally well to any commercial market segment such as financial services, the health care industry, telecommunications, consumer retail, and many others. Moreover, MDM-CDI can be beneficial to any public sector business including government agencies that deal with citizens, employees, tourists, immigration, law enforcement, and others.

While the scope of Master Data Management is extremely broad and includes customers, products, reference data, and other domains, the discussions in this and the follow on chapters (Chapters 3–7) are focused on Customer Data Integration as a framework of processes and technologies designed to deliver authoritative, accurate, complete, and timely customer master data. Focusing on CDI does not make the scope of the discussion smaller. Indeed, customer master is a requirement for any Business-to-Consumer (B2C) or Government-to-Citizen (G2C) organization, which of course is a very broad field.

When dealing with such a large area of CDI coverage, it is important to recognize both the similarities and differences in the way CDI is viewed and implemented across various industries and government sectors. Therefore, let's look at the CDI requirements, approaches, and challenges that different industries and organizations have to deal with in order to achieve the stated CDI goal of creating an authoritative, accurate, timely, and comprehensive system of records. In doing so, we'll first focus on common themes describing the way many organizations are approaching CDI initiatives. These themes are pervasive and typically do not change significantly from industry to industry and from commercial to public sectors.

Clearly, each industry brings its own set of requirements and challenges that are specific to the industry. The following sections discuss some key domain-specific (commercial and public sector) requirements for building and deploying CDI solutions throughout the enterprise.

MDM and CDI are Horizontal Technologies

Master Data Management and Customer Data Integration are horizontal in nature, and apply equally well to any commercial market segment as well as to the public sector.

What Most CDI Implementation Approaches Have in Common

One of the general observations that we can make by analyzing how CDI solutions are implemented across various industries is the strong desire on the part of the enterprise to embark on a CDI initiative in a way that manages and mitigates implementation risk while at the same time realizing tangible business benefits. In practical terms, it often means that CDI initiatives start small and focus on a single high-priority objective such as improving data quality or creating a unified customer profile based on available data. Often, these initial CDI implementations are done using in-house development rather than a vendor CDI tool, and try to leverage existing legacy systems to the extent possible. For example, many organizations try to reuse existing business intelligence, reporting, and profile management applications while providing them with better, more accurate, and more complete data.

As the initial pilots begin to prove their usefulness to the business community, we see a common trend to expand the scope of the project by including additional data sources and new consuming applications. This may include functionality that can leverage new customer identity information and create new service improvement and revenue opportunities driven by more complete knowledge of the customers and their relationships. Ultimately, CDI initiatives mature enough to have a profound impact on the business model of the enterprise by enabling enterprise transformation from account-centric to customer-centric processes.

From the technology point of view, we see that after projects that were initially developed in-house succeed in implementing CDI proof of concept, enterprises start evaluating and implementing best-in-class vendor solutions. Many enterprises ensure that this transition is relatively smooth by adapting a service-oriented architecture (SOA) approach even to the in-house CDI pilot implementations In fact, we see that those enterprises that follow the SOA approach can relatively easily grow their CDI framework by replacing CDI components that were developed in-house with longer-term SOA-based CDI vendor products combined with the enterprise-wide SOA infrastructures, common messaging frameworks, common process management, and even common enterprise-wide information security.

To summarize, some common high-level CDI approaches include implementation strategies aimed at reduction in project and investment risk, and broad adoption of the service-oriented architecture to build, integrate, and deploy a CDI Data Hub as a component of the overall enterprise architecture and infrastructure.

On the business side, enterprises are beginning to see the significant benefits that CDI solutions offer, including growth of revenue and up-sell and cross-sell opportunities, improved customer service, and consistent cross-channel customer experience, increased customer retention rates, and a better regulatory and compliance posture for the enterprise. At the same time, enterprises quickly realize the complexity and multidisciplinary nature of a CDI initiative and therefore often treat a CDI project as corporate initiative that requires large cross-functional teams, multiple work streams, robust and active project management, and a clearly defined set of strategic measurable goals.

The following list presents some of the key technical challenges facing every organization that plans to implement CDI:

▶ Data governance and the ability to measure and resolve data quality issues.

▶ The need to create and maintain enterprise-wide semantically consistent data definitions.

▶ The need to create and maintain an active and accurate metadata repository that contains all relevant information about data semantics, location, and lineage.

▶ Support and management of distributed and/or federated master data especially as it requires business-rules-driven synchronization and reconciliation of data changes across various data stores and applications.

▶ The complexity of the processes required to orchestrate composite business transactions that span systems and applications not only within the enterprise but also across system domains of its business partners.

▶ Scalability challenges that require a CDI solution to scale with data volumes (especially as new entity identification tokens such as Radio Frequency Identification [RFID] solutions for products, universal identification cards for citizens, etc., become available).

▶ Scalability of data types: The need to rationalize and integrate both structured and unstructured content is rapidly becoming a key business requirement not only in the area of product or trading or reference data but even when dealing with customer information, some of which can be found in unstructured files such as word processing files, and images as in a photo gallery.

▶ The need to implement process controls to support audit and compliance reporting.

▶ The challenges of leveraging existing enterprise security framework to protect the new CDI platform and to enable function-level and data-level access control to master data that is based on authenticated credentials and policy-driven entitlements.

Commercial Marketplace: Domain-Specific CDI Features

Let's start with the commercial marketplace, and discuss several CDI drivers and requirements specific to the following industry segments: financial services, the hospitality and gaming industry, the pharmaceutical industry, and the telecommunications industry. We recognize that these industry segments represent only a small portion of the addressable market, but we believe that these segments offer a reasonably good cross-section view of the overall market for Customer

Data Integration. In this discussion we will concentrate on some key features that impact a particular industry more than any other. Common CDI drivers such as those described in the first section of this chapter (i.e., increasing sales productivity and revenue, increasing customer retention rates, improving customer satisfaction, reducing IT infrastructure costs) represent intrinsic CDI properties and thus can be found in CDI implementations for practically every market segment.

Financial Services Industry

Typically, financial services include banking, insurance, and brokerage. Of particular interest to CDI are those institutions that deal with individual customers (as opposed to institutional customers). Throughout this book, we use financial services institutions as a good example of how a customer-facing enterprise can benefit from implementing a CDI solution. The following are some key CDI requirements that drive CDI implementations in financial services:

▶ **Single-customer view**   Retail financial services institutions (FSI) such as consumer banks, life insurance companies, and retail brokerage houses have always faced the challenge of dealing with millions of their customers and prospects in a highly competitive marketplace. In that respect, these types of FSIs are similar to consumer retail businesses such as Wal-Mart and Sears, and they have been on the forefront of creating and using the concept of a single-customer view. This need to have an accurate and complete customer view is not new—as stated in Chapter 1, CDI precursors designed to create a single-customer view included Customer Information Files (CIF), Enterprise Data Warehouses (EDW), and Operational Data Stores (ODS). Financial services organizations were some of the first companies to pioneer and effectively use customer analytics, data mining, and multichannel CRM systems to better understand customer behavior and the factors enforcing the customer's propensity to buy, factors affecting customer brand loyalty, and reasons for customer attrition. Today, financial services institutions embark on CDI initiatives to overcome inefficiencies and limitations of CIF and other CDI precursors to deliver accurate, cross-channel-integrated, current customer information to the point of sales, service, or online channel in a timely fashion to have an impact on the outcome of a customer transaction.

▶ **Regulatory compliance**   Until recently, the single-customer view was the predominant driver of data integration initiatives throughout financial services institutions. However, ever since financial services organizations became subject to numerous regulations such as the Gramm-Leach-Bliley Act, the Sarbanes-Oxley Act, the Basel II Capital Accord, the USA Patriot Act's AML and KYC provisions, and many others, a new and compelling reason to implement CDI has emerged. Indeed, since these and other regulations deal with accuracy of financial information, protection of customer data, and the need to capture and enforce customer privacy preferences, the need to have accurate, complete, secure, and available master data about customers, their portfolios, transactions, sales, and service records became a requirement. Financial services organizations that develop their CDI solutions to comply with the regulations and laws find the justification for building a CDI system to be relatively straightforward.

▶ **Mergers and Acquisitions (M&A)**   Although M&A is not an exclusive business strategy reserved to financial services organizations, the business strategy of many financial services institutions considers M&A as an effective growth vehicle and a competitive differentiator. Obviously, one of the challenges of the merged organization is the integration of their customer bases. This is where CDI capabilities become highly beneficial and in fact, a CDI solution can quickly become a system of record for the new, merged enterprise.

Hospitality and Gaming Industry

The hospitality and gaming industry includes hotels and gambling establishments. It is clear that having an accurate and complete customer master that delivers a timely single-customer view is as beneficial to hotel chain management as it is to a retail bank. At a minimum, a single-customer view can help hotel management to provide better customer service, enable bigger cross-sell and up-sell opportunities, increase marketing campaign effectiveness, and enable better management of hotel inventory. However, this segment and its gaming component in particular bring an additional CDI requirement—to provide a complete customer view together with all his or her relationships and integrate this information with prior history of gambling activities linked with this customer in order to detect fraudulent gamblers, and potential collision between casino employees and players, employees and vendors, employees who are players, etc. In this case, a CDI system would source information from a variety of applications, and after cleaning and transformation, would make a new "player" master file available for advanced analytics.

Pharmaceutical Industry

The pharmaceutical industry deals with research, development, production, and sale of various products for approved medical use. Typically, pharmaceutical companies do not deal directly with consumers but rather with physicians who in turn prescribe the company's products to their customers (patients). Pharmaceutical companies must rationalize and integrate physician/customer information from multiple systems and business units in order to deliver a comprehensive view of their consumers' network and a better insight into the competitive landscape.

In this industry segment where the customers (physicians) also act as participants in the supply chain, CDI is viewed as an enabler of increased efficiency and effectiveness of supply chain operations. Pharmaceutical companies see CDI as an enabler to reconcile various industry-standard identifiers, thus creating an integrated view of the customer (physician, health care organization, medical group).

Having an accurate health care provider (physician, hospital, etc.) master data set that contains all relevant information in one place allows a pharmaceutical company to increase effectiveness of the company's sales representatives; increase the acquisition, retention, and profitability rates of their customers (physicians and physician groups); and enable better regulatory and compliance controls. For example, pharmaceutical companies need to adhere to strict regulations that require them to monitor and limit the total amount of various forms of compensation to their customers (i.e., a physician may attend a conference sponsored by the company, or give a for-pay lecture discussing the latest company product, etc.). And these activities can be performed using different names including a medical group of which this physician is a member. Traditionally, these activities were recorded in different, disconnected systems, and this is where a CDI solution would enable information integration across these disparate systems into a single view in order to assess to the total compensation.

Telecommunications Industry

The telecommunication sector includes companies that provide voice, data, and video communications services. These services can be delivered via wired, wireless, cable, or satellite communications.

Telecommunications companies deal with customers that include individuals as well as business entities. From the individual customer-support point of view, telecommunications companies face mostly the same issues as retail financial services, and having a single customer view is considered a primary driver to improve customer service and create up-sell and cross-sell opportunities. Telecommunication companies are experiencing significant market transformation where the competition for the communications products and services has intensified drastically over the last several years, and today their customers are able to choose and switch to a different service provider with relative ease.

In the days of telecommunication monopoly customer attrition was not even a possibility, but today telecommunication companies are looking into CDI solutions to get a better understanding of customer retention drivers, and to deliver personalized, specially configured and priced service packages that would help increase the customer retention rates.

Other drivers for CDI in telecommunications include support for customer self-service, detection of fraudulent transactions and communication sites, and integration of customer accounts and customer billing for those customers who chose to purchase multiple services from the same provider, but who did that not as a package but rather as individual transactions (it is not unusual today for a customer to receive numerous separate invoices for various telecommunication services from the same provider).

Therefore, CDI initiatives in the telecommunication sector are usually run in conjunction with Master Data Management initiatives focused on delivering a master product environment that can support a single authoritative source of critical product and service bundles.

Public Sector: Domain-Specific CDI Features

When we discuss CDI implementation in the public sector we include not only the departments and agencies of various national governments, but also businesses run by governments (e.g., various utilities, research establishments, transportation companies etc.). Similar to the commercial sector, government organizations dealing with businesses and individuals (G2B and G2C) are also looking to improve efficiencies, reduce expenses, and improve levels of customer service. Government-sponsored businesses and various agencies are concerned that poor service levels may lead to a public outcry that can impact the policies, rules, regulations, staffing levels, and even the management teams running these organizations. Therefore, government organizations are looking to implement CDI solutions that deliver a single-customer (or, as the case may be, a single-citizen) view in order to better understand the needs and behavior traits of their constituencies.

CDI and Public Sector

A CDI-enabled *"citizen master"* can be used by the government agencies to significantly improve usability and accuracy of citizens' self-service channels, thus reducing government costs of service.

In addition to improved service levels, CDI in the government sector holds tremendous promise of providing necessary just-in-time insight into individual behavior, transactions, relationships, and linkages with various terrorist groups and their supporters.

A properly designed CDI solution can help identify and track individuals both inside the country and across the globe. Despite the absence of a national identifier in the United States, a CDI solution used by a public sector entity (we may call it Citizen Data Integration) can be integrated with technologies that implement strong biometrics-based authentication and identification of individuals at points of entry into the country. These capabilities of a CDI solution are very attractive to international, federal, and local law enforcement as well as to various intelligence agencies, and hopefully could be used in the future to prevent acts of terrorism and other harmful activities.

Given the highly confidential nature of some of the information handled by most of the government agencies, it is not surprising that data security, privacy, confidentiality, and integrity concerns are some of the top priorities for implementing CDI solutions in public sector.

Geographic Views: CDI Goes Global

The level of maturity for CDI solutions available in North America significantly exceeds the level of CDI support available for international solutions. Internationalization of CDI is expected to be the next CDI wave. The complexity of international CDI solutions results from the diversity of international requirements and cultural and country-specific standards and regulations. Here are a few examples illustrating this point.

▶ **Russia, Ukraine, and Eastern Europe**   In Russia, the Ukraine, and some other Eastern European countries the second name points to the individual's father's first name. Typically the wife takes her husband's last name, but her last name will have an additional gender-specific suffix, e.g., Ivanov (husband) and Ivanova (wife).

Clearly these rules differ from those typically used domestically in the U.S. and inherited from the European English-, Dutch-, German- and French-speaking countries, where people often have two or more given names. When the wife takes her husband's name their last names are exactly identical without any additional suffixes.

▶ **Spain and Spanish-speaking countries**   In Spain and Spanish-speaking countries people have one or more given names and two family names, one from the father and one from the mother.

▶ **Italy**   In Italy, people may have one or more given names, no middle name, and a family name.

▶ **Thailand**   According to http://www.windowontheworldinc.com/countryprofile/thailand.html, last names have been used in Thailand for only the past 50 years and are difficult even for Thais to pronounce. Two people with the same last name are almost certainly related. According to http://www.apmforum.com/columns/thai4.htm, when immigrants from other countries apply for a Thai last name they have to obey the following procedure that regulates registrations of the new Thai last names:

1. The applicants submit five alternatives to the government officer. Each one has a maximum of ten Thai characters.

2. The officer will search in the database for identical last names. The law requires the uniqueness of the last name.

About one month later, the applicant will check with the officer. If there is no duplication, the applicant can use the new last name. If there is any duplication, the applicant needs to resubmit the application with a new set of proposed surnames. Since Thailand has many immigrants, particularly from China, subsequent applicants have to create new unique last names. This explains why Thais have long surnames and they are getting longer.

There are significant consequences of these rules from a CDI project perspective. Indeed, it is much easier to resolve customer identification issues with the rules just described.

► **Korea**   According to http://www.gaminggeeks.org/Resources/KateMonk/ Orient/Korea/Surnames.htm, until the eighteenth century, only about half the population of Korea had surnames. There are only about 300 or 400 family names used in Korea, of which Lee, Kim, and Park/Pak are particularly common, accounting for almost half the population. People with the same surname are divided into branches often identified by a place name (about 280 in the Kim family and around 5 in most others), and members of these branches could not intermarry until recently when the Korean Supreme Court made a ruling that people from the same clan can marry outside Korea. Women do not take their husband's surname. In addition, Korean names are formed differently than Western names with the family name first, followed by the two-part given name. The first of the two given names is shared by everyone of the same generation in the family, and the second is the individual's given name.

As you can see from these examples, international CDI initiatives have to deal with a wide variety of challenging and fascinating rules. Differences in standards, languages, privacy, compliance, and security regulations, as well as cultural differences drive the complexity of international and global CDI solutions to new heights. In order to be successful in implementing global CDI solutions, enterprises and CDI vendors have to gain a deep understanding of country-specific and cultural rules and regulations. Clearly, global CDI products and solution approaches are still maturing, and a lot of work lies ahead. It is certainly a significant area of growth for Customer Data Integration. Emerging global CDI solutions may have to leverage the trends in developing and deploying global identifiers for individuals as well as advances in authentication technologies that rely on truly global identification attributes that transcend geography and language differences. Examples of these global identification attributes and their usage include multifactor authentication using biometrics such as fingerprints, iris scans,. and retina scans. Practical use of these technologies is in its infancy Multifactor authentication is discussed in more detail in Chapter 8.

Challenges, Concerns, and Risks of Moving Toward Customer Centricity

IN THIS CHAPTER

Business Challenges in Moving Toward Customer Centricity

Technical Challenges in Moving Toward Customer Centricity

This chapter describes the challenges and risks that a company faces on its way toward customer centricity. The process involves a variety of challenges and this chapter will describe them at a high level. Parts II, III, and IV of this book will deal with these issues in more depth.

We start by offering two perspectives that organizations should acknowledge and address in adopting and executing a successful customer-centricity strategy.

► The first perspective addresses business issues: defining a compelling value proposition, project drivers, the new end-state business vision, project organization, competing stakeholder interests, and socialization obstacles.

► The second perspective addresses technical issues such as architecture, data profiling and quality, data synchronization, visibility, and security. Moreover, it examines regulatory and compliance project drivers.

Business Challenges in Moving Toward Customer Centricity

This section discusses challenges and risks associated with the business transformation toward a customer-centric enterprise.

Senior Management Commitment and Value Proposition

Enterprise-scale MDM-CDI implementations tend to be lengthy, expensive, complex, and laden with risks. A typical CDI initiative takes at least a year to deliver, and the initiative's cost can easily reach several million U.S. dollars. Senior management's real commitment in terms of strategy, governance, and resources is foundational for the success of the initiative. Only a compelling value proposition with clearly defined challenges and risks can secure their commitment.

On the surface, defining and socializing a compelling value proposition appears to be a straightforward task. In practice, however, given the diversity of project stakeholders and new concepts that a CDI project often brings to the table, this step will likely take time and energy and may require multiple iterations. Projects may have to overcome a few false starts until finally the organization gains the critical mass of knowledge about what needs to be achieved in all key domains. Only then can the project team obtain and confirm required levels of executive sponsorship, management commitment, and ownership.

Driver Category	Driver
Sales and Marketing	• Screening new prospects • Cross sell/up-sell to existing customers • Effectiveness of marketing campaigns • Recurring revenue from existing customers
Cost Reduction	• Customer acquisition costs • Account setup costs • IT operation costs: duplication and redundancies • Cost of failed tactical initiatives • Reduces costs of planned initiatives due to CDI • Training cost
Customer Service	• Account setup time • Customer service time • Customer intelligence • Customer experience • Improved contact resolution rates
Compliance and Control	• Regulatory fines and penalties • Accurate books & records • Compliance with Basel II, AML, & KYC regulations • Compliance with corporate standards and policies • Fraud protection

Figure 3-1   *Common CDI drivers*

Business Drivers

In order to define the value proposition and end-state vision, we have to clearly understand both business and technical drivers. Figure 3-1 lists typical business drivers grouped by high-level categories such as Sales and Marketing, Cost Reduction, Customer Service, and Compliance and Control. Organizations can use this list as a starting point to prioritize and quantify the importance of the business drivers as they apply to the company.

Once the drivers and the areas of impact are understood and documented, the project team in conjunction with the business stakeholders should perform an in-depth applications and business process analysis that would answer the following questions:

▶   What business requirements drive the need to have access to better quality and more accurate and complete data while still relying on existing processes and applications?

▶ What business activities would gain significant benefits from changing not just applications but also key business processes that deal with customer interactions and customer services at every touch point and across front- and back-office operations?

To illustrate these points, consider a retail bank that decides to develop a CDI platform to achieve several business goals including better customer experience, better compliance posture, and reduced maintenance costs for the IT infrastructure. The bank may deploy a CDI Data Hub solution that would enable aggregation and integration of customer data across various channels, application systems, and lines of business. As a result, existing and new applications may have access to a new customer master that should contain more accurate and complete customer information. The bank's Customer Relationship Management (CRM) and various Business Intelligence (BI) systems may have to be modified to leverage this new data. Improved insights into complete customer profile and past behavior and better anticipation of the customer's needs for products and services translate into better customer service and higher customer satisfaction. These are all valid and valuable benefits that allow the bank to quantify and measure tangible return on investment. However, the core banking business still revolves around the notion of customer accounts, and the bank will continue to service its customers on the basis of their account type and status.

Moving to a customer-centric business model would allow the bank to understand and manage not just customer accounts but the totality of all current and potential customer relationships with the bank, to drastically improve the effectiveness and efficiency of customer interactions with the bank, and even to improve the productivity of the bank's service personnel. To achieve these goals, the bank would have to not only create a new customer master, but also redesign and deploy new, more effective and efficient business processes. For example, in the past the bank may have had an account-opening application that is used to open new customer accounts and modify existing ones. In the new customer-centric world, the bank may have to change its business processes and operational workflows in order to "create a customer" and modify his or her profile or assets (accounts). These new processes will be operating in the context of the integrated holistic customer view. The efficiencies may come from the fact that if the bank deals with the existing customer, it can effectively leverage information already collected about that customer. The bank can leverage this information to shorten the time required to perform the transaction, and to offer better, more personalized and more compelling products and/or services that are configured and priced based on the total view of the customer. Clearly, these new processes are beneficial to the customer and the bank, but they may represent a significant change in the behavior of the bank's application systems and customer service personnel. This is where the customer-centric impact analysis should indicate not only what processes and applications need to change, but what would be the financial impact of the change, and what would be the expected cost-benefit ratio if these changes are implemented as part of the CDI initiative.

Justifying Customer Centricity

The customer-centric impact analysis is one of the key vehicles that should be used to understand and justify the time, resource, and budgetary requirements of the transformational change toward customer centricity.

Customer Centricity and a 360-Degree View of a Customer

The stakeholders often use popular terms like "360-degree view of a customer" or "a single version of truth," "golden customer record," etc. We used this terminology in Chapter 1 as well. It takes time for the organization to understand what these frequently used terms mean for the company and its business. For one thing, these terms by themselves do not necessarily imply customer centricity. Indeed, many CRM systems had a holistic customer view as one of their design and implementation goals, but achieving this 360-degree customer view without changing fundamental business processes did not transform an organization into a customer-centric enterprise, and the traditional account-centric approach continued to be the predominant business model. One way to embark on the road to customer-centric enterprise is to clearly articulate the reasons for the transformation. To accomplish that goal, the project's stakeholders should answer a number of questions:

- ▶ What business processes currently suffer from a lack of customer centricity?

- ▶ Do different lines of business or business functions such as compliance, marketing, and credit card statement processing have identical definitions of a customer, including situations that deal with an institutional customer?

- ▶ Can the company share customer information globally and still comply with appropriate global and local regulatory requirements?

- ▶ What are the benefits of the new customer-centric business processes and how can the company quantify these benefits in terms of ROI?

Answering these questions may not be as simple as it sometimes appears, and often represents a challenge for an organization embarking on an MDM-CDI project. Indeed, many of these questions, if answered correctly, imply a significant financial, resource, and time commitment, so they should not be taken lightly. On the other hand, not answering these questions early in the project life cycle may result in a significant risk to the project when the stakeholders begin to review the project status, goals, budget, and milestones.

Challenges of Selling CDI Inside the Enterprise

By their very nature, MDM-CDI projects enable profound and far-reaching changes in the way business processes are defined and implemented. At the same time, experience shows that enterprise-scale MDM-CDI initiatives tend to take a long time and significant expenditure to implement. These factors make the challenges of socializing the need and benefits of CDI ever more difficult.

Since MDM-CDI initiatives are often considered to be infrastructure projects, the articulation of business benefits and compelling value proposition represents an interesting management challenge that requires considerable salesmanship abilities and a clear and concise business case. Without any application that can rapidly take advantage of a new CDI environment, and without clearly articulated, provable, and tangible ROI, it could be difficult to sell the concept of the MDM-CDI (and justify the funding request) to your senior management and business partners. In fact, selling the idea of a new application that can quickly take advantage of the CDI solution could prove to be the most effective way to define a compelling value proposition. This consumption-based approach often becomes a preferred vehicle for getting the buy-in from the internal stakeholders, especially if the new application delivers certain mandated, regulatory functionality.

In some cases, MDM-CDI initiatives start as information technology process improvement, system re-platforming projects (e.g., moving from mainframe to open system platform, or from IBM DB2 to Oracle, etc.). In these situations the projects may not have a clearly articulated set of business requirements, and the primary justification is based on the enterprise technology strategy direction, cost avoidance, partner integration requirements, or the objectives of improving internal infrastructure, rationalizing the application portfolio, improving data quality, and increasing processing capacity and throughput. If these drivers are sufficiently important to the enterprise, the organization responsible for the delivery of the new capabilities becomes a vocal and powerful champion, and the MDM-CDI project can start without too much resistance.

Whether there are clear and compelling business requirements, or the MDM tasks and deliverables are defined within a more traditional technology-driven project, one thing is clear: large, complex, and costly initiatives such as MDM-CDI projects typically fail without comprehensive buy-in from senior management and other stakeholders.

Complexity of Stakeholders' Landscape

It is important to point out that the answers to the questions for the stakeholders that are listed in the previous section are expected to be multifaceted and would depend on the context and the stakeholder role. Indeed, initiatives and projects of CDI caliber involve multiple stakeholder groups (see Figure 3-2 for a graphical representation of the stakeholder groups).

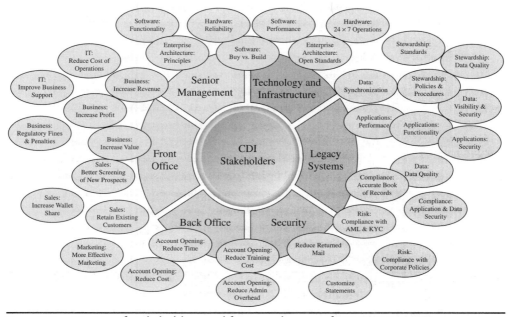

Figure 3-2   *Variety of stakeholders and functional areas of MDM-CDI*

This stakeholder landscape includes executive management and sponsors, line-of-business leaders, front office, back office, corporate and LOB data governance professionals, technology managers, architects and engineers, finance, regulatory, compliance, legal department, information security, technical infrastructure, external technology partners, and possibly other participants. Given their diversity and difference in priorities and goals, these stakeholders will most likely have different opinions and will thus provide different answers to the questions listed earlier. It is crucial to the success of the project that even though the views are different, they must represent different sides of a single consistent "story" about the project's goals, objectives, strategy, priorities, and the end-state vision. It is an ultimate challenge of the project's executive sponsors and project management team to establish, formulate, and disseminate project messages consistently to the appropriate team members, stakeholders, and project sponsors.

From the risk management perspective, human factors outweigh technical factors. For example, the IT organization might decide to implement the CDI project without obtaining an organizational buy-in. Even if the resulting solution is technically sound and perfectly implemented, the efforts would be viewed as a failure if the project is not socialized properly within the organization. In order to mitigate this risk, the initiative should be aligned with business objectives. In this case, project sponsors can "sell" the effort as a major improvement in business processes, customer experience, customer intelligence, business development, marketing, compliance, etc.

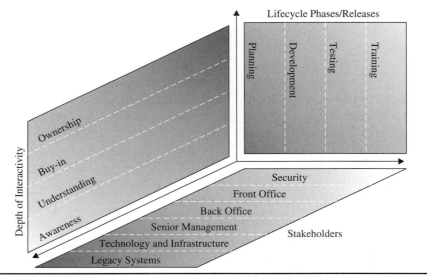

Figure 3-3 *The three-dimensional socialization problem*

Socializing CDI as a Multidimensional Challenge

The socialization challenge of a large scale initiative like MDM-CDI is a multidimensional problem (see Figure 3-3).

We see the socialization problem as having at least three dimensions. The first dimension illustrates a variety of stakeholder groups.

The phases of the life cycle are shown as the second dimension. The role of each group evolves over time as the initiative progresses through the life-cycle phases. For example, business analysts who represent business and define business requirements at the beginning of the initiative may later participate in business acceptance testing. The challenges continue in the road-map development and architecture phase when the solution is defined and the road to the end state is determined. The challenges vary as the project evolves, but they continue to be present throughout the project life cycle. To ensure the success of the MDM-CDI initiative, the project team has to make sure to obtain and regularly renew the organizational commitment from multiple stakeholder groups throughout all phases of development, implementation, deployment, and training.

Need for Organizational Buy-In

Even technically successful CDI projects can be perceived as failures if the project team fails to socialize project goals, and properly organize and orchestrate training for the end-user community.

The third dimension represents the depth of interactivity or the level of user buy-in and involvement. The user involvement begins with awareness. At this level, the stakeholder group becomes aware of the upcoming change, but may have a limited high-level understanding of the initiative. The next level includes understanding of the magnitude and complexity of the effort and its primary implications. Finally, the key stakeholders should participate in the initiative at the ownership level. These stakeholders actively participate in the effort and are responsible for assigned deliverables.

Technical Challenges in Moving Toward Customer Centricity

MDM-CDI projects represent a myriad of technical challenges and risks to IT managers, data architects, security officers, data governance officers, and operations. This section focuses on high-level implementation challenges and risks.

Sometimes, customer-centricity solutions are trivialized by suggesting that the problem can be solved by placing all customer data in a single repository. In reality, this approach is limited, and may be appropriate for small department-level projects. However, CDI projects become much more complex and difficult as the size of the company and the diversity of customer data grows. In midsize and large organizations, it is not unusual to find that customer information is distributed across multiple application systems that provide existing and new business functions and support various lines of business. Rationalizing, integrating, and aggregating this information is not a trivial task, and dealing with the legacy data and applications brings additional complications into the mix. This is especially true if you consider that in many cases legacy systems lack complete and accurate process documentation and stable data definitions—the principal obstacles to seamless semantic integration of heterogeneous data sources.

Of course, an enterprise may adopt a strategy of decommissioning some legacy systems to help deal with this challenge, and can put together an end-state vision for the CDI project that allows for some of these legacy application systems to be phased out over time. However, this strategy can be successful *only* if the candidate legacy systems are carefully analyzed for the potential impact on remaining upstream and downstream application systems. In addition to the impact of decommissioning, a careful analysis needs to take place to see the impact of introducing a CDI platform into the existing application environment even if decommissioning is not going to take place. The project team should develop an integrated project plan that contains multiple parallel work streams, clearly defined dependencies, and carefully allocated resources. The plan should help direct the implementation of a CDI platform in a way that supports coexistence between the old (legacy) and the new (CDI) environments until such time as the organization can decommission the legacy applications without invalidating business processes. We discuss these and other implementation challenges in Part IV of the book.

Most of the technical CDI challenges to achieve customer centricity deal with the following:

▶ Implementation costs and time-to-market

▶ Data governance and data quality

▶ Data synchronization

▶ Data visibility, security, and regulatory compliance

Implementation Costs and Time-to-Market Concerns

As we have already stated, large-scale MDM-CDI projects are risky. The risk is even higher because these projects are supposed to result in significant changes in business processes and impact structural, architectural, and operational models. Achieving all stated objectives of a CDI project may take several iterations that can span years. Therefore, it is not realistic to assume that the project team can deliver a comprehensive end-to-end solution in a single release. Such an unreasonable expectation would represent a significant implementation risk.

The project team can mitigate this risk by devising a sound release strategy. The strategy should include the end-state vision and an implementation plan that defines a stepwise approach in which each step or phase should deliver clear tactical benefits. These benefits should be tangible, measurable, and aligned with the strategic road map and business demands. Project plans should ensure that each release provides a measurable incremental business value on a regular, frequent basis, preferably every six to nine months. When multiple lines of business are involved in the CDI initiative, the first production release should be defined as a trade-off between the business priority of a given line of business and implementation feasibility that minimizes the delivery risk of the first release. We can extend this model by devising a strategy that maintains a trade-off between the business value of the release and release manageability, risk, and complexity, as illustrated in Figure 3-4.

Another implementation risk of a CDI project is caused by a project plan and approach that does not take into account the issues related to existing legacy data stores and applications. For example, consider a CDI project with the goal of delivering a brand new Data Hub. If the project plan does not account for the need to either integrate with or phase out the existing application legacy systems, the resulting CDI Data Hub environment may have questionable value since it will be difficult to synchronize it with various legacy systems and use it as an accurate authoritative customer master. The challenge of concurrently supporting the new customer-centric universe and the old, account-centric "legacy world" may be unavoidable. Both universes must coexist and cooperate in delivering business value, but the risks

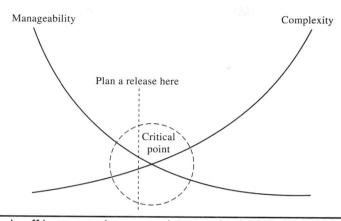

Figure 3-4   *Trade-off between release complexity and manageability*

associated with this approach have to be understood and mitigated through careful planning. For instance, the coexistence and cooperation approach may require significant integration and synchronization efforts, may complicate application and data maintenance, and thus may increase operational risk. Not planning for these efforts may result in a highly visible project failure and could negatively affect the enterprise's ability to transform itself into a new customer-centric business model.

Another concern related to the drive toward customer centricity is its potential organizational impact due to the implementation of new system platforms and new business processes. As we show in Part IV of this book, major CDI implementations lead to significant changes in the business processes that can greatly impact stakeholders' responsibilities and required skills. Some jobs can be significantly redefined. For example, a legacy mainframe application that was the system of record for customer information may lose its significance or may even be decommissioned when the CDI Data Hub becomes available as the new system of record for customer data.

Partnership with Vendors

Given the complexity of major MDM-CDI projects, it is reasonable to assume that no single vendor can provide an all-in-one, out-of-the-box comprehensive MDM-CDI solution that fits the business and technical requirements of every enterprise. This limitation puts MDM-CDI implementers in a position where they have to look for a combination of vendor products and home-grown solutions in order to meet the business demands of the enterprise. Involving multiple vendors is not unusual for any major MDM-CDI implementation. This approach requires that the organization implement a formal process of product evaluation and selection to determine which best-in-class products can make a short list of potentially acceptable solutions. Typically, once the short list is finalized, the organization may start a proof-of-concept activity where one or more vendors would implement working prototypes that would demonstrate both functional and nonfunctional capabilities. While this approach can protect the enterprise from blindly choosing a product based solely on the vendor's claims, it does create a significant management overhead of running one or more proof-of-concept projects, managing additional resources, dealing with the shortage of skilled resources, and balancing conflicting priorities. A strong architectural oversight for the activities that include multiple vendors and implementation partners is a must, and the lack of such an oversight represents a very common and significant implementation risk.

Data Quality, Data Synchronization, and Integration Challenges

Generally speaking, data has a tendency to "decay" and become stale with time as changes to the environment at large occur on a regular or sporadic basis (e.g., products change names, financial systems change accounting rules, etc.). This is especially true for customer data. Indeed, a 2003 study completed by The Data Warehousing Institute entitled "Data Quality and the Bottom Line" stated: "The problem with data is that its quality quickly degenerates over time. Experts say 2 percent of records in a customer file become obsolete in one month because customers die, divorce, marry, and move."

To put this statistic into perspective, assume that a company has 500,000 customers and prospects. If 2 percent of these records become obsolete in one month, that would be 10,000 records per month or 120,000 records every year. So, in two years, about half of all records are obsolete if left unchecked.

Customer Data Integration systems can create and maintain a consistent, accurate, and complete customer view. Critical customer relationship decisions such as promotions, price changes and discounts, marketing campaigns, credit decisions, and daily operations revolve around key customer data. Without an accurate and complete view of the customer, efforts to provide targeted, personalized, and compelling products and services may prove to be ineffective.

In no small measure, a company's success or failure is based on the quality of customer information. The challenge of CDI is to be able to quickly and accurately capture, standardize, and consolidate the immense amount of customer data that comes from a variety of channels, touch points, and application systems.

Many organizations have separate sales, operations, support, and marketing groups. If these groups have different databases of customer data—and different methods for recording and archiving this information—it is extremely difficult for the enterprise to rationalize and understand all of the customer processes and data infrastructure issues simultaneously.

The crux of the problem most companies face is the inability to compile a complete customer view when most of the systems are isolated from each other in their stovepipes and operate independently. By definition, a CDI system effectively bridges the gap between various customer views by rationalizing, integrating, and aggregating customer data collected from disparate data sources and applications in order to provide a single, accurate, consolidated view of the customer.

CDI systems benefit the enterprise by pulling critical customer information from existing internal and external data sources and validating that the data is correct and meets the business needs and data quality standards of the enterprise. Over time, CDI solutions can further enrich customer data with additional internal and external information, and store, manage, and maintain the customer master data as an authoritative system of record for the enterprise.

One approach for maintaining data quality and integrity would be to attack the problem at the operational system level. This seems to be a practical approach. After all, operational systems support applications that manage and execute transactions and maintain transactional properties of atomicity, consistency, isolation, and durability (ACID). To sustain these properties, operational, transactional applications tend to be isolated from nonoperational applications such as data warehousing and business intelligence systems. This "isolation" helps discover and resolve data integrity issues one system at a time.

Correcting data quality is only part of the problem. Once the data has been corrected, the data changes have to be synchronized and integrated with various data sources. Moreover, various data records about the same individual need to be aggregated into a single customer-centric database. Although data integration challenges are not new and are not unique to the CDI space, Customer Data Integration emphasizes their criticality. The challenges of data integration include the following:

▶ **Lack of standardization of customer or company names and addresses** Without standardizing this information, it is difficult to resolve customer lifetime value, as customers may have different representations within databases.

▶ **No common identifier or linking of customers across systems** For example, an individual customer record may be stored in several operational systems, and thus the customer can be represented differently in every system, even using different names and aliases. This representation mismatch may prevent a CDI solution from recognizing the same individual across various applications and data stores.

▶ **Incorrect data** Traditional customer data solutions often use special codes to signify unknown or default data. For example, a phone number of "999-999-9999" or a birth date of "01/01/01" may represent common shortcuts for unspecified or missing data. These special codes may have to be treated in a way that escalates data content questions to the appropriate data steward.

▶ **Stale, outdated data** As we stated earlier, data has a tendency to change over time. Left unchecked and unmanaged, these changes do not get reflected in the customer database, thus significantly reducing the value of data.

One of the stated goals and key requirements of any CDI system is to create and maintain the best possible information about customers regardless of the number and type of the source data systems. To achieve this goal, Customer Data Integration should support an effective data acquisition process (discussed in more detail in Chapter 6). The CDI process requires different steps and rules for different data sources. However, the basic process is consistent, and at a minimum should answer the following questions:

▶ What points of data collection might have customer information?

▶ How does each data source store, validate, and audit customer information?

▶ What sources contain the best customer data?

▶ How can data be integrated across various data sources?

▶ What information about customers is required for current and future business processes?

▶ Where does this customer information reside?

Of course, there are many questions surrounding data quality concerns. Answering these questions can help a CDI solution to determine what business and integration rules are required to bring the best data from the various sources together. This best-available customer data is integrated under the CDI umbrella and should be cleansed, rationalized, integrated, and then synchronized with operational customer data systems.

Data Visibility, Security, and Regulatory Compliance

Solving data quality and data integration challenges allows CDI solutions to enable customer-centric business process transformation. As part of this transformation, the CDI platform creates a fully integrated view of the customers and their relationships with the enterprise, information that most likely has to be protected according to a multitude of various government and industry regulations. Or, stating it slightly differently, integrating customer information in a CDI Data Hub supports enterprise-wide customer-centric transformations that in turn create significant competitive advantages for the enterprise. At the same time, precisely because an MDM-CDI system integrates all customer data in one place called a Data Hub, these implementations face significant security and compliance risks.

The majority of the relevant regulations discussed here focus on the financial services segment and deal with the need to protect customer data from corruption and compromised, unauthorized access and use. In addition, a number of government and industry regulations require an enterprise to capture and enforce customer privacy preferences. Part III of this book provides a detailed look into the requirements for data protection and their impact on the technology of MDM-CDI solutions.

We offer a brief overview of the data protection and privacy regulations in this section for the purpose of completeness and ease of reference.

Basel II and FFIEC

Basel II defines operational risk to include the risk of compromise and fraud. Therefore, when the Federal Financial Institutions Examination Council (FFIEC) stipulated its latest guidance, it immediately affected the scope of Basel II's operational risk in these specific ways:

- ► In order to combat fraud, on October 12, 2005 FFIEC issued new guidance on customer authentication for online banking services. The guidance stated that U.S. banks would be expected to comply with the rules by the end of 2006.

- ► The new regulations guide banks to apply two major methods:

  - ► Risk assessment: Banks must assess the risk of the various activities taking place on their Internet banking site.

  - ► Risk-based authentication: Banks must apply stronger authentication for high-risk transactions.

- ► Specific guidelines require banks to implement

  - ► Layered security

  - ► Monitoring and reporting

  - ► Configurable authentication where its strength depends on degree of risk

  - ► Customer awareness and reverse authentication

  - ► Single-factor and multifactor authentication

  - ► Mutual authentication

The USA Patriot Act's KYC Provision

CDI data protection concerns are driven by regulations such as the USA Patriot Act and Basel Committee's "Customer Due Diligence for Banks" issued in October 2001. The USA Patriot Act specifies requirements to comply with Know-Your-Customers (KYC) provisions. Banks with inadequate KYC policies are exposed to significant legal and reputation risks. Sound KYC policies and procedures protect the integrity of the bank and serve as remedies against money laundering, terrorist financing, and other unlawful activities. KYC is an important part of the risk management practices of any bank, financial services institution, or insurance company. KYC requires Customer Acceptance policy (opt-in/opt-out), customer identification, ongoing monitoring of high-risk accounts, and risk management. CDI-enabled Customer Identification is one of the key drivers for the enterprises to implement systems known as Customer Identity Hub platform.

Customer Fraud Protection

One of the tenets of customer fraud protection is based on sound customer identification and recognition capabilities offered by CDI. According to www.identityguard.com, over 28 million Americans have had their identity stolen in the past three years. According to the California research firm Javelin Strategy & Research, in 2005 there were 8.9 million identity theft victims in the U.S. alone, costing $56.6 billion USD!

The Sarbanes-Oxley Act

The Sarbanes-Oxley Act of 2002 requires public companies to implement internal controls over financial reporting, operations, and assets. The Securities and Exchange Commission (SEC) requires that companies make regular disclosures about the strength, weaknesses, and overall status of these controls. The implementation of these controls is heavily dependent on information technology. The current state of information technology in most of the global companies does not allow them to operate with the required level of data and process transparency. Sarbanes-Oxley's demands for operational transparency, reporting, and controls fuel the needs for CDI-MDM implementations.

OFAC

The Office of Foreign Asset Control (OFAC) of the U.S. Department of the Treasury administers and enforces economic and trade sanctions against target countries, terrorists, international narcotic trafficking, and those entities engaged in activities related to the proliferation of weapons of mass destruction. Executive Order 13224 requires OFAC to make available to customer-facing institutions a list of "blocked individuals" known as Specially Designated Nationals (SDN). The executive order requires institutions to verify their customers' identity against the "blocked list." Clearly, a CDI solution is a valuable platform that can help achieve OFAC compliance.

Gramm-Leach-Bliley Act (GLBA)

The Financial Modernization Act of 1999, also known as the "Gramm-Leach-Bliley Act," includes provisions to protect consumers' personal financial information held by financial institutions. There are three parts of the privacy requirements: the Financial Privacy Rule, the Safeguard Rule, and Pretexting provisions. The Financial Privacy Rule regulates the collection and disclosure of customer information. The Safeguards Rule requires enterprises to design, implement, and maintain safeguards to protect customer information. The Pretexting provisions of the GLBA protect consumers from individuals and companies that obtain the consumers' personal information under false pretenses.

GLBA requires disclosure on what information a company can collect, the usage of the collected information, what information can or cannot be disclosed, and the customer-specific opt-in/opt-out options. The Safeguard Rule includes a disclosure of the procedures used to protect customer information from unauthorized access or loss. For the Internet users, the company must disclose the information collected when the user accesses the company's web site.

Given the potential scope and information value of data stored in CDI Data Hubs, it is easy to see why CDI implementations should consider GLBA compliance as one of the key risk-mitigation strategies.

The UK Financial Services Act

The UK Financial Services Act (1986) requires companies to match customer records against lists of banned individuals (terrorists, money launderers, and others) more rapidly and accurately. CDI Data Hub is an effective data enabler to conduct these matches.

DNC Compliance

As part of their privacy protection campaign, the United States and later Canada accepted Do Not Call (DNC) legislation. In order to avoid penalties, telemarketers must comply with this regulation, which may also require some level of customer recognition and identification. The legislation requires the companies to maintain their customers' opt-in/opt-out options. Customer-centric CDI implementations allow the enterprise to capture and enforce DNC preferences at the customer levels as well as at the account levels. Chapter 5 illustrates this concept by discussing a high-level CDI data model.

CPNI Compliance

The Consumer Proprietary Network Information regulation (CPNI) prohibits telephone companies from using information identifying whom customers call, when they call, and the kinds of phone services they purchased for marketing purposes without customer consent. This creates the need for the opt-in/opt-out support and offers a platform to drive CPNI compliance.

HIPAA

The Health Insurance Portability and Accountability Act (HIPAA) of 1996 (45 CFR Parts 160 and 164) requires the federal government to protect the privacy of personal health information by issuing national standards. A CDI Data Hub for a health care provider or a pharmaceutical company may contain comprehensive and complete personal health information at the customer/patient level. Thus, HIPAA directly affects the design and implementation of CDI solutions that deal with customer health information.

In conclusion, this chapter demonstrates that while MDM-CDI solutions can offer significant benefits to an enterprise, these solutions are not easy to develop and deploy. Further, there are many challenges that an organization has to address when it embarks on a MDM-CDI initiative.

We also showed that MDM, especially its customer-focused variant known as Customer Data Integration (CDI), holds the promise of enabling an enterprise to transform its business model from a traditional account-centric view to a new, effective customer-centric business model, which not only offers significant benefits and competitive advantages but also presents major additional technical, organizational, and business challenges. We discuss many of these challenges, issues, and approaches in more details in Parts II, III, and IV of this book.

Architectural Considerations

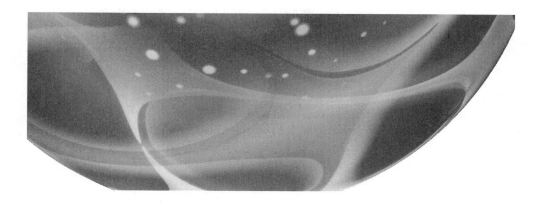

Ⅰn the introductory part of this book, we offered a broad-brush description of the purpose, drivers, and key benefits of Master Data Management and Customer Data Integration. This part of the book discusses the issues of MDM and CDI architecture as a key logical step to building enterprise-wide solutions.

Architecture discussion is important for several reasons:

▶ A comprehensive end-to-end MDM-CDI solution is much more than just a database of customer or product information organized by some kind of a unique key. Some CDI capabilities and components are "traditional" and are a part of a common best-practice design for integrated data solutions, while other, new features came to light primarily in the context of MDM-CDI problem domains. An architectural vision can help organize the "old" and the "new" features into an integrated, scalable, and manageable solution.

▶ MDM-CDI is not just a technology problem—a comprehensive MDM-CDI solution consists of technology components and services as well as new business processes and even organizational structures and dynamics. There are many architecture viewpoints, significant complexity, and a large number of interdependencies to warrant a framework-based approach to the architecture. This multifaceted, multidimensional architecture framework looks at the overall problem domain from different but complementary angles.

▶ Any solution intended to create an authoritative, accurate, and timely system of record that should eventually replace existing legacy sources of the information must be integrated with the enterprise architecture and infrastructure. Given the heterogeneity and the "age" of legacy systems, this requirement is often difficult to satisfy without a comprehensive architecture blueprint.

Thus, we organized this part of the book in the following fashion: First, we discuss the architectural genesis of MDM and CDI. Then, we take a closer look at the enterprise architecture framework and explain how this framework helps us see different aspects of the solution as interconnected and interdependent views. To that end, we organized the architecture discussions into two groups: The first group (Chapter 5) discusses the architectural concerns that are specific to MDM-CDI solutions. The second group (Chapter 6) deals with the more traditional issues of data architecture and data management.

CDI Architecture and Data Hub Components

IN THIS CHAPTER

Architectural Definition of Master Data Management and Customer Data Integration

Evolution of Customer Data Integration Architecture

CDI Architectural Philosophy

CDI Architecture Viewpoints

Architectural Definition of Master Data Management and Customer Data Integration

In order to understand "how" to build a comprehensive Master Data Management solution, we need to define the "what" of Master Data Management and its customer-data-focused version known as Customer Data Integration (CDI).

We have already offered high-level definitions of MDM and CDI in Part I of this book. In this chapter, we are extending those definitions to have a better basis for discussing MDM and CDI architecture. As shown in the previous chapters, the scope of Master Data Management by its very nature is extremely broad and applies equally well to customer-centric, product-centric, and reference-data-centric business problems, to name just a few. A common thread among the solutions to these problems is the ability to create and maintain an accurate, timely, and authoritative "system of record" for a given subject domain. Clearly, such a definition can be refined further for each situation and problem domain addressed by Master Data Management.

The task of defining the "what" is somewhat easier when we focus just on Customer Data Integration. Indeed, since we know the subject to which the MDM has to be applied (in this case, customer data), we can use a working definition of CDI that we offered in Chapter 1:

> ▶   *Customer Data Integration* is a comprehensive set of technology components, services, and business processes that create, maintain, and make available an accurate, timely, integrated, and complete view of a customer across lines of business, channels, and business partners.

To state it slightly differently, a CDI solution takes customer data from a variety of data sources, discards redundant data, and cleanses, rationalizes, and aggregates it to the extent possible. Imagine the CDI environment as a hub and spokes where the spokes are information sources that are connected to the central hub as a new "home" for the accurate, aggregated, and timely customer data (see Figure 4-1). This description helps explain why we often use the term "Data Hub" when discussing CDI and MDM solution space.

Interestingly, using this definition of "what" CDI is does not make our goal of creating architecture much easier to achieve. Indeed, this definition points to the fact that a CDI solution is much more than just a database of customer information, a solution known by many as a Customer Information File (CIF), a data warehouse of customer information, or an operational data store (ODS). In fact, this definition describes an enterprise-scale system that consists of software components, services, processes, data models and data stores, metadata repositories, applications, networks, and other infrastructure components.

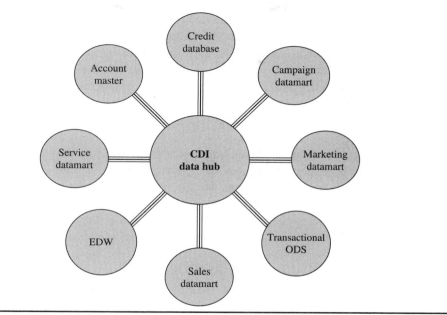

Figure 4-1   *CDI Data Hub*

In order to develop a clear understanding of the "how" of the CDI solution we review the historical roots of Master Data Management and its evolution from early attempts to deliver on the MDM promise to what it has become today.

Evolution of Customer Data Integration Architecture

As we discussed in Chapter 1, the need to create and maintain an accurate and timely "information system of record" is not new, and it applies equally to businesses and government entities. Lately, a number of regulatory requirements that include the Sarbanes-Oxley Act and the Basel II Capital Accord (see discussion on these regulations in Part III of the book) has emphasized this need even further.

In the case of Customer Data Integration, organizations had engaged in creating customer-centric business models, applications, and enabling infrastructure for a long time. However, as the business complexity, number of customers, number of lines of business, and number of sales and service channels continued to grow. This growth often proceeded in a tactical, nonintegrated fashion. As result many organizations ended up with a wide variety of customer information stores and applications that manage customer data.

However, the customer data in those "legacy" environments was often incomplete and inconsistent across various data stores, applications, and lines of business. In many cases, individual applications and lines of business were reasonably satisfied with the quality and scope of customer data that they managed. However, the lack of completeness and accuracy and the lack of consistency across lines of business continue to prevent organizations from creating a complete and accurate view of customers and their relationships with the servicing organization and its partners.

Recognizing this customer data challenge and the resulting inability to transform the business from the account-centric to the customer-centric model, organizations have developed a variety of solutions that attempted to help move the organizations into the new customer-centric world. Although in general these solutions added some incremental value, many of them were deployed in the constraints of the existing lines of business and very few were built with a true enterprise-wide focus in mind. Nevertheless, these solutions and attempts to achieve customer centricity have helped define MDM in general and CDI in particular to become a real enabler of achieving customer centricity, and therefore we need to understand what has been done and what, if any, portions of the existing solutions can and should be leveraged in implementing CDI. These solutions include Customer Information File (CIF); Extract, Transform, and Load Technologies (ETL); Enterprise Data Warehouse (EDW); an Operational Data Store (ODS); Data Quality Technologies (DQ); Enterprise Information Integration (EII); and Customer Relationship Management systems (CRM).

Although these solutions and technologies were discussed briefly in Chapter 1, we want to offer a slightly deeper and more architecture-focused review of these solutions and their suitability to act as components of a Customer Data Integration platform.

▶ **Customer Information File (CIF)**   Many companies have established LOB-specific or company-wide customer information file environments. Historically, CIF solutions used older file management or database management systems (DBMS) technology, and represented some basic point-in-time (static) information about the customers. In other words, CIFs offer limited flexibility and extensibility and are not well suited to capturing and maintaining real-time customer data, customer privacy preferences, customer behavior traits, and customer relationships. Moreover, traditional CIF does not support new complex business processes, event management, and data-level security constraints known as visibility (see Part III for a detailed discussion on this topic). Shortcomings like these prevent traditional CIF environments from becoming a cross-LOB integration vehicle of customer data. Although CIF systems do not deliver a "single version of the truth" about the customer, in most cases existing CIF systems are used to feed the company's Customer Relationship Management systems. Moving forward, a CIF can and should be treated as a key source data file that feeds a new Customer Data Integration Data Hub system.

▶ **Extract, Transform, and Load (ETL)**   These tools are used to extract data from multiple data sources, transform the data to a required target structure, and load the data into the target data store. A key functionality required from the ETL tool is its ability to perform complex transformations from source formats to the target; these transformations may include Boolean expressions, calculations, substitutions, reference table lookup, support for business rules for aggregation and consolidation, and many other features. Contemporary ETL tools include components that perform data consistency and data quality analysis as well as the ability to generate and use metadata definitions for data attributes and entities. Many tools could create output data in the XML format according to the predefined schema. Finally, the enterprise-class ETL tools are designed for high scalability and performance and can parallelize most of their operations to achieve acceptable processing times when dealing with very large data sets. Although typical ETL process runs in batch mode, best-in-class ETL tools can support near-real-time transformations and load functionality. Given that description, it is quite clear that an ETL component can and should be used to put data into a CDI platform—Data Hub—both for the initial load and possibly for the incremental data updates that keep the Data Hub in sync with existing data stores. We discuss MDM-CDI data synchronization approaches using ETL in Chapter 15.

▶ **Enterprise Data Warehouse (EDW)**   Strictly speaking, a data warehouse is an information system that provides its users with current and historical decision support information that is hard to access or present in traditional operational data stores. An enterprise-wide data warehouse of customer information can become an integration vehicle where most of the customer data can be stored. Typically, EDW solutions support business intelligence applications and customer relationship management systems. EDW's design, technology platform, and its data schema are optimized to support efficient storage and processing of complex queries against large amount of historical data. Traditionally, companies use EDW systems as informational environments rather than operational systems that process real-time, transactional data. Since EDW cleanses and rationalizes the data it manages in order to satisfy the needs of the consuming BI and CRM systems, an EDW becomes a good platform from which data should be loaded into the Data Hub.

▶ **Operational Data Store (ODS)**   This technology allows transaction-level detail data records to be stored in a nonsummarized, queryable, and long-lasting form. ODS supports transaction-level analysis and other applications that deal with the low level of details. ODS differs from a data warehouse in that it does not maintain summarized data nor does it manage historical information. ODS allows users to aggregate transaction-level data into higher-level attributes but does not support a drill-down into the underlying detail records. ODS is frequently used in conjunction with the Enterprise Data Warehouse to provide the company with both historical and transactional real-time data. Similar to the EDW, an ODS of customer data can and should be considered a valuable source of information for constructing a CDI solution.

▶ **Data Quality Technologies (DQ)**   From the point of view of a business value proposition, the focus of data quality technologies and tools is to help all applications to produce meaningful and reliable results. These tools are especially important for delivering accurate business intelligence and decision support, improving customer retention, sales and customer service, customer experience, risk management, compliance, and fraud detection. Companies use data quality technologies to profile data, to report anomalies, and to standardize and "fix" data in order to correct data inconsistencies and known data quality issues such as missing or invalid data. Data quality tools are especially effective when dealing with the name and address attributes of customer data records—a key set of attributes required to match several customer records belonging to the same individual or organization. Data quality tools and technologies are some of the key components of any Master Data Management solution including a CDI platform such as a Data Hub.

▶ **Enterprise Information Integration (EII)**   Enterprise Information Integration tools are frequently used to aggregate smaller amounts of distributed data in memory or nonpersistent storage, usually in real time. Companies use EII solutions to perform search queries across distributed databases and aggregate the results of the queries at the application or presentation layer. Contrast that with the data integration solutions that aggregate and persist the information at the back end (i.e., in a data warehouse or a CDI Data Hub). An EII engine, queries a distributed database environment and delivers virtualized aggregated data that appears as if it came from a single source. Some CDI implementations use EII technologies to provide users with a virtualized total view of a customer without creating a persistent physical image of the aggregation, thus providing additional data model flexibility for the target Data Hub.

▶ **Customer Relationship Management (CRM)**   Customer relationship management is a set of technologies and business processes designed to help the company understand the customer, improve customer experience, and optimize customer-facing business processes across marketing, sales, and servicing channels. From the architecture perspective, CRM systems are consumers of customer data and are some of the primary beneficiaries of the CDI Hubs.

CDI Architectural Philosophy

Master Data Management and Customer Data Integration are the milestones on the path of transforming an enterprise from an account-centric to a customer-centric business. In other words, MDM and CDI are not revolutionary since they grew from and are direct beneficiaries of the variety of solutions and approaches described in the previous section. This evolutionary approach allows us to construct many different viewpoints, each of which represents a particular architecture type.

For example, we can create a CDI architecture view that addresses a variety of architectural and management concerns. Specifically, we can develop an architectural view that defines components responsible for the following functional capabilities:

- ▶ Creation and management of the core data stores
- ▶ Processes implementing data governance and data quality
- ▶ Metadata management
- ▶ Extraction, transformation, and load of data from sources to target
- ▶ Backup and recovery
- ▶ Customer analytics
- ▶ Security and visibility
- ▶ Synchronization and persistence of data changes
- ▶ Transaction management
- ▶ Matching and generation of unique identifiers

The complexity of the MDM-CDI architecture and the multitude of the architectural components represent an interesting problem that is often difficult to solve: how to address such a wide variety of architectural and design concerns in a holistic, integrated fashion. One approach to solving this type of a challenge is to use the notion of a top-down, abstracted representation of the MDM-CDI functionality as a stack of the interdependent architecture layers, where a given layer of functionality uses services provided by the layers below, and in turn provides services to the layers above.

Defining Service-Oriented Architecture

Service-Oriented Architecture (SOA) is an architecture in which software components can be exposed as loosely coupled, coarse-grained, reusable services that can be integrated with each other and invoked by different applications for different purposes through a variety of platform-independent service interfaces available via standard network protocols.

We can further enhance the notion of the layered architecture by expressing the functional capabilities of each of the architecture layers in the stack as a set of abstracted services, with a degree of abstraction that varies from high (at the upper layers of the stack) to low (for the bottom layers of the stack). The notion of abstracted services is very powerful and provides architects, designers, and implementers with a number of tangible benefits. We discuss these benefits later in this chapter in the section describing Service-Oriented Architecture (SOA).

Applying the notion of service-level abstraction to the MDM-CDI architecture, we can define its key architecture principle as follows:

▶   An effective MDM-CDI solution should be architected as a metadata-driven Service-Oriented Architecture (SOA) platform that provides and consumes services that allow the enterprise to rapidly move from old account-centric legacy systems to the new customer-centric model.

While the notion of using service-level abstraction is fundamental and even necessary in architecting enterprise-scale MDM-CDI solutions, it is not totally sufficient. Other aspects of the MDM-CDI architecture are better described using alternative architecture representations, or architecture viewpoints, that differ in the content, context, and levels of abstraction. In order to formalize the process of defining and using various architecture viewpoints we need to introduce a notion of the multidimensional enterprise architecture framework. Those readers already familiar with the principles and concepts of the architecture framework can skip this section.

Enterprise Architecture Framework: A Brief Introduction

As stated earlier in this chapter, the complex multifaceted nature of a CDI solution cannot be described using a single architecture view, but instead requires a number of architectural views organized in a multidimensional architecture framework.

Let's illustrate this framework notion using an analogy of building a new community within existing city boundaries. In this case, the city planners and the architects need to create a scale-down model of the new area including buildings, streets, parks, etc. Once this level of architecture is completed and approved, the building architects would start developing building blueprints. Similarly, the road engineers would start designing the streets and intersections. Utilities engineers would start planning for underground cabling, water, and sewerage. City planners would start estimating the number and type of schools and other public facilities required to support the new community. And this list goes on.

Clearly, before the work can get started, the city planners will have to create a number of architecture views all of which are connected together to enable a cohesive and complete picture of *what*, *when, where,* and *how* the individual parts of the new city area will be built.

To state it differently, any complex system can be viewed from multiple angles each of which can be represented by a different architecture type. To organize these various architecture types into a holistic and connected picture we will use an enterprise architecture framework first pioneered by John Zachman. This framework helps architects, designers, and engineers to develop a complex solution in a connected, cohesive, and comprehensive fashion.

Zachman's principal insight was the way to solve the complexity of the enterprise architecture by decomposing the problem into two main dimensions each of which consisted of multiple subcategories. The first dimension defines the various levels of abstraction that represent business scope, conceptual level (business model), logical level (system model), and physical level (technology model). The second dimension consists of key decision-driving questions—what, how, where, who, when, and why. In the context of the enterprise architecture, these questions are considered at the different levels of the first dimension as follows:

- ▶ "What" answers the question about what data flows throughout the enterprise.

- ▶ "How" describes the functions and business processes performed by different parts of the enterprise.

- ▶ "Where" defines the network that provides interprocess and intercomponent connectivity and information delivery.

- ▶ "Who" defines the people and organizational structures affected by the target architecture.

- ▶ "Why" represents business drivers for this architecture-based initiative.

- ▶ "When" defines the timing constraints and processing requirements.

Each question of the second dimension at every level of the first dimension represents a particular architecture viewpoint, for example, a logical data model

Figure 4-2   *Zachman's enterprise architecture framework*

view or a physical network architecture view. All these 30 viewpoints are organized together in the framework to comprise a complete enterprise architecture.

Figure 4-2 shows a graphical representation of Zachman's Framework.

The representation in Figure 4-2 is based on the work published by Zachman's Institute for Framework Advancement (ZIFA).

The value of such an architecture framework is its ability to act as a guide for organizing various design concerns into a set of separate but connected models. The framework benefits become apparent as the complexity and the heterogeneity of the system that is being designed increases. In the case of Master Data Management and Customer Data Integration, the framework approach helps address the complexity of the individual functions and components, integration of the new MDM-CDI environment with the legacy systems, and the need to implement an effective, efficient, secure, and manageable solution in a stepwise, controlled fashion.

CDI Architecture Viewpoints

Because of its broad coverage of the business-to-technology dimensions, an architecture framework can also help organize and promote different points of view for an enterprise. Different people within the enterprise may express these points of view differently based on their organizational affiliation, skill sets, and even the political landscape of the workplace. Since a full-function MDM solution tends to be truly an enterprise-scale initiative that spans organizational and lines-of-business boundaries, the benefit of using the framework approach helps gain organizational buy-in and support for usually expensive and lengthy MDM projects.

Of course, we do not want to create an impression that any MDM and CDI solution has to be architected using Zachman's Framework. In fact, very few enterprise-wide initiatives use this framework in its entirety with all its 30 viewpoints. Many architecture-savvy organizations use a subset of the complete enterprise architecture framework or different architecture viewpoints. The goal of the preceding architecture framework discussion was simply to illustrate the principles and benefits of the enterprise architecture framework approach as a way to solve the design and implementation challenges of any large and complex software system.

We would like to use the principles of the architecture framework to define the most relevant architecture viewpoints for a successful design and implementation of a MDM-CDI solution, with a specific emphasis on the CDI Data Hub implementations. In this context, we will focus the framework viewpoints discussion on the conceptual and logical levels of the architecture, and shall consider the following set of architecture viewpoints:

► Consumption and reconciliation architecture

► Data Hub implementation styles

- ► Conceptual architecture
- ► High-level reference architecture
- ► Services architecture
- ► Data architecture

From the framework perspective, we recognize many different but equally important architecture viewpoints. However, since describing a complete framework set is beyond the scope of this book, we'll focus the follow-on discussion in this chapter on three viewpoints: services view, consumption view, and reference architecture view. We discuss additional architecture details and specific data architecture views in Chapters 5 and 6, while data security and visibility architecture views are discussed in Chapter 10.

Services Architecture View

A services architecture viewpoint is a perfect example of how we can extend the architecture framework approach to describe complex systems such as MDM-CDI systems. Indeed, even though Zachman's Framework does not explicitly show a services architecture viewpoint, we can define such a viewpoint for a Data Hub system and show how this viewpoint can be mapped to Zachman's Framework.

Introduction to Service-Oriented Architecture

We define *service-oriented architecture (SOA)* as an architecture in which software components can be exposed as loosely coupled, coarse-grained, reusable services that can be integrated with each other and invoked by different applications for different purposes through a variety of platform-independent service interfaces available via standard network protocols.

The World Wide Web Consortium (W3C) has developed a comprehensive definition of the service-oriented architecture in its February 2004 Working Group publication.

W3C Definition of Service-Oriented Architecture

A Service-Oriented Architecture (SOA) is a form of distributed systems architecture that is typically characterized by the following properties:

- ► **Logical view** The service is an abstracted, logical view of actual programs, databases, business processes, etc., defined in terms of what it does, typically carrying out a business-level operation.

▶ **Message orientation**   The service is formally defined in terms of the messages exchanged between provider agents and requester agents, and not the properties of the agents themselves.

▶ **Description orientation**   A service is described by machine-processable metadata.

▶ **Granularity**   Services tend to use a small number of operations with relatively large and complex messages.

▶ **Network orientation**   Services tend to be oriented toward use over a network, though this is not an absolute requirement.

▶ **Platform-neutral**   Messages are sent in a platform-neutral, standardized format delivered through the interfaces.

Similar to the architecture framework discussion, we can define SOA in a way that recognizes multiple views of service orientation and clearly relies on the messaging paradigm implemented over a network. In addition to these views, we can also show that the Service-Oriented Architecture can be mapped to the viewpoints of the Enterprise Architecture Framework. Specifically, SOA is not a technology or a product. Rather it can be described as a design philosophy for the Application Architecture portion of the framework. If we use the SOA definition to represent information technology assets as services, then SOA can be mapped to the framework at the Logical level within the Function domain.

We can logically extend this approach to show that the set of functional services represents business processes, and since SOA is based on the network-aware messaging paradigm, the notion of the service orientation can be realized in several architecture framework viewpoints that connect process models and network-based messaging.

We offer these considerations simply to demonstrate that the framework approach and service-oriented architecture are closely connected and continuously evolving concepts that together help describe and plan the design and implementation of complex systems such as Master Data Management and Customer Data Integration.

SOA Benefits

Additional insights into the SOA include the following key principal benefits:

▶ SOA offers access mechanisms to the application logic as a service to users and other applications where

   ▶ Service interfaces are independent of user interfaces.

   ▶ Services are business-process-oriented.

- ▶ Business-level services are coarse-grained and can be easily mapped to business functions.

- ▶ Coarse-grained services can be combined or assembled from lower-level, fine-grained service primitives at run time.

- ▶ Services are published in a standard fashion for discovery and execution.

- ▶ Services can be used/reused by existing applications and systems.

▶ SOA permits the construction of scalable applications over the network.

▶ SOA supports asynchronous communications.

▶ SOA supports application-level conversations and state management.

SOA can significantly simplify and accelerate the development of new applications by invoking a variety of published services and organizing or orchestrating them to achieve the desired business functionality. Since SOA allows business-level services to be assembled at run time, developers do not have to design all possible variations of services in advance. This reduces the development time and helps minimize the number of errors in the application code.

One of the benefits of SOA is its ability to leverage the power and flexibility of Web Services across the enterprise by building loosely coupled, standards-based applications that produce and consume services.

Introduction to Web Services

Web Services is a concept that enables a shift in distributed computing toward loosely coupled, standards-based, service-oriented architectures that help achieve better cross-business integration, improved efficiency, and closer customer relationships.

A short definition of *Web Services* states that Web Services are *encapsulated, loosely coupled, contracted* software objects that are published and consumed using standard interfaces and protocols. The true power of Web Services lies in three related concepts that describe how Web Services change the fundamental nature of distributed computing:

- ▶ Web Services offer a standard way of supporting both synchronous and asynchronous messages—a capability essential to perform *long-running* B2B transactions.

- ▶ Web Services are loosely coupled, enabling *reduction in the integration costs* as well as facilitating *federation* of systems.

- ▶ Web Services support *coarse* granularity of the application programming interfaces (APIs). A coarse-grained interface rolls up the functions of many different API calls into a small number of business-oriented messages—a key to *business process automation.*

Web Services

Web Services are encapsulated, loosely coupled, contracted software objects that are published and consumed using standard interfaces and protocols.

A high-level view of Service-Oriented Architecture is shown in Figure 4-3.

Another, more structured view of the service-oriented reference architecture has been developed by the standards organization called Organization for the Advancement of Structured Information Standards (OASIS), and it is depicted in Figure 4-4.

Web Services are rapidly evolving from intraenterprise usage to interenterprise communities of interest to general-purpose business-to-business environments, enabling significant reductions in the cost of integration among established business partners. Web Services have changed the way companies do business. For example, business transactions that use Web Services can offer new per-use or subscription-based revenue opportunities by exposing value-added services via public, Internet-accessible directories. Combined with the benefits of the client-centric transformations offered by the CDI Data Hub solutions, Web Services and Service-Oriented Architecture are powerful tools that can have a direct and positive impact on the design, implementation, and benefits of the new customer-centric business strategies.

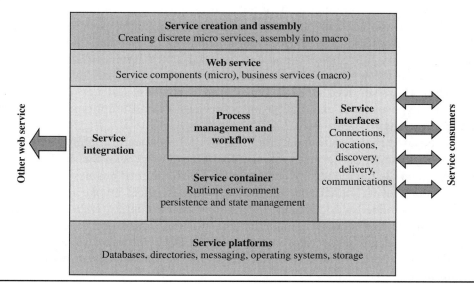

Figure 4-3   *Service-Oriented Architecture*

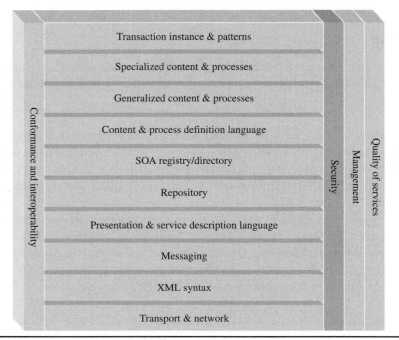

Figure 4-4   *OASIS service-oriented reference architecture*

Specifically, applying SOA principles to the CDI solutions, we can construct a high-level service-oriented view of the CDI Data Hub (see Figure 4-5). Here, the Data Hub acts as a services platform that supports two major groups of services: internal, infrastructure-type services that maintain Data Hub data integrity and enable necessary functionality; and external, published services. The latter category of services maps well to the business functions that can leverage CDI Data Hub. These services are often considered as business services, and the Data Hub exposes these external business services for consumptions by the users and applications.

As we stated in the section defining MDM-CDI architectural philosophy, we can organize all the services into a layered framework with the services consumers on the top requesting and using the coarse-grained business services on the second layer. These published, business-level services invoke appropriate internal, fine-grained services in the layer below. In this context, Data Hub internal services enable data access and maintain data integrity, consistency, security, and availability. The internal services interact with the Data Hub as a Data Service provider, and potentially with other data stores for the purpose of data acquisition, synchronization, and delivery.

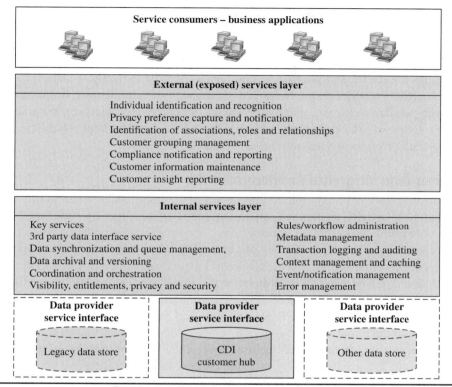

Figure 4-5   *CDI Data Hub as a service platform*

The services invoke executable components and implement methods that perform requested actions. Following the principles of the service-oriented architecture and Web Services, the lower-level Data Hub services can be combined to form more coarse-grained, composite, business-level services that execute business transactions. In general, the service-oriented nature of the Data Hub platform would allow this service assembly to take place at run time. In this case, a Data Hub would help establish an appropriate execution environment including the support for transactional semantics, coordination, compensation, and orchestration of services. A full-function CDI Data Hub system would deliver these features through a dedicated set of internal services and functional components. It is important to note that this description applies to a general service-oriented design of a Data Hub solution. While many Data Hub vendor products support this functionality, support for the scalability, flexibility, and granularity of the business services varies significantly from product to product. We discuss additional details of the Data Hub as an instance of a service-oriented architecture in Chapter 5. We describe the Data Hub components view in the context of the reference architecture later in this chapter.

Consumption and Reconciliation Viewpoint

Many industry analysts define versions of Data Hub architecture as architecture styles, for example, a Registry style or a full Transactional Hub style. These definitions are useful and provide a good handle on how to design a Data Hub to exhibit certain behavior traits. However, armed with the architecture framework approach, we can recognize that these "styles" represent architecture viewpoints that determine the way the Data Hub is intended to be used and be kept reliably in synch with its data providers (data sources) and data consumers.

Customer Data Integration Architectural Styles

The consumption and reconciliation architecture viewpoints described in this section offer valuable insights on how to construct a scalable and function-rich Data Hub. These viewpoints represent an intersection of the functional and data dimensions of the enterprise architecture framework at the logical, conceptual, and contextual levels. The resulting design constructs are a direct consequence of the different breadth and depth of the CDI data model coverage. These design styles vary in the context of other dimensions of the enterprise architecture framework including the organizational need and readiness to create and fully deploy a new system of records about customer data. And of course, these design styles manifest themselves in different service-oriented architecture viewpoints. Let's briefly describe the four predominant CDI architecture styles in the context of data content and consumption and reconciliation services. We discuss the implementation concerns of these architecture styles in Chapter 11.

CDI Architecture Styles

CDI architecture and design styles include

▶ External reference

▶ Registry

▶ Reconciliation engine

▶ Transaction hub

In general, a Data Hub data model may contain all data attributes about the customer, or just some attributes, while other attributes remain in their original data stores. It is logical to assume that the Data Hub should be the "master" of those data attributes it manages. This assumption is one of the drivers defining the Data Hub design options. Let's consider the following CDI Data Hub design styles:

▶ **External Reference Style**   In this case, a Data Hub is a reference database pointing to all source customer data stores, but does not usually contain actual customer data.

> ▶ This is the most extreme case where a Data Hub contains only a reference to customer data that continues to reside in the legacy data stores. In this case, the Data Hub acts as a special "directory" and points to the customer data that continues to be created and updated by the existing legacy applications. This design option is known as the *External Reference Data Hub*, and it is the least complex of the Data Hub styles.

▶ **Registry Style**   This style of a Data Hub represents a registry of unique customer identifiers (created using identity attributes); it maintains links with data sources that were used to obtain the identity attributes, and it allows the consuming application to either retrieve or assemble customer view at run time.

> ▶ A *Registry-style Data Hub* maintains some, usually key, customer profile attributes that the Hub uses to generate a unique customer identifier. Such attributes may include customer name, address, date of birth, and externally assigned identifiers (e.g., social security number, an employer identification number, a business reference number such as DUNS number, etc.).

> ▶ The Registry-style Data Hub should automatically generate and maintain links with all upstream systems that maintain data about the customers. Consuming applications query the Registry for a given customer or a set of customers, and the Registry would use its customer identification number and legacy pointers or links to allow the application to retrieve and construct a view of the customer from the underlying data.

> ▶ This style of the Data Hub is the "master" of the unique customer identifiers, but does not change the actual customer data, so in a situation where the customer data quality is questionable or unsatisfactory, this style of the Data Hub does not provide any value-added data enrichment or data hygiene capabilities.

▶ **Reconciliation Engine**   This design style is a system of record for some customer attributes; it provides active synchronization between itself and the legacy systems.

> ▶ In this case, the Data Hub is the master for those data attributes that it maintains. The *Reconciliation Engine Data Hub style* relies on the upstream source system to maintain other data attributes. One implication of this approach is the fact that *some* applications that handle customer data may have to be changed or redesigned based on the business processes, application interfaces, and the data they use. The same is true for the corresponding business processes. The other implication is that

the Data Hub has to maintain, create, and change those data attributes
for which it is the master. The Data Hub has to propagate changes
for these attributes to the upstream and downstream systems that use
these attributes. The result is a data environment that continuously
synchronizes the data content among its participants to avoid data
inconsistencies. The complexity of synchronization increases as some of
the data attributes maintained in the Data Hub are derived from the data
attributes maintained in other systems. A typical Reconciliation Engine-
style Data Hub has to create and maintain unique customer identification
as well as references to the legacy systems and data stores where the
customer data is sourced or continues to reside. This design style is more
sophisticated than the Registry-style Data Hub, and in many situations is
a viable evolutionary step toward the full Transaction Hub.

► **Transaction Hub**   This is the most sophisticated option, in which the Data
Hub becomes the primary source of and the system of record for the customer
data and its references.

  ► This is the case where the Data Hub maintains *all* data attributes about the
  customer (individuals or businesses). Then the Hub becomes a "master"
  of customer information, and as such should be the source of all changes
  to any attribute about the customer. In this case, the Data Hub has to be
  engineered as a complete transactional environment that maintains its
  data integrity and is the sole source of changes that it propagates to all
  downstream systems that use the customer data. Clearly, this approach
  has some profound implications for the overall environment—the existing
  applications and business processes in place. For example, an existing
  account maintenance application may have to undergo modifications to
  update the Data Hub instead of an existing legacy system, and appropriate
  synchronization mechanisms have to be in place to propagate and apply
  the changes from the Data Hub to some or all downstream systems.
  Moreover, most of the previously deployed transactions that change
  customer information should be redesigned to work directly with the Data
  Hub, which may also change existing business processes, workflows, and
  user navigation. This is the most complex case, which is known as a Full
  Transaction Hub.

   With the exception of the first, the External Reference style, these architecture
and design styles have one thing in common—they define, create, and manage a
centralized platform where customer data is integrated either virtually (e.g., Registry)
or physically (Reconciliation Engine and Transaction Hub) to create a reliable and
sustainable system of record for customer information.

Reference Architecture Viewpoint

In the previous sections we looked at the key components and architecture viewpoints of the CDI architecture, and showed its complexity and the variety of the approaches you could take to select, build, and implement a CDI solution.

As in the previous discussions, we will address the complexity of the solution and the rational way to make CDI design choices by employing a notion of the enterprise architecture framework and an appropriate architecture viewpoint. One of the best known complexity-reducing architecture viewpoints is a Reference Architecture viewpoint.

Let's informally define reference architecture as follows:

> *Reference architecture* is a set of interlinked components, services, processes, and interfaces organized into functional layers, where each layer provides services to the layers above and consumes services from the layers below.

Using this definition of the reference architecture, we can construct a reference architecture viewpoint (see Figure 4-6) as a multilayered architecture stack that consists of services, components, processes, and interfaces.

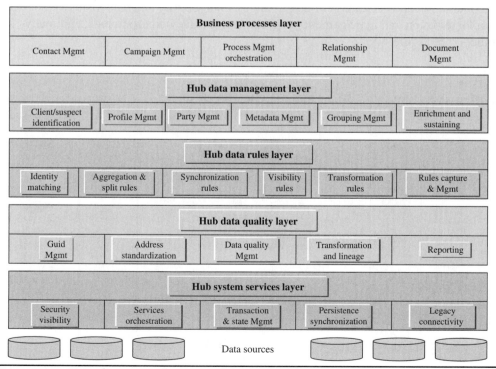

Figure 4-6 *CDI reference architecture of the Data Hub*

While at a high level this reference architecture appears to be deceptively simple, a close look will reveal that most of the components and services of the architecture have to be present in order to accomplish the goal of creating a CDI system. Moreover, many of these components are complex objects that in turn contain many lower-level components and services. We will offer a more detailed discussion of some of the components in the subsequent chapters of the book. To set the stage for the detailed discussion, we will organize the components, services, and layers of this high-level conceptual reference architecture into two major groups—traditional architecture concerns of information management, and new, emerging concerns driven by the goals of Master Data Management and Customer Data Integration.

The traditional architecture concerns focus on data and data management. These concerns include data architecture and data modeling; data extractions, transformation, and loading; metadata repository and metadata management; database management system performance and scalability; transaction management; backup and recovery; and others (see Figure 4-7).

New MDM- and CDI-specific concerns include areas such as identity recognition, matching and generation of global unique customer identifiers, persistence of customer identification, rules-based and data-content-based synchronization to/from legacy, reconciliation and arbitration of data changes, data security and data visibility, service implementation and management integration with legacy environments, and many others (see Figure 4-8).

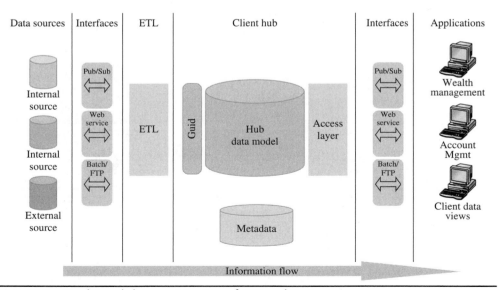

Figure 4-7   *Traditional data-centric view of CDI architecture*

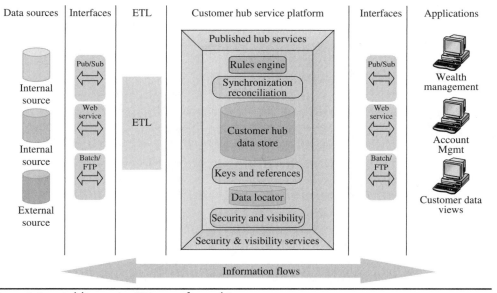

Figure 4-8   *Adding new CDI-specific architecture concerns*

We discuss these emerging and traditional concerns of the MDM and CDI architecture in more details in Chapters 5, 6, and 10. The material in these chapters offers additional insights and architecture viewpoints that should help CDI managers, designers, and implementers to achieve measurable results using a structured and disciplined architecture approach.

CHAPTER 5

Architecting for Customer Data Integration

IN THIS CHAPTER

Emerging Architecture Concerns of MDM-CDI Solutions

What Is Required to Create and Maintain the MDM-CDI Platform?

CDI Solution as Service-Oriented Architecture Platform

Identity Recognition, Matching, and Generation of Unique Party Identifiers

Aggregating Customer Information

Data Hub Keys and Management Services

Emerging Architecture Concerns of MDM-CDI Solutions

In the previous chapter, we discussed several general topics related to Master Data Management architecture. We paid particular attention to the architecture issues and concerns of Customer Data Integration solutions, often referred to as CDI Data Hubs.

We organized these discussions in the context of the enterprise architecture framework and its various viewpoints, which we used to help address the complexity and the interconnected nature of components of the MDM and CDI solutions. Using the principles and goals of the architecture framework, we demonstrated some key requirements and features of the MDM-CDI architecture. We also showed key differences and common features between two classes of data management solutions: Master Data Management and Customer Data Integration on the one hand, and the technologies from which MDM and CDI have evolved, including Customer Information File, Data Warehousing, Operational Data Stores, and Customer Relationship Management, on the other hand.

The features and functions that have evolved into contemporary MDM-CDI solutions from their various predecessor technologies are driving our approach to leverage already-familiar data architecture and data management concepts and components. These concepts and components include, among other things, scalable and manageable database technology; metadata management; extract, transform, and load (ETL) technologies; and data quality measurement and improvement technologies. We discuss the architecture viewpoints and design constructs dealing with these technologies in Chapter 6.

Using the MDM definition offered in preceding chapters, we can assert that Master Data Management architecture cannot be complete without considering components, functions, and services that enable transformation of record-level detail data into cleaned, rationalized, aggregated, sustainable, and leverageable system of record.

These architecture constructs are primarily relevant to Master Data Management and may not apply to predecessor technologies such as CIF, EDW, and others. In order to discuss these MDM-specific architecture concerns, we will use the already familiar approach of analyzing and demonstrating MDM-specific features and architecture viewpoints in the context of the enterprise architecture framework. Furthermore, we will apply enterprise architecture framework concepts to the specific, well-defined variant of Master Data Management known as Customer Data Integration, and concentrate our discussions on CDI solutions known as Data Hubs.

CDI and Customer Relationships

The specific concerns relevant to CDI Data Hub solutions include capabilities that allow an organization to uniquely identify, recognize, and possibly aggregate (or enable aggregation of) individual records about the customers into groups or clusters of records all of which describe a particular aspect of an individual.

Recognizing Individuals, Groups, and Relationships

One of the key design goals of a CDI solution is the ability to identify and recognize not just individual customers but all of their existing and potential relationships with the organization.

Equally important, a CDI solution has to be able to recognize when two or more detail-level records belong to the same party (individual or organization).

For example, let's consider a hypothetical Johnson family. We will start with Mike Johnson, who has just become a customer of the neighborhood bank by opening a savings account with a minimum deposit. Such action is considered trivial by the bank, and Mike is categorized by the bank's CRM platform as a low-priority customer. However, the situation would change drastically if the bank knew that Mike Johnson is a member of a very affluent family and has relationships with other, already established customers of the bank's Wealth Management and Private Banking business units. The immediate implication of this situation is that Mike Johnson and his extended household represent high-net-worth customers that may already provide or in the future will provide significant revenue to the bank.

Let's further assume that Mike Johnson's network of relationships includes family relationships, business relationships, and investment/trust relationships as follows:

- ► Mike Johnson's extended family consists of six individuals:
    - ► Dan (Daniel) Johnson and Kathy Johnson—parents
    - ► Mike Johnson and his wife Susan
    - ► Mack Johnson—Mike and Susan's son
    - ► George Patterson—Susan's brother
    - ► Ann Patterson—George's wife
- ► Johnson's family owns two businesses:
    - ► Advanced Computer Graphics Inc.
    - ► Leading Edge Marketing LLP
- ► Johnson's family established and owns three trusts:
    - ► Dan and Kathy Johnson Trust
    - ► Mack Johnson Trust
    - ► Patterson Trust Company

▶ Mike Johnson is a chief designer in the Advanced Computer Graphics company where his father is the CEO. He is also a board member of the Patterson Trust Company and is a senior technical advisor for Leading Edge Marketing.

▶ Dan and Kathy Johnson have several accounts with the bank, and Dan often uses his nickname (Rusty). The bank classifies Dan and Kathy as high-net-worth, high-priority customers.

▶ George Patterson has established a business account with the bank and is considering opening a joint Wealth Management account with his wife.

A simplified graphical representation of the Johnson-Patterson family is shown in Figure 5-1.

An effective CDI solution would deliver a customer integration platform that contains a complete, integrated view not only of each individual in the Johnson household but also of the entire extended Johnson family. In order to accomplish this goal, the CDI platform would support data models and functional capabilities that, for example, can recognize all accounts that Dan Johnson has with the bank as belonging to the same individual even though Dan used an alias when he opened his Private Banking account. But even more importantly, the bank should recognize any

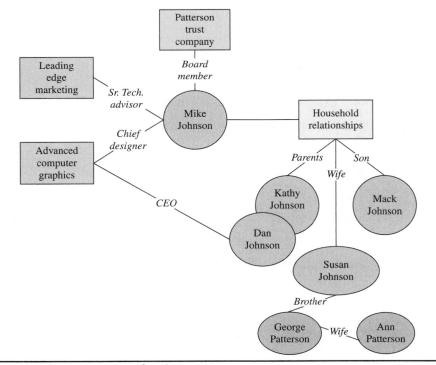

Figure 5-1 *Johnson-Patterson family*

member of the extended Johnson family as belonging to this extended family entity, and should be able to obtain a data view that shows the totality of the relationships the Johnson family and its members have already established and may establish with the bank in the future.

In other words, a CDI platform would enable a transformation of an account-centric view of the Johnson household to a customer-centric view that facilitates the new, better, and more rewarding customer experience that the bank can provide to both the Johnson and Patterson households and their business associations (see Figure 5-2).

The ability to recognize and maintain these relationships is one of the key properties of Data Hub solutions, especially as these solutions evolve from the Registry-style Data Hub into a full-function Transaction Hub (see Chapter 4 for the discussion on the CDI architecture styles). The process of creating the relationship links, which collects or groups individual records into higher-level clusters, starts at the very granular account-level data and can extend its scope to include higher levels of abstractions such as households, business associations, and other customer groups.

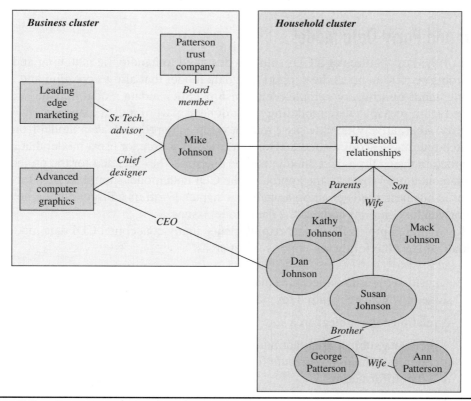

Figure 5-2   *Customer relationship clustering.*

This process requires that a CDI solution implement a comprehensive data model and provide a set of functional services designed to support customer recognition, matching, and linking. We discuss these capabilities in more details later in this chapter and in Chapters 12 and 13.

Customer Groupings

The ability to recognize individual entities as members of arbitrary complex groups (e.g., households and extended families for individuals, holding companies, and other organizational hierarchies for business entities) is one of the key properties of Master Data Management. This feature applies equally well to Customer Data Integration solutions, Reference Data Management, Product Master Hubs, etc., with the complexity of the associations and grouping depending in large part on the completeness and accuracy of the data, and the business rules driving the resolution of conflicting or undetermined links.

CDI and Party Data Model

One of the key features of a CDI solution designed to handle the matching and grouping requirements is the support of a data model that allows creation and maintenance of arbitrary complex relationships. Such a data model may be reused from previous data modeling work done as part of a data management activity. Alternatively, an enterprise may develop an appropriate data model from scratch internally, acquire a model from an external source, or use a model that is included in the CDI product bundle that the enterprise has selected for the project implementation. Whatever the approach, the CDI data model should address the specific business needs of an organization. Chapter 17 offers a discussion on how major vendor solutions address the data model issues.

To support complex functional requirements, many conceptual CDI data models contain at least the following major subject areas:

▶ A customer profile subject area that is populated with relevant customer attributes, some of which are required for matching and linking of individual records

▶ A relationships subject area

▶ A metadata subject area that maintains record-level and attribute-level location information, attribute formats, domain constraints, and other relevant information

▶ An audit subject area

The first two subject areas are often industry-specific and may be customized to support a particular line of business. For example, several industry-proven data models support property and casualty insurance or a retail banking business. These data models maintain customer profiles and relationships in the context of the industries they support. We briefly illustrate the key components of the conceptual domain-specific subject area in this chapter and offer more implementation-level concerns in Part IV of the book.

The remaining subject areas are created to support the Data Hub's ability to become a reliable, accurate, and timely system of record. Some of these subject areas are created as part of the Data Hub data model, while others are created as separate data domains. For example, the metadata subject area is often implemented not as a part of the Data Hub data model but rather as a logical component of the metadata repository (metadata and other supporting subject areas of the Data Hub are discussed in more details later in this chapter).

A conceptual CDI data model that can support a customer-centric business such as retail banking or personal insurance is known as a *party-centric* model, and it may consist of a number of data entities and attributes including party/customer, profile, account, party group, location, demographics, relationships, channels, products, events, and privacy preferences. Some of the key attributes of this model include identity attributes used to uniquely identify the party as a collection or cluster of individual detail-level records. Such a party-centric data model supports multiple party types including organizations, customers, prospects, etc. Figure 5-3 illustrates

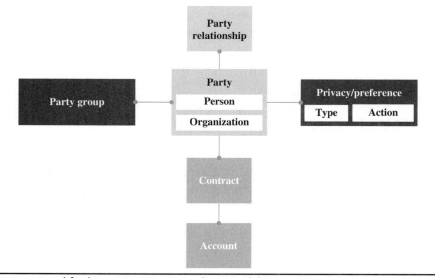

Figure 5-3   *Simplified generic CDI party data model*

a highly simplified version of this conceptual model that is aligned with the insurance domain. Fundamental entities in this conceptual party model include the following:

▶ The Party entity, which represents a person or an organization, and can support an existing customer or a prospect. In our relationship example (see previous section in this chapter), a party could represent a member of the Johnson family.

▶ The Party group is an entity that represents a collection of individual parties affiliated with each other based on specific, well-defined criteria (e.g., household).

▶ Relationship-enabling entities that support party-to-party relationships.

▶ Party-level privacy preferences that can differ from one contract or account to another.

▶ The party entity may have one or more contracts each of which may have one or more accounts.

In practice, CDI implementations have to support party models that are much more extensive and complex.

What Is Required to Create and Maintain the MDM-CDI Platform?

In order to create and maintain an authoritative, accurate, timely, and secure system of record, an MDM-CDI solution must support a number of capabilities that are designed not only to maintain the content, scope, and integrity of the core data model but also to enable the CDI Data Hub to integrate and interoperate with established business processes, systems, and applications.

Key MDM-CDI Capabilities

Several key MDM and CDI capabilities have to be supported by all major Data Hub architecture styles from Registry to Transaction Hub. These capabilities are data-domain-independent and are relevant to Data Hub systems that integrate and manage customer data, organization data, reference data, and product data alike. In the context of Customer Data Integration, these capabilities include but are not limited to

▶ Identity recognition; matching and generation of global unique customer identifiers

- ▶ Persistence of the customer identification and other information for which Data Hub is the master
- ▶ Rules-based and data-content-based synchronization to/from legacy
- ▶ Reconciliation and arbitration of data changes
- ▶ Attribute location service
- ▶ Data security and visibility

Figure 5-4 illustrates these capabilities in the form of functional components at a conceptual level. There, we show that the core CDI data store is surrounded by additional functional components that work in concert to enable the desired CDI functionality.

However, this picture represents only a high-level conceptual component architecture. It does not show a view in which CDI functionality is available as a set of services that are published and consumed by the Data Hub in accordance with the Service-Oriented Architecture (SOA) paradigm. In the previous chapter we discussed the rationale and the benefits of the service-oriented architecture approach to designing

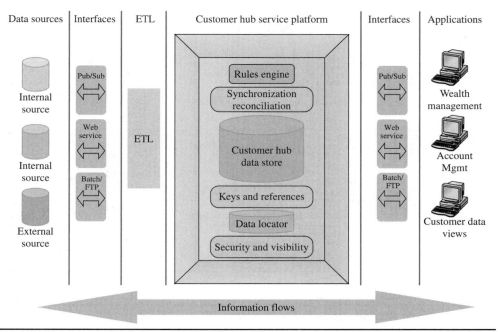

Figure 5-4   *The conceptual architecture view addresses CDI-specific problem domains.*

complex integration-enabled software systems. Customer Data Integration solutions by their very nature belong to the category of complex integration-enabled systems. Therefore, applying SOA principles and concepts to the design of a CDI architecture is not only an appropriate but also an effective approach. The next section describes a high-level services view of the CDI platform.

CDI Solution as Service-Oriented Architecture Platform

Let's start the discussion of the functional aspects of the CDI platform in the context of the CDI Data Hub reference architecture viewpoint described in Chapter 4 (see Figure 4-6). We modified this CDI Reference Architecture in Figure 5-5 by applying

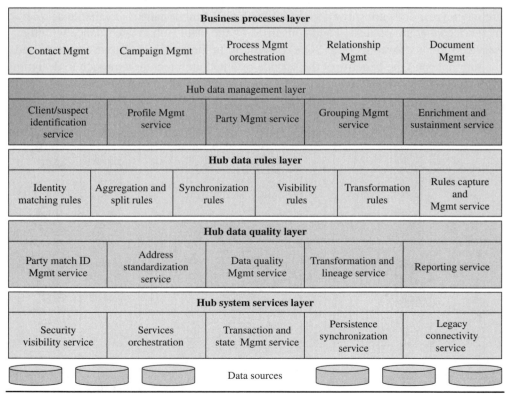

Figure 5-5   *Data Hub reference architecture for CDI*

Service-Oriented Architecture (SOA) principles and focusing on key services that enable CDI functionality. As a reminder, we offer an abbreviated definition of Services-Oriented Architecture.

SOA

Service-Oriented Architecture (SOA) is a software architecture in which software components can be exposed as services on the network, and so can be reused as necessary for different applications and purposes.

As shown in Figure 5-5, the CDI reference architecture includes a number of components and services designed to enable enterprise-scale CDI solutions. We arrange these components and services into functional architecture layers that emphasize CDI service taxonomy. From a business point of view, CDI Data Hub publishes and consumes coarse-grained functional business services that usually correspond to business functional requirements. However, under the covers, the CDI platform supports fine-grained, lower-level services some of which represent primitive, atomic services used to compose the business services (we discuss this important point in Chapter 4). The CDI platform also supports internal, system-level and infrastructure-level services that make the entire environment operational and manageable by the enterprise in a production environment. These supporting, infrastructure-level services include service coordination and orchestration, integration with the enterprise infrastructure and legacy systems, systems instrumentation and management, error processing, and many others.

By applying SOA principles to the CDI Data Hub reference architecture, we can construct a high-level service-oriented view of the Data Hub (see Figure 5-6). We offered an overview of the CDI solution as a service platform in Chapter 4. In this chapter, we offer several additional considerations on how the CDI services framework enables both business functionality and enterprise-level integration between a CDI Data Hub and other systems and applications.

Specifically, in addition to the published business services, we can differentiate between two major groups of interoperable internal services. The first group includes atomic functional services such as Create, Read, Update, and Delete (CRUD). These can be combined to assemble higher-level, coarse-grained composite business services that execute business transactions (for example, a coarse-grained business service could be "Find a Customer by Name," or "Create Customer Profile"). This abstraction is very powerful; it enables the reuse of services and components and easy, almost declarative-style integration.

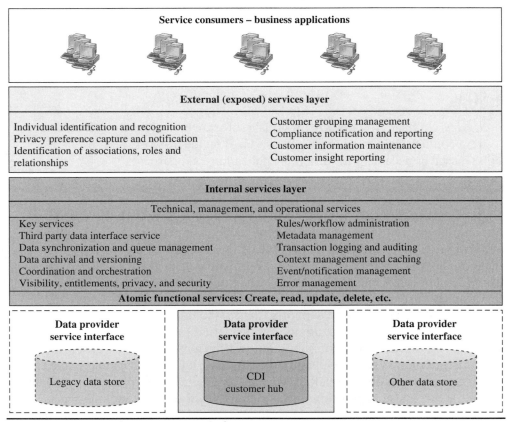

Service consumers – business applications

External (exposed) services layer

Individual identification and recognition
Privacy preference capture and notification
Identification of associations, roles and
relationships

Customer grouping management
Compliance notification and reporting
Customer information maintenance
Customer insight reporting

Internal services layer

Technical, management, and operational services

Key services
Third party data interface service
Data synchronization and queue management
Data archival and versioning
Coordination and orchestration
Visibility, entitlements, privacy, and security

Rules/workflow administration
Metadata management
Transaction logging and auditing
Context management and caching
Event/notification management
Error management

Atomic functional services: Create, read, update, delete, etc.

Data provider
service interface

Data provider
service interface

Data provider
service interface

Legacy data store

CDI
customer hub

Other data store

Figure 5-6   *Data Hub as a service platform*

The second group is a set of technical management and operational services that hide the technical complexity of the design from the application and business service developers. The services in this group include support for transactional semantics, coordination, compensation, orchestration, synchronization, recovery, error management, auditing, etc. Although these services abstract application developers from the underlying technical complexity, these services interoperate with both atomic and business services in order to manage and execute business transactions against a CDI data Hub.

Following the same approach defined in Chapter 4, we can illustrate the service-oriented nature of a CDI Data Hub by "wrapping" the core Data Hub platform in the layers of internal and external services. We have shown a high level graphical representation of this SOA wrapping in Chapter 4, Figure 4-8. Figure 5-7 builds on the view shown in Figure 4-8 and provides additional service details.

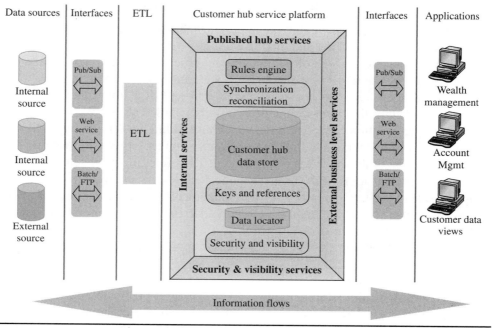

Figure 5-7   *Services and CDI platform*

Identity Recognition, Matching, and Generation of Unique Party Identifiers

As we stated in the preceding section, one of the primary goals of a CDI solution is to enable business transformation from an account-centric to a customer-centric enterprise by creating an authoritative system of record that provides an accurate and complete view of the individual customers, their groups, relationships, and hierarchies.

The ability to recognize the fact that two or more detail-level records belong to the same party (individuals or organizations) is a paramount requirement for any CDI solution.

Technologies and services that enable this type of recognition include *matching and linking* of detail records and *creation and maintenance of unique identifiers* as primary links to indicate the affinity of detail records to the same party.

Matching and Linking Services

Matching and linking is a highly specialized set of technologies that allows the user to identify party entities with a high degree of confidence. The operation resulting in party identification allows a user of the CDI platform to construct a total view of a party from the detail-level records. The matching and linking technologies are very sophisticated, and many commercial products that offer these capabilities try to differentiate their matching and linking engines by using three value dimensions: *accuracy* of the match, *speed* of the match, and processing *scalability*. These characteristics are the result of the techniques and implementation approaches of the matching algorithms. It is not surprising, therefore, that many vendors keep their matching algorithms and techniques a closely guarded secret! We will discuss specific implementation concerns of the matching and linking services in Part IV.

The variety of matching and linking techniques is rather large, and it would be beyond the scope of this book to cover them all. Therefore, in this chapter, we will take a closer look at some of the best-known techniques that are used to achieve a high degree of accuracy in matching individual records. The algorithms we are discussing in this section are highly regarded within the area of the research and technology domain known as data quality.

At a high level, we can classify all algorithmic approaches to record matching into the following groups:

▶ **Deterministic algorithms**   These algorithms offer predictable behavior of the comparison and matching process that is based on the data itself. In a deterministic algorithm, each attribute is compared byte by byte against the same attribute in another record, which results in either a match or a no-match. For example, the deterministic algorithm would compare a social security number in one record with the social security number in another, an operation that would find a match if these two values are equal. Because of this relative simplicity, a deterministic algorithm can deliver a very high performance and throughput. Deterministic algorithms often require cleansing of the input data and format standardization in order to perform the match. Traditionally, deterministic algorithms had limited capability to handle such common data anomalies as blank fields, transposition of characters, common misspelling of known names and addresses, or abbreviations. Today, however, advanced deterministic algorithms can overcome this limitation by employing various fuzzy logic techniques.

▶ **Probabilistic algorithms**   These matching algorithms are based on various statistical probability theories. The advantage of the probabilistic algorithm is that it can learn to match records that initially had to be resolved by a direct user intervention. The matching process of a probabilistic algorithm consists of several steps:

  ▶ An analysis of the input data to determine precise frequencies for weighting and matching individual data elements

  ▶ A determination of the outcome of matching between records using derived statistical distribution of value frequencies

> ▶ An assignment of the weight values for match attributes and predefined match threshold

> ▶ A refinement of the match values through the user-guided value assignment process for those cases where the match confidence level is below the threshold

▶ **Machine learning algorithms**   These sophisticated techniques are based on advanced research and development in the area of machine learning and artificial intelligence. These techniques allow the system not only to detect similarities between two entities based on a number of factors and rules, but also to learn to refine the matching process automatically over time. Many machine learning approaches are somewhat similar to fuzzy logic techniques and allow the matching engine to learn how to match records based on calculated proximity values. These algorithms can discover and measure similarities between attributes and entire record values in a way similar to how a human brain may recognize two objects as being similar.

▶ **Hybrid algorithms**   As the name implies, these algorithms may use multistep processes that combine deterministic, probabilistic, and machine learning techniques that can also be enhanced by applying more advanced techniques, including phonetic conversion and matching. Hybrid algorithms may use formal matching rules in a deterministic fashion. Alternatively, they can enhance probabilistic relevance of the variables (attributes) and weights to achieve higher matching rates. Many advanced algorithms may use heuristics (algorithmic techniques that use the observed and understood experience of searching for matches within a given domain), pattern-based matching techniques, and a number of other techniques. Of course, as new techniques become available, their implementations could be either a hybrid or a "pure" deterministic or probabilistic matching engine.

Regardless of how sophisticated and innovative the matching algorithms are, in practice no single technique or single algorithm can satisfy all diverse matching requirements of the enterprise, especially if the enterprise already developed and successfully used empirical, proven, business-area-specific matching rules that may contain a large number of exceptions. When deciding on which linking and matching technique is best suited for any given environment, the CDI designers and match solution architects should consider the following factors:

▶ **Match accuracy**   This requirement is self-explanatory. Higher accuracy allows the enterprise to construct a more complete integrated view of the customer, be it an individual or an organization, and to reduce the errors associated with assigning false positives (for example, incorrectly recognizing an individual as a member of a wrong household) or false negatives (for example, missing a key member of the household).

▶ **Linking and matching speed**   This requirement is especially important in the case of online applications designed to recognize an individual in real time, for example, a patient who is being admitted to the hospital and requiring an emergency blood transfusion, or an airport security control point that has to recognize an individual as a potential threat before the airplane boarding starts.

▶ **Uniqueness and persistence of the link keys**   The linking and matching process can be very fast and accurate, but if the results of the match cannot be stored reliably in the Data Hub or another facility for follow-on processing, then the value of the matching becomes questionable. Thus, a matching engine needs to be able to generate a unique identifier that the Data Hub would persist in its data store as a unique key. These key values must be unique in the name space of all possible Data Hub entity keys. In other words, if we're dealing with a CDI Data Hub for a global retail enterprise that serves 100 million customers, each of which has one or more detail records (e.g., account-level records), the link key should have a sufficient range of values to support the cardinality of all Hub customer entities (in our example, 100 million) rather than all detail-level records.

▶ **Deterministic outcome**   Key generation service must be deterministic in the sense that if the underlying data did not change, then the key value for the same cluster of records should not change either.

▶ **Scalability of the solution**   This is a classical system requirement. In the case of the linking and matching engine, it has to address numerous scalability concerns. These include the number of records to be matched, number of various data sources, number of user-defined matching rules, and the number of concurrent users that may request the matching operation either to recognize individuals or to generate unique identification keys. The latter requirement should address the concurrency and throughput concerns of the Data Hub environment where the matching engine has to support a prerequisite number of concurrent users, each of which is able to perform a required number of tasks in a unit of time (e.g., a predefined number of transactions per second [TPS]).

▶ **Ease of use**   The algorithm and the engine that implements it should provide an easy-to-use, intuitive way for the users to define or customize matching criteria, to understand the reasons for the matching outcome, and to resolve potential uncertainties. The engine should not require the user to be an expert in mathematics or computer science. The intuitive way the users can use the tool may make all the difference between user acceptance or rejection.

▶ **Ease of implementation and administration**   If the matching engine is external from the CDI platform (that is, not built in as a components of the CDI vendor product), the engine should not require a highly specialized computing platform such as a supercomputer. The engine should comply with the enterprise infrastructure standards and should be easily integratable into the enterprise system architecture and infrastructure environments. And finally, an external matching engine should interoperate with the CDI platform of choice (server hardware, software, and the DBMS).

▶ **Flexibility**   The matching engine should be flexible to conform to ever-changing business requirements. For example, if the organization decides not to use certain data elements in order to protect customer privacy and confidentiality and to comply with applicable privacy regulations (for example, not to use social security numbers or unlisted telephone numbers), the CDI administrator should be able to easily configure the matching engine to implement these changes.

▶ **Ability to adapt to the business requirements and to implement proven existing matching rules**   Many matching algorithms are very sophisticated and are finely tuned to achieve high matching accuracy. The engines that implement these algorithms are designed to preserve the integrity (and in many cases, significant intellectual property) of these algorithmic techniques. This approach works for many organizations that would like to rely on the matching engine rather than on home-grown matching rules. However, there are organizations and/or business situations where custom-defined matching rules must be followed to achieve the desired business outcome. In these cases, the matching engine should be able to use user-defined custom rules in conjunction with the internal algorithms in such a way that the custom rules can override the internal processing or at a minimum defer the match decision to a user-driven manual process of asserting the matching result.

▶ **Ability to support linking and matching as a service**   This is a technical requirement of the service-oriented architecture that helps implement and manage the linking and matching engine as a part of the enterprise architecture. If the engine makes its capabilities available as services, then the consumer (a user or an application) is isolated from the intricacies and complexities of the underlying algorithms and is only concerned with the consumption of the service and the interpretation of the results.

To summarize, the most effective matching engine will utilize a combination of deterministic, probabilistic, and machine learning algorithms to achieve the highest accuracy in the shortest time. And at the end of the day, the flexibility of the matching engine to support the business rules of the enterprise creates a winning combination of sophisticated technology and intuitive behavior that enables the best linking and matching process for the enterprise.

Matching and Linking Service

The outcome of the Matching and Linking process is the identification of groups or clusters of records associated with each other based on some criteria. An effect of this process on the CDI data content is the ability of the Matching and Linking service to generate, insert, and persist for each record a unique identifier that can be used to organize individual records into clusters of affinity known as match groups. The Matching and Linking service applies the notion of uniqueness to the match groups rather than to the individual detail records themselves.

Aggregating Customer Information

Using the Matching and Linking service described in the preceding section, the Data Hub will recognize similar records and assign unique link keys to all records in such a way that all records with a given link key value can be grouped together or aggregated into a single entity. In the case of the CDI party model shown in Figure 5-3, this entity is the Party, and the link key becomes the Party's unique identifier and its primary key.

In principle, this process can be iterative, and can match and link party entities using some business-defined criteria. Therefore, a Matching and Linking service can use various business rules to generate different identifiers used to aggregate individual party objects into even higher-level entities. Examples of these higher-level entities are households, business associations, or other types of customer groups. Depending on the desired depth of aggregation, the Matching and Linking service can generate a number of keys or identifiers that are unique in the corresponding name space of entities for which the matching operation is performed.

Once the identifiers are generated, the CDI Data Hub can use its Aggregation Service to merge appropriate records into the next-level entity. This merge operation can be automatic or user-guided. For example, the Aggregation Service component of the CDI Data Hub may use the unique identifiers to automatically "merge" account-level records into clusters representing individuals, and use next-level identifiers to merge individual-level records into uniquely identified groups such as households see Figure 5-8). We discuss the merge process in more details in Chapter 12.

In practice, however, an automatic merge may be undesirable. This is because the matching algorithm may create false positive and false negative outcomes. Another consideration for not using an automatic merge is that in some cases, the matching business rules are so complex and the number of exceptions is so great that the users would prefer that the system suggests a potential merge suspect while leaving the

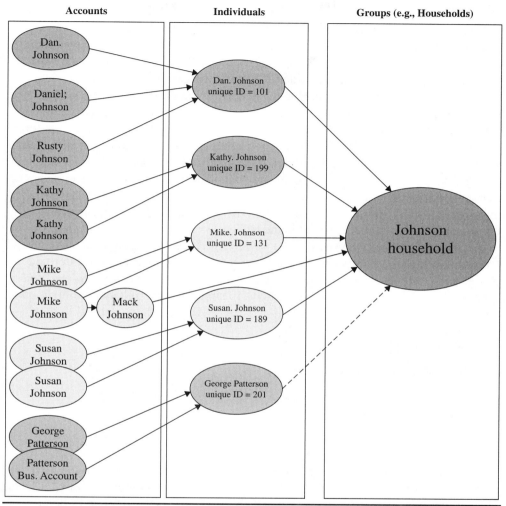

Figure 5-8   *Mapping accounts to individuals and group*

final decision to the user. Thus, the Aggregation Service of the CDI Data Hub should be able to support both modes of operation: automatic and user-guided, or supervised aggregation.

Data Hub Keys and Management Services

The previous sections discussed the CDI Data Hub services designed to match and link individual records by generating persistent unique identifiers. These identifiers, while critically important, are not sufficient to synchronize and maintain the content of the

Data Hub in relationship to the upstream and downstream data stores and applications. Indeed, the CDI Data Hub is not an isolated and disconnected environment. It should be a system of record for some information such as customer profile, organizational profile, and other data domains. Depending on the CDI architecture style, the Data Hub may be just a Registry of the identification information, or a federated data environment that allows the Data Hub to "peacefully" coexist with other systems by maintaining some information inside the Hub and some pointers to data in external data stores, data for which the Data Hub is *not* the master. Ultimately, a CDI platform could be the full Transaction Data Hub and a completely self-contained master of the information that it manages. Regardless of the architecture style, a CDI Data Hub has to support a comprehensive data model and a number of specialized services designed to maintain data integrity inside the Data Hub. These specialized services have to also support Data Hub's ability to keep its content in sync with the providers and consumers of the data that is stored in the Hub.

Keeping a Data Hub in sync is not a trivial task. It requires comprehensive design and availability of a number of carefully orchestrated services and well-defined processes. To illustrate this point, let's define several *interdependent cooperative* service classes designed to work in concert to support Data Hub synchronization consistency and data integrity:

▶   Key Generation service

▶   Record Locator service

▶   Synchronization service

▶   Reconciliation service

▶   Attribute Location service

We briefly discuss Key Generation and Record Locator services in the next sections. The other services and additional architecture considerations for CDI Data Hub solution are discussed in Chapter 6. Part IV of this book offers an in-depth look at the implementation aspects of these and other CDI services.

Key Management and Key Generation Service

First, let's review some basic concepts related to creation and management of Data Hub keys. As we stated in the beginning of this chapter, the CDI Data Hub data model contains a number of data entities and the relationships between the entities. The general principles of the enterprise data architecture and the relational data model dictate that every entity has at least one unique key, and depending on how the model is defined, one of these unique keys is known as a primary key. A *data modeler* defines the interrelationships between entities through the assignment and maintenance of the primary and foreign keys. These keys enable a key data model constraint of *referential integrity* where a primary key of one entity (e.g., a table) should exist in a related table as a foreign key. For example, a profile table may have a unique profile key. This table may be related to the account table, which in turn contains unique account keys. Further, each profile may have one or more accounts. To link these two tables, profile keys are inserted into the account table as foreign keys for easy reference in such a way that for each profile key in the account table, there is a record in the profile table with this key value.

Referential integrity is one of the functional features of the majority of Relational Database Management Systems (RDBMS) that support the CDI application. Many CDI solutions are deployed on standards-based commercial RDBMS platforms. However, since a typical CDI solution uses a number of other keys, many CDI engines offer additional key management services designed to maintain the integrity and consistency of the CDI Data Hub.

At design time, a Hub data modeler constructs the logical and physical data models that include primary and foreign keys. However, having a key placeholder is not enough—the values of these keys need to be available for any operation where data in the Data Hub is added, changed, or deleted. Moreover, the values of these keys need to be created and placed in appropriate records in such a way that it does not violate referential integrity and other constraints. These key values need to be available prior to loading records into the Data Hub so that the load operation can create a well-formed Data Hub data store. Likewise, any action that results in the addition of a data record (e.g., a new account) has to make sure that the appropriate values for the primary and foreign keys are available and that the resulting operation does not violate referential integrity of the Data Hub.

The generation and maintenance of all keys required for the operation and sustainability of the CDI Data Hub is the responsibility of the Key Generation service. This service has to be flexible, adaptable, and scalable, and should support any number of keys defined in the Hub data model. For example, the Key Generation Service should effectively generate primary keys for every record stored in the Hub and foreign keys for all related entities inside the Data Hub data model. This service also needs to capture and maintain "native" keys that get loaded into the Data Hub from all data sources. Key generation service needs to interface with the Matching and Linking service (discussed in previous sections) in order to store and manage various unique identifiers created by the Matching and Linking process.

As the Data Hub matures and begins to support additional data attributes and entities, the Key Generation service would need to rapidly and easily adapt to new requirements and generate new sets of keys as required by the service consumers, which includes data load processes as well as business applications that can add, change, and delete records.

Record Locator Services

A Data Hub is an information integration platform that, by definition, integrates information collected from various data sources. A Data Hub data model is designed to easily aggregate individual records that came into the Data Hub from a variety of sources into linked groups. The resulting logical and physical data structures inside the Data Hub are different from the data stores used to load the Hub. In other words, in the majority of all CDI implementation cases, there is no simple one-to-one mapping between the records in the Data Hub and its sources. And this is the reason why a CDI Data Hub needs to support a service capability that enables such mapping.

This mapping becomes necessary as soon as the Data Hub is loaded with data and properly seeded with entity keys. At that point, the Data Hub can act as the authoritative reference of the customer information. However, as the consuming applications begin to use Data Hub information, a number of use cases need to be considered to maintain the integrity and accuracy of the data:

▶ Consuming applications may request information that is only partially stored in the Hub, with the remainder still residing in the source system from which the Hub was initially loaded—a typical scenario for the Registry and Coexistence Hub architecture styles.

▶ As data in the Data Hub gets updated by users and application, the Data Hub would have to propagate the changes to the systems that were used to load the Data Hub in the first place (*Hub-to-Source Synchronization*).

▶ The data for which the Data Hub is not the master resides in the old legacy systems of record. If this data is also loaded into the Data Hub, it has to be updated in step with the updates to the original source system (*Source-to-Hub Synchronization*).

The challenge of these use cases is to find appropriate records in the sourcing systems based on the records stored in the Data Hub, and vice versa. This is the responsibility of another important Data Hub service—the Record Locator service.

The Record Locator service is a metadata-based service that creates and maintains a persistent transactional subject area inside a metadata repository store. The Record Locator service leverages a metadata repository and maps Data Hub keys and keys used by other systems as they participate in the loading and updating of data inside the Data Hub. This mapping represents a special type of metadata that may be implemented as a subject area in the Data Hub Metadata Repository (metadata is briefly discussed in the next chapter).

Conceptually, this metadata area can be represented as a table that contains a row for each Data Hub record. Each row contains a primary key of the Data Hub detail record, and as many columns as there are external record keys. Again, this is certainly only a conceptual view. Logical and physical model would require normalization. The key values are loaded into this table during operations that create records in the Hub. The primary key can be obtained from the Linking and Matching service, or if desired, from the Key Generation service, as long as that key value exists in the Data Hub record.

In our Source-to-Hub use case, the Record Locator service would identify the impacted records in the Data Hub caused by the changes received by one or more source systems. In the Hub-to-Source scenario, the Record Locator service would perform a reverse operation and would identify external (to the Hub) systems and individual records impacted by changes applied to the Data Hub.

The Key Generation service and Record Locator service are necessary functional components of any CDI solution whether developed in-house or implemented as a CDI vendor product. The architecture requirements for these services include service-oriented implementation, scalability, reliability, flexibility, and support for transactional semantics. The latter means that when, for example, a Data Hub creates, updates, or deletes a data record, this operation will succeed only if the update operations for Key Generation and Record Locator services also complete successfully. In this case, the Data Hub will commit all the changes to the Hub data store and to the metadata repository. If any of the component transactions (Hub data operation, Key Generation, or CRUD operations on Record Locator metadata) fail, then the entire transaction should fail, and the Data Hub has to roll the partial changes back to their pretransaction state.

The foregoing discussion of Data Hub services would not be complete if we did not mention other CDI functions and services such as Transaction Coordination, Synchronization and Reconciliation service, Rules Management service, Metadata-driven Attribute Location service, Change Management service, Hub Data Load service, Security and Visibility service, and many others. We discuss some of these services in the next chapters, and their implementation aspects in Part IV of the book.

Data Management Concerns of MDM-CDI Architecture

IN THIS CHAPTER

Data Strategy
Managing Data in the Data Hub

The preceding chapters discussed the enterprise architecture framework as the vehicle that helps resolve a multitude of complex and challenging issues facing MDM and CDI designers and implementers. As we focused on the Customer Data Integration aspects of the MDM architecture, we showed how to apply the Enterprise Architecture Framework to the service-oriented view of the CDI platform, often called a Data Hub. And we also discussed a set of services that any Data Hub platform should provide and/or support in order to deliver key data integration properties of matching and linking detail-level records—a service that enables the creation and management of a complete view of the customers, their associations and relationships.

We also started a discussion of the services required to ensure the integrity of data inside the Data Hub as well as services designed to enable synchronization and reconciliation of data changes between the Data Hub and surrounding systems, applications, and data stores.

We have now reached the point where the discussion of the Data Hub architecture cannot continue without considering issues and challenges of integrating a Data Hub platform into the overall enterprise information environment. To accomplish this integration, we need to analyze the Data Hub architecture components and services that support cross-systems and cross-domain information management requirements. These requirements include challenges of the enterprise data strategy, data governance, data quality, a broad suite of data management technologies, and the organizational roles and responsibilities that enable effective integration and interoperability between the Data Hub, its data sources, and its consumers (users and applications).

An important clarification: as we continue to discuss key issues and concerns of the CDI architecture, services, and components, we focus on the logical and conceptual architecture points of view. That means that we express functional requirements of CDI services and components in architecture terms. These component and service requirements should not be interpreted literally as the prescription for a specific technical implementation. Some of the concrete implementation approaches—design and product selection guidelines that are based on the currently available industry best practices and state of the art in the MDM and CDI product marketplace—are provided in Part IV of this book.

Data Strategy

This chapter deals primarily with issues related to data management, data delivery, and data integration between a Data Hub system, its sources, and its consumers. In order to discuss the architecture concerns of data management we need to expand the context of the enterprise architecture framework and its data management dimensions by introducing key concerns and requirements of the enterprise data strategy. While these concerns include data technology and architecture components, the key insights of the enterprise data strategy are contained in its holistic and multidimensional approach to the issues and concerns related to enterprise-class information management. Those readers already familiar with the concepts of data strategy, data governance, and data stewardship can easily skip this section and proceed directly to the section titled "Managing Data in the Data Hub."

The multifaceted nature of the enterprise data strategy includes a number of interrelated disciplines such as data governance, data quality, data modeling, data management, data delivery, data synchronization and integrity, data security and privacy, data availability, and many others. Clearly, any comprehensive discussion of the enterprise data strategy that covers these disciplines is well beyond the scope of this book. However, in order to define and explain Data Hub requirements to support enterprise-level integration with the existing and new applications and systems, at a minimum we need to introduce several key concepts behind data governance, data quality, and data stewardship. Understanding these concepts helps explain the functional requirements of those Data Hub services and components that are designed to find the "right" data in the "right" data store, to measure and improve data quality, and to enable business-rules-driven data synchronization between the Data Hub and other systems. We address the concerns of data security and privacy in Part III of this book, and additional implementation concerns in Part IV.

Data Governance

Let's consider the following working definition of data governance.

Data Governance

Data governance is a process focused on managing the quality, consistency, usability, security, and availability of information. This process is closely linked to the notions of data ownership and stewardship.

Clearly, according to this definition, data governance becomes a critical component of any Data Hub initiative. Indeed, an integrated CDI data architecture contains not only the Data Hub but also many applications and databases that more often than not were developed independently, in a typical stovepipe fashion, and the information they use is often inconsistent, incomplete, and of different quality.

Data governance strategy helps deliver appropriate data to properly authorized users when they need it. Moreover, data governance and its data quality component are responsible for creating data quality standards, data quality metrics, and data quality measurement processes that together help deliver acceptable quality data to the consumers—applications and end users.

Data quality improvement and assurance are no longer optional activities. For example, the 2002 Sarbanes-Oxley Act requires, among other things, that a business entity should be able to attest to the quality and accuracy of the data contained in their financial statements. Obviously, the classical "garbage in—garbage out" expression is still true, and no organization can report high-quality financial data if the source data used to produce the financial numbers is of poor quality. To achieve compliance and to successfully implement an enterprise data governance and data quality strategy, the strategy itself should be treated as a value-added business proposition, and sold to the organization's stakeholders to obtain a management buy-in and commitment like any other business case. The value of improved data quality is almost self-evident, and includes factors such as the enterprise's ability to make better and more accurate decisions, to gain deeper insights into the customer's behavior, and to understand the customer's propensity to buy products and services, the probability of the customer's engaging in high-risk transactions, the probability of attrition, etc. The data governance strategy is not limited to data quality and data management standards and policies. It includes critically important concerns of defining organizational structures and job roles responsible for monitoring and enforcement of compliance with these policies and standards throughout the organization.

Committing an organization to implement a robust data governance strategy requires an implementation plan that follows a well-defined and proven methodology. Although there are several effective data governance methodologies available, a detailed discussion of them is beyond the scope of this book. However, for the sake of completeness, this section reviews key steps of a generic data governance strategy program as it may apply to the CDI Data Hub:

▶ *Define a data governance process.* This is the key in enabling monitoring and reconciliation of data between Data Hub and its sources and consumers. The data governance process should cover not only the initial data load but also data refinement, standardization, and aggregation activities along the path of the end-to-end information flow. The data governance process includes such data management and data quality concerns as the elimination of duplicate entries and creation of linking and matching keys. We showed in Chapter 5 that these unique identifiers help aggregate or merge individual records into groups or clusters based on certain criteria, for example, a household affiliation or a business entity. As the Data Hub is integrated into the overall enterprise data management environment, the data governance process should define the mechanisms that create and maintain valid cross-reference information in the form of Record Locator metadata that enables linkages between the Data Hub and other systems. In addition, a data governance process should contain a component that supports manual corrections of false positive and negative matches as well as the exception processing of errors that cannot be handled automatically.

►   *Design, select, and implement a data management and data delivery technology suite.* In the case of a CDI Data Hub both data management and data delivery technologies play a key role in enabling a fully integrated CDI solution regardless of the architecture style of the Data Hub, be it a Registry, a Reconciliation Engine, or a Transaction Hub. Later in this chapter we will use the principles and advantages of service-oriented architecture (SOA) to discuss the data management and data delivery aspects of the Data Hub architecture and the related data governance strategy.

►   *Enable auditability and accountability for all data under management that is in scope for data governance strategy.* Auditability is extremely important as it not only provides verifiable records of the data access activities, but also serves as an invaluable tool to help achieve compliance with the current and emerging regulations including the Gramm-Leach-Bliley Act and its data protection clause, the Sarbanes-Oxley Act, and the Basel II Capital Accord. Auditability works hand in hand with accountability of data management and data delivery actions. Accountability requires the creation and empowerment of several data governance roles within the organization including data owners and data stewards. These roles should be created at appropriate levels of the organization and assigned to the dedicated organizational units or individuals.

To complete this discussion, let's briefly look at the concept of data stewards and their role in assessing, improving, and managing data quality.

Data Stewardship and Ownership

As the name implies, data owners are those individuals or groups within the organization that are in the position to obtain, create, and have significant control over the content (and sometimes, access to and the distribution of) the data. Data owners often belong to a business rather than a technology organization. For example, an insurance agent may be the owner of the list of contacts of his or her clients and prospects.

The concept of data stewardship is different from data ownership. Data stewards do not own the data and do not have complete control over its use. Their role is to ensure that adequate, agreed-upon quality metrics are maintained on a continuous basis. In order to be effective, data stewards should work with data architects, database administrators, ETL (Extract-Transform-Load) designers, business intelligence and reporting application architects, and business data owners to define and apply data quality metrics. These cross-functional teams are responsible for identifying deficiencies in systems, applications, data stores, and processes that create and change data and thus may introduce or create data quality problems. One consequence of having a robust data stewardship program is its ability to help the members of the IT organization to enhance appropriate architecture components to improve data quality.

Data stewards must help create and actively participate in processes that would allow the establishment of business-context-defined, measurable data quality goals. Only after an organization has defined and agreed with the data quality goals can the data stewards devise appropriate data quality improvement programs.

These data quality goals and the improvement programs should be driven primarily by business units, so it stands to reason that in order to gain full knowledge of the data quality issues, their roots, and the business impact of these issues, a data steward should be a member of a business team. Regardless of whether a data steward works for a business team or acts as a "virtual" member of the team, a data steward has to be very closely aligned with the information technology group in order to discover and mitigate the risks introduced by inadequate data quality.

Extending this logic even further, we can say that a data steward would be most effective if he or she can operate as close to the point of data acquisition as technically possible. For example, a steward for customer contact and service complaint data that is created in a company's service center may be most effective when operating inside that service center.

Finally, and in accordance with data governance principles, data stewards have to be accountable for improving the data quality of the information domain they oversee. This means not only appropriate levels of empowerment but also the organization's willingness and commitment to make the data steward's data quality responsibility his or her primary job function, so that data quality improvement is recognized as an important business function required to treat data as a valuable corporate asset.

Data Quality

Data Quality

Data quality is one of the key components of any successful data strategy and data governance initiative, and is one of the core enabling requirements for Master Data Management and Customer Data Integration.

Indeed, creating a new system of record from information of low quality is almost an impossible task. Similarly, when data quality is poor, matching and linking records for potential aggregation will most likely result in low match accuracy and produce an unacceptable number of false negative and false positive outcomes.

Valuable lessons about the importance of data quality are abundant, and data quality concerns confronted data architects, application designers, and business users even before the problem started to manifest itself in the early data integration programs such as Customer Information Files (CIF), early implementations of data warehouses (DW), Customer Relationship Management (CRM), and Business Intelligence (BI) solutions. Indeed, if you look at a data integration solution such as a data warehouse, published statistics show that as high as 75 percent of the data warehouse development effort is allocated to data preparation, validation, and extraction, transformation, and loading (ETL). Over 50 percent of these activities are spent on cleansing and standardizing the data.

Although there is a wide variety of ETL and data cleansing tools that address some of the data quality problem, data quality continues to be a complex, enterprise-class challenge. Part of the complexity that needs to be addressed is driven by the ever-increasing performance requirements. A data cleansing tool that would take more than 24 hours to cleanse a customer file is a poor choice for a real-time or a web-based customer service application. As the performance and throughput requirements continue to increase, the functional and technical capabilities of the data quality tools are sometimes struggling to keep up with the demand.

But performance is not the primary issue. A key challenge of data quality is an incomplete or unclear set of semantic definitions of what the data is supposed to represent, in what form, with what kind of timeliness requirements, etc. These definitions are ideally stored in a metadata repository. Our experience shows that even when an enterprise adapts a metadata strategy and implements a metadata repository, its content often contains incomplete or erroneous (poor quality) definitions. We'll discuss metadata issues in more details later in this chapter.

The quality of metadata may be low not because organizations or data stewards do not work hard on defining it, but primarily because there are many data quality dimensions and contexts, each of which may require a different approach to the measurement and improvement of the data quality. For example, if we want to measure and improve address information about the customers, there are numerous techniques and reference data sources that can provide an accurate view of a potentially misspelled or incomplete address. Similarly, if we need to validate a social security number or a driver license number, we can use a variety of authoritative sources of this information to validate and correct the data. The problem becomes much harder when you deal with names or similar attributes for which there is no predefined domain or a business rule. For example, "Alec" may be a valid name or a misspelled "Alex." If evaluated independently, and not in the context of, say, postal information about a name and the address, this problem often requires human intervention to resolve the uncertainty.

Finally, as the sophistication of the data quality improvement process grows, so do its cost and processing requirements. It is not unusual to hear that an organization would be reluctant to implement an expensive data quality improvement system because, according to them, "...so far the business and our customers do not complain, thus the data quality issue must not be as bad as you describe." This is not an invalid argument, although it may be somewhat shortsighted from the strategic point of view, especially since many aspects of data quality fall under government- and industry-regulated requirements.

Data Quality Tools and Technologies

There are many tools that automate portions of the tasks associated with cleansing, extracting, loading, and auditing data from existing data stores into a new target environment, be it a data warehouse or a CDI Data Hub. Most of these tools fall into several major categories:

▶ **Auditing tools** These tools enhance the accuracy and correctness of the data at the source. These tools generally compare the data in the source database to a set of business rules that are either explicitly defined or automatically inferred from a scan operation of the data file or a database catalog. Auditing tools can determine the cardinality of certain data attributes, value ranges of the attributes in the data set, and the missing and incomplete data values, among other things. These tools would produce various data quality reports and can use their output to automate certain data cleansing and data correction operations.

▶ **Data cleansing tools** These tools would employ various deterministic, probabilistic or machine learning techniques to correct the data problems discovered by the auditing tools. These tools generally compare the data in the data source to a set of business rules and domain constraints stored in the metadata repository or in an external rules repository. Traditionally, these tools were designed to access external, reference data such as a valid name and address file from an external "trusted" data provider (e.g., Acxiom or Dun & Bradstreet), or an authoritative postal information file (e.g., National Change of Address [NCOA] file), or to use a service that validates social security numbers. The data cleansing process improves the quality of the data and potentially adds new, accurate content. Therefore, this process is sometimes referred to as *data enrichment*.

▶ **Data parsing and standardization tools** The parsers would break a record into atomic units that can be used in subsequent steps. For example, such a tool would parse one contiguous address record into separate street, city, state, and zip code fields. Data standardization tools convert the data attributes to what is often called a *canonical* format or canonical data model—a standard format used by all components of the data acquisition process and the target Data Hub.

Canonical Data Format

Canonical data format is a format that is independent of any specific application. It provides a level of abstraction from applications' native data formats by supporting a common format that can either be used by all applications or may require transformation adapters that convert data between the canonical and native formats. Adding a new application or a new data source may only require a new adapter or modifying an old one, thus drastically reducing the impact on applications. A canonical format is often encoded in XML.

► **Data extraction, transformation, and loading (ETL) tools** are not data quality tools in the pure sense of the term. ETL tools are primarily designed to extract data from known structures of the source systems based on prepared and validated source data mapping, transforming input formats of the extracted files into a predefined target data store format (e.g., a Data Hub), and loading the transformed data into a target data environment, e.g., the Data Hub. Since ETL tools are aware of the target schema, they can prepare and load the data to preserve various integrity constraints including referential integrity and the domain integrity constraints. They can filter out records that fail a data validity check, and usually produce exception reports used by data stewards to address data quality issues discovered at the load stage. This functionality helps ensure data quality and integrity of the target data store, which is the reason we mentioned ETL tools in this section.

► **Hybrid packages**   These packages may contain a complete set of ETL components enriched by a data parser and a standardization engine, the data audit components, and the data cleansing components. These extract, parse, standardize, cleans, transform, and load processes are executed by a hybrid package software in sequence and load consistently formatted and cleansed data into the Data Hub.

Managing Data in the Data Hub

Armed with the knowledge of the role of the enterprise data strategy, we can discuss CDI Data Hub concerns that have to deal with acquiring, rationalizing, cleansing, transforming, and loading data into the Data Hub as well as the concerns of delivering the right data to the right consumer at the right time. In this chapter, we also discuss interesting challenges and approaches of synchronizing data in the Data Hub with applications and systems used to source the data in the first place.

Let's start with the already familiar Data Hub conceptual architecture that we first introduced in Chapter 5. This architecture shows the Data Hub data store and supporting services in the larger context of the data management architecture (see Figure 6-1). From the data strategy point of view, this architecture depicts data sources that feed the loading process, data access and data delivery interfaces, Extract-Transform-Load service layer, the Data Hub platform, and some generic consuming applications.

However, to better position our discussion of the data-related concerns, let's transform our Data Hub conceptual architecture into a view that is specifically designed to emphasize data flows and operations related to managing data in and around the Data Hub.

Data Zone Architecture Approach

To address data management concerns of the Data Hub environment, we introduce a concept of the data zones and the supporting architectural components and services. The Data Zone architecture illustrated in Figure 6-2 employs sound architecture principles of the separation of concerns and loose coupling.

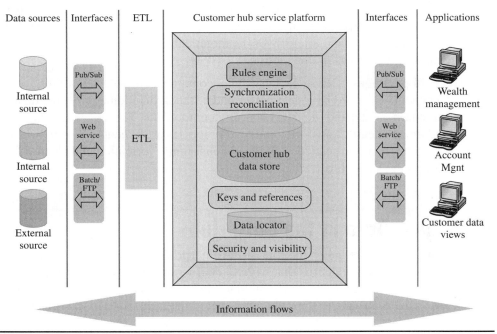

Figure 6-1   *Conceptual Data Hub components and services architecture view*

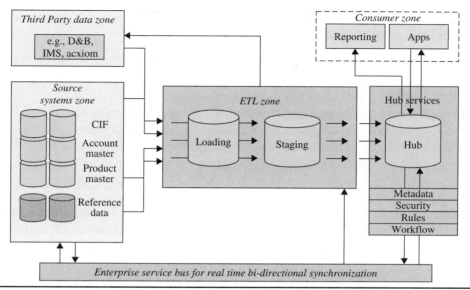

Figure 6-2   *Data Hub architecture—Data Zone view*

Separation of Concerns

In software design, the principle of *separation of concerns* is linked to specialization and cooperation: When designing a complex system, the familiar trade-off is between a few generic modules that can perform various functions versus many specialized modules designed to work together in a cooperative fashion. In complex systems, specialization of components helps address the required functionality in a focused fashion, organizing groups of concerns into separate, designated, and specifically designed components.

Turning to nature, consider the difference between simple and complex organisms. Where simple organisms contain several generic cells that perform all life-sustaining functions, a complex organism (e.g., an animal) is "built" from a number of specialized "components" such as heart, lungs, eyes, etc. Each of these components performs its functions in a cooperative fashion together with other components of the body. In other words, when the complexity is low to moderate, having a few generic components simplifies the overall design. But, as the complexity of the system grows, the specialization of components helps address the required functionality in a focused fashion, by organizing groups of concerns into separate specifically designed components.

We briefly discussed the principle of Loose Coupling in the previous chapter when we looked at service-oriented architectures.

Loose Coupling

In software design, *loose coupling* refers to the design approach that avoids rigid, tightly coupled structures where changes to one component force that change to propagate throughout the systems, and where a failure or a poor performance of one component may bring the entire system down.

When we apply these architecture principles to the data architecture view of the Data Hub, we can clearly delineate several functional domains, which we call *zones*. The Data Zones shown in Figure 6-2 include the following:

- ► Source Systems zone
- ► Third-Party Data Provider zone
- ► ETL/Acquisition zone
- ► Hub Services zone
- ► Information Consumer zone
- ► Enterprise Service Bus zone

To make it very clear, this zone structure is a logical design construct that should be used as a guide to help solve the complexity of data management issues. The Zone Architecture approach allows architects to consider complex data management issues in the context of the overall enterprise data architecture. As a design guide, it does not mean that a Data Hub implementation has to include every zone and every component. A specific CDI implementation may include a small subset of the data zones and their respective processes and components.

Let's review the key concerns addressed by the data zones shown in Figure 6-2.

- ► **The Source Systems zone** is the province of existing data sources, and the concerns of managing these sources include good procedural understanding of data structures, content, timeliness, update periodicity, and such operational concerns as platform support, data availability, data access interfaces, access methods to the data sources, batch window processing requirements, etc. In addition to the source data, this zone contains enterprise reference data, such as code tables used by an organization to provide product-name-to-product-code mapping, state code tables, branch numbers, account type reference tables, etc.

This zone contains "raw material" that is loaded into the Data Hub and uses information stored in the metadata repository to determine data attributes, formats, source system names, and location pointers.

► **The Third-Party zone** deals with external data providers and their information. An organization often purchases this information to cleanse and enrich input data prior to loading it into a target environment such as a Data Hub. For example, if the Data Hub is designed to handle customer information, the quality of the customer data loaded into the Data Hub would have a profound impact on the linking and matching processes as well as on the Data Hub's ability to deliver an accurate and complete view of a customer. Errors, use of aliases, and lack of standards in customer name and address fields are most common and are the main cause of poor customer data quality. To rectify this problem an organization may decide to use a third-party data provider that specializes in maintaining an accurate customer name and address database (for example, Acxiom, D&B, etc.). The third-party data provider usually would receive a list of records from an organization, would match them against the provider's database of verified and maintained records, and would send updated records back to the organization for processing. Thus the third-party zone is concerned with the following processes:

  ► Creating a file extract of customer records to be sent to the provider

  ► Ensuring that customer records are protected and that only absolutely minimal necessary information is sent to the provider in order to protect confidential data

  ► Receiving an updated file of cleansed records enriched with accurate and perhaps additional information

  ► Making the updated file available for the ETL processing

  ► Making appropriate changes to the content of the metadata repository for use by other data zones

► **The ETL/Acquisition zone** is the province of data extract, transformation, and loading (ETL) tools and corresponding processes. These tools are designed to extract data from known structures of the source systems based on prepared and validated source-to-target data mapping; transforming input formats of the extracted files into a predefined target data store format (e.g., a Data Hub); and loading the transformed data into the Data Hub using either a standard technique or a proprietary one. The transformations may be quite complex and can perform substitutions, aggregations, and logical and mathematical operations on data attribute values. ETL tools may access an internal or external metadata repository to obtain the information about the transformation rules, integrity constraints, and target Data Hub schema, and therefore can prepare and load the data while preserving various integrity constraints. Many proven, mature solutions can perform ETL operations in an extremely efficient, scalable fashion.

They can parallelize all operations to achieve very high performance and throughput on very large data sets. These solutions can be integrated with an enterprise metadata repository and a BI tool repository.

▶ An effective design approach to the data acquisition/ETL zone is to use a multistage data acquisition environment. To illustrate this point, we consider a familiar analogy of using loading dock for "brick-and-mortar" warehouse facility. Figure 6-2 shows a two-stage conceptual Acquisition/ETL data zone where the first stage, called *Loading zone*, is acting as a recipient of the data extraction activities. Depending on the complexity and interdependencies involved in data cleansing, enrichment, and transformation, a Loading zone may serve as a facility where all input data streams are normalized into a common, canonical format. The third-party data provider usually receives an appropriate set of data in such a canonical format. The Loading zone is a convenient place where the initial audit of input records can take place.

▶ The *Staging zone*, on the other hand, is a holding area for the already cleansed, enriched, and transformed data received from the Loading zone as well as the data processed by and received from a third-party data provider. The Staging zone data structure could be similar to that of the Data Hub. The benefits of having a Staging zone include efficiency in loading data into the Data Hub (most often using a database utility since the transformations are already completed). The Staging zone offers access to a convenient area to perform a record-level audit before completing the load operation. Finally, a Staging zone provides for an easy-to-use, efficient, and convenient Data Hub reload/recovery point that does not depend on the availability of the source systems.

▶ **The Hub Service data zone** deals with the data management services that create and maintain the structures and the information content inside the Data Hub. We discussed several of these services in the previous chapter. In this chapter, we discuss Data Hub services that support data synchronization and reconciliation of conflicting data changes. Some Data Hub services use a metadata repository to enforce semantic consistency of the information. Other services include linking, matching, record locator, and attribute locator services.

▶ **The Information Consumer zone** is concerned with data-delivery-related issues such as formats, messages, protocols, interfaces, and services that enable effective and easy-to-use access to the required information whether it resides in the Data Hub or in the surrounding systems. The Information Consumer zone is designed to provide data to support business applications including Business Intelligence applications, CRM, and functional applications such as account opening and maintenance, aggregated risk assessment, and others. The Information Consumer zone enables persistent and virtual, just-in-time data integration technologies including Enterprise Information Integration (EII) solutions. Like other data zones, the information consumer zone takes advantage of the metadata repository to determine data definitions, data formats, and data location pointers.

▶ **The Enterprise Service Bus (ESB)** zone deals with technologies, protocols, message formats, interfaces, and services that support a message-based communication paradigm between all components and services of the CDI data architecture. The goal of ESB is to support the loosely coupled nature of the Data Hub service-oriented architecture (SOA) by providing a message-based integration mechanism that ensures guaranteed, once and only once, sequence-preserving, transactional message delivery.

Now that we have reviewed the content and purpose of the architecture zones, we can expand these concepts by including several high-level published services that are available to various data architecture components including Data Hub. These services include

1. Data acquisition services
2. Data normalization and enrichment services
3. Data Hub management services
4. Data synchronization and reconciliation services
5. Data location and delivery services

We discuss some of these services in Chapter 5. The following sections offer a discussion on additional data management services in the context of the Data Zone architecture.

Loading Data into the Data Hub

Data architecture concerns discussed in the beginning of this section have a profound impact on the overall Data Hub architecture and in particular, its data management and data delivery aspects. The Data Zone architecture view shown in Figure 6-2 can help define new effective design patterns, additional services and components that would support any generic data integration platform, and in particular, a Data Hub system for Customer Data Integration.

The level of abstraction of the data zone architecture is sufficiently high to be applicable equally well to all major styles of the Data Hub design including Registry style, Reconciliation Hub style, and ultimately, full Transaction Hub style. However, as we take a closer look at these design styles, we discover that the way the data is loaded and synchronized varies significantly from one style to another.

Indeed, consider the key difference between these styles—the scope of data for which the Hub is the master, specifically:

- **The Registry style of a Data Hub** represents a master of unique identifiers of customer "match groups" and all key attributes (often called identity attributes) that allow Data Hub Linking and Matching services to generate these unique persistent identifiers. The Registry-style Data Hub maintains links with data sources for the identity attributes to provide a clear synchronization path between data sources and the Data Hub. The Registry-style Data Hub allows the consuming application to either retrieve or assemble an integrated view of customers or parties at run time.

- **The Reconciliation Engine style** (sometimes also called Coexistence Hub) supports an evolutionary stage of the Data Hub that enables coexistence between the old and new masters, and by extension, provides for a federated data ownership model that helps address both inter- and intraorganizational challenges of who controls which data. The Data Hub of this style is a system of record for *some* but not all data attributes. It provides active synchronization between itself and the systems that were used to create the Hub data content or still maintain some of the Hub data attributes inside their data stores. By definition of the "master," the data attributes for which the Data Hub is the master need to be maintained, created, and changed in the Data Hub. These changes have to be propagated to the upstream and downstream systems that use these data attributes. The goal is to enable synchronization of the data content between the Data Hub and other systems on a continuous basis. The complexity of this scenario increases dramatically as some of the data attributes maintained in the Data Hub are not simply copied but rather *derived* using business-defined transformations on the attributes maintained in other systems.

- **The Transaction Hub** represents a design style where the Hub maintains *all* data attributes about the target subject area. In the case of a CDI Data Hub, the subject area is the customer (individuals or businesses). In this case, the Data Hub becomes a "master" of customer information, and as such should be the source of all changes that affect any data attribute about the customer. This design approach demands that the Data Hub is engineered as a complete transactional environment that maintains its data integrity and is the sole source of changes that it propagates to all downstream systems that use this data.

A conceptual Data Hub architecture shown in Figure 6-1 and its Data Zone viewpoint shown in Figure 6-2 should address several *common* data architecture concerns:

▶ **Batch and real-time input data processing**   Some or all data content in the Data Hub is acquired from existing internal and external data sources. The data acquisition process affects the Source System zone, theThird-Party Data Provider zone, and the Data Acquisition/ETL zone. It uses several relevant services including data acquisition services, data normalization and enrichment services, and Data Hub management services such as Linking and Matching, Key Generation, Record Locator, and Attribute Locator services (see Chapters 4 and 5 for more details). Moreover, the data acquisition process can support two different modes—initial data load and delta processing of incremental changes. The former implies a full refresh of the Data Hub data content, and it is usually designed as a batch process. The delta processing mode may support either batch or real-time processing. In the case of batch design, the delta processing, at least for the new inserted records, can leverage the same technology components and services used for the initial data load. The technology suite that enables the initial load and batch delta processing has to support high-performance, scalable ETL functionality that architecturally "resides" in the Acquisition/ETL data zone and usually represents a part of the enterprise data strategy and architecture framework. Real-time delta processing, on the other hand, should take full advantage of service-oriented architecture including the Enterprise Service Bus zone, and in many cases is implemented as a set of transactional services that include Data Hub management services and synchronization services.

▶ **Data quality processes**   To improve the accuracy of the matching and linking process, many Data Hub environments implement data cleaning, standardization, and enrichment preprocessing in the Third-Party Data Provider and Acquisition/ ETL zones before the data is loaded into the Data Hub. These processes use data acquisition and data normalization and enrichment services, and frequently leverage external, industry-accepted reference data sources such as Dun & Bradstreet for business information, or Acxiom for personal information.

NOTE

A note about mapping Data Hub service to the data zones. Using a service-oriented architecture approach allows Data Hub designers to abstract and isolate services from the actual location of the methods and functions that execute them regardless of which architecture zone these methods reside.

Data Synchronization

As data content changes, a sophisticated and efficient synchronization activity between the "master" and the "slaves" has to take place on a periodic or an ongoing basis depending on the business requirements. Where the Data Hub is the master, the synchronization flows have to originate from the Hub toward other systems. Complexity grows if an existing application or a data store acts as a master for certain attributes that are also stored in the Data Hub. In this case, every time one of these data attributes changes in the existing system, this change has to be delivered to the Data Hub for synchronization. One good synchronization design principle is to implement one or many unidirectional synchronization flows as opposed to a more complex bidirectional synchronization. In either approach, the synchronization process may require transactional conflict-resolution mechanisms, compensating transaction design, and other synchronization and reconciliation functionality.

A variety of reasons drive the complexity of data synchronization across multiple distributed systems. In the context of a CDI Data Hub, synchronization becomes difficult to manage when the entire data environment that includes Data Hub and the legacy systems is in a peer-to-peer relationship. This is not a CDI-specific issue; however, if it exists, it may defeat the entire purpose and benefits of building a CDI platform. In this case, there is no clear master role assigned to a Data Hub or other systems for some or all data attributes, and thus changes to some "shared" data attributes may occur simultaneously but on different systems and applications. Synchronizing these changes may involve complex business-rules-driven reconciliation logic. For example, consider a typical non-key attribute such as telephone number. Let's assume that this attribute resides in the legacy Customer Information File (CIF), a customer service center (CRM) system, and also in the Data Hub, where it is used for matching and linking of records. An example of a difficult scenario would be as follows:

▶ A customer changes his/her phone number and makes a record of this change via an online self-service channel that updates CIF. At the same time, the customer contacts a service center and tells a customer service representative (CSR) about the change. The CSR uses the CRM application to make the change in the customer profile and contact records but mistypes the number. As the result, the CIF and the CRM systems now contain different information, and both systems are sending their changes to each other and to the Data Hub for the required record update.

▶ If the Data Hub received two changes simultaneously, it will have to decide which information is correct or should take precedence before the changes are applied to the Hub record.

▶ If the changes arrive one after another over some time interval, the Data Hub needs to decide if the first change should override the second, or vice versa. This is not a simple "first-in first-serve" system since the changes can arrive into the Data Hub after the internal CIF and CRM processing is completed, and their timing does not have to coincide with the time when the change transaction was originally applied.

► Of course, you can extend this scenario by imagining a new application that accesses the Data Hub and can make changes directly to it. Then all systems participating in this change transaction are facing the challenge of receiving two change records and deciding which one to apply if any.

This situation is not just possible but also quite probable, especially when you consider that the Data Hub has to be integrated into an existing large enterprise data and application environment. Of course, should the organization implement a comprehensive data governance strategy and agree to recognize and respect data owners and data stewards, it will be in a position to decide on a single ownership for each data attribute under management. Unfortunately, not every organization is successful in implementing these data management structures. Therefore, we should consider defining conceptual Data Hub components that can perform data synchronization and reconciliation services in accordance with a set of business rules enforced by a business rules engine (BRE).

Overview of Business Rules Engines

Let's first define a business rules engine.

Business Rules Engine

A *business rules engine (BRE)* is a software application or a system that is designed to manage and enforce business rules based on a specified stimulus, for example, an event of attribute value changes. Business rules engines are usually architected as pluggable software components that separate the business rules from the application code. This separation helps reduce the time, effort, and costs of application maintenance by allowing the business users to modify the rules as necessary without the need for application changes.

In general, a BRE may help register, classify, and manage the business rules it is designed to enforce. In addition, a BRE can provide functionality that detects inconsistencies within individual business rules (for example, a rule that violates business logic), as well as rule sets.

Rule Set

A *rule set* is a collection of rules that apply to a particular event and must be evaluated together.

In the context of the CDI Data Hub, BRE software manages the rules that define how to reconcile the conflicts of bidirectional synchronization. For example, if a date-of-birth attribute is changed in the CRM system supporting the service center and in the self-service web channel, an organization may define a business rule that requires the changes to this attribute that came from the self-service channel to take precedence over any other changes. A more complex rule may dictate to accept changes to the date of birth only if the resulting age of the customer does not exceed the value of 65. There may be another business rule that would require a management approval in the case when the age value is greater than 65. The BRE would evaluate and enforce all rules that apply to a particular event.

At a minimum, a full-function BRE will include the following components:

▶ **Business Rule Repository**   A database that stores the business rules defined by the business users

▶ **Business Rule Designer/Editor**   An intuitive, easy-to-use, front-end application and a user interface that allows users to define, design, document, and edit business rules

▶ **A Query and Reporting Component**   Allows users and rules administrators to query and report existing rules

▶ **Rules Engine Execution Core**   Actual code that enforces the rules

There are several types of business rules engines available today that differ by at least the following two dimensions: by the way they enforce the rules and by the types of rules they support. The first dimension differentiates the engines that *interpret* business rules in a way similar to a script execution, from the engines that "compile" business rules into an internal executable form to drastically increase the performance of the engine. The second dimension is driven by the types of rules—inference rules and reaction rules:

▶ **Inference Engines** support complex rules that require an answer to be inferred based on conditions and parameters. For example, an Inference BRE would answer a question like "Should this customer be offered an increased credit line?"

▶ **Reaction Rules Engines** evaluate reaction rules automatically based on the context of the event. The engine would provide an automatic reaction in the form of real-time message, directive, feedback, or alert to a designated user. For example, if the customer age in the Data Hub was changed to qualify for mandatory retirement distribution, the reaction BRE would initiate the process of the retirement plan distribution by contacting an appropriate plan administrator.

Advanced BRE solutions support both types of business rules in either translator / interpreter or compilation mode. In addition, these engines support rules conflict detection and resolution, simulation of business rules execution for "what-if" scenarios, and policy-driven access controls and rule content security. Clearly, such an advanced BRE would be useful in supporting complex data synchronization and conflict reconciliation requirements of the Data Hub. Architecturally, however, a BRE may be implemented as a component of a Data Hub or as a general business rules engine that serves multiple lines of business and many applications. The former approach leads to a specialized BRE that is fine-tuned to effectively process reconciliation rules of a given style and context of the Data Hub. The latter is a general-purpose shared facility that may support a variety of business rules and applications, an approach that may require the BRE to support more complex rules-definition language syntax and grammar, and higher scalability and interoperability with the business applications. To isolate Data Hub design decisions from the specifics of the BRE implementation, we strongly recommend that companies take full advantage of the service-oriented approach to building a Data Hub environment and to encapsulating the BRE and its rules repository as a set of well-defined services that can be consumed by the Data Hub on an as-needed basis.

Data Delivery and Metadata Concerns

The complexities and issues of populating Data Hub give rise to a different set of concerns. These concerns have to be solved in order to enable data consumers (systems, applications, and users) to find and use the right data and attest to its quality and accuracy. The Information Consumer zone addresses these concerns by providing a set of services that help find the right data, package it into the right format, and make available the required information to the authorized consumers. While many of these concerns are typical for any data management and data delivery environment, it is important to discuss these concerns in the context of the CDI Data Hub and its data location service.

As we look at the overall enterprise data landscape, we can see the majority of data values spread across the Data Hub and many heterogeneous source systems. Each of these systems may act as a master of some data attributes, and in extreme cases, it is even possible that some data attributes have many masters. Every time a consumer requests a particular data record or a specific data attribute value, this request can be fulfilled correctly only when the requesting application "knows" what system it should query to get the requested data. This knowledge of the master relationship for each data attribute, as well as the knowledge of the name and location of the appropriate masters, is the responsibility of the *Attribute Location service*. Architecturally, it is an enterprise-wide data service that hides the implementation details from the applications and other service consumers. Conceptually, this service acts as a directory for all data attributes under management, and this directory is active, that is, the directory is continuously updated as data attributes migrate or get promoted from old masters to the Data Hub—a natural evolution of a CDI environment from a Registry style to the Transaction Hub. Logically, however, this service is a subset of a larger service framework that represents an enterprise-wide *metadata repository*—a key component of any enterprise-wide data strategy and data architecture. As we mentioned in Chapter 5, the Metadata Repository role is much broader than just providing support for the Attribute Locator service, and also includes such internal Data Hub services as Record Locator and even Key Generation services.

Although a detailed discussion of metadata is beyond the scope of this book, we briefly discuss the basic premises behind metadata and the metadata repository in the section that follows. This section describes how a metadata repository helps enable just-in-time data delivery capabilities of some Data Hub implementations as well as some end-user applications such as real-time or operational Business Intelligence applications.

Metadata Basics

In simple terms, *metadata* is "data about data," and if managed properly, it is generated whenever data is created, acquired, added to, deleted from, or updated in any data store and data system in scope of the enterprise data architecture.

Metadata provides a number of very important benefits to the enterprise, including:

▶ **Consistency of definitions**   Metadata contains information about data that helps reconcile the difference in terminology such as "clients" and "customers," "revenue" and "sales," etc.

▶ **Clarity of relationships**   Metadata helps resolve ambiguity and inconsistencies when determining the associations between entities stored throughout data environment. For example, if a customer declares a "beneficiary" in one application, and this beneficiary is called a "participant" in another application, metadata definitions would help clarify the situation.

▶ **Clarity of data lineage**   Metadata contains information about the origins of a particular data set and can be granular enough to define information at the attribute level; metadata may maintain allowed values for a data attribute, its proper format, location, owner, and steward. Operationally, metadata may maintain auditable information about users, applications, and processes that create, delete, or change data, the exact timestamp of the change, and the authorization that was used to perform these actions.

There are three broad categories of metadata:

▶ **Business metadata** includes definitions of data files and attributes in business terms. It may also contain definitions of business rules that apply to these attributes, data owners and stewards, data quality metrics, and similar information that helps business users to navigate the "information ocean." Some reporting and business intelligence tools provide and maintain an internal repository of business-level metadata definitions used by these tools.

▶ **Technical metadata** is the most common form of metadata. This type of metadata is created and used by the tools and applications that create, manage, and use data. For example, some best-in-class ETL tools maintain internal metadata definitions used to create ETL directives or scripts. Technical metadata is a key metadata type used to build and maintain the enterprise data environment. Technical metadata typically includes database system names, table and column names and sizes, data types and allowed values, and structural information such as primary and foreign key attributes and indices. In the case of CDI architecture, technical metadata will contain subject areas defining attribute and record location reference information.

▶ **Operational metadata** contains information that is available in operational systems and run-time environments. It may contain data file size, date and time of last load, updates, and backups, names of the operational procedures and scripts that have to be used to create, update, restore, or otherwise access data, etc.

All these types of metadata have to be persistent and available in order to provide necessary and timely information to manage often heterogeneous and complex data environments such as those represented by various Data Hub architectures. A metadata management facility that enables collection, storage, maintenance, and dissemination of metadata information is called a metadata repository.

Topologically, metadata repository architecture defines one of the following three styles:

▶ Centralized Metadata repository

▶ Distributed Metadata repository

▶ Federated or Hybrid Metadata repository

The centralized architecture is the traditional approach to building a metadata repository. It offers efficient access to information, adaptability to additional data stores, scalability to capture additional metadata, and high performance. However, like any other centralized architecture, centralized metadata repository is a single point of failure. It requires continuous synchronization with the participants of the data environment, may become a performance bottleneck, and may negatively affect quality of metadata. Indeed, the need to copy information from various applications and data stores into the central repository may compromise data quality if the proper data validation procedures are not a part of the data acquisition process.

A distributed architecture avoids the concerns and potential errors of maintaining copies of the source metadata by accessing up-to-date metadata from all systems' metadata repositories in real time. Distributed metadata repositories offer superior metadata quality since the users see the most current information about the data. However, since distributed architecture requires real-time availability of all participating systems, a single system failure may potentially bring the metadata repository down. Also, as source systems configurations change, or as new systems become available, a distributed architecture needs to adapt rapidly to the new environment, and this degree of flexibility may require a temporary shutdown of the repository.

A federated or a hybrid approach leverages the strengths and mitigates the weaknesses of both distributed and centralized architectures. Like a distributed architecture, the federated approach can support real-time access of metadata from source systems. It can also centrally and reliably maintain metadata definitions or at least references to the proper locations of the accurate definitions in order to improve performance and availability.

Regardless of the architecture style of the metadata repository, any implementation should recognize and address the challenge of semantic integration. This is a well-known problem in metadata management that manifests itself in the system's inability to integrate information properly because some data attributes may have similar definitions but have completely different meanings. The reverse is also true. A trivial example is the task of constructing an integrated view of the office staff hierarchy for a company that was formed because of a merge of two entities. If you use job titles as a normalization factor, a "Vice President" in one company may be equal to a "Partner" in another. Not having these details explained clearly in the context becomes a difficult problem to solve systematically. The degree of difficulty grows with the diversity of the context. Among the many approaches to solving this challenge is the metadata repository design that links the context to the information itself and the rules by which this context should be interpreted.

Enterprise Information Integration and Integrated Data Views

Enterprise Information Integration (EII) is a set of technologies that leverage information collected and stored in the enterprise metadata repository to deliver accurate, complete, and correct data to all authorized consumers of such information without the need to create or use persistent data storage facilities.

The fundamental premise of EII is to enable authorized users to just-in-time and transparent access to all information they are entitled to. Part III of this book discusses the concepts of the "authorized user" and "entitlements."

Conceptually, EII technologies complement other solutions found in the Information Consumer zone by defining and delivering virtualized views of integrated data that can be distributed across several data stores including a Data Hub.

EII data views are based on the data requests and metadata definitions of the data under management. These views are independent from the technologies of the physical data stores used to construct these views.

Moreover, advanced EII solutions can support information delivery across a variety of channels including the ability to render the result set on any computing platform, including various mobile devices. Looking at EII from a CDI Data Hub architecture viewpoint, and applying service-oriented architecture principles, we can categorize EII technologies as components of the Information Consumer zone. The EII components that deliver requested data views to the consumers (users or applications) should be designed, implemented, and supported in conjunctions with the data location and delivery services depicted in Figure 6-2.

Although, strictly speaking, EII is not a mandatory part of the Data Hub architecture, it is easy to see that using EII services allows a Data Hub to deliver the value of an integrated information view to the consuming applications and users more quickly, at a lesser cost, and in a more flexible and dynamic fashion.

In other words, a key part of any CDI Data Hub design is the capability of delivering data to consuming applications periodically and on demand in agreed-upon formats. But being able to deliver data from the Data Hub is not the only requirement for the Information Consumer zone. Many organizations are embarking on the evolutionary road to a Data Hub design and implementation that makes the Data Hub a source for analytical and operational data management including support for the Business Intelligence and Servicing CRM systems. This approach expands the role of the Data Hub from the data integration target to the master data source that feeds value-added business applications. This expanded role of the Data Hub and the increased information value of data managed by the Data Hub require an organizational recognition of the importance of enterprise data strategy, broad data governance, clear and actionable data quality metrics with specially appointed data stewards that represent business units, and the existence and continuous support of an enterprise metadata repository.

The technical, business, and organizational concerns of data strategy, data governance, data management and data delivery that were discussed in this and the previous chapter are some of the key factors necessary to make any CDI initiative a useful, business-value-enhancing proposition.

Data Security, Privacy, and Regulatory Compliance

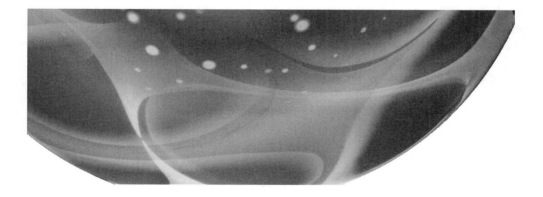

A s we stated in the beginning of the book, one of the major goals of Master Data Management and Customer Data Integration strategy is the creation of an authoritative, cleansed, and integrated system of record for a specific business domain such as customers, products, partners, etc. Integrating such information in one place creates an extremely useful, valuable, and highly leverageable information management opportunity. At the same time, it makes these integrated data platforms attractive targets for unauthorized access and subject to various types of information security risk, including risks of noncompliance with numerous government and industry regulations and laws.

This heightened risk exposure has become a key concern of information security officers and regulatory compliance groups and therefore has to be well understood in order to create business-driven, value-added MDM-CDI solutions that don't put the enterprise in jeopardy. This part of the book, therefore, will review various aspects of information security risks and key regulatory compliance requirements driving the issues of security and privacy to the forefront of MDM-CDI implementations, with the emphasis on Customer Data Integration solutions such as Data Hubs that integrate and need to protect confidential data about customers, prospects, business partners, service providers, and other parties. In addition, this part discusses approaches and strategies for managing and mitigating information security risks. This discussion includes information technology architecture and infrastructure implications of developing and deploying secure and integrated MDM-CDI solutions. The discussion of these topics is organized in the following fashion: Chapter 7 discusses regulatory requirements for security, privacy, and confidentiality of information. Chapter 8 provides an introduction to information security and identity management technologies, Chapter 9 talks about information content protection, and Chapter 10 concludes with a discussion of data security and visibility concerns and implications for the MDM-CDI architecture and design.

Overview of Risk Management for Integrated Customer Information

IN THIS CHAPTER

Risk Taxonomy

Regulatory Compliance Landscape

Emerging Regulatory Compliance Requirements and Their Impact on MDM IT Infrastructure

Key Information Security Risks and Regulatory Concerns

Key Technical Implications of Data Security and Privacy Regulations on MDM Architecture

W hen we discuss risk, we should recognize and be concerned about various types of risks including financial, legal, operational, transactional, reputational, and many others. While these types of risks don't represent formal risk taxonomy, it is easy to see that they all have some elements in common and are closely related. Unfortunately, more often than not various risk types are treated differently by different organizations within the enterprise, often without proper coordination between the organizations and without the ability to effectively recognize and aggregate the risks to understand the root causes and thus the most effective approaches to mitigate the risks.

This chapter offers a high-level overview of various types of risk, risk management strategies, and the implications of the major risk types for Master Data Management and Customer Data Integration. It is not intended to provide readers with a complete set of definitions, processes, and concerns of the integrated risk management and regulatory impact analysis. Rather, the goal of this chapter is to help information technology teams and MDM-CDI designers to be aware of the concerns and high-level requirements of the integrated risk management. This awareness should help MDM-CDI practitioners to better understand the impact of integrated risk management on the architecture, design, and implementation of Master Data Management and Customer Data Integration solutions.

Risk Taxonomy

The interconnected nature of various risk types became highly visible with the emergence of a broad set of government regulations and standards that focus on increased information security threats and terrorist activities that can result in unintended and unauthorized information exposure and security compromise. The types of risks companies are facing include:

▶ ***Transaction risk***   Sometimes also referred to as operational risk, transaction risk is the primary risk associated with business processing. Transaction risk may arise from fraud, error, or the inability to deliver products or services, maintain a competitive position, or manage information. It exists in each process involved in the delivery of products or services. Transaction risk includes not only production operations and transaction processing, but also areas such as customer service, systems development and support, internal control processes, and capacity planning. Transaction risk may affect other risk types such as credit, interest rate, compliance, liquidity, price, strategic, or reputational risks.

▶ ***Reputational risk***   Errors, delays, omissions, and information security breaches that become public knowledge or directly affect customers can significantly impact the reputation of the business. For example, a failure to maintain adequate business resumption plans and facilities for key processes may impair the ability of the business to provide critical services to their customers.

▶ *Strategic risk*   Inaccurate information can cause the management of an organization to make poor strategic decisions.

▶ *Compliance (legal) risk*   Inaccurate or untimely data related to consumer compliance disclosures or unauthorized disclosure of confidential customer information could expose an organization to significant financial penalties and even costly litigation. Failure to track regulatory changes and provide timely accurate reporting could increase compliance risk for any organization that acquires, manages, and uses customer data.

NOTE

There are other ways to represent various types of risks. We will discuss a different representation of the risk taxonomy later in this chapter when we review how the emerging regulatory and compliance requirements are driving risk management approaches.

To address these various risks, companies have to develop and maintain a holistic risk management program that coordinates various risk management activities for a common goal of protecting the company and its assets.

Defining Risk

In general, we can define *risk* as the probability that a threat agent will be able to exploit a defined vulnerability that would adversely impact the business.

Using this definition, an organization can calculate the risk if it understands the possibility that a vulnerability will exist, the probability that a threat agent will exploit it, and the resulting cost to the company. In practical terms, the first two components of this equation can be analyzed and understood with a certain degree of accuracy. The cost component, on the other hand, is not always easy to figure out since it depends on many factors including business environments, markets, competitive positioning of the company, etc. Clearly, not having a cost component makes the calculation of the risk management ROI a challenging proposition. For example, in the case of the risk of a computer virus attack, one option to calculate the cost could be based on how many computers have to be protected using appropriate antivirus software—the cost of software licenses and software patch management. The other option could be to calculate the cost based on the assumption that infected computer systems prevent the company from serving their customers for an extended period of time, let's say one business day. In that case, the cost could be significantly larger than the one assumed in the first option.

Furthermore, consider the risk of a computer system theft or a data compromise. The resulting potential exposure and loss of customer data may have significant cost implications, and the cost to the company could vary drastically from a reasonable system recovery expense to the hard-to-calculate cost of potentially irreparable damage to the company's reputation. Combining this cost with the cost of a highly probable case of litigation against the company, this risk can result in loss of potential and unrealized customer revenue, loss of market share and, in the extreme case, even liquidation of the business.

Risk Analysis

Risk analysis brings together all the elements of risk management (identification, analysis, and control) and is critical to an organization for developing a effective risk management strategy. There are two types of risk analysis: qualitative and quantitative. Quantitative risk analysis attempts to assign an objective numeric value (cost) to components (assets and threats.) Qualitative risk analysis is scenario-driven and does not attempt to assign values to components.

Quantitative risk analysis uses the following variables to calculate the risk exposure:

▶ **SLE** is the single loss expectancy (expressed as the monetary value of the loss).

▶ **ARO** is the annualized rate of occurrence.

▶ **ALE** is the annualized loss expectancy.

Using these variables we can define the following expression for risk calculations:

```
ALE = SLE x ARO
```

The implication of this definition is clear: To manage the risks properly, the company must understand all of its vulnerabilities and match them to specific threats. This can be accomplished by employing a formal risk management methodology and a formal risk management process that includes the following four steps:

1. Identify the assets and their relative value.
2. Define specific threats and the frequency and impact that would result from each occurrence.
3. Calculate annualized loss expectancy (ALE).
4. Select appropriate safeguards.

This four-step process allows an organization to be in a position to define a risk management strategy that includes options to either find a way to avoid the risk, accept the risk, transfer the risk (for example, by purchasing the insurance), or mitigate the risk by identifying and applying the necessary actions (known as *countermeasures*).

While a comprehensive discussion of risk management and various types of risks is well beyond the scope of this book, understanding and managing information security risks by defining appropriate countermeasures is key to designing and deploying Master Data Management solutions, especially CDI Data Hub solutions that deal with customer information. Therefore, we will discuss the notion of customer-level risks, causes of information security risks, regulatory and compliance drivers that elevate the concerns of the information security risks to the highest levels of the organization, and principles used to develop information risk management strategies.

Regulatory Compliance Landscape

Businesses in general, and financial services firms in particular, are beginning to recognize and adopt the concept of Integrated Risk Management (IRM) as a means to manage the complex process of identifying, assessing, measuring, monitoring, and mitigating the full range of risks they face. One of the drivers for IRM is the expansion of the traditional risk management scope to include the notion of *customer risk*—a notion that, in addition to the already-familiar personal credit risk and probability of default, now includes the risks of fraudulent and terrorism-related behavior, the risk of violating customer privacy, and the risk of customer identity theft. Many of these customer-level risk concerns have become significantly more visible and important as organizations started to integrate and aggregate all information about its customers using advanced CDI solutions. The reason for this elevated level of concerns is straightforward: Customer data protection, confidentiality, and integrity risks have become subject to new regulatory and compliance legislation and industry-wide rules. In many cases, compliance is mandatory, with well-publicized implementation deadlines. Depending on a particular regulation and legal interpretation, noncompliance may result in stiff penalties, expensive litigation, damaged reputation, and even an inability to conduct business in certain markets. To achieve timely compliance, to manage these and other types of risks in a cohesive, integrated fashion, companies around the world are looking to adopt technology, data structures, analytical models, and processes that are focused on delivering effective, integrated, enterprise-wide risk management solutions. But the technology is just an enabler of the Integrated Risk Management (IRM). IRM cannot be implemented without direct participation of the business units. For example, the Office of the Comptroller of the Currency (OCC) is forcing financial organizations to place risk management directly at the business unit level. These IRM-related regulations are forcing companies to ensure that the business managers own and manage risk. This approach results in integrated risk management solutions that provide a single, cohesive picture of risk exposure across the entire organization.

Integrated Risk Management: Benefits and Challenges

An effective information risk management strategy provides improved accuracy for risk and compliance reporting, and can mitigate transaction risk by reducing operational failures. Some of the benefits of an integrated information risk management strategy are shown in the following list:

▶   The ability to provide accurate, verifiable, and consistent information to internal and external users and application systems.

▶   The ability to satisfy compliance requirements using clean, reliable, secure, and consistent data.

▶   The ability to mitigate transaction risk associated with the data issues. For example, in financial services, companies embarked on implementing IRM strategies are better positioned to avoid data-related issues that affect successful implementation of Straight Through Processing and next-day settlement environments (STP and T+1).

▶   Flexibility in implementing and managing new organizational structures and the cross-organizational relationships that can be caused by the increase in the Merger and Acquisition (M&A) activity as well as in forming new partnerships.

▶   The ability to define, implement, and measure enterprise-wide data quality strategy and metrics.

▶   The ability to avoid delays related to data issues when delivering new products and services to market.

Many organizations struggle when attempting to implement a comprehensive and effective information risk management strategy, often because they underestimate the complexity of the related business and technical challenges. Moreover, these risks and challenges have to be addressed in the context of delivering integrated customer data solutions such as those enabled by MDM-CDI platforms. Some of these challenges include:

- ▶ Business Challenges

  - ▶ Some risk management and information strategy solutions may have a profound impact on the organization at large, and thus may require continuous executive-level sponsorship.

  - ▶ Data ownership and stewardship have organizational and political implications that need to be addressed prior to engaging in implementation of the information risk management strategy.

  - ▶ Determining real costs and calculating key business metrics such as Return on Investment (ROI), Return on Equity (ROE), and Total Cost of Ownership (TCO) is difficult; the calculations are often based on questionable assumptions and thus produce inaccurate results and create political and budgetary challenges.

  - ▶ New regulatory requirements introduce additional complexity into the process of defining and understanding intra- and interenterprise relationships; this is one of the areas where Customer Data Integration can help mitigate the complexity risks.

  - ▶ The product and vendor landscape is changing rapidly. Although technology solutions continue to mature, this causes additional uncertainty and increases the risk of not achieving successful, on-time, and on-budget project delivery.

  - ▶ Global enterprises and international business units often face conflicting regulatory requirements, cross-border data transfer restrictions, and various local regulations pertaining to outsourcing and offshoring data that include access, storage, and transfer components.

- ▶ Technical Challenges

  - ▶ Risk management solutions must be scalable, reliable, flexible, and manageable. This challenge is particularly important for financial services institutions with their need to support enterprise-level high throughput required for the high-value global transactions that traverse front-office and back-office business systems (e.g., globally distributed equities or currency trading desks).

  - ▶ Risk-related data already resides in a variety of internal repositories including enterprise data warehouses and CRM data marts, but its quality and semantic consistency (different data models and metadata definitions) may be unsuitable for business transaction processing and regulatory reporting.

▶ Similarly, risk data is acquired from a variety of internal and external data sources that often contain inconsistent or stale data.

▶ Risk data models are complex and are subject to new regulations and frequently changing relationships between the organizations and its customers and partners.

▶ Even business-unit-specific risks can have a cascading effect throughout the enterprise, and risk mitigation strategies and solutions should be able to adapt to rapidly changing areas of risk impact. Specifically, a business unit (BU) may be willing to accept a particular risk. However, a security compromise may impact the company brand name and reputation well beyond the scope of a particular channel or a business unit. For example, a major bank may have tens of business units. A security breach within a mortgage BU can affect retail sales, banking, wealth management, consumer lending, credit card services, auto finance, and many other units.

All these challenges have broad applicability to all enterprise-class data management issues, but they are particularly important to organizations that embark on implementing Master Data Management and Customer Data Integration solutions.

Emerging Regulatory Compliance Requirements and Their Impact on MDM IT Infrastructure

As we stated in previous sections, a number of new regulatory and compliance legislations have become the primary drivers for the emergence of the Integrated Risk Management concept. Let's consider two industry segments that by definition have to deal with customer personal data—financial services and health care. In this case, regulations that are focused on handling customer data and the risks associated with its misuse include but are not limited to those on the following list:

▶ **The Sarbanes-Oxley Act of 2002 (SOX)** defines requirements for the integrity of the financial data and availability of appropriate security controls.

▶ **The USA Patriot Act** includes provisions for Anti-Money Laundering (AML) and Know Your Customer (KYC).

▶ **The Gramm-Leach-Bliley Act (GLBA)** mandates strong protection of personal financial information through its data protection provisions.

▶ **The Basel II Capital Requirements Accord** defines various requirements for operational and credit risks.

- **FFIEC guidelines** require strong authentication to prevent fraud in banking transactions.

- **The Payment Card Industry (PCI) Standard** defines the requirement for protecting sensitive cardholder data inside payment networks.

- **California's SB1386** is a state regulation requiring public written disclosure in situations when a customer file has been compromised.

- **Do-Not-Call** and other opt-out preference requirements protect customers' privacy.

- **International Accounting Standards Reporting IAS2005** defines a single, high-quality international financial reporting framework.

- **The Health Insurance Portability and Accountability Act (HIPAA)** places liability on anyone who fails to properly protect patient health information including bills and health-related financial information.

- **New York Reg. 173** mandates the active encryption of sensitive financial information sent over the Internet.

- **Homeland Security Information Sharing Act (HSISA, H.R. 4598)**, prohibits public disclosure of certain information.

- **The ISO 17799 Standard** defines an extensive approach to achieve information security including communications systems requirements for information handling and risk reduction.

- **The European Union Data Protection Directive** mandates protection of personal data.

- **Japanese Protection for Personal Information Act**, Kojin Joho Hogo HouA, May 2003.

- **Federal Trade Commission, 16 CFR Part 314** defines standards for safeguarding customer information.

- **SEC Final Rule, Privacy of Consumer Financial Information (Regulation S-P)**, 17 CFR Part 248 RIN 3235-AH90.

- **OCC 2001-47** Third-party data-sharing protection.

- **17 CFR Part 210** defines rules for records retention.

- **21 CFR Part 11** (SEC and FDA regulations) define rules for electronic records and electronic signatures.

- **NASD rules 2711 and 3010** define several supervisory rules including the requirement that each member establish and maintain a system to supervise the activities of each registered representative and associated person.

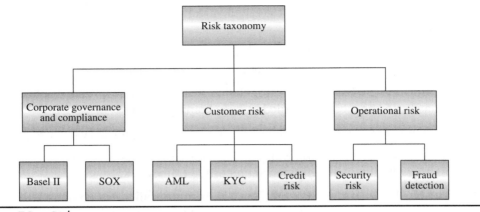

Figure 7-1 *Risk taxonomy*

This is far from a complete list, and it continues to grow and expand its coverage and impact on the way the businesses must conduct themselves and protect their customers.

Many of these regulations are "connected" to each other by their risk concerns and the significant implications for the IT infrastructure and processes that are required to comply with the law. If we were to map the types of risks discussed in this chapter to the key regulations that are designed to protect the enterprise and its customers from these risks, we might end up with the mapping shown in Figure 7-1.

Using this risk taxonomy diagram as a guide, the following sections discuss some of the regulatory compliance requirements and their impact on the information management infrastructures.

The Sarbanes-Oxley Act

The Sarbanes-Oxley Act (SOX) is a set of business risk management concerns that contains a number of sections defining specific reporting and compliance requirements. Some of the key requirements of the Act are defined in Sections 302, 404, 409, and 906, and they require that the company's CEO/CFO must prepare quarterly and annual certifications that attest that

▶ The CEO/CFO has reviewed the report.

▶ The report does not contain any untrue or misleading statement of a material fact or omit to state a material fact.

▶ Financial statements and other financial information fairly present the financial condition.

- ▶ The CEO/CFO is responsible for establishing and maintaining disclosure controls and has performed an evaluation of such controls and procedures at the end of the period covered by the report.

- ▶ The report discloses to the company's audit committee and external auditors:

  - ▶ Any significant deficiencies and material weaknesses in Internal Control over Financial Reporting (ICFR)

  - ▶ Any fraud that involves personnel that have a significant role in the company's ICFR

SOX requires each annual report to contain an "internal control report" that

- ▶ Defines management's responsibilities for establishing and maintaining ICFR

- ▶ Specifies the framework used to evaluate ICFR

- ▶ Contains management's assessment of ICFR as of the end of the company's fiscal year

- ▶ States that the company's external auditor has issued an attestation report on management's assessment

SOX also requires that

- ▶ The company's external auditor reports on management's internal control assessment.

- ▶ Companies have to take certain actions in the event of changes in controls.

In addition, Section 409 specifies the real-time disclosure requirements that need to be implemented by every organization. This represents a new challenge for the companies that have predominantly offline, batch business reporting processes.

The events requiring real-time disclosure include

- ▶ Loss of major client (bundled service purchaser or significant component of product portfolio)

- ▶ Increased exposure to industries that are "in trouble" (significant portion of portfolio)

- ▶ Impact of external party changes (e.g., regulators, auditors)

- ▶ Write-offs of a significant number of loans or portfolios

- ▶ Cost over-runs on IT or other major capital project

These and similar material events will require reporting to interested parties within 48 hours. From a technical capabilities point of view, Section 409's real-time disclosure requires

► Real-time analytics instead of batch systems

► The ability to report on a wide range of events within 48 hours

► Real-time notification and event driven alerts

► Deep integration of information assets

Clearly, achieving SOX Section 409 compliance would be easier using an MDM-CDI solution to provide flexible and scalable near-real-time reporting capabilities.

Gramm-Leach-Bliley Act Data Protection Provisions

The Gramm-Leach-Bliley Financial Modernization Act was signed into law on November 11, 1999 as Public Law 106-102. The GLBA Section 501 defines the Data Protection Rule and subsequent safeguards that are designed to

► Ensure the security and confidentiality of customer data

► Protect against any reasonably anticipated threats or hazards to the security or integrity of data

► Protect against unauthorized access to or use of such data that would result in substantial harm or inconvenience to any customer

Specifically, GLBA key privacy protection tenets are defined in the following paragraphs:

► **Paragraph A** "Privacy obligation policy—It is the policy of the Congress that each financial institution has an affirmative and continuing obligation to respect the privacy of its customers and to protect the security and confidentiality of those customers' nonpublic personal information."

► **Paragraph B3** "… to protect against unauthorized access to or use of such records or information which could result in substantial harm or inconvenience to any customer."

The term "nonpublic personal information" (NPI) referenced in Paragraph A of GLBA means personally identifiable financial information that is

► Provided by a customer to a financial institution

▶ Derived from any transaction with the customer or any service performed for the customer, or

▶ Obtained by the financial institution via other means

In January 2003 the Federal Financial Institutions Examination Council (FFIEC) issued new guidance that expanded GLBA. The new guidance requires financial institutions to protect *all* information assets, not just customer information. FFIEC recommended a security process that the financial institutions have to put in place to stay compliant with the expanded requirements. This process includes the following components:

▶ Information security risk assessment including employee background checks

▶ Security strategy development including:

  ▶ Response programs for unauthorized events

  ▶ Protective measures against potential environmental hazards or technological failures

▶ Implementation of security controls (these controls and technologies enabling the controls are discussed in some detail in Chapters 8–10):

  ▶ Access controls and restrictions to authenticate and permit access by authorized users only

  ▶ Encryption of data-in-transit (on the network) and data-at-rest (on a storage device)

  ▶ Change control procedures

▶ Security testing

▶ Continuous monitoring and updating of the security process including monitoring systems and procedures for intrusion detection

GLBA makes an organization responsible for noncompliance, even if the security breach and the resulting data privacy violation are caused by an outside vendor or service provider.

Specifically, according to GLBA the organization must establish appropriate oversight programs of its vendor relationships, including:

▶ Assessment of outsourcing risks to determine which products and services are best outsourced and which should be handled in-house

▶ Creation and maintenance of an inventory list of each vendor relationship and its purpose

▶ Prioritization of the risk of each relationship consistent with the types of customer information the vendor can access

▶ Routine execution of proper due diligence of third-party vendors

▶ Execution of written contracts that outline duties, obligations, and responsibilities of all parties

A number of federal and state agencies are involved in enforcing GLBA, for example:

▶ Federal banking agencies (i.e., Board of Governors of the Federal Reserve System; Comptroller of the Currency, FDIC, Office of Thrift Supervision, and others)

▶ National Credit Union Administration

▶ Secretary of the Treasury

▶ Securities and Exchange Commission

▶ Federal Trade Commission

▶ National Association of Insurance Commissioners

It is easy to see that the requirements imposed by the Sarbanes-Oxley and Gramm-Leach-Bliley acts have clear implications for the way organizations handle customer and financial data in general, and by extension, how the data is managed and protected in data integration platforms such as Master Data Management systems, and Customer Data Integration solutions in the form of Data Hubs.

Other Regulatory/Compliance Requirements

Of course, in addition to SOX and GLBA, there are numerous other regulations that have similarly profound implications for the processes, technology, architecture, and infrastructure of the enterprise data strategy and particularly on the initiatives to develop MDM-CDI solutions. We'll discuss some of these regulations briefly in this section for the purpose of completeness.

OCC 2001-47

GLBA makes an organization responsible for noncompliance even if the breach in security and data privacy is caused by an outside vendor or service provider. Specifically, the Office of the Comptroller of the Currency (OCC) has defined the following far-reaching rules that affect any institution that plans to share sensitive data with an unaffiliated third party:

▶ A financial institution must take appropriate steps to protect information that it provides to a service provider, regardless of who the service provider is or how the service provider obtains access.

▶ The Office of the Comptroller of the Currency defines oversight and compliance requirements that require a company's management to

  ▶ Engage in a rigorous analytical process to identify, measure, monitor, and establish controls to manage the risks associated with third-party relationships.

  ▶ Avoid excessive risk-taking that may threaten the safety and integrity of the company.

The OCC oversight includes the review of the company's information security and privacy protection programs regardless of whether the activity is conducted directly by the company or by a third party. OCC primary supervisory concern in reviewing third-party relationships is whether the company is assuming more risk than it can identify, monitor, manage, and control.

USA Patriot Act: Anti-Money Laundering (AML) and Know Your Customer (KYC) Provisions

Money laundering has become a serious economic and political issue. Indeed, the International Monetary Fund has estimated that the global proceeds of money laundering could total between two and five percent of world gross domestic product, which is equivalent to $1–3 trillion USD every year.

With the advent of the International Money Laundering Abatement and Anti-Terrorism Financing Act of 2001 (Title 3 of the USA Patriot Act), the U.S. Department of the Treasury has enacted far-reaching regulations aimed at detecting and deterring money-laundering activities and events. These regulations apply to all financial institutions, and have direct implications for all Master Data Management and Customer Data Integration initiatives as activities that deal with the totality of customer information.

The USA Patriot Act affects all financial institutions, including banks, broker-dealers, hedge funds, money service businesses, and wire transfers by requiring them to demonstrate greater vigilance in detecting and preventing money-laundering activity. It defines implementation milestones that include mandatory suspicious activity reporting (SAR) and mandatory adoption of due diligence procedures to comply with these regulations.

USA Patriot Act Technology Impact   Business process requirements of the USA PATRIOT Act include

▶ Development of the AML policies and procedures.

▶ Designation of a compliance officer.

▶ Establishment of a training program.

▶ Establishment of corporate testing/audit function.

► Business units that manage private banking accounts held by noncitizens must identify owners and source of funds.

► For the correspondent accounts processing, implement restrictions that do not allow account establishment with foreign shell banks; implement strict and timely reporting procedures for all corresponding accounts with a foreign bank.

► Organizations must develop and use "reasonable procedures" to know their customer when opening and maintaining accounts.

► Financial institutions can share information on potential money-laundering activity with other institutions to facilitate government action; this cooperation will be immune from privacy and secrecy-based litigations.

The USA Patriot Act requires banks to check a terrorist list provided every two weeks by the Financial Crimes Enforcement Network (FinCEN). Another list to be checked is provided by the Treasury's Office of Foreign Assets Control (OFAC). Additional information sources may become available as the system matures.

Key technical capabilities that support USA PATRIOT Act requirements include

► Workflow tools to facilitate efficient compliance procedures, including workflow processes to prioritize and route alerts to appropriate parties

► Analytical tools that support ongoing detection of hidden relationships and transactions among high-risk entities, including the ability to detect patterns of activity to help identify entities utilizing the correspondent account (the customer's customer)

► Creation and maintenance of account profiles and techniques like scenario libraries to help track and understand client behavior throughout the life of the account

► Support of risk-based user segmentation and a full audit trail to provide context for outside investigations

► Policy-driven comprehensive monitoring and reporting to provide a global view and to promote effective and timely decision making

Many of the required capabilities can be enabled by effective leverage of the data collected and maintained by the existing CRM or new CDI systems. However, the USA Patriot Act and its "know your customer" (KYC) directives require additional customer-focused information. This requirement of knowing your customers and being able to analyze their behavior quickly and accurately is one of the benefits and a potential application of the customer-centric solutions enabled via Customer Data Integration.

Basel II Capital Accord Technical Requirements

In 1988, the Basel Committee on Banking Supervision introduced a capital measurement system, commonly referred to as the Basel Capital Accord. This system addressed the design and implementation of a credit risk measurement framework for a minimum capital requirement standard. This framework has been adopted by more than a hundred countries.

In June 1999, the Committee issued a proposal for a New Capital Adequacy Framework to replace the 1988 Accord. This capital framework consists of three pillars:

- ▶ **Pillar I**   Minimum capital requirements
- ▶ **Pillar II**   Supervisory review of an institution's internal assessment process and capital adequacy
- ▶ **Pillar III**   Effective use of disclosure to strengthen market discipline as a complement to supervisory efforts

One key departure from the 1988 Basel Accord was that banks are required to set aside capital for operational risk. The Basel Committee defines operational risk as "the risk of direct or indirect loss resulting from inadequate or failed internal processes."

The Basel II Accord seeks to align risk and capital more closely, which may result in an increase in capital requirements for banks with higher-risk portfolios.

To comply with Basel II requirements financial institutions have begun creating an *Operational Risk Framework and Management Structure*. A key part of this structure is a set of facilities that would track and securely store loss events in Loss Data Warehouses (includes Loss, Default, and Delinquency data) so that at least two years of historical data are available for processing. This Loss Data Warehouse (LDW) is a primary vehicle to provide accurate, up-to-date analysis of capital adequacy requirements, and is also a source of disclosure reporting.

In the context of Master Data Management, an LDW should become an integrated platform of accurate, timely, and authoritative data that can be used for analysis and reporting.

FFIEC Compliance and Authentication Requirements

On October 12, 2005 the Federal Financial Institutions Examination Council (FFIEC) issued new guidance on customer authentication for online banking services. According to the FFIEC guidance, the authentication techniques employed by the financial institution should be appropriate to the risks associated with those products and services used by the authenticated users. The new regulation guides banks to apply two major methods:

- ▶ **Risk assessment**   Banks must assess the risk of the various activities taking place on their internet banking site.
- ▶ **Risk-based authentication**   Banks must apply stronger authentication for high-risk transactions.

Technical implications of the FFIEC regulations include

- ▶ The ability to provide multifactor authentication for high-risk transactions
- ▶ Monitoring and reporting capabilities embedded into all operational systems
- ▶ Appropriate strength of authentication that is based on the degree of risk
- ▶ Customer awareness and ability to provide reverse authentication where customers are assured they communicate with the right institution and not a fraudulent site
- ▶ Implementation of layered security framework

Let's consider these requirements in the context of MDM-CDI. A CDI Data Hub solution designed and deployed by a financial institution will most likely represent the authoritative source of customer personal and potentially financial data. Therefore, a Data Hub platform must be designed to support the adaptive authentication and information security framework required by the FFIEC regulations. Key details of this enterprise security framework are discussed in Chapter 10.

State Regulations: California's SB1386

California's SB1386 requires that companies dealing with residents of the State of California disclose breaches of their computer systems, when such breaches are suspected of compromising certain confidential information of the California customers. The most unique feature of this law is that it allows for class-action lawsuits against companies in the event of noncompliance.

SB1386 and Sarbanes-Oxley Compliance   In the beginning of this chapter we stated that many of the regulations affecting the processes and methods of information management are interconnected. This section describes one such example of the connected nature of the regulations.

The Committee of Sponsoring Organizations of the Treadway Commission (COSO) has established a framework against which a company's internal controls may be benchmarked for effectiveness and compliance with the Sarbanes-Oxley Act and other applicable laws. According to the COSO framework, the companies are required to identify and analyze risks, establish a plan to mitigate that risk, and have well-defined policies and procedures to ensure that management objectives are achieved, and risk mitigation strategies are executed.

The implication of these requirements is that failure to deal with regulations such as California SB1386 effectively could be interpreted as the failure of a company's management in establishing and maintaining appropriate internal controls to deal with the risk of customer data compromise, thus violating the principal requirements of the Sarbanes-Oxley Act. Litigation and the resulting SB1386 judgments could potentially trigger Sarbanes-Oxley–related violations and its consequences.

Key Information Security Risks and Regulatory Concerns

Identity Theft

Numerous government and private sector reports from sources such as the FTC, the FBI, and the Computer Security Institute repeatedly indicate that identity theft is rapidly becoming one of the fastest-growing white-collar crimes. According to published reports and the latest crime statistics, identity theft continues to be on the rise, and the size of the problem is becoming quite significant. For example, according to a recent report by the California-based Javelin Strategy & Research, in 2005 there were 8.9 million identity theft victims in the U.S. alone, costing $56.6 billion USD, with the average fraud amount of $6,383 per individual, and the average problem resolution time of 40 hours!

There are two primary classes of economic crime related to identity theft:

▶ *Account takeover* occurs when a thief acquires a person's existing credit account information and uses the existing account to purchase products and services. Victims usually learn of account takeover when they receive their monthly account statement.

▶ In true *identity theft*, a thief uses another person's SSN and other identifying information to fraudulently open new accounts and obtain financial gain. Victims may be unaware of the fraud for an extended period of time—which makes the situation that much worse.

In general, credit card fraud is the most common application of the account takeover style of identity theft, followed by phone or utility fraud, bank fraud, real estate rent fraud, and others.

Phishing and Pharming

Traditionally, the most common approach to stealing one's identity was to somehow get hold of the potential victim's personal information. In pre-Internet days thieves went after one's wallet or a purse. Then they increased the area of "coverage" by collecting and analyzing the content of the trash of the intended victims. With the advent of electronic commerce, the Internet and the web, the thieves embarked on easy-to-implement phishing scams, in which a thief known as a "phisher" takes advantage of the fact that some users trust their online establishments such as banks and retail stores, by creating compelling e-mail messages that lead unaware users to disclose their personal data. For example, a frequent phishing scam is to send an e-mail to a bank customer that may look like a totally legitimate request from the bank to verify the user's credentials (e.g., user ID and password) or worse, to verify the individual's social security number. Phishers use frequent mass mailings in the hope that even a small percentage of respondents will financially justify the effort.

A variant of phishing known as *spear-phishing* targets a phishing attack against a selected individual. The phishing text contains correct factual elements (personal identifiers) that correspond to the target/reader. This targeted phishing messages are quite effective in convincing their intended victims of the presumed authenticity of the message.

Pharmers, on the other hand, try to increase the success ratio of stealing other people's identification information by redirecting as many users as possible from legitimate commercial websites to malicious sites. The users get redirected to the false websites without their knowledge or consent, and these pharming sites usually look exactly the same as the legitimate site. But when users log in to the sites they think are genuine by entering their login name and password, the information is captured by criminals.

Of course, there are many other types of scams that are designed to steal people's identities. These criminal actions have reached almost epidemic proportions and have become subject to numerous laws and government regulations. The variety of scams is so large that a number of advisory web sites publish new scam warnings on a regular basis. Examples of these watchdog sites include www.LifeLock.com and the Identity Theft Resource Center (www.idtheftcenter.org).

MDM-CDI and Identity Theft

The key reason we're discussing identity theft in this chapter is the fact that by design, Master Data Management and Customer Data Integration solutions are some of the most attractive targets for identity thieves including phishers and pharmers. To protect customers' identities from being stolen from an MDM-CDI system, these solutions have to be designed and deployed in such a way that the access to and the content of the information these solutions manage are protected and that proper security controls are put in place as CDI Data Hubs are being deployed.

GLBA, FCRA, Privacy, and Opt-Out

Other relevant regulations include National Do Not Call lists and the ability of customers to declare their privacy preferences as well as to opt-out from sharing their personal information to other companies or nonaffiliated third parties. The ability to opt-out is a provision of legislations such as the Gramm-Leach-Bliley Financial Modernization Act (GLBA) and the Fair Credit Reporting Act (FCRA).

The term *opt-out* means that *unless and until* the customers inform their financial institution that the customer does not want them to share or sell customer data to other companies, the company is free to do so. The implication of this law is that the initial burden of privacy protection is on the customer, not on the company.

Contrast this with a stronger version of expressing the same choices—*opt-in*. This option prohibits the sharing or sale of customer data *unless* the customer explicitly agreed to allow such actions.

In addition to the opt-out options, additional privacy protection regulations are enabled by the National Do Not Call (DNC) Registry. National Do Not Call Registry (www.DoNotCall.org) is a government organization that maintains a protected registry of individual phone numbers that their owners have opted to make unavailable for most telemarketing activities.

Recognizing customer privacy preferences such as opt-outs and DNC allows companies to enhance the customer's perception of being treated with respect and thus improves customers' experience and strengthens their relationships with the organization. The ability to capture and enforce customer privacy preferences including opt-out choices is one of the design requirements for data integration solutions in the form of customer information files, CRM systems, and CDI Data Hubs.

Key Technical Implications of Data Security and Privacy Regulations on MDM Architecture

As you can see from the foregoing discussion, regulations such as the Sarbanes-Oxley Act, the Gramm-Leach-Bliley Act, and many others have profound implications for the technical architecture and infrastructure of any data management solution. Of course, Master Data Management is becoming a focal point where these implications are clearly visible and have a significant impact. If we focus on the issues related to protection of and controlling access to the information managed by a Master Data Management solution, we can summarize the technical implications of key regulations into a concise set of requirements that should include the following:

► Support for layered information security framework.

► Support for flexible multi-factor authentication with the level of authentication strength aligned to the risk profile

► Support for policy-based, roles-based, and entitlements-based authorization.

► The ability to protect data managed by a CDI platform whether data is in transit (on the network) or at rest (on a storage device or in memory).

► Support for data integrity and confidentiality.

► Business-driven data availability.

▶ The ability to aggregate personal profile and financial reporting data only to an authorized individual.

▶ Auditability of the transactions and data access and manipulation activities.

▶ Support for intrusion detection, prevention, and monitoring systems.

▶ Support for an inventory list of each third-party vendor relationship and its purpose.

▶ Support for event and document management.

▶ Support for real-time analytics and reporting.

▶ The ability to recognize and categorize all data that needs to be protected, including customer records, financial data, product and business plans, and similar information that can impact the market position of the organization.

▶ Support for a structured process that can keep track of all input and output data to mitigate business risk associated with disclosing private, confidential information about the company and its customers. This includes not only the authoritative data source but also all copies of this data. Indeed, unlike other auditable assets, a copy of data has the same intrinsic value as the original. Therefore, the tracking process should include an active data repository that maintains a current, up-to-date inventory of all data under management that needs to be protected and accounted for.

To sum up, the regulatory landscape that defines the "rules of engagement" related to the protection of information assets and identities of customers has some profound implications for any IT infrastructure. By their very nature, Master Data Management and Customer Data Integration solutions are natural targets of the majority of the regulations mentioned in this chapter. Thus, an MDM-CDI solution that is designed to integrate private confidential or financial data has to be architected and implemented to achieve a verifiable compliance state. The remaining chapters of this part of the book describe design approaches that mitigate various information security risks while addressing the multitude of regulatory and compliance requirements.

Introduction to Information Security and Identity Management

IN THIS CHAPTER

Traditional and Emerging Concerns of Information Security

Overview of Security Technologies

Integrating Authentication and Authorization

Web Services Security Concerns

Putting It All Together

Traditional and Emerging Concerns of Information Security

In medieval times, commerce was conducted in city-states that were well protected by city walls, weapons, and an army of guards and soldiers. In modern times, as commerce rapidly moved to a global marketplace, the goal of keeping potential participants out was replaced by the desire to invite and keep potential customers in.

In today's business environment, we see a similar transformation—instead of keeping everything hidden behind proprietary secure networks protected by firewalls, commerce is done on the public Internet, and every business plans to take advantage of the potentially huge population of prospective customers. Denying access to corporate information is no longer a viable option—inviting new customers and enticing them to do business is the new imperative.

Clearly, this imperative brings with it a new set of security challenges—challenges that are reinforced by numerous pieces of legislation that promote various forms of e-commerce and even e-government and require new approaches to security that can protect both the customer and corporate information assets. We discussed a number of these regulations in Chapter 7.

What Do We Need to Secure?

The Internet has become a de facto standard environment where corporations and individuals conduct business, "meet" people, perform financial transactions, and seek answers for questions about anything and everything. In fact, all users and all organizations that have some form of Internet access appear to be close (and equidistant) to each other.

The Internet has moved the boundaries of an enterprise so far away from the corporate data center that it created its own set of problems. Indeed, together with the enterprise boundaries the traditional security mechanisms have also been moved outward, creating a new "playing field" for customers, partners, and unwanted intruders and hackers alike. As a result, enterprise security requirements have become much more complex.

One way to discuss these requirements is to look at what areas of the business environments need to be secured, and from what kind of danger. Figure 8-1 illustrates the areas of security concerns and corresponding security disciplines that are defined in the following section.

Layered Security Framework

The security domains can be organized into a layered framework that looks at security from "outside in": perimeter security, network security, platform (host) security, and application, data, and user security.

This model describes security "zones" that need to be protected regardless of whether the threat is originating from outside or from within the organization.

Technologies that enable the implementation of the layered security framework may offer overlapping functionality and can span several security domains. For example, the security disciplines of authentication, authorization, and administration (3A) play equally important roles in securing the network resources, the enterprise perimeter, the computing platform, and the applications, data, and users.

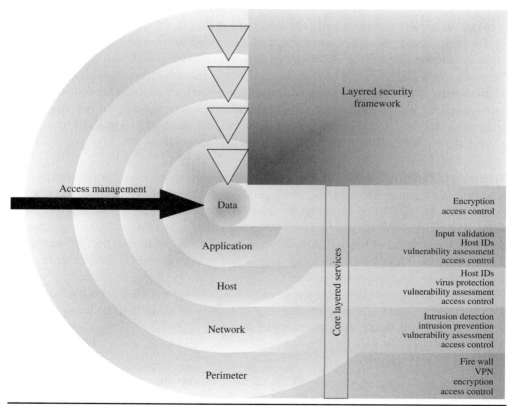

Figure 8-1 *Layered security model*

Perimeter Security

Perimeter security deals with the security threats that arrive at the enterprise boundary via a network. By definition, the perimeter security has to handle user authentication, authorization, and access control to the resources that reside inside the perimeter. The primary technology employed to achieve perimeter security is known as *firewalls*.

A firewall is placed at the network node where a secure network (i.e., an internal enterprise network) and an insecure network (i.e., the Internet) meet each other. As a general rule, all network traffic, inbound and outbound, flows through the firewall, which screens all incoming traffic, and blocks that which does not meet the restrictions of the organization's security policy.

In its most simple form, the role of the firewall is to restrict incoming traffic from the Internet into an organization's internal network according to certain parameters. Once a firewall is configured, it filters network traffic, examines packet headers, and determines which packets should be forwarded or allowed to enter and which should be rejected.

Network Security

Network security deals with authenticating network users, authorizing access to the network resources, and protecting the information that flows over the network.

Network security involves authentication, authorization, and encryption, and often uses technologies like Public Key Infrastructure (PKI) and Virtual Private Network (VPN). These technologies are frequently used together to achieve the desired degree of security protection. Indeed, no security tool, be it authentication, encryption, VPN, firewall, or antivirus software, should be used alone for network security protection. A combination of several products needs to be utilized to truly protect the enterprise's sensitive data and other information assets.

Network and Perimeter Security Concerns   A common approach to network security is to surround an enterprise network with a defensive perimeter that controls access to the network. However, once an intruder has passed through the perimeter defenses, he, she, or it may be unconstrained and may cause intentional or accidental damage. A perimeter defense is valuable as a *part* of an overall defense. However, it is ineffective if a hostile party gains access to a system inside the perimeter or compromises a single authorized user.

Besides a defensive perimeter approach, an alternative network security model is the model of mutual suspicion where every system within a critical network regards every other system as a potential source of threat.

Platform (Host) Security

Platform or host security deals with the security threats that affect the actual device and make it vulnerable to outside or internal attack. The platform security issues include the already-familiar authentication, authorization, and access control disciplines, and the security of the operating system, file system, application server, and other computing platform resources that can be broken into, or taken over by a hacker.

Platform security solutions include security measures that protect physical access to a given device. For example, platform security includes placing a server in a protected cage; using sophisticated authentication and authorization tokens that may include biometrics; using "traditional" physical guards to restrict access to the site to the authorized personnel only; developing and installing "hardened" versions of the operating system; and using secure application development frameworks like the Java Authentication and Authorization Service (JAAS). (JAAS defines a pluggable, stacked authentication scheme. Different authentication schemes can be plugged in without having to modify or recompile existing applications.)

Application, Data, and User Security

Application, data, and user security concerns are at the heart of the overall security framework. Indeed, the main goal of any malicious intent is to get a hold of the protected resource and use it, whether it is information about a company's financial state or an individual's private activities, functionality of the electronic payment funds transfer, or as the case may be, the identity of a person the intruder wants to impersonate for personal, political, or commercial gains.

The security disciplines involved in this are already familiar: the 3As (authentication, authorization, administration), encryption, digital signatures, confidentiality, data integrity, privacy, accountability, and virus protection.

End-to-End Security Framework

To sum up the discussions in the previous sections, when we talk about security, we may want to look at the entire security space from "outside in," using the diagram in Figure 8-1. An important point that needs to be emphasized here is that neither of the disciplines taken separately—network, perimeter, platform, application, data and user security—could offer a complete security assurance.

The events of recent history and the heightened awareness of the real dangers that can be exploited by various terrorist organizations and unscrupulous opportunists have taught us that in order to be and feel secure, we need to achieve "end-to-end security"—an environment that does not intentionally or by omission expose security holes, and that can provide the business benefits of security—privacy, confidentiality, integrity, and trust (see Figure 8-2).

Only a strong understanding of potential security vulnerabilities and an effective combination of various security technologies and disciplines can ensure that this goal can be achieved.

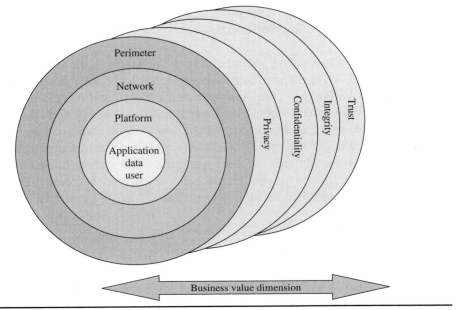

Figure 8-2   *Security and business value dimensions*

Traditional Security Requirements

Today's business environment has different security requirements than traditional commerce. Enterprise networks are no longer defined by the physical boundaries of a single company location but often encompass remote sites and include mobile and remote users all over the world. Also, organizations often use many contractors who are not employees and thus do not undergo employee-level screening and vetting, but may have similar or even greater access than many employees.

Traditional security requirements include:

▶ **Authentication**   The ability to verify that an individual or a party are who they claim they are; authentication is a verification component of the process known as identification.

▶ **Authorization**   A business process of determining what information and computing resources the authenticated party is allowed to access; authorization processes and technologies enforce the permissions expressed in the user authorization *entitlements*. An authorization mechanism automatically enforces entitlements that are based on a security policy dealing with the use of the resource, and in general, the policy could be roles-based, rules-based, or a combination of the two. Clearly, authorization is driven by and depends on reliable authentication (see the discussion on various authorization concerns later in this and the following chapters).

▶ **Confidentiality**   A business requirement that defines the rules and processes that can protect certain information from unauthorized use.

▶ **Integrity**   A business requirement that data in a file or a message traversing the network remains unchanged or that any received data matches exactly what was sent; data integrity deals with the prevention of accidental or malicious changes to data or message content.

▶ **Verification and Nonrepudiation**   This requirement deals with the business and legal concepts that allow a systematic verification of the fact that an action in question was undertaken by a party in question, and that the party in question cannot legally dispute or deny the fact of the action (*nonrepudiation*); this requirement is especially important today when many B2C and B2B transactions are conducted over the network.

  ▶ Traditional paper-based forms are now available over the network and are allowed to be signed electronically.

  ▶ Recently adopted eSign legislation made such signatures acceptable in the court of law (see section on eSign law later in the chapter).

▶ **Auditing and Accountability**   The requirement that defines the process of data collection and analysis that allows administrators and other specially designated users, such as IT auditors, to verify that authentication and authorization rules are producing the intended results as defined in the company's business and security policy. Individual accountability for attempts to violate the intended policy depends on monitoring relevant security events, which should be stored securely and time-stamped using a *trusted time source* in a reliable log of events (also known as an audit trail or a chain of evidence archive); this audit log can be analyzed to detect attempted or successful security violations. The monitoring process can be implemented as a continuous automatic function, as a periodic check, or as an occasional verification that proper procedures are being followed. The audit trail may be used by security administrators, internal audit personnel, external auditors, government regulatory officials, and in legal proceedings.

▶ **Availability**   This requirement provides an assurance that a computer system is accessible by authorized users whenever needed.

▶ **Security management**   This requirement includes user administration and key management:

  ▶ In the context of security management, user administration is often referred to as *user provisioning*. It is the process of defining, creating, maintaining, and deleting user authorizations, resources, or the authorized privilege relationships between users and resources. Administration translates business policy decisions into an internal format that can be used to enforce policy definitions at the point of entry, at a client device, in network devices such as routers, and on servers and hosts. Security administration is an ongoing effort because business organizations, application systems, and the users are constantly changing.

▶ Key management deals with a very complex process of establishing, generating, saving, recovering, and distributing private and public keys for the security solutions based on PKI (see more on this topic later in the chapter).

These traditional security concerns apply to any software system or application that has to protect access to and use of information resources regardless of whether the system is Internet-based or is a more traditional client-server design. However, as businesses and government organizations continue to expand their Internet channels, new security requirements have emerged that introduce additional complexity into an already complex set of security concerns.

Emerging Security Requirements

Let's briefly discuss several security concerns and requirements that have emerged in recent years. These requirements include identity management and user provisioning, intrusion detection and prevention, antivirus and antispyware capabilities, and concerns about privacy, confidentiality, and trust.

Identity Management

This security discipline is concerned with some key aspects of doing business on the Internet. These aspects include:

▶ The need to develop and use a common and persistent identity that can help avoid endless checkpoints that users need to go through as they conduct business on different web sites

▶ The need to prevent the theft and unauthorized use of user identities

The first requirement is not just a user convenience—the lack of a common identity management results in multiple instances of the same user being known but being treated differently in different departments of the same organization. For example, a services company may have a Mike Johnson in its sales database, M. W. Johnson in its services database, and Dr. Michael Johnson and family in its marketing database—clearly, this organization would have a difficult time reconciling this individual's sales and services activity, and may end up bombarding him and his household with marketing offers for the products he already has—the result is a poor customer relationship!

The second requirement is also very important. As we stated in Chapter 7, identity theft continues to be on the rise, and the size of the problem is becoming quite significant. For example, according to the independent research firm Javelin Strategy & Research (Pleasanton, California), in 2005 there were 8.9 million identity theft victims in the U.S. alone, costing $56.6 billion USD, with an average fraud amount of $6,383 per individual, and the average problem resolution time of 40 hours!

This growth of identity theft incidents is estimated to continue at an alarmingly high rate, and many analysts agree that identity theft has become the fastest-growing white collar crime in the Unites States and probably around the world.

Identity management is also a key requirement for a success of Web Services. For Web Services to become a predominant web-based e-Business model, companies need to be assured that web-based applications have been developed with stringent security and authentication controls. Not having strong identity management solutions could prevent Web Services from evolving into mature web-based solutions.

Identity management consists of many components, services, and complex interrelated processes. In order to better visualize the complexity and multitude of identity management, we would like to use a notion of conceptual reference architecture. Such identity management reference architecture is shown in Figure 8-3.

Federated identity layer		
Cross-enterprise provisioning	Cross-enterprise identity mapping	Cross-enterprise trust models

Identity provisioning and life cycle management layer				
Provisioning	Customer self service	Policy Management	Credentials & profile management	Customer preferences management

Access control and management layer				
Authentication	Access control	Authorization	Entitlements	Monitoring
SSO	RBAC	Permissions	Roles & rules management	Auditing and reporting

Identity and security infrastructure layer			
Directory services	Workflow management	XML web services	Data security PKI, tokens
Network security	Perimeter security		Platform security
System directory store	User identity store		Policy store

Figure 8-3   *Identity management reference architecture*

There are a number of standards-based and industry-driven initiatives that attempt to address various aspects of identity management, including such initiatives as Liberty Alliance. However, the topic of identity, anonymity, and privacy involves the sociology of personal information and of information more generally. Therefore, the identity management should by itself be considered as a cross-discipline, multifaceted area of knowledge and technology. A diagram in Figure 8-4 shows a typical architecture of identity management.

User Provisioning

This requirement has emerged to address identity life-cycle management and its user administration aspects that deal with creation, maintenance, and termination of digital identities. User provisioning deals with automating the process of granting users access rights (entitlements) to computing and network resources. Therefore, it is often referred to as *entitlements provisioning*. By automating time- and cost-consuming manual procedures, user provisioning can sharply reduce the costs of provisioning new employees, customers, partners, and suppliers with the necessary credentials, tools, and access privileges. Conversely, the process can also be used to deprovision ex-employees, customers, partners, suppliers, and expired accounts. User provisioning provides a greater degree of corporate efficiency and lowers administrative costs by facilitating account creation and tightly controlling access privileges, and enhances security by tracking, managing, and controlling access. It is also very important to note that by automating the processes of creating and

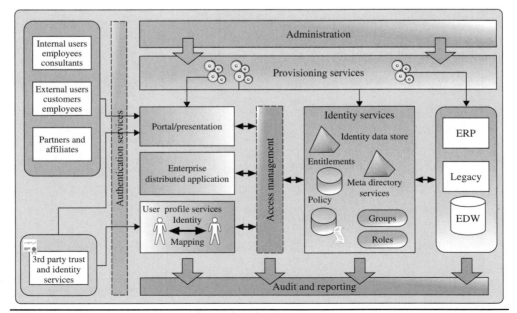

Figure 8-4   *Identity management logical architecture*

removing user accounts and their entitlements, user provisioning and deprovisioning are widely viewed as some of the key capabilities that are required to enable compliance with various regulations including those defined in GLBA, SOX, and the USA Patriot Act's Know Your Customer (KYC).

Intrusion Detection and Prevention

This truly is a traditional requirement that has been revitalized in recent years due to increased incidents of break-ins and similar security violations, all due to the networked and interconnected nature of today's business. According to a recent study by the Computer Security Institute (CSI) and the Federal Bureau of Investigation (FBI), a staggering 70 percent of organizations surveyed reported at least one security incident (breach, data compromise, etc.). This figure is growing significantly year after year. Considering the typical enterprise's reluctance to admit to incidents or their inability to detect them, the true figure is likely to be higher than what has been reported.

Intrusion detection is the process of monitoring the events occurring in a computer system or network and analyzing them for signs of intrusion. Intrusion detection is a necessary business, technical, and even legal requirement that cannot be addressed by simply relying on firewalls and Virtual Private Networks. Indeed, as the attackers are getting smarter and their intrusion techniques and tools are getting more effective, reliable intrusion detection solutions have to offer a degree of sophistication and adaptability that requires unprecedented levels of industry collaboration and innovative "out-of-the-box" approaches to designing intrusion detection systems.

While intrusion detection systems were designed to detect unauthorized access or misuse of computing resources, the new breed of security systems called *Intrusion Prevention Systems (IPS)* has emerged to change the focus from detection of attack to the prevention of attack before actual damage has occurred. Contemporary IPS solutions are designed to protect against such common threats as worms, viruses, Trojan horses; installation and activation of back doors; modifications to system files; changes in user entitlements and privilege levels; buffer overflow attacks; various spyware applications; and many others.

Information and Software Integrity and Tamper-Resistance

Protection of software and data against illegitimate use and modifications is a pressing security issue for software developers, software publishers, and intellectual property distributors (e.g., music, digital video, DVD) alike. Many existing software-based mechanisms are too weak (e.g., having a single point of failure) or too expensive to apply (e.g., heavy run-time performance penalty). Software tamper-resistance deals with a serious threat where a malicious user obtains a copy of the software and modifies its protection mechanism so that the modified software can change its original behavior to satisfy the attacker's intent. For example, a program can be modified to create an unauthorized copy of the software that can be illegally distributed to the public, to a business competitor, to a criminal organization, etc.

Privacy, Confidentiality, and Trust

These requirements became critical as more organizations and users started to use the internet for many aspects of business and personal life. The issue of trust revolves around keeping confidential information confidential, respecting and maintaining user privacy according to his or her privacy preferences, and providing a systematic means of verifying that the privacy and confidentiality aspects of the trusted relationship are not violated. In general, different forms of trust exist to address different types of problems and mitigate risk in certain conditions. Various forms of trust have to be managed and reinforced differently based on the nature of the business and its corporate policies. When we look at the traditional network security solution, we can identify two principal forms of trust: direct trust and third-party trust.

▶ *Direct trust* refers to a situation in which two entities (for example, individual users) have established a trusted relationship in order to exchange information. When direct trust is applied to secure communications, it is the responsibility of each entity to ensure that they are comfortable with their level of personal trust in one another.

▶ *Third-party trust* refers to a situation in which two entities implicitly trust each other even though they have not previously established a personal relationship. In this situation, two entities implicitly trust each other because they each share a relationship with a common third party, and that third party vouches for the trustworthiness of the two entities in question. As an example, when classical security users named Alice and Bob want to exchange trustworthy credentials, they can use passports and/or driver licenses since they implicitly trust the government agencies that issued those credentials. Third-party trust is a fundamental requirement for any large-scale implementation of a network security product based on public key cryptography since it's impractical and unrealistic to expect each user to have previously established relationships with all other users.

Trust and Business Semantics

The nature of trust in relationship to security varies based on the business processes that require different degrees and procedures to establish trust. A Russian proverb, adopted by former President Ronald Reagan, says, "Trust, but verify." This is especially true for the financial services industry, and more specifically, for securities trading. The notion of trust is paramount there and is the key to enable securities trading. However, the business trust in securities trading is different from the trust relationship between two individuals. Business trust implies the ability to rely on others to assume certain risks, the assurance that business commitments will be honored, and the certainty that there is an effective avenue of recourse. To establish and maintain these trusted relationships, a security system should support the notion that *acting as if* you don't trust the *counterparty* forces you to find ways to trust the *transaction*. This concept of trust drives new developments in security standards, systems, and solutions.

Overview of Security Technologies

This section provides a cursory overview of several major security technologies. This overview is by necessity brief—a complete and comprehensive discussion on this topic is well beyond the scope of this book.

Confidentiality and Integrity

Let's start the overview of the security technologies with a high-level discussion of two key security requirements—information confidentiality and integrity.

Cryptography, Cryptology, and Cryptanalysis

Cryptography is the process of converting data into an unreadable form via an *encryption algorithm*. Cryptography enables information to be sent across communication networks that are assumed to be insecure, without losing confidentiality or integrity of information being sent. Cryptography also can be used for user authentication by enabling verification of the sender identity to the recipient.

Cryptanalysis is the study of mathematical techniques designed to defeat cryptographic techniques. Collectively, a branch of science that deals with cryptography and cryptoanalysis is called *cryptology*.

An encryption algorithm transforms plain text into a coded equivalent, known as the cipher text, for transmission or storage. The coded text is subsequently decoded (decrypted) at the receiving end and restored to plain text. The encryption algorithm uses a key, which typically is a large binary number. The length of the key depends on the encryption algorithm and determines the strength of the encryption.

The data that needs to be protected is "locked" for sending by using the bits in the key to transform the data bits mathematically. At the receiving end, the same or a different but related key is used to unscramble the data, restoring it to its original binary form. The effort required to decode the unusable scrambled bits into meaningful data without knowledge of the key—known as "breaking" or "cracking" the encryption—typically is a function of the complexity of the algorithm and the length of the keys. In most effective encryption schemes, the longer the key, the harder it is to decode the encrypted message.

Two types of algorithms are in use today: shared key (also known as "secret key" or symmetric key) and public key (or asymmetric key).

Symmetric vs. Asymmetric Key Encryption

There are two principally different approaches to creating, applying, and managing the encryption keys: one is known as *symmetric cipher* (the encryption and decryption keys are identical, and all communicating parties have to know the key in order to communicate successfully and confidentially); the second one is an *asymmetric* cipher and it is the foundation of the *Public Key Infrastructure* (*PKI*).

The obvious problems with the symmetric cipher include:

▶ The key distribution problem.
  ▶ The need to exchange the secret key between all intended recipients of the sender.
  ▶ Communication difficulties between unknown parties (i.e., the challenge is for the sender to distribute a secret key to a party unknown to the sender).
▶ The scalability issue; for example, in a group of 100 participants a sender may have to maintain 99 secret keys.

These problems of symmetric ciphers were addressed by the discovery made by Whitfield Diffie and Martin Hellman in the mid-1970s. Their work defined a process in which the encryption and decryption keys were mathematically related but sufficiently different that it would be possible to publish one key with very little probability that anyone would be able to derive the other. This notion of publishing one key in the related key pair to the public gave birth to the term Public Key Infrastructure (PKI). The core premise of PKI is based on the fact that while deriving the other key is possible, it is computationally and economically infeasible.

While symmetric encryption is using a shared secret key for both encryption and decryption, PKI cryptography is based on the use of public/private key pairs. A public key is typically distributed in the form of a certificate that may be available to all users wishing to encrypt information, to be viewed only by a designated recipient using his or her private key.

A *private key* is a distinct data structure that is always protected from unauthorized disclosure and is used by the owner of the private key to decrypt the information that was encrypted using the recipient's public key. The beauty of the PKI is in its mathematics, which allows the encryption key to be made public, but it still would be computationally infeasible to derive a private decryption key from the public key.

Allowing every party to publish its public key PKI solves the major key distribution and scalability problems of symmetric encryption that we mentioned earlier.

The mathematical principles, algorithms, and standards used to implement public key cryptography are relatively complex and their detailed description is well beyond the scope of this book. Moreover, creation and management of the public-private key pairs is a complex and elaborate set of processes that include key establishment, life-cycle management, recovery, key escrow, and many others. These and other details about various aspects of PKI are too complex and numerous to be discussed in this book. However, there are a number of mature PKI products on the market today, and in many cases the technology has been made sufficiently easy to use to become practically transparent to the user.

PKI, Nonrepudiation, and Digital Signature

Digital signatures are one of the major value-added services of the Public Key Infrastructure. Digital signatures allow the recipient of a digitally signed electronic message to authenticate the sender and verify the integrity of the message. Most importantly, digital signatures are difficult to counterfeit and easy to verify, making them superior even to handwritten signatures.

Digital Signatures

A digital signature fundamentally relies on the concept of a key pair, where a private "signing" key is known only to the sender (Alice) so that when she signs some data, the data is uniquely and explicitly tied to her. Alice's public key is available to a broad audience of potential recipients so that the signature can be verified and associated with the owner of the private key (Alice). Because of the nature of public-key encryption algorithms, only the public key can decrypt a message encrypted with the corresponding private key. This process thus establishes that only the holder of the private key (Alice) could have created the digitally signed message.

Most analysts and legal scholars agree that digital signatures will become increasingly important in establishing the authenticity of the record for admissibility as evidence. The adoption of the Electronic Signatures in Global and National Commerce Act (eSign) legislation into law by the U.S. Congress is one confirmation of the importance of digital signatures. However, the status of explicit digital signature legislation varies from country to country. For example, some countries, such as Australia, have decided to hold off on drafting detailed digital signature law, whereas others, such as the Netherlands, allow digital signatures and electronic documents to be submitted in court.

Digital signatures received serious legal backing from organizations such as the American Bar Association (ABA), which states that to achieve the basic purpose of a signature, it must have the following attributes:

▶ **Signer authentication**   A signature should indicate who signed a document, message, or record, and should be difficult for another person to produce without authorization.

▶ **Document authentication**   A signature should identify what is signed, making it impracticable to falsify or alter either the signed matter or the signature without detection.

The ABA clarifies that these attributes are mandatory tools used to exclude impersonators and forgers and are essential ingredients of a "nonrepudiation service."

Nonrepudiation

Nonrepudiation is the term used for a service that assures, to the extent technically possible, that entities cannot deny the fact that a particular action has been taken by the entity in question. In the context of PKI, we can distinguish several types of nonrepudiation:

▶ *Nonrepudiation of origin* in which a user cannot falsely deny having originated a message or a document

▶ *Nonrepudiation of receipt* in which a user cannot falsely deny having received a message or a document

▶ Other forms of nonrepudiation including nonrepudiation of *creation*, *delivery,* or *approval*

Network and Perimeter Security Technologies

This group of security technologies is relatively mature and widely deployed throughout corporate and public networks today.

Firewalls

Network firewalls enforce a site's security policy by controlling the flow of traffic between two or more networks. A firewall system provides both a perimeter defense and a control point for monitoring access to and from specific networks. Firewalls often are placed between the corporate network and an external network such as the

Internet or a partnering company's network. However, firewalls are also used to segment parts of corporate networks.

Firewalls can control access at the network level, the application level, or both. At the network level, a firewall can restrict packet flow based on the protocol attributes such as the packet's source address, destination address, originating TCP/UDP port, destination port, and protocol type. At the application level, a firewall may base its control decisions on the details of the conversation (e.g., rejecting all conversations that discuss a particular topic or use a restricted keyword) between the applications and other available information such as previous connectivity or user identification.

Firewalls may be packaged as system software, hardware and software bundles, and, more recently, dedicated hardware appliances (embedded in routers, for example). Known as firewall "appliances," they are easy-to-configure integrated hardware and software packages that run on dedicated platforms. Firewalls can defend against a variety of attacks including:

- Unauthorized access
- IP address "spoofing" (a technique where hackers disguise their traffic as coming from a trusted address to gain access to the protected network or resources)
- Session hijacking
- Spyware, viruses, and trojans
- Malicious or rogue applets
- Traffic rerouting
- Denial of Service (DoS)

With the emergence of spyware as one of the fastest-growing security threats, advanced firewalls, and other perimeter defense solutions are extending their features to support the capability to recognize and eradicate spyware modules that reside on end-user computers and corporate servers.

Many popular firewalls include VPN technology, where a secure "tunnel" is created over the external network via an encrypted connection between the firewalls to access the internal, protected network transparently.

Virtual Private Networks

Virtual Private Network (VPN) solutions use encryption and authentication to provide confidentiality and data integrity for communications over open and/or public networks such as the Internet. In other words, VPN products establish an encrypted tunnel for users and devices to exchange information. This secure tunnel can only be as strong as the method used to identify the users or devices at each end of the communication.

Typically, each VPN node uses a secret session key and an agreed-upon encryption algorithm to encode and decode data, exchanging session keys at the start of each connection using public key encryption. Both end points of a VPN link check data integrity, usually using a standards-compliant cryptographic algorithm (e.g., SHA-1 or MD-5).

S-HTTP/SSL/TLS/WTLS

These communication protocols address issues of secure communication between clients and server on the wired (and in the case of WTLS, wireless) network. We discuss these protocols very briefly in this section for completeness.

Secure HyperText Transport Protocol   The primary protocol used between web clients and servers is the HyperText Transport Protocol (HTTP). Secure HTTP (S-HTTP) extends the basic HTTP protocol to allow both client-to-server and server-to-client encryption. S-HTTP provides three basic security functions: digital signature, authentication, and encryption. Any message may use any combination of these (as well as no protection). S-HTTP provides multiple-key management mechanisms including password-style manually distributed shared secret keys, public-key key exchange, and Kerberos ticket distribution. In particular, provision has been made for prearranged symmetric session keys to send confidential messages to those who have no established public/private key pair.

Secure Sockets Layer   SSL is the most widely used security technology on the web. In contrast with S-HTTP, which secures application-to-application communications, SSL provides end-to-end security between browsers and servers, always authenticating servers and optionally authenticating clients. SSL is application-independent (compared to S-HTTP's dependence on the HTTP protocol) because it operates at the transport layer rather than at the application layer. It secures connections at the point where the application communicates with the IP protocol stack so it can encrypt, authenticate, and validate all protocols supported by SSL-enabled browsers, such as FTP, Telnet, e-mail, and so on. In providing communications channel security, SSL ensures that the channel is private and reliable and that encryption is used for all messages after a simple "handshake" is used to define a session-specific secret key.

Transport Layer Security Protocol (TLS)   The Internet Engineering Task Force renamed SSL as the Transport Layer Security protocol in 1999. TLS is based on SSL 3.0 and offers additional options for authentication such as enhanced certificate management, improved authentication, and new error-detection capabilities. Three levels of server security include server verification via digital certificate, encrypted data transmission, and verification that the message content has not been altered.

Wireless Transport Layer Security   The Wireless Transport Layer Security (WTLS) protocol is the security layer of the Wireless Application Protocol (WAP). The WAP WTLS protocol was designed to provide privacy, data integrity, and authentication for wireless devices. Even though the WTLS protocol is closely modeled after the well-studied TLS protocol, there are a number of potential security problems in it, and it has been found vulnerable to several attacks including chosen plaintext data recovery attack, a datagram truncation attack, a message forgery attack, and a key-search shortcut for some exportable keys.

Security experts are continuously working on addressing these concerns, and new wireless security solutions are rapidly becoming available not only to corporate local area networks but to all wireless devices including personal computers, PDAs, and even mobile phones. Therefore, information stored in a MDM/CDI Data Hub can be accessed securely as long as the wireless access point or a router and the wireless users exercise appropriate precautions and employ wireless security protocols of enterprise-defined strength. These protocols include Wireless Equivalent Privacy (WEP), Wi-Fi Protected Access (WPA), Extensible Authentication Protocol (EAP), and others.

Application, Data, and User Security

In this section, we'll discuss application, data, and user security technologies and their applicability to the business requirements of authentication, integrity, and confidentiality.

Introduction to Authentication Mechanisms

Authentication mechanisms include passwords and PINs, one-time passwords, digital certificates, security tokens, biometrics, Kerberos authentication, and RADIUS.

Passwords and PINs   Authentication most commonly relies on passwords or personal identification numbers (PINs). Passwords are typically used while logging into networks and systems. To ensure mutual authentication, passwords can be exchanged in both directions.

Challenge-Response Handshakes   These techniques offer stronger authentication than ordinary passwords. One side starts the exchange, and is presented with an unpredictable challenge value. Based on a secretly shared value, an appropriate response is then calculated and sent. This procedure defeats the unauthorized use of simple passwords.

One-Time Password   One-time passwords are designed to remove the security risks presented by traditional, static passwords and PINs. The same password is never reused, so intercepted passwords cannot be used for authentication. Implementations of this approach vary, often using time values to provide the basis on which the current password is based. For example, RSA Security's SecurID card displays a value on its LCD screen that changes every minute. This value, plus the user's PIN, is submitted to an authentication server, where it is compared to a value computed for that user's card at that particular time. This form of authentication is sometimes referred to as two-factor authentication.

Digital Certificates   Digital certificates work like their real-life counterparts that are issued by a trusted authority to contain and present the user's credentials (e.g., passports, driver's license). Digital certificates contain encryption keys that can be used to authenticate digital signatures. Certificates are often based on PKI technology and mathematically bind a public encryption key to the identity (or other attribute) of a principal. The principal can be an individual, an application, or another entity such as a web server. A trusted certificate authority creates the certificate and vouches for its authenticity by signing it with the authority's own private key. There are several commercial certificate issuers such as RSA Security (now a part of EMC^2), Entrust, and VeriSign. An organization can issue certificates for its own applications by using an internally managed Certificate Authority. A certificate-issuing server can also be installed as a part of the web server suite (e.g., IBM, Lotus, and Microsoft integrate a certificate server with their web server software). PKI security vendors like Entrust and RSA Security/EMC^2 offer a variety of mature certificate-enabled products for businesses.

Other authentication techniques include Kerberos and Remote Authentication Dial-In User Service (RADIUS) Authentication.

Multifactor Authentication Technologies

In principle, any authentication process deals with one or more questions that help define the user's identity. These questions include:

- ▶ Something you have (e.g., a smart card or a hardware token)
- ▶ Something you know (e.g., a password or a PIN)
- ▶ Something you are (e.g., an intrinsic attribute of your body including fingerprint, iris scan, face geometry)
- ▶ Something you do (e.g., typing characteristics, handwriting style)

The concept of multifactor authentication uses more than one of these options. Clearly, multifactor authentication systems are more difficult to get used to for the user. However, the security benefits of multifactor authentication are significant. Multifactor authentication can successfully withstand a number of impersonation attacks, and therefore can eventually overcome many perceived drawbacks of this technology.

Biometrics   The goal of biometric identification is to provide strong authentication and access control with a level of security surpassing password and token systems. This goal is achievable because access is allowed only to the specific individual, rather than to anyone in possession of the access card.

Biometric techniques usually involve an automated process to verify the identity of an individual based on physical or behavioral characteristics. The first step in using biometrics is often called the *enrollment*. Predefined biometric templates, such as a voiceprint, fingerprint, or iris scan, are collected in a database for each individual. The template data then is used during a verification process for comparison with the characteristic of the person requesting access. Depending on the computer and network technologies used, verification takes only seconds. Biometric techniques fall into two categories: physiological and behavioral.

- ▶ **Physiological biometrics**   Face, eye, fingerprint, palm print, hand geometry, or thermal images

- ▶ **Behavioral biometrics**   Voiceprints, handwritten signatures, and keystroke/ signature dynamics

Biometric measures are used most frequently to provide hard-to-compromise security against impersonation attacks, but they also are useful for avoiding the inconveniences of needing a token or of users forgetting their passwords.

When considering biometric techniques, care must be taken to avoid a high rate of false positives (erroneous acceptance of the otherwise compromised identity) and false negatives (erroneous rejections or otherwise valid identity). For example, a fingerprint scan can produce a false negative because the individual's finger was dirty, covered with grease, etc. Among the biometric techniques available to date, the iris scan produces the highest degree of confidence (indeed, an iris scan is unique for each eye for each individual for as long as the individual is alive; the number of all possible iris scan codes is in the order of 10^{72}—a very large number that exceeds the number of observable stars in the universe!).

Smart Cards

Smart cards represent another class of multifactor authentication solutions that offer a number of defenses against password-based vulnerabilities.

Smart cards—plastic cards about the same size as a credit card, but with an embedded computer chip—are increasingly used in a wide variety of applications, from merchant loyalty schemes to credit/debit cards, to student IDs, to GSM phones. According to several reports by Gartner Group and other research organizations, smart cards are the highest-volume semiconductor-based product manufactured today, with GSM phones and financial-service applications leading this boom—the GSM subscriber information module (SIM) remains the single-largest smart card application.

Authentication, Personalization, and Privacy   The tension between *privacy* with its intrinsic property of not disclosing personal information unless and to the extent absolutely necessary, and *personalization,* which requires access to personal information, transactional behavior, and even knowledge of the party-to-enterprise relationships, is well known. To put it slightly differently, enabling personalization requires a certain amount of privacy disclosure.

But personalization is not the only threat to privacy. We have stated repeatedly that effective, strong authentication is a prerequisite to protecting an individual's privacy. However, it can also threaten privacy since depending on the situation, the risk profile of the users, and their transactions, the stronger the authentication the more personal, sensitive, identifying information may be needed before access to an information resource or permission to execute a transaction can be granted. Solving these tensions is one of the drivers for an integrated MDM-CDI solution that can support privacy preferences of the users as a part of the CDI data model.

Integrating Authentication and Authorization

While PKI addresses the issues of authentication, integrity, confidentiality, and nonrepudiation, we need to define an overarching conceptual framework that addresses a set of issues related to the authorization of users and applications to perform certain functions, to access protected resources, to create and enforce access control policies, and to "provision" users to automatically map appropriate policies, permissions, and entitlements at the time of their enrollment into a security domain.

As we mentioned earlier, a successful authorization relies on the ability to perform reliable authentication. In fact, these two disciplines should go hand in hand in order to create a robust and fully functional and auditable security framework. To help discuss these topics let's take a brief look at access control mechanisms and Single Sign-On (SSO) technologies as a contemporary access control solution for the web and beyond.

Access control simplifies the task of maintaining the security of an enterprise network by cutting down on the number of paths and modes through which attackers might penetrate network defenses. A more detailed discussion on access control can be found in Chapter 10.

SSO Technologies

Single Sign-On (SSO) is a technology that enables users to access multiple computer systems or networks after logging in once with a single set of authentication credentials. This setup eliminates the situation where separate passwords and user IDs are required for each application. SSO offers three major advantages: user convenience, administrative convenience, and improved security. Indeed, having only one sign-on per user makes administration easier. It also eliminates the possibility that users will keep their many passwords in an easily accessible form (e.g., paper) rather than try to remember them all, thereby compromising security. Finally, SSO enhances productivity by reducing the amount of time users spend gaining system access.

SSO is particularly valuable in computing environments where users access applications residing on multiple operating systems and middleware platforms, and correspondingly, where its implementation is most challenging.

One disadvantage of the SSO approach is that when it is compromised, it gives the perpetrator access to all resources the user can access via single sign-on.

Web Services Security Concerns

We discussed Web Services in Part II when we looked at service-oriented architecture (SOA). While Web Services offer a number of truly significant benefits, they bring with them interesting and challenging security concerns that need to be addressed in order to design, develop, and deploy a security Web Services system.

Authentication

Since Web Services, like any other services and interfaces, should allow only authorized users to access service methods, authenticating those users is the first order of business. This is similar to the username and password authentication of users that ordinary web sites may require. However, the main difference here is that in the context of Web Services, the users are other computers that want to use the Web Service.

Data Integrity and Confidentiality

If an organization decides to expose an internal application as a Web Service, it may have to also expose supporting data stores (databases, registries, directories). Clearly, special care is necessary to protect that data, either by encryption (which often means a performance impact) or by guarding its accessibility.

Similarly, data may be in danger of interception as it is being processed. For example, as a Web Service method gets invoked on user request, the temporary data that the Web Service uses locally may be exposed to an attacker if unauthorized users gain access to the system.

Eavesdropping in a Web Services context implies acquiring the information that users get back from a Web Service. If the Web Services output can be intercepted on its way to the user, the attacker may be in a position to violate the confidentiality and integrity of this data. One preventive measure is to use data-in-transit encryption (e.g., SSL) for returned information.

Attacks

In the Web Services model, special care needs to be taken with regard to input parameter validation. In a poorly designed service, a set of invalid input parameters can bring the service or a system down. One solution to this problem could be to use a standard object transport protocol such as Simple Object Transport Protocol (SOAP) to define an acceptable value for all input parameters in a Web Service.

Denial-of-service (DoS) attacks, especially the ones where an attacker can overload the service with requests, will prevent legitimate users from using the service and thus disrupt the business. Furthermore, a flood of requests on one component or service can propagate to other components, affecting them all in a cascading, "domino" effect. Since component A may receive requests from sources B and C, this means that an attack on B disrupts A, and may also affect users of C.

The loosely coupled nature of Web Services also leads to other security issues. The chain of components always has a component that is most vulnerable to attack (the weakest link). If attackers can compromise such a weak-link component, they can exploit this opportunity in a variety of ways:

▶ Intercept any data that flows to that particular component from either direction.

▶ Acquire sensitive, personal, or valuable information.

▶ Manipulate the streams of data in various ways including data alteration, data redirection, or using innocent servers to mount denial-of-service attacks from the inside.

▶ Shut down the component, denying its functionality to the other components that depend upon it; this will effectively disrupt many users' activities from many different access points.

WS-Security Standard

As we discussed in the preceding section, Web Services are concerned with the issues of authenticity, integrity, and confidentiality of messages, and are subject to various penetration and denial-of-service attacks. A dedicated OASIS standard—*WS-Security*—has been developed to provide quality of protection through message integrity, message confidentiality, and single-message authentication.

These mechanisms can be used to accommodate a wide variety of security models and encryption technologies.

WS-Security also provides a general-purpose mechanism for associating security tokens with messages. No specific type of security token is required by WS-Security. It is designed to be extensible (e.g. support multiple security token formats). For example, a user might provide proof of identity and proof that they have a particular business certification. Additional information about WS-Security can be found on the OASIS Web Services Security Technical Committee web site, www.oasis-open .org/committees/wss/.

Putting It All Together

Given the multitude and complexity of security technologies and the size constraints of the book, we were able only to "scratch the surface" of security concerns. However, general security practices and common sense dictate that enterprises should develop a comprehensive end-to-end security framework and reference architecture in order to protect data, users, and application platforms to a degree that makes good business, economic, and even legal sense. The key concerns of information security that are driven by risk management imperatives as well as regulatory and compliance requirements can and should be addressed by carefully designing and implementing a holistic, integrated, and manageable information security architecture and infrastructure that are based on established and emerging standards as well as industry- and enterprise-specific policies. Experience shows that as long as you design your security solution holistically and do not concentrate only on one aspect of security, be it authentication, firewall, or encryption, the current state of the art in security technologies can enable you to create robust and secure Master Data Management and Customer Data Integration solutions. The layered security framework shown in Figure 8-1 can be applied directly to the MDM-CDI solutions, and in fact, the security framework shows that the outer layers of security are "wrapped" around the data core that naturally represents a Data Hub.

The last two chapters in this part of the book focus on two key aspects of information security that are particularly important to Master Data Management and Customer Data Integration solutions: protecting CDI information from a security breach and unintended, unauthorized access and use.

To that end, we'll show how to design an MDM-CDI solution to enable appropriate levels of information security and security-related compliance. We'll also show how to integrate MDM-CDI information management architecture, which was discussed in Part II of the book, with the security and compliance concerns discussed in this and the previous chapters.

Protecting Content for Secure Master Data Management

IN THIS CHAPTER
Data Security Evolution
Data Security Overview
Enterprise Rights Management

Data Security Evolution

The Internet has brought about an information and connectivity revolution where enterprises, governments, and individuals all act as participants in the global interconnected, networked information ecosphere.

The information assets available in this networked ecosphere continue to grow and expand their scope. Moreover, as enterprises aggregate data into large data warehouses and MDM-CDI Data Hub systems that use networked storage devices, these information assets become increasingly more valuable and at the same time more accessible.

This networked ecosphere and the information it contains has become an attractive target for identity thieves, information thieves, and other malicious attackers who have learned to take advantage of the ubiquitous nature of the Internet. And even as security practitioners are working diligently to develop new security solutions, the hackers do not stay idle. They continue to develop new security compromise techniques and approaches. These approaches include not only phishing and pharming. The hackers and information thieves keep on building and distributing new spyware and malware at an ever-increasing rate. As a result, the number, the variety, and the size of security breaches continue to grow with no signs of slowing down.

For example, consider a high-profile security breach at BJ's Wholesale Club that occurred in March 2004. In that well-publicized case, 6 million accounts were compromised, and $16 million in claims were filed from credit card issuers. This cost included $10 million in credit-card reissuing and monitoring costs. If a breach were to compromise not 6 but 100 million accounts or more, the resulting costs could be significantly higher.

A joint 2005 PGP/Ponemon Institute's Benchmark Study of the data breach impact estimated the average cost of a data breach at about $139 per person. Hence, a compromise of a million-customer file can cost as much as $139 million to remediate. This would include explicit costs such as

▶ Discovery of the breach

▶ Escalation procedures

▶ Notification of the potential victims

▶ Recovery from security incidents in the form of fraud write-offs, legal costs, investigation costs, audits, credit report monitoring, IT and operational costs, and other redress activities

The overall cost of a security breach would also include implicit costs often characterized by lost opportunity, legal liabilities, and noncompliance with federal and state regulations. The result could be not just a significant loss of revenue but potential termination of business. As indicated by the industry research and analysis firm Gartner Group: "...the loss of trust in a vendor by consumers or in a payment service provider by vendors can result in the termination—not just interruption—of revenue as customers change their practices or suppliers."

Incidents of data compromise are often classified as identity theft—the fastest-growing white collar crime in the United States (we introduced identity theft in Chapter 7). The Federal Bureau of Investigation (FBI), the Computer Security Institute (CSI), and various identity theft watchdog organizations estimate that organized crime globally makes more money from identity theft than from selling illegal drugs.

What appears to be even more alarming is that the sources of these incidents and the security threats to organizations are no longer coming from the outside the enterprise. Disgruntled or irresponsible employees and contractors can easily bypass traditional perimeter defenses and cause significant, long-lasting damage to organizations, their customers, and their reputation. According to published FBI reports, internal threats that originated inside the enterprise account for 50–80% of all security attacks.

Emerging Information Security Threats

The vast majority of information that is stored in digital form contains some confidential data—data that is the real target of a wide variety of security threats. We described some of these threats in previous chapters and the preceding section. In addition, rapid growth of spyware and various forms of viruses has become one of the major threats to the security of the enterprise information.

Spyware

Spyware is malicious software that installs itself onto a user's computer and sends information from that computer to a third party without the user's permission or knowledge.

Some of the better known types of spyware include:

- ▶ General compromise enablers such as
    - ▶ Botnet worms that can create a network of infected computers that can work in concert to perform any malicious activity including but not limited to running Distributed Denial-of-Service (DDoS) attacks
    - ▶ Downloaders that are designed to install potentially malicious programs on computers without the user's knowledge or consent

▶ Identity grabbers that "complement" phishing and pharming activities by performing actions such as

    ▶ Theft of user identification, passwords, and other sensitive or confidential personal information

    ▶ Monitoring and capturing keystrokes that can enable a thief to steal user information such as passwords (this type of spyware is known as *keylogger*)

    ▶ Hijacking a web browser in order to modify browser settings so that it can redirect the user to a pharming location or another bogus site

▶ Data theft enablers include:

    ▶ **Banking trojans**   Specialized software agents that monitor information entered into banking applications

    ▶ **Backdoor trojans**   A type of spyware that may allow hackers unrestricted remote access to a computer system when it is online

These and other types of spyware represent a real threat to enterprises and individual users alike. However, those spyware programs that are focused specifically on data compromise represent a serious challenge to the enterprise's ability to comply with data protection regulations (many of these regulations are mentioned in Chapter 7 and also listed in the next section). These regulations are designed to protect sensitive and confidential customer and business financial data, including the following data categories:

▶ Customer and patient data

▶ Financial transactions

▶ Finance and accounting data

▶ Human resource data

▶ Confidential company performance and planning data

▶ Military data

▶ Legal data

▶ Intellectual property including design and research data

Interestingly, these data categories represent primary areas of the activities surrounding Master Data Management initiatives. As we discussed in Part II of the book, MDM and CDI solutions are information integration platforms that create and manage authoritative, accurate, timely, and secure systems of record for their respective areas of focus (e.g., customer, product, etc.). The goal of these MDM-CDI Data Hub solutions is to collect, integrate, and manage confidential data from a wide variety of sources in order to create a new system of record for the enterprise. Obviously, enterprises implementing these MDM-CDI solutions need to protect information stored in Data Hub systems from the compromise of unauthorized access and use.

Moreover, this information may represent highly confidential intellectual property that requires additional considerations for protecting the use of the information content even after the data is legitimately delivered to an authorized user. The latter information protection concern is the province of a special category of information asset protection technology known as Enterprise Rights Management (ERM). We briefly discuss ERM later in this chapter. In general, however, the need to protect information assets is driven by a number of factors including customer expectations, business demands, competitive pressures, industry regulations, business policies, etc. Recent adoption of regulatory compliance requirements—some of which are general, while others are specific to a particular domain such as public sector, life sciences, and financial services—has further emphasized this need for data protection.

Regulatory Drivers for Data Protection

Concerns over confidential data in general and customer data privacy and data security in particular have resulted in a broad range of legislative and regulatory requirements for data security. Failure to comply with these rules can result in civil and criminal liability. We have discussed some of these regulations in previous chapters of this book, and they are listed here for ease of reference. Examples of regulatory requirements that directly or indirectly focus on information security include:

▶ **The Sarbanes-Oxley Act** requires that executives know who has access to what information, and that proper security controls are in place to ensure data confidentiality and integrity.

▶ **The Gramm-Leach-Bliley Act (GLBA)** dictates that organizations must preserve the security and confidentiality of nonpublic personal information including personal financial data.

▶ **The Health Information Portability and Accountability Act (HIPAA)** directs health care providers to preserve the confidentiality of individual medical records. To the extent that some of this data becomes visible to the benefits departments of any organization (i.e., Human Resources and Payroll departments), HIPAA may have broader applicability than just health care providers.

▶ **21 Code of Federal Regulations (CFR) Part 11** In the pharmaceutical industry, the Federal Drug Administration (FDA) has established guidelines for any individual or organization governed by the FDA that uses electronic recordkeeping and electronic signatures, including requirements for auditable procedures to ensure the integrity of that data.

▶ **The Children's On-Line Privacy Protection Act (COPPA)** establishes privacy protection guidelines for any organization holding information about children.

- ▶ **California Senate Bill 1386** requires that any organization that loses a California citizen's personal data must alert its California customers via "notification to major statewide media."

- ▶ **The European Data Protection Directive** establishes a set of rules that address the handling of *all* types of personal data. This directive requires organizations to ensure that

  - ▶ Personal data must be kept confidential.

  - ▶ Individuals should know in advance what information is collected about them, how it will be used and by whom, who has access/permissions to change that data, and how it will be stored.

Risks of Data Compromise

To summarize the concerns discussed in the preceding section, data security, privacy, integrity, and confidentiality are no longer optional requirements, and data compromises that violate these requirements can put an organization at significant risk. Some risk types associated with data security compromises include:

- ▶ **Reputation risk**   Risk to earnings or revenue arising from negative public opinion.

- ▶ **Compliance risk**   Companies are now subject to numerous regulations such as the Sarbanes-Oxley Act, the Basel II Accord, the USA Patriot Act, the Gramm-Leach-Bliley Act, and California's SB 1386.

- ▶ **Operational/transactional risk**   Risk of direct or indirect loss from inadequate or failed internal processes, people, and systems, or from external events, including fraud. Data compromised at the enterprise level can increase operational risk by potentially impacting the stability and availability of the key enterprise systems.

- ▶ **Third-party information sharing risk**   According to the letter and spirit of GLBA and the Office of the Comptroller of Currency (OCC) regulations such as OCC 2001-47, an organization is responsible for data privacy and confidentiality breaches even if these events happened at or were caused by an unaffiliated third-party data or service provider. This risk is particularly relevant as organizations move toward outsourcing and offshore implementation of many customer service and support tasks.

Managing these risks is a focus of data security and identity management (we introduced the concepts of identity management in Chapter 8). Identity management and data security are complementary technology disciplines that offer a number of significant business benefits including organizational ability to

- ▶ Minimize fraud
- ▶ Meet compliance requirements of existing and emerging legislation
- ▶ Minimize legal exposure
- ▶ Improve competitive advantage
- ▶ Increase brand equity
- ▶ Enhance customer retention/loyalty

Data Security Overview

The foregoing discussion shows that data protection is a key business requirement of any organization. However, solving the data protection problem is a massive and very complex undertaking that requires a holistic view of information security and in particular, knowledge of identities that can either cause harm or become victims of these new types of crime. As stated earlier, the set of technologies and processes dealing with issues related to digital identities is known as identity management. Information security is an overarching concept that in addition to identity management includes multilayered defense approaches, authentication, authorization and access control, entitlements and provisioning, enterprise rights management, and various data encryption solutions.

This chapter deals with one particular aspect of identity management and information security—data security and protection.

Data Security

Data security refers to the protection of data from either accidental or unauthorized viewing, modification, destruction, duplication, or disclosure during input, processing, storage, transmission, or output operations.

The practice of safeguarding data is at the core of the Information Security discipline and is primarily concerned with the following factors:

- ▶ **Data privacy and confidentiality**   Information should be available only to those who rightfully have access to it.
- ▶ **Data integrity**   Information should be modified only by those who are authorized to do so via authorized actions.
- ▶ **Data availability**   Information should be accessible to those who need it, when they need it.

In the context of data security, the term "data" includes, but is not limited to, data in databases or files, transactional data, operational policies and procedures, system design, organization policies and procedures, system status, and personnel schedules.

Layered Security Framework

The protection of data can only be effective if considered as part of a comprehensive security strategy and end-to-end security framework. We started general discussion of the layered security framework in Chapter 8. This chapter will take a closer look at this framework from the perspective of data protection. In the context of data protection, a layered security framework considers information as the core that needs to be protected from outside attackers and internal compromises caused by incompetence, lack of appropriate due diligence, or malicious intent.

The comprehensive end-to-end security framework defined in Chapter 8 offers a multilayered "defense-in-depth" approach that surrounds data and its users in several layers of security controls. This layered security framework consists of the following layers:

1. Perimeter
2. Network
3. Platform (host)
4. Application
5. Data
6. User

The diagram shown in Figure 9-1 depicts the security layers as well as core security services for each layer.

We discussed specific security concerns for each layer of the framework in Chapter 8 of this book, and summarize these concerns in the following list for ease of reference.

▶   **Perimeter security** deals with security threats that arrive at the enterprise boundary via a network. Perimeter security has to support user authentication, authorization, and access control to the resources that reside inside the perimeter. The perimeter may consist of one or more firewalls protecting a network perimeter demilitarized zone (DMZ). The DMZ may contain web servers, e-mail gateways, network antivirus software, and Domain Name Servers (DNS) exposed to the Internet. It may also implement intrusion detection and intrusion prevention systems.

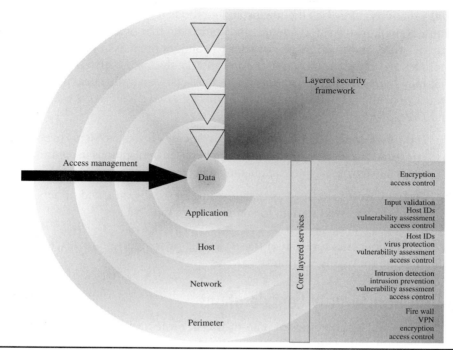

Figure 9-1   *Layered security framework*

▶ **Network security** deals with the authentication of the network user, authorizing access to the network resources, and protecting the information that flows over the network. Network security often uses technologies like transport layer security (SSL/TLS or IPSec), Public Key Infrastructure (PKI), and Virtual Private Network (VPN). It may also implement intrusion detection and intrusion prevention systems.

▶ **Platform/host security** deals with the security threats that affect the actual device and make it vulnerable to external or internal attacks. Platform security issues include authentication, authorization, and access control disciplines, and the security of the operating system, file system, application server, and other computing platform resources that can be broken into or taken over by a hostile agent.

▶ **Application security** deals with the need to protect not just access to the application execution environment but also access to the application code itself. Poorly protected applications can provide easy access to confidential data. Unprotected application code can be stolen or modified to create "back doors," to insert spyware, worms, and Trojans. Therefore, it is very important to define and enforce a comprehensive set of application security standards and controls.

▶ **Data security** addresses the means and methods to protect the *content* of transactional, historical, dynamic, and static data that organizations acquire, create, store, and manipulate in order to conduct business operations. This includes not only traditional data files and databases but also the software that may represent significant information assets. Generally speaking, content security for all data under management falls into two categories: *Data-in-Transit* and *Data-at-Rest*.

  ▶ **Data-in-Transit** is defined as any data moving between systems over network connections as well as data transferred between applications using file transfer mechanisms, messaging and queuing mechanisms, and/or ETL tools.

  ▶ **Data-at-Rest** is defined as data residing in locally attached or networked data stores as well as data in archives (e.g., tape backup).

Data security concerns for each of these two major categories are described in more detail in the following section.

Data-In-Transit Security Considerations

The techniques and technologies of data-in-transit protection represent a mature area of data protection and are reasonably well understood. These technologies include transport layer security (SSL/TLS or IPSec) as well as secure tunneling using Virtual Private Networks (VPN). In the case of proprietary network protocols (for example, IBM Systems Network Architecture APPC/LU6.2), encryption options are available in some implementations, and typically, these protocols are implemented over nonpublic wide-area networks that offer a certain degree of security by design.

The main principles behind the techniques used for data-in-transit protection include:

▶ Authentication between the sender and the receiver

▶ Encryption of the message payload while it traverses the network fabric

The advantages of using these data-in-transit techniques include:

▶ Maturity of the technology solutions.

▶ Protection of data content while in transit.

▶ Predictable performance impact.

▶ Application transparency; as a rule, networked applications don't have to be changed to send messages/data over a secure network protocol.

One consideration concerning data-in-transit solutions includes the need for client-resident components. For example, in a web-based environment, SSL/TLS solutions rely on the web browser's security features and usually do not require additional client-side software.

IPSec, on the other hand, requires client-side software installation. Since a typical legacy environment is not web-based, IPSec may be the right choice for data-in-transit protection for legacy applications.

Another interesting approach to protecting data-in-transit deals with the message-level security that can be implemented on top of the transport layer protection. The message payload itself can be protected using a variety of techniques, for example, by using encryption for messages that are moving into and from message queuing systems. One approach to secure e-mail messaging is to use S/MIME (this feature is available in popular e-mail clients such as Microsoft Outlook and Outlook Express, and does not require additional software distribution).

A key consideration for data protection relates to the scope of protection. For example, some data-in-transit techniques protect data only between the client and the server (e.g., between a web browser and a web server), thus leaving data in the open on the sending and receiving systems. An attacker can exploit these exposure points with relative ease. Therefore, security architects need to consider additional security measures that can complement "out-of-the-box" transport-level security to ensure a reasonable degree of data protection.

Security architects and system designers have to consider the following key requirements and considerations for data-in-transit protection:

- ▶ Minimize the number of encryption/decryption points to ensure a reasonable level of performance, throughput, and latency.

- ▶ Develop an integrated key management strategy across different network segments, especially if they use different encryption algorithms (e.g., TLS and IPSec between web-based networks and legacy systems).

To sum up, data-in-transit protection addresses some of the security concerns about data that is moving over networks. However, by itself, this protection is limited and does not address a number of security concerns discussed earlier. For example, a network can be compromised, data payload can be intercepted (hijacked), data can be replayed or redirected to unintended destinations, and the network can become unavailable or can be used for denial-of-service or other types of attacks.

Therefore, relying on just data-in-transit protection is a necessary but not a sufficient approach to protecting data privacy, confidentiality, integrity, and availability.

Data-at-Rest Protection

Even if the network is secure, and appropriate access controls are in place, the sophistication of the attackers continues to outpace the defenders' ability to detect and prevent new types of attacks in a timely manner, which can put the entire enterprise at risk.

Therefore, the scope of data security includes an approach that aims to protect data if/when all other security controls failed and the attacker got hold of data that is stored on a storage device. The goal of data-at-rest protection is to address this risk by making data unusable to unauthorized users even if such a user has managed to obtain proper network access credentials. Data-at-rest protection provides complementary protection capability that works equally well for defending the enterprise from both external and internal compromise. The latter point is very important since a majority of all security breaches occur because of inappropriate, erroneous, or malicious action on the part of the employees.

In general, the technologies of data-at-rest security rely on authentication, access authorization and control, and payload encryption techniques. This section looks closely at the data-at-rest techniques that make the data unusable when the access controls and perimeter defenses are compromised. These techniques include:

▶ **Compression** Data-loss-less protection schemes are often used to provide certain levels of protection while improving the operational throughput of data due to the reduced record/message length.

▶ **Encryption** Data encryption schemes are commonly implemented at the data, application, and operating-system levels. Almost all schemes involve encryption/decryption keys that must be available to all parties accessing the data. When the data is at-rest on a storage device, we can apply these general techniques at the following levels of granularity:

   ▶ **Field-level protection** In this case, the protection mechanism would encrypt or scramble the data in place, thus protecting each sensitive field individually. The data type and the field length would not change. This technique would not require any addition of new fields to any files.

   ▶ **File or database protection** In this case, the protection mechanism would encrypt the entire file or database, without separating sensitive data from the total data content.

   ▶ **Block-level protection** encrypts the entire device block.

In addition, as a general principle we should also consider physical security as an accepted means of protecting any facilities including data centers and data storage facilities (i.e., security gates, hard-to-compromise identification badges, background checks, security guards, etc.).

We need to consider these levels of data-at-rest protection in the context of the business and technical requirements that help determine technical and economical viability. The key requirements for software and hardware-based data-at-rest security approaches include:

▶ **Data type support**   Support for any form of data-at-rest, including files, databases, messages, etc.

▶ **Total application transparency**   If data is encrypted on a storage device, it has to be decrypted for every access to preserve and sustain application functionality; applications that use the protected data should not be aware of the cryptographic operations.

▶ **Preserved database functionality**   If attributes used for database access are encrypted (e.g., primary and foreign keys, indexes, search arguments), then the database may become unusable.

▶ **Encryption**   Use of strong encryption that is based on industry standards and proven encryption algorithms.

▶ **Key management**   This is a key requirement for any data-at-rest encryption to be viable; for example, key management needs to address the following:

   ▶ Encryption/decryption keys have to be available to all applications producing and consuming protected data; this requirement presents a key distribution challenge.

   ▶ Keys have to change regularly so that the data protection scheme does not become stale and thus become vulnerable to being broken by a brute force attack.

   ▶ Keys have to be available for a long period of time so that the data can be recovered and used long after it was first encrypted (e.g., recovery from an archive storage).

▶ **Performance**   The encryption/decryption operations are very computing-cycles-intensive and can drastically impact the performance of the entire environment.

▶ **Manageability**   Support for operations and system/network management.

▶ **Scalability**   Data-at-rest security solutions should scale up functionally and technically to cover the current and future data landscape.

Data-at-Rest Solution Selection Considerations

When choosing a data-at-rest solution, we have to map the requirements listed in the preceding section and the business needs of the organization to the solution's capabilities.

We should consider and assess these capabilities in line with the organization's risk management strategy. For example, we can start by analyzing whether the solution is configurable and customizable in order to protect the highest risk areas first. Once the most vulnerable areas are covered, we have to assess the scalability and flexibility of the solution to easily and quickly cover other areas of data protection concerns. Some of the considerations for choosing a solution may be as follows:

▶ In general, field-level encryption has the largest negative impact on performance and may affect application transparency.

▶ Newer operating systems offer file-level encryption (e.g., Microsoft's Encrypted File System [EFS]).

▶ Some database management systems have built-in encryption capabilities.

▶ Some storage vendors offer proprietary encryption engines that operate on the storage device to perform encrypt/decrypt operations.

▶ Some specialized data-at-rest security vendors offer dedicated software and hardware appliances that operate on the entire storage subsystem.

While the last three options offer application transparency and deliver better performance than a field-level encryption, they are specific to the data formats and platforms supported. For example, database encryption will not support protection of non-database file structures. Similarly, EFS is not supported outside Microsoft operating environments. And built-in crypto-engines only work with the storage devices they are built for.

Specialized vendors of data-at-rest solutions differ in the choice of technologies, approaches, capabilities, performance, and supported platform. Many support block-level encryption on the device. A large number of vendors offer hardware-based appliances that are installed on the I/O channel between the computer and the storage subsystem. These appliances deliver the best performance and the least performance penalty (some solutions claim to have under 1 percent performance penalty), total application transparency, manageability of the devices, and scalability for the size of the protected data, and the number of consuming applications. Most of the current limitations of the appliance-based solutions revolve around the types of storage subsystems and the channel protocols used to exchange data between the CPU and the storage. For instance, almost all vendor solutions support Storage Area Network (SAN) and Network Attached Storage (NAS) architecture over Fibre Channel. Examples of the hardware-based data-at-rest security appliance include solutions from companies such as DeCru (a NetApp company), Ingrian Networks, NeoScale, and others.

Enterprise Rights Management

The collaborative nature of work in today's global enterprise results in the need for individual workers and organizations to engage in frequent interactions with their colleagues, partners, suppliers, government agencies, and other parties. These interactions often include the need to exchange information over the network in order to achieve common business goals.

The information exchanged between collaborating parties is often of a very sensitive nature, and enterprises have to protect it to satisfy regulatory requirements and company's fiduciary obligations to their customers and other owners of this information.

Three main concerns related to protecting data in collaborative environments have become painfully obvious. We already discussed two key concerns in this and the previous chapters:

▶ Access to any data that requires protection needs to be controlled, enforced, and audited based on the appropriate policies, user entitlements, and regulations.

▶ The information content needs to be protected from unauthorized use both while it traverses communication networks and while it "rests" on storage devices.

The third concern is a direct consequence of the proliferation of the digital content, a collaborative nature of the work, and the recognition of the intrinsic information value of data regardless whether it is in the "original" form or in copies. To put it slightly differently, any copy of the data is as valuable as the "original" data itself.

Indeed, according to numerous studies, over 90 percent of all information created by corporations now exists in electronic form. Moreover, a significant portion of this information contains intellectual property that represents key market value for many business and individual content creators (authors, artists, etc.) alike. According to studies by companies such as PricewaterhouseCoopers, a significant component of the market value of a typical U.S. company resides in its intellectual property assets.

Thus, the third concern deals with the need to understand and protect the rights of access to and use of data content and to prevent potential IP leakage. Such concern becomes a reality when, for example, the data is initially acquired by an authorized user and then shared with a person who has no authority to use all or some of this data.

This concern often comes to light when a business defines a collaborative process that creates or uses protected intellectual property information. Such information may include research, discovery, or patent description; legal documents requiring protection; business transactions or business plans related to a proposed merger or acquisition; medical diagnosis and medical history of a patient being referred to another physician or a hospital; and many similar cases. In a collaborative situation, an authorized user can legitimately create and access this information, and then share it with a recipient outside the protected enterprise in order to perform a particular business task (e.g., an external reviewer of the patent application). Clearly, sharing the protected information in this case creates opportunities for data leakage, misuse, and outright theft.

For example, imagine that confidential information regarding a merger between two companies has been organized and stored as an Excel spreadsheet document. This document can be stored in a highly secured enterprise server that is protected by robust policy-based authentication and access control mechanisms. However, if this highly confidential document is accessed legitimately by a member of the M&A team and then given to an unauthorized third party either via e-mail, as a printed document, or as a copy on a removable storage device, the document no longer enjoys the protection it requires.

In other words, while secure data access can prevent unauthorized users from accessing confidential information, this may not stop the authorized user from copying the information and sharing it with the others. And once that information moves outside the protection of the secured enterprise network, anyone can do with it what they will, and the owner's ability to control that information is lost. This last point has become a business driver for the intellectual property protection of digital content in the retail marketplace. A well-known example of the need for IP and copyright protection includes electronic distribution and sharing of music and/or books over the Internet.

The area of concern we've just described is the focus of technologies collectively known as Digital Rights Management (DRM). And as the collaborative nature of today's networked business continues to embed itself tighter and tighter into the daily enterprise activities, DRM has often been referred to using a broader term, Enterprise Rights Management (ERM). Since the focus of this book is on enterprise solutions for Master Data Management, we will use the term ERM when discussing issues related to protection of the digital content. To be specific, let's define ERM.

Enterprise Rights Management

Enterprise Rights Management (ERM) is a set of technologies designed to manage and enforce information access policies and use rights of electronic documents within an enterprise. ERM enables protection of intellectual property embedded in the electronic documents. ERM provides protection persistence that enforces information access policies. ERM-enforced polices allow an organization to control access to information that needs to be secured for privacy, competitive, or compliance reasons. ERM's protection persistence should prevent users and administrators from disabling protection mechanisms.

In order to show specific functional components of ERM, we can restate the ERM definition as follows:

Enterprise Rights Management (ERM) is a set of technologies designed to

- ▶ Secure content using strong encryption.
- ▶ Enable protection persistence that prevents users and administrators from disabling the protection mechanisms.

▶ Provide security controls that automatically and assuredly monitor and audit all data access operations and events including traditional Create, Read, Update, Delete (CRUD) operations as well as print, e-mail, copy/paste, file transfer, and screen capture.

▶ Minimize the impact of content protection on users and applications both from usability and performance points of view.

▶ Leverage existing enterprise authentication and authorization methods including enterprise directory and provisioning systems to manage and control authorized users.

Master Data Management environments by their very nature require that the authoritative master data created and managed by MDM systems should be protected in a comprehensive and holistic way. This includes user authentication, authorization and access controls, data-in-transit and data-at-rest protections, and the post-retrieval protection of the secured content based on the concepts of ERM. To put it another way, secure Master Data Management should integrate several information security disciplines and technologies including ERM.

We can apply the capabilities and requirements of ERM solutions to Master Data Management environments. Similar to the requirements of data protection in-transit and at-rest (see previous sections), one of the key requirements in developing an ERM system is the potential impact of ERM technologies and processes on user experience. Any system that creates drastically different or difficult-to-use methods to gain access to the content will make ERM adoption at best long and at worst impractical.

Combining these factors with the high visibility and strategic positioning of any Master Data Management initiative makes the transparency and the ease of use of the ERM solution some of the key success factors not only for selecting and deploying an ERM solution but for the entire MDM initiative.

ERM Processes and MDM Technical Requirements

Since an MDM solution may contain confidential or sensitive information assets, an MDM data integration platform such as a Data Hub for customer or product information would have to enable or implement some key ERM/DRM capabilities including data model extensions, processes, and technologies.

Contemporary ERM systems can leverage basic ideas of symmetric and asymmetric encryption algorithms of the Public Key Infrastructure (PKI) technology and the latest rights management policy and the XML licensing standard known as XrML.

An ERM-enabled MDM system uses XrML-expressed policies and rules, and should support at least two key processes: authoring and viewing.

An example of the authoring process that uses both symmetric and asymmetric key encryption would include the following steps:

► Create a publishing license that uses the XrML standard to define content entities and their rights.

► Encrypt the content, usually with a symmetric content key.

► Protect the content key by encrypting it with the public key of the ERM server.

► Digitally sign the publishing license and the encrypted content key.

► Attach the package that contains signed publishing license to the content.

A corresponding viewing process will act in reverse and should include the following steps:

► Authenticate the user.

► Extract the content key and decrypt it using the user's private key.

► Create a use license specifying the rights outlined in the publishing license.

► Decrypt the content and apply the use license to it to comply with the publishing license restrictions.

These processes may appear complex. However, there are a number of ERM products on the market today that implement these types of processes and transparently enforce ERM rules. One of the better-known ERM solutions that enable ERM in a Microsoft Windows environment is Microsoft's Rights Management System (RMS).

ERM Examples

Let's illustrate the way an ERM/DRM solution could be deployed in a Master Data Management Data Hub environment that is designed to store and manage confidential and sensitive data.

Ensuring Regulatory Compliance of Customer Information

Customer Data Integration solutions collect and aggregate customer information in the data integration systems known as CDI Data Hubs. As we stated in the previous chapters of this book, a CDI Data Hub is the integration point of *all* information about the Customer. As such, a CDI Data Hub must enable the following functions:

► Protect customer information in the Data Hub from inappropriate or unauthorized access by internal and external users.

► In financial services in particular, a Data Hub must enforce strict visibility rules where a broker or an account manager must be able to access the information associated only with their customer and accounts, and prevent users from accessing information about other customers (we discuss visibility concerns and architecture approaches in greater details in Chapter 10).

▶ Protect customer information from unintended usage by those who have been authorized to access the information.

HIPAA Compliance and Protection of Personal Health Information

At a high level, the Health Insurance Portability and Accountability Act (HIPAA)'s Security and Privacy Rules define similar concerns. According to HIPAA regulations, health care organizations must, among other controls, implement the following:

▶ Establish policies, procedures, and technical measures that protect networks, computers, and other electronic devices.

▶ Protect the privacy of all individually identifiable health information that is stored and/or transmitted electronically.

▶ Restrict disclosures of protected health information (PHI) to the minimum needed for healthcare treatment and business operations.

▶ Establish new business agreements with business partners that would safeguard their use and disclosure of PHI.

▶ Assess and modify systems to ensure they provide adequate protection of patient data.

End users, health care providers, and organizations can easily violate these requirements if the appropriate controls are not put in place. Indeed, consider the following: a hospital's office manager may have a perfectly legitimate reason to access patient health, insurance, and financial information. A common business practice may be to capture the patient's profile, account, medical diagnosis, and treatment information into specially designed Microsoft Office documents or forms for planning, referral, or contact management purposes. However, since these documents can be printed or e-mailed, the very fact of their existence creates a new risk of exposure that can put the hospital at risk of noncompliance and privacy preference violations. These risks could easily translate into significant reputational damage to the hospital and potentially to the parent company managing a network of health care providers.

Other ERM Examples

Other examples of situations where ERM/DRM can play a significant role include Master Data Management implementations that support highly confidential information about impending mergers and acquisitions, equities research, scientific research, and patent processing and filing. In the government sector, ERM/DRM may protect information assets of military, law enforcement, and national security agencies as well as other government organizations. As you can see, the area of ERM applicability is very large, and as MDM solutions begin to proliferate across various industries and areas of business focus, their respective implementations would have to enable the protection of the information assets that these solutions are designed to aggregate and integrate.

Thus, sophisticated information security and visibility architecture is a key component of any MDM implementation, especially those Data Hub systems that deal with customer information. Therefore, in addition to authentication, authorization, access control, and content protection, the security architecture for an MDM solution should consider and include an implementation of the ERM/DRM processes and technology as a part of the overall information security design.

Sound information-protection architecture should enforce policy-based and roles-based security to protect access to information from unauthorized users. Such architecture should enable an audit of data access actions and archiving of information for legally required or enterprise-defined duration based on industry and government regulations. In addition, such comprehensive security architecture should employ an ERM/DRM solution to identify information objects such as documents and e-mail messages that contain regulated content (i.e., account numbers, social security numbers); apply appropriate protection techniques; and ensure that authorized users use confidential protected information in approved ways.

Let us conclude this discussion with the following observations:

The need for information protection has become one of the key priorities of government agencies and commercial organizations—a priority that is driven and reinforced by regulatory and compliance pressures. However, while information protection is no longer an option for any commercial or government organization, there is no single "silver bullet" to accomplish this goal. Therefore, we strongly recommend using a layered "defense-in-depth" approach to protecting information assets.

In the area of information protection, data-at-rest protection and ERM have emerged as hotly competitive areas of information security, the areas that could easily become a competitive differentiator in situations when customers and organizations are looking for assurances that even if a security breach has occurred, the data acquired by such an action continues to be secure. This confidence in information security, confidentiality, and integrity reinforces the notion of trusted relationships between organizations and their customers.

Enterprise Security and Data Visibility in Master Data Management Environments

IN THIS CHAPTER

Access Control Basics
Policies and Entitlements
Entitlements and Visibility
Integrating CDI Solutions with Enterprise Information Security

Ａs we stated in previous chapters, a core component of any Master Data Management solution is its data integration platform, which is designed to provide a complete and accurate view of the customer, product, account, etc. Customer Data Integration solutions, often referred to as CDI Data Hubs, are perfect examples of such platforms.

By design a CDI Data Hub contains a wealth of information about individuals, companies, or products, and thus represents an attractive target for various forms of information security attacks. Thus, as a repository maintaining an authoritative system of record for the enterprise, a CDI Data Hub would require extra levels of protection for the information it manages.

The preceding chapter discussed various concerns and approaches to the protection of the information content.

This chapter will focus on protecting and controlling access to the Data Hub and the information stored there.

Access Control Basics

In general, when we talk about controlling access to a resource, be it a computer, network device, a program, or an application, we intuitively accept that such a control should be based on the individual or group credentials and permissions that are defined according to the security policies.

As we showed in the previous chapters, the credentials are acquired or provisioned and verified through the activities called *authentication*. We also discussed that authentication can be weak or strong, single factor or multifactor. Whatever the approach, the end result of the authentication action is twofold: the user is identified using supplied credentials such as user ID and password, hardware, or a biometric token; and the user's identity is verified (authenticated) by comparing the supplied credentials with the ones stored in the authentication store such as an enterprise directory.

However, the authentication alone does not solve the access control portion of the security equation unless authenticated users are given total access to all resources in the system to which they are authenticated and authorized.

In practice, most users should have access to some but not all resources, and we need to find a way to limit access rights per user based on some form of authorization rule that is based on user-authenticated credentials and the security policy in force at the time of the access request. To state it differently, each authenticated user should be able to access only those resources that he or she is authorized to use. The authorization decision is based on who the user is and on the security policy that defines the access.

This decision-making process could be implemented and enforced easily if an enterprise has individual policies for each user. Clearly, this approach is not realistic since the number of authenticated users can easily reach thousands (i.e., employees and contractors) or even millions in the case of enterprise customers. Managing such a large number of policies is a labor-intensive and error-prone activity that can also create significant security vulnerabilities.

One way to "avoid" creating and managing this large policy set is to implement access control logic inside the applications. Many applications have traditionally been developed with these access control capabilities as a part of their code—an approach that historically has proved to be expensive, inflexible, and hard to maintain.

A better approach is to abstract the authorization functionality away from applications into a common set of authorization functions. This approach would deliver a much more flexible and scalable solution. There are design patterns that implement common authorization functionality while reducing the number of policies that need to be managed. The goal of these designs is to provide sufficient flexibility, scalability, and fine-level granularity for data access. Naturally, these techniques and design options are the domain of the security discipline called authorization. And as we stated in previous chapters, authentication, authorization, access control, and related concerns including entitlements and provisioning are all components of the information security discipline known as *identity management*.

Groups and Roles

One of the main principles in reducing the required number of policies is to introduce the notion of user groups and roles, and to provide access decisions based on user groups and/or roles. Since the number of groups and roles is typically much smaller than the overall number of users, this approach can be quite effective. Groups can help reduce errors in permissions and opportunities for a user to have unnecessary and potentially dangerous access.

Group-Based Access Control

The basic principles of group-based access controls are as follows:

► A security administrator creates groups and roles with the various permissions.

► Then the administrator assigns users to one or more groups/roles.

► An individual's access permission set is the aggregate of all group/role permissions to which the person is assigned.

► Updating user access is as simple as adding/deleting the user to a group, or changing the permissions for a defined group/role.

Some of the group-based approaches for a common authorization facility are based on what is known as Access Control Lists (ACLs), where the typical ACL structure would maintain a name-value pair with the "name" being the user ID or a group ID, and the "value" being the reference or an address of the resource this user or this group can access. For example, an ACL may contain a list of functional groups such as Managers, HR Administrators, and Database Administrators, and where each employee is assigned to one or more groups. Each of the groups will have one or more resources they are allowed to access, with the specific access authorization (Create, Read, Update, Delete, Execute [CRUDE]). Such ACL structures have been widely implemented in many production environments protected by legacy security systems including Resource Access Control Facility (RACF), ACF2, and Top Secret. Several popular operating systems such as UNIX and ACL-controlled Windows Registry also use Access Control List–based authorization schemas.

ACLs work well in situations with well-defined and stable (persistent) objects, such as the IBM DB2 subsystem or the Windows System Registry. In these cases, the ACL can be mapped to the object, and access decisions can be made based on group membership and the CRUDE contents of the ACL. However, ACLs have some well-documented shortcomings. Among them are the following items:

▶ The ACL model does not work well in situations where the authorization decisions are often based not only on the group membership but also on business logic. For example, an authorization may depend on the value of a particular attribute (e.g., outstanding payment amount), where if a value exceeds a predefined threshold it can trigger a workflow or an authorization action.

▶ A common administrative task of reviewing and analyzing access given to a particular user or group can become difficult and time-consuming as the number of objects/resources grows, since the ACL model will require reviewing every object to determine if the user had access to the object. Generally speaking, the administration of large ACL sets can become a management nightmare.

▶ ACLs do not scale well with the growth of the number of users/groups and resources. Similarly, ACLs do not scale well as the granularity of the user authorization requests grows from coarse to fine level. In other words, to take full advantage of the group metaphor, the administrator would create a small number of groups and assign all users to some or all of the groups. However, if the organization has a relatively large number of individuals that are organized in a number of small teams with a very specialized set of access permissions, the ACL administrator would have to define many additional groups, thus creating the same scalability and manageability issues stated in the preceding list. An example of the last point can be a brokerage house that defines groups of traders specialized in a particular financial instrument (e.g., a specific front-loaded mutual fund). The business rules and policies would dictate that these traders can only access databases that contain information about this particular mutual fund. To support these policies, the ACL administrator may have to define a group for each of the specialized instruments.

Roles-Based Access Control (RBAC)

A better approach to authorization is to use user roles as the basis for the authorization decisions. Roles tend to be defined and approved using a more rigorous and formalized process known as *roles engineering*, which can enable the enterprise to better align the roles with the security policies. The approach and technologies of providing access control based on user credentials and roles are known as Roles-Based Access Control (RBAC). Although some of the goals of Roles-Based Access Control can be accomplished via permission groups, we will focus on RBAC since it offers a framework to manage users' access to the information resources across an enterprise in a controlled, effective, and efficient manner. The goal of RBAC is to allow administrators to define access based on a user's job requirements or "role." In this model an administrator follows a two-step process:

1. Define a role in terms of the access privileges for users assigned to a given role.
2. Assign individuals to a role.

As the result, the administrator controls access permissions to the information assets at the role level. Permissions can be queried and changed at the role level without touching the objects that have to be protected. Once the security administrator establishes role permissions, changes to these permissions will be rare compared to changes in assigning users to the roles.

Clearly, for RBAC to be effective the roles of the users have to be clearly defined and their access permissions need to be closely aligned with the business rules and policies.

Roles-Engineering Approach

When we discuss user roles, we need to recognize the fact that similarly named roles may have different meanings depending on the context of how the roles and permissions are used. For example, we may be able to differentiate between roles in the context of the Organization, Segment, Team, and a Channel:

▶ The *Organization* role defines the primary relationship between the user and the organization. An example of the organization role could be an Employee, Customer, Partner, Contractor, etc. Each user can only have one Organization role for a given set of credentials.

▶ The *Segment* role defines the user's assignment to a business domain or segment. For example, in financial services a segment could be defined by the total value of the customer's portfolio such as high priority customers, active traders, etc. Each of these segments can offer its members different types of products and services. Segment roles can be set either statically or dynamically, and each user may be assigned to multiple Segment roles.

▶ The *Team* role defines the user's assignment to a team, for example, a team of software developers working on a common project, or a team of analysts working on a particular M&A transaction. The Team role can be set either statically or dynamically. Each user may be assigned multiple Team roles.

▶ The *Channel* role defines user permissions specific to a channel (channel in this context means a specific platform, entry point, application, etc). For example, a user may have a role of a plan administrator when having personal interactions with the sales personnel (e.g., a financial advisor). At the same time, in the self-service online banking channel the same user can be in the role of a credit card customer who can perform online transactions including funds transfers and payments. Each user may be assigned multiple Channel roles.

The role classification shown in the preceding list is only one example of how to view and define the roles. More formally, we need a rigorous roles-engineering process that would help define the roles of the users in the context of the applications and information assets they need to access.

There are a number of methodological approaches on how to define roles and to engineer roles-based access controls. The details of these approaches are beyond the scope of this book. However, it would be helpful to further clarify these points by reviewing some key role-designing principles:

▶ The roles need to be defined in the context of the business and therefore should not be done by the IT organization alone.

▶ Like any other complex cross-functional activity, the roles-engineering process requires sound planning and time commitment from both business and IT organizations. Planning should start with a thorough understanding of security requirements, business goals, and all the components essential to the implementation of the RBAC.

▶ Some core roles-engineering components include:

  ▶ Classes of users

  ▶ Data sources

  ▶ Applications

  ▶ Roles

►   Business rules

►   Policies

►   Entitlements

The last three components are discussed in greater detail later in this chapter.

Sample Roles-Engineering Process Steps   The roles-engineering process consists of several separate steps necessary to build the access management policies. The following steps illustrate how the process can be defined:

►   Analyze the set of applications that would require role-based access controls. This analysis should result in a clear inventory of application features and functions, each of which can be mapped to a specific permission set.

►   Identify a target user base and its context dimensions (e.g., organizations, segment, team, etc.). Use a generally accepted enterprise-wide authoritative source of user credentials to perform this task, for example, a human resources database for employees.

►   Create role definitions by associating target functional requirements with a target user base.

Once the role definitions are created, we recommend identifying and mapping business rules that should be used for user-role assignment. For example, a rule may state that a user is assigned the role of a teller if the HR-supplied credentials are verified and if the user operates from the authorized channel (e.g., a branch). Another example can be a business rule that states that an employee does not get assigned a Segment role.

RBAC Shortcomings

While Roles-Based Access Control can be very effective in many situations and represents a good alternative to Access Control Lists, it does have a number of shortcomings. Some of these shortcomings are described in the following list:

►   Roles-Based Access Control does not scale well as the granularity of protected resources grows. In other words, if you need to define access controls to sensitive data at the record or even attribute levels, you should define a set of roles that would map to each possible data record and/or attribute thus resulting in a very large and difficult-to-manage set of roles.

►   Roles can be difficult to define in an enterprise-wide uniform fashion especially if the enterprise does not have a formal process that guides the creation and differentiation of roles. For example, an enterprise may define a role of an analyst in its marketing department and a similarly named role of the analyst for the IT department. However, these roles represent different capabilities, responsibilities, compensation, etc.

▶   Roles alone do not easily support access constraints where different users with equal roles have access only to a portion of the same data object. This particular requirement is often called "data visibility" and is discussed in more detail later in this chapter.

Policies and Entitlements

The limitations of Roles-Based Access Control that we discussed in the preceding section make it difficult to implement many complex business-driven access patterns. These access patterns are particularly important when you consider all potential uses of a Master Data Management environment. MDM-CDI designers should consider these use cases and usage patterns in conjunction with the need to protect information from unauthorized access. At the same time, MDM solutions should streamline, rationalize, and enable new, more effective, and efficient business processes. For example, let's consider a CDI Data Hub implementation that is positioned to replace a number of legacy applications and systems. To take full advantage of the CDI Data Hub as a system of record for the customer information, an enterprise should change several core processes (e.g., the account-opening process). So instead of accessing legacy data stores and applications, a modified account-opening process should use the CDI Data Hub's data, services, and RBAC-style access controls as a centralized trusted facility. But in a typical enterprise deployment scenario, existing legacy applications contain embedded business-rules-driven access controls logic that may go beyond RBAC. Thus, the Data Hub cannot replace many legacy systems without analyzing and replicating the embedded functionality of the access control logic in the Data Hub first. This means that all access decisions against Data Hub need to be evaluated based on the user attributes, the content of the data to be accessed, and the business rules that take all these conditions into considerations before returning a decision.

Analysis of typical legacy applications shows that access permissions logic uses a combination of user roles and the business rules, where the business rules are aligned with or derived from the security and relevant business policies in place.

The problem of providing flexible access control solutions that would overcome many known RBAC limitations is not a simple replacement of Roles-Based Access Control with Rules-Based Access Controls (using the RBAC analogy, we will abbreviate Rules-Based Access Control as RuBAC). Indeed, RuBAC can implement and enforce arbitrary complex access rules and thus offers a viable approach to providing fine-grained access control to data. However, RuBAC does not scale well with the growth of the rule set. Managing large rule sets is at least as complex a problem as the one we showed during the RBAC discussion.

Therefore, a hybrid roles-and-rules-based access control (RRBAC) may be a better approach to solving access control problems. This hybrid approach to defining access controls uses more complex and flexible *policies* and processes that are based on *user identities, roles, resource entitlements,* and *business rules.* The semantics and grammar of these policies can be quite complex, and are the subject of a number of emerging standards. An example of these standards is the WS-Security standard and its WS-Policy—a Web Services standard allowing users to create an XML document that unambiguously expresses the authorization rules.

Entitlements Taxonomy

As we just stated, the key concepts of the hybrid approach are policies, identity-based entitlements, roles, and rules. We already discussed roles in the preceding sections of this chapter. However, the discussion on the hybrid approach to access controls would not be complete if we don't take a closer look at policies and entitlements.

Policies

In the context of authorization and access control, we will define a *policy* as the encoding of rules particular to a business domain and its data content, and the application systems designed to operate in this domain on this set of data.

Whenever a user requests an access to a resource, an appropriate policy acts as a "rule book" to map a given request to the entitlements of that user.

Entitlements

An *entitlement* is an expression stating that a *party* has *permission* to do something with respect to some *entity* or an *object when certain conditions are met.*

For example, you may create an entitlement for your college-age daughter stating that she has permission to withdraw money from your checking account as long as the withdrawal amount does not exceed $500. In this example, we established the party (daughter), object (checking account), nature of the permission or the action (withdrawal), and the condition of the permission ($500 limit).

It is easy to see that entitlements contain both static and dynamic components, where static components tend to stay unchanged for prolonged periods. The value of the dynamic component (e.g., a $500 limit), on the other hand, may change relatively frequently and will most likely be enforced by applying business rules at run time.

Another interesting observation about entitlements is the fact that on one hand, they can be categorized as functional and data entitlements, and on the other hand as coarse- and fine-grained entitlements (see Figure 10-1).

This entitlements taxonomy has interesting implications for the complexity of the business rules and the applicability of the already-discussed ACL and RBAC approaches.

Indeed, at a coarse level of granularity, there are many situations where ACL or RBAC solutions would provide an adequate level of access controls. But given their shortcomings, a different approach had to be found for fine grain entitlements. This different approach is based on a relatively recent set of technologies known as policy authorization servers or policy servers for short. As the name implies, policy servers evaluate all access control requests against the appropriate set of polices in the context of authenticated user identities, roles, entitlements, and business rules. To state it differently, policy servers help ensure proper alignment of access control enforcement with the security policies of the enterprise. Policy servers avoid the scalability and manageability issues of ACL and RBAC by combining the roles-based and rules-based approaches to authorization. Consequently, policy servers abstract the authorization decisions away from the application. Specifically, the network administrators or security managers define users, authentication methods (such as passwords, token-based authentication, or X.509 certificates), and access controls. The applications no longer handle access control directly. Instead, they interact with the policy server whenever a user issues a request to use a resource.

Typically, a policy server answers the question "Can user U perform action A on object O?" A number of commercial products offer robust policy server functionality.

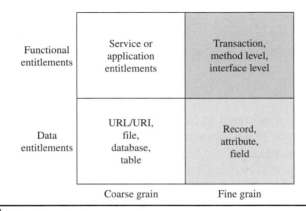

	Coarse grain	Fine grain
Functional entitlements	Service or application entitlements	Transaction, method level, interface level
Data entitlements	URL/URI, file, database, table	Record, attribute, field

Figure 10-1 *Entitlements taxonomy*

Some products use a group-based policy, where a user's group might be determined by user role (e.g., cashiers), or the group's placement in an enterprise authentication directory (e.g., LDAP tree). Other products support policies of higher complexity, where user privilege might be based on certain attributes (e.g., a policy defines the authorization level of 1 to 5, where 1 is the highest level of access or similar privilege). Role- or attribute-based policies place users into groups based on user attributes. For example, greater access might be granted to the holder of an American Express Platinum card, or an airline upgrade entitlement is determined by the status and level of the frequent flyer.

Yet more advanced approaches use complex policies where the policy paradigm is extended to drive access control decisions based on events. For example, if a user is not registered for a particular service, the policy can redirect the user to the enrollment/registration page. Conversely, trying to enter an invalid password more than a predetermined number of times can redirect the user to a customer service page. All of these decisions can be further enhanced by using user attributes as factors in the policy evaluation.

Transactional Entitlements

Event-based access controls can be used to support coarse-grained and fine-grained entitlements as well as *transactional* entitlements—an emerging approach to policy-based authorization designed to solve complex access control problems in real time.

Transactional entitlements allow authenticated users to check their permissions against specific parameters by evaluating business policy rules in real time on an individual basis. For example, a transactional entitlement can control a user's ability to execute a requested transaction (e.g., complete a funds transfer, update a log, search a particular database). Transactional entitlements can control various business-defined actions, including updates to a personnel file; execution of a particular transaction only on a certain day and/or at a certain time; in a given currency; and within a specified spending/trading limit. In our college student example earlier, checking for a $500 withdrawal limit is a transactional component of the entitlement structure.

In transactional entitlements, logical expressions can be arbitrarily complex to address real-world requirements. And ideally, the expressions are strongly typed and reusable, written once to support similar transactions, not just one transaction at a time.

The key differences between transactional and nontransactional entitlements are twofold:

▶ Transactional entitlements are evaluated (and can be updated) in real time.

▶ Transactional entitlements can support transactional semantics by performing their actions within transactional brackets.

Transactional entitlements are vital to providing just-in-time authorization decisions for real-time applications such as online banking, trading, purchasing, and similar activities. Transactional entitlements are especially useful when business applications rely on dynamic policy-driven access controls to a Master Data Management environment and its information, which represents the authoritative system of records.

Entitlements and Visibility

The definition of entitlements makes it clear that the entitlements, being a resource-dependent expression, have to be enforced locally, close to the target resources. This enforcement should be done in the context of the access request, user credentials, and resource attributes. And by extension, the resource access request should not be decided by a central, resource-agnostic authority because of performance, scalability, and security concerns. As mentioned in previous sections, technology solutions that provide entitlement enforcement are known as policy servers. These servers are designed to be resource-aware and thus can enforce entitlement rules in the context of the specific access requests.

Policy servers can support fine-grained access controls, but are especially well-suited to support functional-level authorization at the method and interface level, since the policy semantics are easily adaptable to include the access rules.

However, fine-grained access control for data access and fine-grained data entitlements represent an interesting challenge. The area of fine-grained data access, shown in the lower-right corner of Figure 10-1, is known as *data visibility challenge*. It is the primary data access control concern for Master Data Management platforms such as Data Hub systems supporting CDI. This challenge is a direct result of the complexity of the business rules defining who can access what portion of the data, when, and under what conditions. Solving this data visibility challenge requires a new policy evaluation and policy enforcement approach that should complement the functional entitlement enforcement provided by the current generation of policy servers. The following sections look more closely at this data visibility challenge and a potential architecture of the visibility solution in more detail. This chapter also discusses approaches that allow for effective integration of functional and data entitlements in the context of the overarching enterprise security architecture framework.

Customer Data Integration Visibility Scenario

Let us illustrate the data visibility challenges with an example of a Data Hub solution for a hypothetical retail brokerage. As we stated previously, one of the key goals of a CDI solution is to enable transformation of the enterprise from an account-centric to a customer-centric business model.

To that end, a retail brokerage company has embarked on the initiative to build a Customer Data Integration platform (Data Hub) that eventually would become a new system of record for all customer information. The data model designed for the new Data Hub will have to satisfy the specific business need to support two types of entities—customers with their information profiles, and the brokers who provide advisory and trading services to the customers. In order for this scheme to work, the project architects decided to build a reference facility that would associate a broker with his or her customers.

To improve customer experience and to enforce broker-customer relationships, the company has defined a set of business policies that state the following access restrictions:

- ▶ A customer may have several accounts with the company, and have relationships with several brokers to handle the accounts separately.

- ▶ A broker can see and change information about his or her customer but only for the accounts that the broker manages. The broker cannot see any customer account data owned by another broker.

- ▶ A broker's assistant can see and change most but not all customer information for the customers that have relationships with this broker.

- ▶ A broker's assistant can support more than one broker and can see the customer data of all of the brokers' customers but cannot share this information across brokers, nor can this information be accessed at the same time.

- ▶ A customer service center representative can see some information about all customers but explicitly is not allowed to see the customers' social security numbers.

- ▶ A specially appointed manager in the company's headquarters can see and change all data for all customers.

It is easy to see that this list of restrictions can be quite extensive. It is also easy to see that implementing these restrictions in the Data Hub environment where all information about the customers is aggregated into customer-level data objects is not a trivial task. Specifically, the main requirements of data visibility in Data Hub environments are twofold:

- ▶ Create customer and employee entitlements that would be closely aligned with the authorization policies and clearly express the access restrictions defined by the business (for example, the restrictions described in the preceding list).

- ▶ Implement a high-performance, scalable, and manageable enforcement mechanism that would operate transparently to the users, be auditable to trace back all actions taken on customer data, and ensure minimal performance and process impact on the applications and the process workflow used by the business.

The first requirement calls for the creation of the entitlement's grammar and syntax, which would allow the security and system administrators to express business rules of visibility in a terse, unambiguous, and complete manner. This new grammar has to contain the set of primitives that can clearly describe data attributes, conditions of use, access permissions, and user credentials. The totality of these descriptions creates a *visibility context* that changes as the rules, variables, and conditions change. This context allows the designers to avoid an inflexible approach of using hard-coded expressions, maintenance of which will be time-consuming, error-prone, and hard to administer. The same considerations apply to the functional permissions for the data services (e.g., a permission to invoke a "Find Customer by name" service), as well as usage permissions for certain attributes based on the user role (e.g., SSN restriction for customer service representative). Another consideration to take into account is that the role alone is not sufficient—for example, a broker's assistant has different permissions on data depending on which broker that assistant supports in the context of a given transaction.

The second requirement is particularly important in financial services: Performance of a system can be a critical factor in a company's ability to conduct trading and other business activities in volatile financial markets. Thus, the enforcement of the visibility rules has to be provided in the most effective and efficient manner that ensures data integrity but introduces as little latency as technically feasible.

Policies, Entitlements, and Standards

One way to define the policy and entitlement language and grammar is to leverage the work of standards bodies such as the Organization for the Advancement of Structured Information Standards (OASIS) and the World Wide Web Consortium (W3C). At the time of this writing, the most relevant standards to implement policy-enforced visibility are eXtensible Access Control Markup Language (XACML), eXtensible Resource Identifier (XRI), and WS-Policy, a component of the broader WS-Security framework of standards for Web Services security.

XACML

XACML is designed to work in a federated environment consisting of disparate security systems and security policies. In that respect, XACML can be very effective in combination with the Security Assertion Markup Language (SAML) standard in implementing federated Roles-Based Access Control.

XACML and XRI

The XACML standard provides a clear and unambiguous expression of permissions for the user to perform certain actions on a specific resource (defined in XRI), and obligations of how to enforce a given permission.

These standards can be used to encode the policies and entitlements and therefore design policy evaluation systems that can provide clear and unambiguous access control decisions. For example, XACML policy can define a condition that allows users to log in to a system only after 8 A.M. A fragment of this policy in XACML that uses standard references to XML schema for the "time" data type may look like this:

```
<Condition FunctionId="urn:oasis:names:tc:xacml:1.0:function:and">
        <Apply FunctionId="urn:oasis:names:tc:xacml:1.0:function:time-
greater-than-or-equal"
. . . . .
AttributeId="urn:oasis:names:tc:xacml:1.0:environment:current-time"/>
        </Apply>
        <AttributeValue
DataType="http://www.w3.org/2001/XMLSchema#time">08:00:00</AttributeValue>
        </Apply>
</Condition>
```

While XACML offers a vehicle to clearly express access policies and permissions, XRI, on the other hand, allows users to create structured, self-describing resource identifiers. For example, XRI can describe the specific content of the library of research documents where the documents and books are organized by author, title, ISBN number, and even the location of the library, all in one comprehensive expression. To illustrate this power of XRI, consider a book search application that would allow users to find a book on a given subject that is available from one or more bookstores and library branches. Using XRI we can define the following resources:

```
xri://barnesandnoble.store.com/(urn:isbn:0-123-4567-8)/(+new)
xri://borders.store.com/(urn:isbn:0-123-4567-8)/(+used)
xri://NY.Public.Library.org/(urn:isbn:0-123-4567-8)/(+used)
```

In this example, XRI is used to identify the same book title (identified by its ISBN number), which is available from three different locations, two of which are bookstores—Barnes and Noble, and Borders—and the third one is the New York Public Library. Furthermore, XRI allows fine-grained resource definition attributes such as new or used book types.

Additional Considerations for XACML and Policies

The OASIS technical committee and the XACML working group have defined a number of details about XACML language, policies, rules, the way the policies are to be evaluated, and the decisions to be enforced. While these details are beyond the scope of this book, we will briefly look at some key XACML components and features that can help MDM-CDI architects, designers, and implementers to protect access to the information stored in MDM-CDI Data Hub systems.

Using the definition of the Policy as the encoding of Rules particular to a business domain, its data content, and the application systems designed to operate in this domain on this set of data, we can review several basic XACML components:

▶ XACML specifies that each Policy contains one or more Rules, where each Policy and Rule has a *Target*.

▶ XACML Target is a simple predicate that specifies which *Subjects, Resources, Actions*, and *Environments* the Policy or Rule has to apply to.

▶ XACML is designed to support policy expressions across a broad range of subject and functional domains known as *Profiles*.

Profiles and Privacy Protection   The notion of XACML profiles is very useful and provides for a high degree of reuse and manageability. For example, among several XACML-defined profiles there is a Profile for Access Control and a Profile for Privacy Protection. The latter should be particularly interesting to MDM-CDI designers since it shows the power and extensibility of XACML as a policy language even for privacy policies that, unlike most traditional access control policies, often require a verification that the purpose for which information is accessed should match the purpose for which the information was gathered.

XACML Privacy Profile

The *XACML Privacy Profile* defines standard attributes for describing the purpose for which information was gathered and the purpose for which information is being accessed. A Privacy policy may require that in order to gain access to data, these two values must match.

In addition to defining the privacy attributes, the XACML Privacy Profile describes how to use them to enforce privacy protection. This is a very important argument in favor of using XACML in defining and enforcing policies in the CDI environments where customer privacy preferences have to be captured, maintained, and enforced according to the explicit and implicit requests of the customers.

XACML is emerging as a flexible, useful, and powerful language that allows organizations to implement systematic creation, management, and enforcement of security and privacy policies. What follows is a brief discussion on how to use XACML to help MDM-CDI architects, designers, and implementers to address complex issues related to information security and data visibility in MDM and CDI environments.

Integrating CDI Solutions with Enterprise Information Security

The challenge of implementing data visibility and security in Master Data Management and Customer Data Integration environments is twofold:

▶ First, it is a challenge of enforcing the access restrictions rules in a new system of record.

▶ Second, it is a challenge of integrating new visibility controls with the existing enterprise security infrastructure using comprehensive and overarching security architecture.

The situation is complicated by the fact that most of the commercially available MDM-CDI solutions on the market today do not support either or both of these requirements. Moreover, the standards defining the fine-grained data-level entitlements are still immature, and as the result, current Policy Servers cannot yet enforce the visibility rules of required complexity in high-performance, low-latency environments.

However, experience shows that the visibility problem can be solved when you architect the solution (e.g., a Data Hub) using a component-based services-oriented architecture approach and applying the key principle of the "separation of concerns."

We discussed some basics of the "separation of concerns" principle in Part II of this book.

Separation of Concerns and Data Visibility

In the context of security and visibility, separation of concerns means that making policy-based access control decisions is a general function that is different and should be separated from the actions related to the enforcement of these access decisions.

The decision maker in this context is called a *Policy Decision Point* (*PDP*), and the decision enforcement is performed by a *Policy Enforcement Point* (*PEP*). The third component is a policy administration facility known as *Policy Administration Point* (*PAP*), sometimes referred to as Policy Management Authority (PMA). As the name implies, the role of PAP is primarily to perform out-of-band policy creation, administration, editing, and reporting—functionality that is clearly separate and distinct from run-time decision making and enforcement.

The benefits of separating the actions of policy administration, decision making, and access decision enforcement into separate components and services include the ability to better manage the complexity of fine-grained access control enforcement as well as the ability to change policy or add additional resources or new entitlements without requiring any changes to the consuming applications that initiate data access requests.

The conceptual distributed security architecture that shows the role of PDP, PEP, and PAP components is shown in Figure 10-2.

The details of the PDP, PEP, and PAP roles and responsibilities are defined by the OASIS distributed security standard described in detail in the OASIS document library available on www.oasis.org.

Overview of Key Architecture Components for Policy Decision and Enforcement

The OASIS standard defines a Policy Enforcement Point (PEP) that is responsible for intercepting all attempts to access a resource (see Figure 10-2). It is envisioned to be a component of the request-processing server such as a web server that can act as an interceptor for all requests coming into the enterprise through a network gateway. Since resource access is application-specific, the PEP is also application- or resource-specific. The PEP takes its orders from the Policy Decision Point (PDP), a component that processes resource access requests and makes authorization decisions.

The PDP is divided into two logical components. The "Context Handler" is implementation-specific. It knows how to retrieve the policy attributes used in a particular enterprise systems environment. The PDP core is implementation-

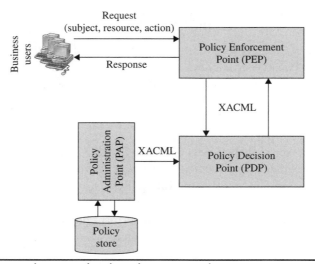

Figure 10-2 *Conceptual OASIS distributed security architecture*

independent and represents a common, shared facility. It evaluates policies against the information in the access request, using the Context Handler to obtain additional attributes if needed, and returns a decision of *Permit, Deny, Not Applicable*, or *Indeterminate*. The last two values are defined as follows:

- ▶ *Not Applicable* means that there is no policy used by this PDP that can be applicable to the access request.

- ▶ *Indeterminate* means that some error occurred that prevents the PDP from knowing what the correct response should be.

Policies can contain *Obligations* that represent actions that must be performed as part of handling an access request, such as "Permit access to this resource but only when an audit record is created and successfully written to the audit log."

The PDP exchanges information with PEP via XACML-formatted messages. PDP starts evaluating a decision request in the following sequence:

- ▶ Evaluate the Policy's Target first.

- ▶ If the Target is *FALSE,* the Policy evaluation result is *Not Applicable*, and no further evaluation is done of either that Policy or of its descendants.

- ▶ If the Target is *TRUE*, then the PDP continues to evaluate Policies and Rules that are applicable to the request.

- ▶ Once all levels of Policies are evaluated to *TRUE*, PDP applies the Rule's *Condition* (a Boolean combination of predicates and XACML-supplied functions).

- ▶ Each Rule has an *Effect*, which is either *Permit* or *Deny*. If the Condition is *TRUE*, then the Rule returns a valid *Effect* value. If the Condition is *FALSE*, then *Not Applicable* is returned.

Each Policy specifies a *combining algorithm* that says what to do with the results of evaluating *Conditions* from the Policies and Rules. An OASIS-defined example of such algorithm is *Deny Override*. Here, if any detail-level Policy or Rule evaluates to *Deny*, then the entire high-level Policy *set* that contains these detail policies and rules evaluates to *Deny*. Of course, other combining algorithms are also possible, and should be defined based on the business requirements and business-level security policies.

Integrated Conceptual Security and Visibility Architecture

The foregoing brief discussion offers an insight into how PDP and PEP components operate and communicate with each other. We also discussed how policies, rules, and obligations have to be expressed in order to provide a clear set of directives for access control decisions. Together, these components represent building blocks of the Data Hub *Visibility and Security Services*. Let's apply the principles of separation of concerns and service-oriented architecture framework to these Data Hub visibility and security services to define a comprehensive end-to-end security and visibility architecture that would enable policy-based fine-grained access control to the information stored in a Data Hub system.

First, let's adjust the architecture shown in Figure 10-2 to accommodate the following enterprise requirements:

▶ To ensure appropriate performance and transaction latency requirements, the policy enforcement has to be performed as "close" to the data being protected as possible. For example, when a Data Hub is built on a a relational database platform, a Policy Enforcement Point may be implemented as a stored procedure or other appropriate SQL-based technique.

▶ Most enterprise environments contain a large number of heterogeneous resources each of which may implement a different, resource-specific PEP. We'll reflect this concern by introducing additional resources and PEP components as shown in Figure 10-3.

▶ Many resource requests issued by end users could come from within the enterprise boundary (in other words, from the users inside the firewall). Thus, it may be inefficient to use a central server to intercept and route all requests to different resources. Therefore, we can modify the data flows in such a way that a resource-independent PDP will receive a data request, make a *Permit* or *Deny* decision, and send the result to the appropriate PEP component as part of the XACML obligations.

▶ Finally, since a global enterprise data environment typically contains a wide variety of data stores, it is reasonable to assume that a business application may request data not just from the Data Hub but from multiple, often heterogeneous data stores and applications. Such complex requests have to be managed and *orchestrated* to support distributed transactions including compensation in case of a partial or complete failure. Therefore, let's introduce a conceptual Request Management Service Component that would receive data requests from consuming applications, communicate with the Policy Decision Point, and in general, manage request execution in an appropriate, policy-defined order. Note that we're defining the Request Management function as a service in accordance with the principles of the service-oriented architecture. Thus, as the enterprise adds additional resources and develops new workflows to handle data requests, the business applications will continue to be isolated from these changes since all authorization decisions are performed by the PDP.

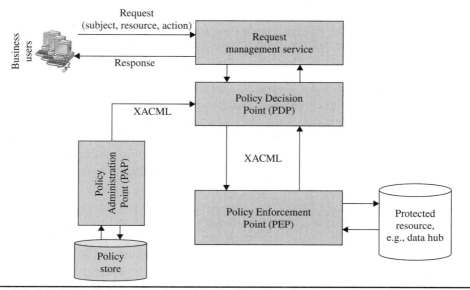

Figure 10-3 *Policy enforcement architecture adjusted to enterprise requirements*

The resulting architecture view is shown in Figure 10-3.

Let's define specific steps aimed at implementing this architecture of distributed, enterprise-scale data visibility solution:

▶ Define business visibility requirements and rules.

▶ Design a Data Hub data model that can enable effective visibility-compliant navigation (for example, by introducing data tags that can be used for highly selective data retrieval).

▶ Decompose data visibility rules into decision logic and decision enforcement components.

▶ Develop an entitlements grammar (or extend the existing policy grammar) to express visibility rules.

▶ Map visibility rules to user credentials and roles.

▶ Design and develop Policy Decision Point (PDP)—a component of the architecture that would analyze every data request to the Data Hub and evaluate it against the policies and entitlements of the requester (user). The PDP can be an implementation of a specialized proprietary or a commercial rules engine.

▶ Design and develop a Policy Enforcement Point (PEP) as a data-structure and data-content-aware component that performs requested data access operations in the most technically efficient manner. For example, in the case of a Data Hub implementation that is using a Relational Database Management System (RDBMS), the PEP can be a library of stored procedures, a set of database triggers, or built-in functions.

▶ Ensure that all policies are created, stored, and managed by a Policy Administration Point (PAP). This component stores the policies and policy sets in a searchable policy store. PAP is an administration facility that allows an authorized administrator to create or change user entitlements and business rules. Ideally, if the enterprise has already implemented a policy database that is used by a Policy server, a visibility policy store should be an extension of this existing policy store.

However, data visibility is only a part of the overall data security and access control puzzle. Therefore, while these steps can help develop a policy-based Visibility Architecture, we need to extend this process and the architecture itself to integrate its features and functions with the overall enterprise security architecture. It is reasonable to assume that the majority of functional enterprises have no choice but to implement multilayered security architecture that includes perimeter defense, network security, enterprise-class authentication, roles-based or policy-based authorization, a version of a single-sign-on (SSO) facility, and an automated provisioning and deprovisioning of user entitlements.

Let's add the following steps to the architecture definition and design process outlined in the preceding list . These steps are designed to ensure that the resulting architecture can interoperate and be integrated with the existing enterprise security architecture:

▶ Develop or select a solution that can delegate authentication and coarse-grained authorization decisions to the existing security infrastructure including Policy Servers.

▶ Similarly, ensure that user credentials are captured at the point of user entry into the system and carried over through the PDP and PEP components to the Data Hub, thus supporting the creation and management of the auditable log of user actions.

▶ Make sure that PDP, PEP, and the Enterprise Audit and Compliance system can interface with each other and interoperate in supporting business transactions so that all data access actions can be captured, recorded, and reported for follow-on audit analysis.

Applying these additional steps to the architecture shown in Figure 10-3 may result in the following high-level conceptual integrated enterprise security and visibility architecture shown in Figure 10-4.

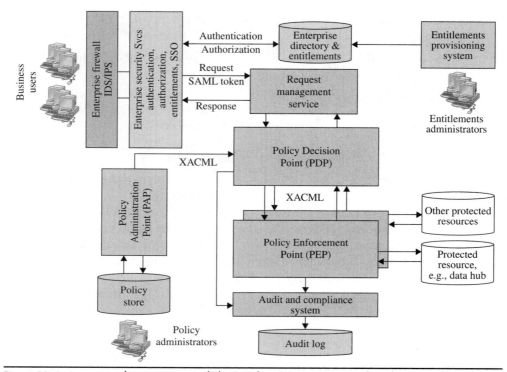

Figure 10-4   *Integrated enterprise visibility and security conceptual architecture*

This architecture shows how major components of the visibility and security services can be integrated and configured to provide seamless and transparent access control to the data stored in the CDI platform (i.e., a Data Hub). As we stated earlier, the core components in this architecture include:

► Policy Administration Point (PAP)

► Policy Store that contains visibility and entitlements policies and rules

► Policy Decision Point (PDP)

► Policy Enforcement Point (PEP)

These components are integrated with the enterprise security architecture that includes but is not limited to

► Perimeter defense and firewalls

► Enterprise directory

- ► Entitlements and access control policy store that supports policy authorization server

- ► Enterprise authentication and authorization service (possibly including enterprise-class single-sign-on solution)

- ► Enterprise provisioning system

- ► Regulatory and compliance auditing and reporting system

Visibility and Security Architecture Requirements Summary

The foregoing discussion of the visibility and security components and services helps illustrate the complexity of the integrated visibility design. This complexity is one of the drivers for making the "buy vs. build" decision for PDP, PEP, PAP, and other components and services. This decision must be made very carefully in order to protect the entire CDI initiative from the risk of embarking on a complex, unproven, error-prone, and extensive implementation. To help make this decision, we would like to offer the following list of functional requirements that MDM-CDI and security architects should consider during the evaluation of the available products and solutions. At a high level, the PDP and PEP components of the architecture should support

- ► XACML properties

- ► Domain independence

- ► Protection of XML documents

- ► Distributed policies

- ► Optimized indexing of policies

- ► Rich set of standard functions and data types

- ► Profiles

- ► Policy administration and delegation

These functional requirements are listed here as a template and a reference, Specific implementation requirements may differ and should be evaluated in a formal, objective, and verifiable fashion like any other enterprise software purchase decision.

Visibility and Security Information Flows

The integrated security and visibility architecture shown in Figure 10-4 is designed to support user requests to access data stored in the CDI platform by implementing a number of run-time interaction flows. These flows have been adapted from the

OASIS-defined PDP and PEP interactions briefly mentioned in the previous section. We discuss these flows in this section to illustrate the key processing points:

▶ The user gains access to the CDI environment by supplying his or her credentials to the network security layer.

▶ After passing through the firewall the user interacts with the enterprise authentication and authorization service where the user credentials are checked and the user is authenticated and authorized to use the CDI platform (this is a functional authorization to use CDI services that is enforced by a Policy Server).

▶ The authenticated user issues the request for data access, probably using a business service call (e.g., *Find Party*).

▶ The authorization system reviews the request and makes an authorization decision for the user to *permit* or *deny* invocation of a requested service and/or method (in this case, a service method that implements *Find Party* functionality).

▶ Once the affirmative decision is made, the user credentials and the request are passed to the Policy Decision Point, where the request is evaluated against user entitlements in the context of the data being requested. If the PDP decides that the user is allowed to access or change the requested set of data attributes, it will assemble an XACML-formatted payload using one of the standard message formats (possibly a SAML message). This message would include user credentials, authorization decision, and obligations containing enforcement parameters and the name of the enforcement service or interface (e.g., the name of the stored procedure and the value for the predicate in the SQL WHERE clause). The authorization decision and corresponding parameters comprise policy obligations that can be expressed in XACML and XRI.

▶ If the decision evaluates to *Permit,* PDP sends the message with the XACML payload to the appropriate Policy Enforcement Point (PEP).

▶ PEP parses the payload, retrieves the value of the obligation constraints that should form data access predicates (e.g., list of values in the SQL WHERE clause), and invokes the appropriate PEP service or function.

▶ Once the PEP-enforced data access operation completes successfully, the query result set is returned to the requesting application or a user.

▶ PEP retrieves the user credentials and uses them to create a time-stamped entry in the audit log for future analysis and recordkeeping.

▶ If necessary, PEP will encrypt and digitally sign the audit log record to provide nonrepudiation of the actions taken by the user on the data stored in the CDI/Data Hub.

For these steps to execute effectively at run time, several configuration activities need to take place. These configuration flows may include the following:

► Use the Enterprise Provisioning System to create and deliver user credentials and entitlements from the authoritative systems of user records (e.g., an HR database for employees) to all consuming target applications including the Enterprise Directory.

► If necessary, extend, modify, or create new entries in the Visibility and Rules Repository.

► Configure and execute audit reports to obtain regular snapshots of the list of active users, their entitlements, and summary of their actions, so that system administrators can tune the overall system to avoid performance bottlenecks. At the same time, the security administrators can use the activity logs to integrate them with the enterprise Intrusion Detection System.

While these steps may appear simple, the task of architecting and integrating data visibility and user entitlements into the overall enterprise security framework is very complex, error-prone, and time-consuming, and will require a disciplined, phased-in approach that should be managed like any other major enterprise integration initiative.

We conclude this part of the book with the following observation: Master Data Management environments are designed to provide their consumers with an accurate, integrated, authoritative source of information. Often, environments such as MDM solutions for Customer Data Integration deliver radically new ways to look at the information. In the case of a Data Hub for customer information, the CDI platform can deliver an authoritative and accurate customer-centric operational data view. But a CDI Data Hub can deliver much more. Indeed, it may also make integrated customer data available to users and applications in ways that extend and sometimes "break" traditional processes and rules of the business that define who can see which part of what data. Therefore, the majority of CDI implementations need to extend the existing policy grammar and policy server or develop and deliver new capabilities that support fine-grained functional and data access entitlements while at the same time maintaining data availability, presentation flexibility, and alignment with the legacy and new improved business processes.

To sum up, the entitlements and data visibility concerns of Customer Data Integration represent an important challenge. To solve this challenge, the demands of data security and visibility have to be addressed in an integrated fashion in conjunction with the enterprise security architecture.

Implementing Customer Data Integration for the Enterprise

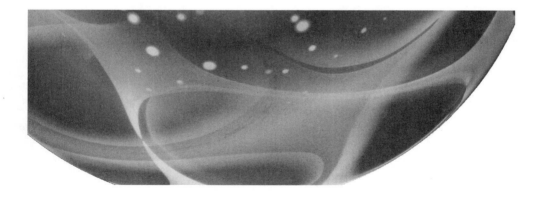

U p to this point, our discussion has been focused on issues and concerns surrounding Master Data Management and Customer Data Integration. We took a close look at the business and technology drivers for MDM and CDI, discussed architecture considerations and design concerns, and offered an architectural approach to addressing some of the key challenges presented by the MDM-CDI goal of integrating data across the enterprise, and especially the challenges related to data security and visibility.

This part of the book deals with the practical aspects of implementing MDM-CDI solutions as complex, multidisciplinary, enterprise-wide projects or programs. The complexity and multidisciplinary nature of MDM-CDI systems is such that implementing these solutions requires an approach that may be even broader than a single project, and should be managed as an initiative-level, enterprise-wide program that consists of multiple projects, phases, steps, tasks, and activities that are organized into a cohesive set of concurrent but interdependent work streams. The terms "project," "program," and "initiative" are often defined according to the rules, structures, processes, and standards of an individual organization, and are often treated as synonyms. Therefore, to avoid confusion related to the appropriate use of these terms, we will use the familiar term "project" when discussing implementation concerns of MDM-CDI systems.

CHAPTER

11

Project Initiation

IN THIS CHAPTER

Implementation Begins

Scope Definition

Customer Data Hub Solution Architecture

Project Work Streams

Implementation Begins

Let us assume at this point that the business drivers, objectives, and value propositions for the MDM-CDI project have been established and agreed upon within the organization. This agreement should result in senior management's issuing marching orders to the information technology organization to proceed with the project. Senior management wants to know how the project will be organized and planned—major milestones and releases. Senior management will also want to know how much this project would cost to develop and deploy. What should the IT organization do to translate business objectives into IT vision, strategy, actionable road map, and resource-loaded project plans, in order to successfully implement the project? Senior management will want to see the end-state vision across all business and technology domains, and will ask a number of key questions such as how the currently ongoing projects should be modified, aligned, and prioritized in the context of the MDM-CDI project. These and other critical questions are discussed in this chapter.

One of the key management challenges of MDM-CDI projects is the need to define the project's success criteria. When asked informally, IT executives may provide very different answers to the question of how to decide if the project is successful, including answers such as "Have better quality data," "Improve application functionality," "Achieve regulatory compliance faster," and "Keep the end users happy." In practice, MDM-CDI projects should follow a capabilities road map with a sound release strategy that defines what will be implemented and deployed, and when. A key component of this road map is clearly defined short-term and long-term success criteria that need to be understood and agreed upon by all stakeholders.

Of course, the tasks of defining the road map and success criteria would be so much easier to accomplish if there were a single strategy and solution architecture that works for all MDM-CDI implementations. Unfortunately, that is not the case. As we mentioned earlier, MDM-CDI projects address multiple, often diverse business requirements, involve a broad spectrum of technical disciplines, and can be extremely complex.

At a high level all MDM-CDI projects are quite similar. For example, all CDI projects have common goals of delivering an authoritative system of record for customer data that includes a complete, 360-degree view of customer data including the totality of the relationships the customer has with the organization. At this high level, project management and all key stakeholders are enthusiastic and are in "violent" agreement about the capabilities and opportunities offered by a CDI system.

The devil is in the details. And there are *many* details to consider. At the beginning and in the course of an MDM-CDI project, the wide variety of questions, issues, and dependencies may appear so overwhelming that the initiative's stakeholders feel like the fishermen in the movie "Perfect Storm." The characters of the film were practically

Key Senior Management Concerns

► How will the equity value and market capitalization of the company change as a result of the MDM-CDI project?

► What is the first set of applications and business functions that would become the early adopters and beneficiaries of the MDM-CDI project?

► What is the phase-by-phase and total project cost/ROI?

► How will the new business processes be different?

► What will it take to accomplish the transition to the new business processes?

► What additional skills, both business and technology, will the organization's staff members have to acquire and how?

► Will the organizational structure be affected, and to what extent?

► What legacy systems and functions will be affected and how?

► How will the project be organized and planned?

► What are the major milestones and releases?

► Does the technology organization have adequate knowledge, resources, and understanding of industry best practices in order to translate business objectives into IT vision, strategy, actionable road map, and project plans, and successfully implement the project?

► What are the investment and delivery risks and mitigation strategies?

► What is the end-state vision that would impact business and technology domains?

► How should the current in-flight initiatives be modified, aligned, and prioritized in light of starting a CDI project?

► What are the success criteria for each phase and for the project overall?

helpless before the fury of the ocean. The situation may seem similarly unmanageable for the participants of some MDM-CDI projects. Many large MDM-CDI projects failed with dire consequences for the company and people who worked on the project. We will discuss risks and reasons for project failure in Chapter 18.

In short, due to the variety of conditions and the complexity of the MDM-CDI projects, it is difficult to define a single one-size-fits-all set of recommendations. Experience shows that an effective working approach to complex and diverse problems like the one presented by MDM-CDI is to define a comprehensive solution framework that is designed around sound problem-solving architecture principles including separation of concerns, layered architecture, federation, and service orientation (please see Part II for more details on the architecture framework and design principles). Such a framework allows us to use industry best practices for particular areas of concern, and to break down the problem domain into smaller and more manageable pieces. At a more granular level the tasks and decision-making points are much more common and manageable across MDM-CDI projects. We will follow this approach and break down the CDI problem domain into work streams and components that support and are supported by what we define as the CDI "ecosystem." The areas of concerns and key components that constitute a CDI "ecosystem" are shown in Figure 11-1. We discuss most of them throughout this book in more detail.

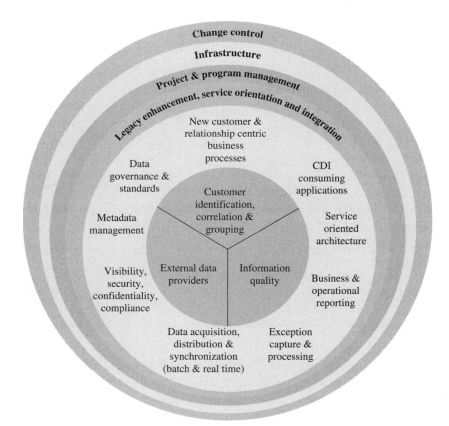

Figure 11-1 *CDI "ecosystem"— high-level areas of the solution*

The CDI "ecosystem" is a layered construct that includes business processes and technical domains of change. The core CDI functional area includes:

► Customer identification, matching, correlation, hierarchies, relationships, and grouping

► Information quality

► External data providers

The layer immediately surrounding the CDI core is a key part of the CDI "ecosystem" even though it includes some components that support both CDI and non-CDI environments. We discuss various aspects of these components throughout the book.

As we continue to "peel" the layers of the CDI "ecosystem," we can see the components and services that do not necessarily represent "pure" CDI functionality, but are affected and/or required by the CDI solution to function. For example, the legacy layer demonstrates these dual properties—it is usually the source of CDI data and is a key consumer of new functionality enabled by the CDI platform.

Similarly, the outer layers of the CDI "ecosystem" cover Infrastructure, Project/Program Management, and Change Control. These areas of concern are vital for any successful CDI implementation. Indeed, it is hard to imagine a project of MDM-CDI magnitude that can be successful without considering infrastructure issues or providing adequate program management and change control.

CDI-related areas of the "ecosystem" contain components that have to be acquired or built. Thus, the CDI "ecosystem" also provides a framework for "buy vs. build" decisions. These decisions are not easy to make, especially considering that many vendor products in the CDI space overlap, and the resulting market focus and positioning of many CDI vendors continues to change. For example, ETL and data synchronization vendors are moving into the Information Quality space, and Information Quality vendors are extending their capabilities towards CDI Data Hubs. The discussion of the vendor landscape and their product features can be found in Chapter 17.

The complexity of the MDM-CDI problem space requires participation of multiple stakeholders. This in turn, creates a formidable socialization problem. The idea of bringing all people onto the same page on all issues can easily paralyze any initiative. While consensus building is a good strategy, we need to remember that both unlimited democracy and military-style decision making can cause large initiatives to fail. Best practices suggest to set up a small leadership group that can successfully combine principles of strong management control and decision making with principles of sharing information and keeping all participants on common ground in key areas.

Workshop Agenda

▶ State project goals and senior management concerns.

▶ Define and agree on the end-state of the solution and what it means from both business and technology points of view.

▶ Discuss the types of partners and vendors that will be required to achieve the objectives.

▶ Define and socialize the project's organizational structure and project governance.

▶ Discuss a high-level road map.

▶ Determine project success criteria.

▶ Analyze cost benefits of the project.

▶ Discuss the timeline, content, and the deliverables of the project on a phase-by-phase basis.

▶ Build consensus between business and technology teams as the decision on "What should the first release look like?" is made.

Of course, every time you want diverse groups such as business and technology teams to agree, you have to overcome the challenge of each group looking at the problem from its own perspective. Using the comprehensive solution framework described throughout this book should help the reader to manage the discussions about the project and to make decisions that each project team can be comfortable with.

It is a good idea to start an MDM-CDI project with a well-structured workshop where business vision and technology approach will be discussed. Two or three days spent as a team can be very beneficial to jump-start the project by getting high-level agreement on a number of key issues.

Using a multiphased approach to a CDI project is clearly a good strategy. The outcome of the first phase (first release of the CDI solution) should be thought of as a trade-off between what the business ultimately needs and what is achievable in a single release. A practical rule of thumb is that each phase should not exceed six to eight months and should deliver tangible, business-recognizable benefits. Credibility of the project will be at stake if a year has gone by and no changes have been implemented. Enterprise-level planning should be in place to ensure successful cross-departmental delivery.

When a CDI project is initiated, IT group should have access to a business-sponsored document that defines business case by business function and line of business. This business requirements document should include the following:

- ▶ Formulation of business problems as they relate to MDM-CDI
- ▶ Definition of the business scope including articulations of the new business processes
- ▶ Strategic business vision and objectives
- ▶ Business drivers and priorities
- ▶ ROI estimation for MDM-CDI implementation

Considering the complexity and potential breadth of the impact a CDI solution may have on the organization, defining the scope is one of the key factors that determines the actual or perceived success or failure of the CDI project.

Scope Definition

When we discuss CDI projects, we should realize that the scope of these projects is a multidimensional matter. The most important dimensions are shown in Figure 11-2 and discussed in this section.

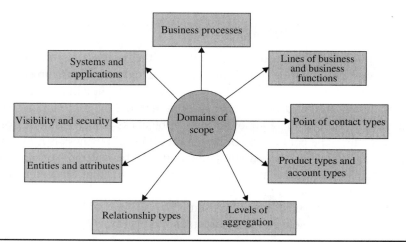

Figure 11-2 *Domains of Scope*

Business Processes

It is critically important to understand what business processes need to be improved. Without a clear understanding of what business processes will be improved and how, the entire effort may turn into a costly and most likely useless endeavor. Starting from the business objectives, drivers, and value propositions, the technology group should work with the business team to document the current state of the business processes that need to be improved. There are many methodologies on how to define and document business processes. Rational Unified Process (RUP) is one of the better-known methodologies used for this purpose. RUP uses a concept of use cases as the core of business process analysis and definition.

Once the current state of the business processes and their weaknesses are defined and documented, the target-state business processes need to be determined. There are many techniques and methodologies on business process improvement and re-engineering. For example, see *Business Process Management: Practical Guidelines to Successful Implementations* by John Jeston and Johan Nelis (Butterworth-Heinemann, 2006).

What level of granularity in the business process definition is sufficient? If you need to describe the process of lawn mowing you can do it at a high level, e.g., get the lawn mower, turn it on, mow the lawn, clean the lawn mower, and put it back. Alternatively, you can describe this process with more granularity and show decision points, e.g. what happens if you do not have enough gas, or what you do if the device breaks, or how do you trim corners that cannot be reached by the lawn mower. The required granularity of the business process should be at the level of detail that is sufficient to define the logical data model of the CDI solution. This brings us to an important point. The data modelers should work closely with the business process development team to provide input and pose questions driving the depth of the business process coverage.

Lines of Business and Functions

One of the outcomes of the creation and analysis of the business requirements for the project is the determination of new and impacted legacy business processes. At the same time, the requirements should specify the needs of key lines of business and business functions that drive the change. At that point, the requirements analysis should determine whether there are other lines of business that can benefit from the CDI-driven change. The perspective of these other lines of business is important for the enterprise to understand that additional benefits can be realized from implementing the CDI project. These additional requirements and benefits may strengthen the CDI business case and its value proposition.

In addition, a comprehensive view presented by all lines of business and functions early in the project life cycle can help understand constraints that otherwise would be revealed at later phases of the project with additional risks and costs always accompanying late changes in project planning and execution.

An understanding of all impacted lines of business should also help in building a project team that adequately represents all interested parties.

Customer Touch Points, Product Types, and Account Types

Modern enterprises frequently have multiple channels that support various customer touch points. For instance, customers interact with a hotel chain by phone, personally in the hotel lobby, online over e-mail and the Internet, by mail, etc. The same channels may provide additional touch points for customers who participate in hotel membership clubs or are hotel credit card holders. Similar variety in the touch points exists in the financial services and other industries.

Analyzing the channel and touch-point requirements helps bring into focus additional perspectives and questions that can impact the scope of the CDI project. Specifically, the customer data presented at different touch points may vary significantly, and as the result, may impact the identification and matching process, data visibility, and security approaches. We will discuss customer identification and matching in more detail in Chapter 12. Visibility and security are discussed in depth in Part III of the book.

A typical enterprise normally offers and serves many product types to its customers. In the financial services industry, for example, products are often linked to or represented by account types such as Wealth Management Account, Cash Management Account, 401K Retirement Account, etc. Other industries also have a strong emphasis on products. For example, a telecommunications company can offer and provide local, long distance, and international phone service, DSL, wireless connectivity services, satellite or cable TV services, etc. They may also offer their private label credit card and other financial instruments.

As industries define their specific portfolios of products and services, this view is also important to adequately define the scope and priorities of the planned MDM-CDI effort. This understanding can help bring a valuable perspective from the groups of existing or new stakeholders of the CDI project.

Levels of Aggregation and Relationship Types

This dimension of scope defines how the data should be aggregated. Typically data aggregation is an area discussed within data warehousing projects. If a data warehouse has already been built, the CDI project scope should answer the question of whether the CDI Data Hub will feed the data warehouse in the future and how the existing processes will be impacted. If the data warehouse is not available yet, we do not recommend mixing the MDM-CDI Data Hub project and a data warehousing effort, even though interdependencies between the two efforts should be well understood.

Even though creation of multiple data aggregation layers is not the primary focus of the CDI Data Hub, we should consider a data aggregation view that is directly associated with CDI Data Hubs. This particular data aggregation view is also known as a "single version of truth" for customer data. We defined this new, additional view in Parts I and II of the book. Indeed a typical enterprise does not want to get rid of all of its customer records even though some of them may exist in multiple versions. The discussion on customer data aggregation may reveal an enterprise's intent to preserve and maintain the existing redundant customer records along with the new single version of truth for customer data. Since by definition, a CDI platform integrates all available data about the customer into the authoritative system of record, this single version of truth represents an aggregated data view. We discuss CDI data aggregation in more detail in Chapter 12.

A discussion of relationship types that have to be supported and managed by the CDI platform is another important dimension of scope. CDI and customer relationships are discussed in Chapter 13.

Entities and Attributes

As the CDI project is initiated, an initial logical/canonical data model of the integrated solution should include all entities, key attributes, and other attributes (to the extent possible at this early project stage) required by the integrated solution regardless of which systems these data elements reside in at present. The canonical data model, described in Chapter 8, defines the entities in scope, and the relationships between the entities and data attributes in scope no matter where they physically reside.

Clearly, to enable proper CDI functionality, the data attributes used for customer identification and matching should be included in the model. However, some of the data attributes and entities may not be available in any of the existing systems at all. Such a logical data model provides the organization with a technique to abstract their analysis from the complexities of the existing data structures and develop a desired consolidated data model that represents business vision correctly.

It is not always easy to conceptualize the enterprise vision and abstract it from the organizational realities. Therefore, we highly recommend finding the right external partners specializing in logical data modeling, preferably with deep expertise in an appropriate subject area domain (i.e., customer, product, subscriber, etc.). Some domain-specific data models are published by their owners or vendors. As an example, please see *The Data Model Resource Book,* Vol. 1, *A Library of Universal Data Models for All Enterprises*, and Vol. 2, *A Library of Data Models for Specific Industries* by Len Silverston (Wiley, 2001).

If you feel that the data models recommended by your partners do not entirely fit your organizational needs, which is not uncommon, your organization would still benefit from the experience of data modelers who built industry-specific models. It is also very useful for project direction to acquire a clear understanding of why the industry model does not fit your organizational business model. Whether you buy a data model from an external source or decide to develop it internally, discussions about the choices you need to consider in developing and deploying the data model for the CDI platform will enable the organization to establish a logical data model that defines the scope of the solution from the data attributes' perspective.

There are other considerations that drive the scope of the canonical model. In addition to the initial scope, the team should determine the scope of the incremental data model changes as the CDI platform evolves from one release to the next.

Systems and Applications in Scope

Systems and applications are another important dimension of scope. Specifically, in a typical Customer Data Hub the data is sourced from multiple systems. When the Customer Data Hub is in production, how will the current systems be affected? Some applications and systems may have to be phased out, which is a significant scope issue that also determines the end state of the solution and work in the legacy system areas that must be planned.

Alternatively, existing legacy systems may have to coexist with the Data Hub. The discussion of what such coexistence means will lead us to the topic of the next section about the Customer Data Hub solution architecture.

Customer Data Hub Solution Architecture

As the process of the project scope definition reaches a point where the team gains a consensus about entities, data attributes, products/account types, and lines of business, the CDI project can move into the next phase to decide upon architectural choices for the CDI Customer Data Hub. CDI products and solutions known as Customer Data Hubs are designed to support data structures, functions, and services that enable rationalization, integration, and delivery of customer data. A conceptual CDI Data Hub architecture, described in detail in Part II of the book, recognizes a number of options that can be used to solve customer data integration problems in the context of the business requirements of a given enterprise. Let's review these architecture options as they have been defined by the industry research firm Gartner Group. The follow-on section in this chapter provides an analysis of the architecture styles and offers some insights into and variations of the architecture options, which are based on the authors' practical experience implementing CDI solutions.

Data Hub Architecture Styles

A well-known industry research firm, the Gartner Group, has defined the following architecture styles for typical Data Hub implementations.

Registry Hub

The Registry-style Data Hub uses a metadata repository, or a stand-alone Data Attribute directory that points to the locations of the data attributes using specialized Data Hub services called Attribute Locator service and the Metadata service (see Chapter 5 for more details on the Data Hub services). Figure 11-3 illustrates the way the Registry-style Hub operates. For instance, the metadata repository should store the rules about the retrieval of the "best" customer name, the "best" (i.e., authoritative) source for account type, etc. The rules can be complex enough to take into account multiple conditions and scenarios. The Data Hub of this style stores only key identifiers and links them to the fragments of master data in source systems. In addition, the Registry-style Data Hub supports data transformations necessary to achieve semantic consistency and reconciliation (please refer to Chapter 14 for additional discussion on semantic reconciliation). The Registry-style Data Hub provides a real-time reference by dynamically assembling an integrated but read-only customer view from the source systems.

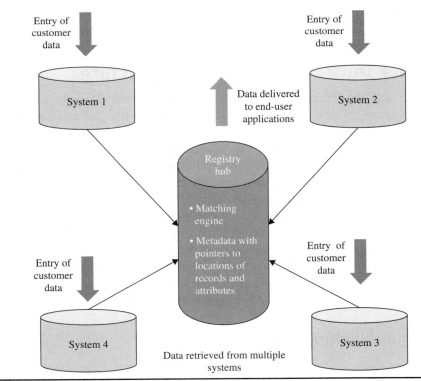

Figure 11-3 *Registry Hub*

The Registry Hub is the right choice if the company's strategy is to preserve the existing systems and invest their development funds to fix and enhance legacy systems over time. Considerations for and against a Registry-style Data Hub are shown in the following list.

Pros:

▶ The lowest-cost customer data integration solution.

▶ The data flow changes are limited and implementation risks are minimized.

▶ Only limited data reconciliation between the legacy and the new data Hub systems is required.

Cons:

▶ If the Data Hub has to support complex business rules including data survivorship, the data access (query) performance of the Hub can be an issue. The term "data survivorship" refers to the rules defining how to assemble a single record from two or more records with overlapping attributes that may contain conflicting values. In this case the attributes "compete" for survivorship to resolve the conflicts.

▶ Query performance represents an even bigger concern when multiple systems must be accessed to retrieve the data.

Coexistence Hub

The Coexistence Hub architecture style of the Data Hub (see Figure 11-4) physically stores some master data along with referencing some other data in the source systems. This Data Hub style is not used to directly originate transactions, but is updated from the source systems that initiate transactions. The source systems serve as the systems of record. The Data Hub is used as a central reference point for customer data. In addition to the customer data, the Data Hub can also store relationship data, customer groups, etc. with specifics dependent on the industry and organizational needs.

Identity Hub

A slight variation of the Registry-style Hub design that enables primarily matching and linking services is known as the *Identity Hub*. It is similar to the Registry Hub in that it stores pointers to data attributes that reside in external systems, but it is designed to store and manage only those data attributes that are required to perform record matching, linking, and party identification.

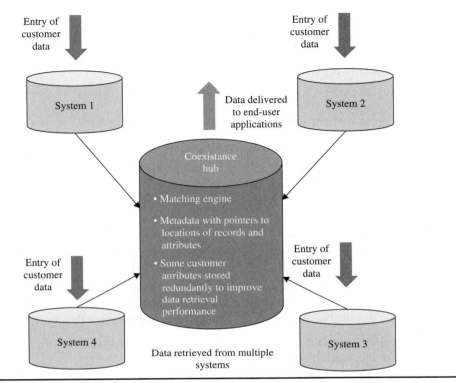

Figure 11-4 *Coexistence Hub*

The Coexistence Hub bridges some gaps in the existing systems. It is the right choice if the company's strategy is to partially preserve the existing systems and decommission at least some of the legacy systems. The Coexistence Hub style is sometimes used as a step towards a Transaction Hub. Its advantages and disadvantages are summarized in the following list.

Pros:

▶ The Coexistence Data Hub solution cost is relatively low.

▶ Data flow is limited to one-directional synchronization.

▶ Data retrieval performance issues are resolved by storing certain data attributes in the Data Hub. The complexity of data transformation is moved to ETL.

Cons:

▶ ETL transformations that are required to maintain Data Hub content can be fairly complex.

▶ Since the Coexistence-style Data Hub assumes some data redundancy, its design should provide for synchronization and reconciliation of data changes between the source systems and the Data Hub.

Transaction Hub

This Data Hub style physically stores the customer data and is used as the authoritative system of record for customer data, as shown in Figure 11-5. This style of Data Hub supports services that apply data access transactions directly to the Hub and generate messages or batch files that publish the results of the transactions to the external systems. The Transaction Hub is the right choice when the organization does not intend to invest additional money and resources in the source systems for the data domains where the Data Hub must become the master. In this case, a prudent approach is to prepare to support significant data flow changes in the

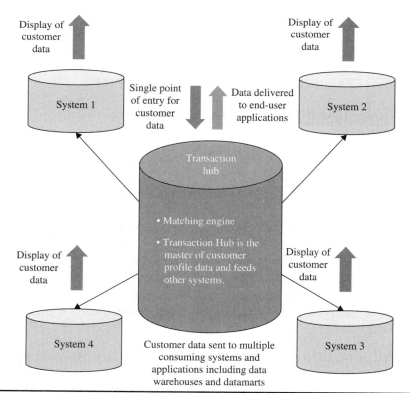

Figure 11-5 *Transaction Hub*

existing system structure including decommissioning of some of the legacy systems. Transaction hub advantages and disadvantages are shown in the following list.

Pros:

▶ This is a comprehensive solution that can be used to phase out obsolete legacy systems.

▶ This architecture style of the Data Hub allows organizations to achieve at least one of the major CDI goals—the creation of an accurate, timely, and complete system of record that maintains just-in-time data accuracy and integrity.

Cons:

▶ This architecture style of the Data Hub results in the highest complexity of ETL implementation.

▶ This style also requires complex real-time synchronization and reconciliation. Therefore, it usually demands the highest cost and implementation risk. The complexity of data synchronization is discussed in Chapter 15.

The taxonomy of these architecture styles illustrates an interesting pattern: the richness of the Data Hub functionality and the complexity and the associated risks of CDI implementations increase as the Hub stores and manages more and more customer data. Therefore, CDI projects need to carefully evaluate the benefits and risks associated with each approach and decide on the appropriate road map for implementing a CDI solution in a phased, risk-managed fashion.

Phased Implementation of Customer Data Hub

Even though an ultimate goal of the CDI project may be to develop a Transaction Hub solution, in order to achieve this goal and to manage the risks and impact of implementing a Transaction Hub, a CDI project typically begins with a "slim" Data Hub implementation. The plan should be to evolve the Data Hub by increasing the number of data attributes for which it acts as a master. As the Data Hub data scope grows, so does the value that the Data Hub provides to the organization. From the project management point of view, this evolutionary change should be organized into well-defined project phases. Of course, it is clear that this chapter discusses a phase of the CDI project called the Initiation phase.

Using this approach as a guide, we recommend a somewhat different categorization of the Customer Data Hub styles that are more aligned with phased implementation as shown in Figure 11-6.

Artifacts That Should Be Produced in the Project Initiation Phase

Typical artifacts that are to be produced at the end of the Project Initiation phase are shown in the following list:

Phase 1: Hub "Slave"	Phase 2: Hub "Slave" enhanced	Phase 3: Hub "Master"
Data governance • Reference data • Data cleansing in source • Data cleansing during Transformations Buy vs build and client hub vendor selection • Data-model-specific • Data-model-agnostic Customer identification (matching) & data quality vendor selection • Deterministic match • Probabilistic match Key generation cross-reference loading and synchronizing the hub Visibility & security at the record level limited to view only	Additional attributes, LOBs and systems Attribute level visibility & security solution All account types, party types, domestic vs international Enhanced customer identification capabilities based on improved data quality and stewardship Comprehensive reference data translations Visibility & security at the attribute level Legacy system/functionality phase out road map	Direct updates against the hub Inverse data flows to support hub master scenario for selected fields Customer identification enhanced by end-user input • Merge • Split • Data enrichment Comprehensive visibility & security implementation Legacy system/functionality phase-out Comprehensive transactional semantics Comprehensive visibility & security solution including support for direct data changes in the hub

Figure 11-6 *Data Hub phased implementation*

- ▶ Business process analysis (current state)
- ▶ Requirements for business process improvement and re-engineering (desired target state of the business processes)
- ▶ Incremental business process changes by release
    - ▶ Incremental benefits by business function and line of business
    - ▶ State of the solution architecture by release
- ▶ Conceptual and logical data model of the integrated solution and how it ties back to the business processes
- ▶ Scope and priority definitions in terms of data attributes, products/account types, and lines of business
- ▶ Solution architecture and the architecture road map indicating how the architecture evolves with the implementation releases
- ▶ Vendor product evaluation criteria, buy vs. build decision, and tool recommendation/selection for the key areas of CDI Data Hub functionality

Project Work Streams

In the beginning of this chapter we mentioned that an effective methodology to managing complex projects such as a CDI Data Hub is to use a phased approach and organize the work and resources into a number of interconnected and interdependent work streams. The following work streams typically represent the body of work that needs to be planned and executed.

- ▶ Customer identification
- ▶ Customer/account groups and relationships
- ▶ Data governance, standards, quality, and compliance
- ▶ Data architecture
- ▶ Metadata and related services including record locator and attribute locator metadata and services
- ▶ Initial data load
- ▶ Inbound data processing (batch and real-time)
- ▶ Outbound data processing (batch and real-time)
- ▶ Changes to legacy systems and applications
- ▶ Visibility and security
- ▶ Exception processing
- ▶ Infrastructure
- ▶ Data Hub applications
- ▶ Reporting requirements of a stratified user community
- ▶ Testing
- ▶ Release management
- ▶ Deployment
- ▶ Training
- ▶ Project management

To sum up, if you are planning to embark on an MDM-CDI effort, this list can be used as a guide to build a detailed project plan including appropriate resources and the project team composition. Each of these work streams should have clearly defined deliverables that have to be aligned at the entire project level in order to produce a cohesive and comprehensive solution. Although these work streams define different interdependent efforts that prevent them from being executed in a totally parallel fashion, many of these work streams can be structured so that their dependence on each other is minimized and the overall project timeline is optimized to parallelize as much work as possible. We will cover the areas addressed by these work streams in the chapters that follow.

Customer Identification

IN THIS CHAPTER

A 360-Degree View of a Customer: Frequently Used Terms and Definitions

Attributes and Attribute Categories Commonly Used for Matching and Customer Identification

Customer Identification, Matching Process, and Models

Summary of Data-Matching Requirements and Solutions

A s we already mentioned in Chapter 1 and discussed in more detail in Chapter 5, Customer Identification is at the heart of CDI. The goal of Customer Identification is to have accurate and timely information about each individual and organization that has past, current, or potential future relationships with the enterprise regardless of what business unit actually owns those relationships. Clearly, the sales and marketing department will want to know the nature of interested parties that have or had some relationships or points of contact with the company but may never have been the company's customer. Furthermore, a party may have multiple relationships with the enterprise. These relationships should be tracked across channels, lines of business, and contact types. For a variety of businesses, for legal and compliance reasons the company may need to know about the employees who are also the company's customers. A more complex question the company may want to answer is whether its employee or an existing customer has a professional relationship with other existing customers, for example, their attorney, accountant, or any other interested party.

The first step in customer identification is the ability to identify a party in the most granular way that makes sense for the enterprise. The granularity level also depends on the way the source data is stored in legacy systems. Reconciling various degrees of granularity represents one of the challenges that needs to be addressed for efficient customer identification.

Customer data resides in multiple systems that represent different business area silos. Figure 12-1 illustrates the integration of multiple disparate systems. In the enterprise environment, it is quite common that the number of systems that need to be integrated ranges from 10 to 30 and sometimes even higher. Customer data in these systems is formatted, stored, and managed differently since these application systems tend to be

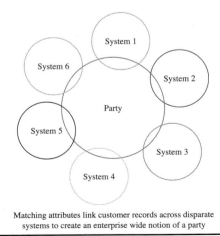

Matching attributes link customer records across disparate
systems to create an enterprise wide notion of a party

Figure 12-1   *System integration and a 360-degree view of customer*

highly heterogeneous because they are created and maintained by different departments and used for different purposes. Often various application systems maintain overlapping attributes and may support different levels of granularity and different data structures, e.g., account-centric data vs. customer-centric data, household-level data, different touch points, channels, etc.

A 360-Degree View of a Customer: Frequently Used Terms and Definitions

In order to recognize each individual that has one or more relationships with the firm, the information about the individuals must be assembled from all relevant records across the enterprise. This comprehensive view of an individual is frequently referred to by business as a 360-degree view of a customer. What are some key challenges in creating this view?

It is not always clear if the records that read Mike Johnson and M. Johnson represent the same individual even if the records show the same address, home phone number, and credit card number, as in Figure 12-2. Two records with the name M. Johnson at the same address may still belong to different people, e.g. father and son. Indeed, if we consider Mike's son Mack Johnson, then M. Johnson may represent Mike Johnson or Mack Johnson. Other scenarios are also possible.

On the other hand, two records for Mike Johnson at two different addresses may still represent the same individual who moved from one address to another. In this scenario one of the addresses was occupied by this individual in the past; see Figure 12-3.

In the case of United States residences, a service that can access National Change of Address (NCOA) information, which is maintained by the U.S. Postal Service, may be required to link the records in Figure 12-3 and associate them with the same individual. Another variation on the theme could be a situation where Mike Johnson may have two or more addresses at a time, e.g. the primary residence and a vacation home. In addition, both names and addresses can have different spellings, aliases, etc.

Any attempt to create a comprehensive 360-degree view of a customer faces the challenge of *overmatching*. This scenario occurs when the records belonging to two or more customers are mistakenly assigned to a single individual. If the matching data is used for a marketing campaign, such an error may result in the marketing department

Full Name	Address	Phone Number	Credit Card Number
Mike Johnson	123 Main St. Bordentown, NJ 08513	(609) 987-6543	4213 0001 1234 6789
M. Johnson	123 Main St. Bordentown, NJ 08513	(609) 987-6543	4213 0001 1234 6789

Figure 12-2 *Two records for Mike Johnson and M. Johnson with the same phone number and credit card number*

Full Name	Address	Phone Number	Credit Card Number
Mike Johnson	123 Main St. Bordentown, NJ 08513	(609) 987-6543	4213 0001 1234 6789
M. Johnson	767 Central Ave. Bordentown, NJ 08513	(609) 987-6543	4213 0001 1234 6789

Figure 12-3   *Two records for Mike Johnson at different addresses*

not sending a marketing letter to a customer. However, when data is used for legal or financial purposes, a customer can be incorrectly linked to legal documents, financial statements, or medical records, which can have serious consequences for both the customer and the firm. For example, the firm may send a dividend check to a wrong individual or disclose sensitive information to a stranger.

Errors in Matching

Two or more records erroneously matched to the same individual are frequently referred to as *false positives*. Conversely, two or more records that are not matched even though they do belong to the same individual are referred to as *false negatives*.

Business must identify the required match accuracy in terms of the level of confidence for both false negatives and false positives. Legal, financial, medical, and certain other applications of customer data integration typically require high-confidence data with the primary focus of avoiding false positives at any cost. Some compliance applications are relatively tolerant to false positives but need to avoid false negatives, for example, identifying suspects potentially involved in money laundering, drug trafficking, terrorism, or other criminal activities. In the latter case, the law enforcement officer wants to see all suspects who meet given suspect criteria, while realizing that some records may be false matches. False negatives in this scenario would mean an exclusion of potential criminals from the list of suspects. Once the initial "wide-net" list of records is produced systemically, a manual effort and analysis will be required to exclude false positives and finalize the list.

The sections that follow summarize some common reasons responsible for producing false positives and false negative matches.

Reasons for False Positives

With a typical match based on the name, address, phone, and some other attributes the primary reasons for false positives are as follows:

▶ Family members living at the same address with the same or similar first names or initials and possibly having joint accounts or trusts on which they have different roles, e.g. Mike Johnson Sr. vs. Mike Johnson Jr.

▶ Lack of differentiation between party types. For instance, if a customer Tom Kent opened a checking account with a firm, created a trust where he is a trustee, and has an account for his small business called "Tom Kent Associates," the system may not be able to recognize the three parties as distinct entities (individual, trust, and small company).

▶ The use of invalid or incorrect data for multiple records, e.g. records with social security number (SSN) 999-99-9999.

Reasons for False Negatives

There are many reasons for false negative matches, most of them being related to data quality:

▶ The use of multiple versions of the same name

    ▶ Nicknames and aliases (Bill vs. William, Larry vs. Lawrence are the most common)

    ▶ Misspelled names

    ▶ Names for international customers that may not fit the standard First Name–Middle Initial–Last Name structure

▶ Name changes

    ▶ As a result of marriage

    ▶ As a result of the naturalization process

    ▶ Organizational name changes as a result of rebranding, mergers, acquisitions, and company spin-offs

▶ Addresses

    ▶ Incorrect spelling

    ▶ Different abbreviations and spelling including full spellings (Street vs. St., Avenue vs. Ave, Ave vs. Rd, St vs. Ct., etc.)

    ▶ Inability to parse certain formats

    ▶ Vanity addresses (multiple towns associated with a single zip code; the towns are used interchangeably in the mailing address)

    ▶ Address changes

- ▶ Phone numbers
  - ▶ Inability to systemically parse some of the phone number formats

Attributes and Attribute Categories Commonly Used for Matching and Customer Identification

The fields used for matching and customer identification can be divided into the following three major categories:

- ▶ **Identity attributes**   Used for direct matching
- ▶ **Discrimination attributes**   Used to disqualify similar records
- ▶ **Record type attributes**   Used to determine which identification rules to apply

Identity Attributes

Identity attributes are the primary attributes (e.g. name and/or SSN) used by the matching algorithm to directly identify a customer. If identity attributes match two or more records, there is a good chance that the customer records are matched correctly. If a high-confidence matching is required, a match on a single identity attribute may not be sufficient and multiple attributes should be taken into account. Good candidates for identity attributes include:

- ▶ Name
  - ▶ Individual names (first, last, and middle initial) for persons and full business name for organizations are the most well-known identity attributes. Indeed, names were invented for identification purposes. From this perspective, the customer identification problem is as old as humankind.
- ▶ Key identifiers
  - ▶ Since the vast majority of individuals' names are not universally unique, people invented key identifiers such as social security numbers, tax identification numbers, driver's license numbers, patient numbers, student IDs, employee IDs, etc. to identify individuals and organizations.
- ▶ Address
  - ▶ The customer's address is frequently used for customer identification. It is not uncommon for a marketing campaign to target households (typically a family living in the same physical location) rather than individual customers.

- ▶ Phone
    - ▶ Home phone numbers and cell phone numbers are frequently used for identification. Automated customer security systems shortcut security questions when they recognize the customer phone number.
- ▶ Online identity attributes
    - ▶ IP address
    - ▶ Internet provider
    - ▶ E-mail address
    - ▶ Other online identifiers
- ▶ Product type, account number, and role
    - ▶ In account-centric enterprises (the majority of businesses across all industry segments today belong to this category), the most credible customer information is stored and maintained at the account level. The firm recognizes a customer by examining the product type (e.g., mortgage) provided by a line of business, account number, and customer's role (e.g., coborrower) on the account. Typically account information is maintained by multiple systems across the enterprise, which makes these attributes good candidates for matching.
- ▶ Customer affiliations
    - ▶ Customer affiliation information is frequently used as additional identity information. A typical example of affiliation is customer employment information.
- ▶ Customer relationships and hierarchies
    - ▶ This information is particularly critical and frequently used by organizations servicing high-net-worth customers. Every customer in these organizations is defined through a relationship with the firm or with other customers (individuals or groups) and then by name, address, etc. Customer relationships can also be used as additional identification information. Hierarchies of institutional customers may also be important as identification attributes. We will discuss this in more detail in Chapter 13.

Note that most of the identity attributes can change over time, due to life events and normal business activities. Changes in identity attributes create significant CDI challenges. Indeed, people and businesses move and change addresses, phones, and professional affiliations. For institutional customers, mergers and acquisitions cause additional complexities. Name change is not unusual either. And it is not limited to the name change as the result of a marriage. The immigration and naturalization process in many countries includes a name change as part of the naturalization process.

Discrimination Attributes

Discrimination attributes are the attributes that are not typically used to match two parties. Instead, they are used to disqualify two or more similar records; e.g., father and son with the same name and address can be differentiated by the discrimination attribute "Date of Birth." Typically, a strong discrimination attribute candidate should be static and have a well-defined set of distinct values, e.g., Date of Birth or Gender.

Even if some identity attributes match across two or more records, there is a chance that the records still belong to different customers. Discrimination attributes help to distinguish between similar records that may or may not belong to the same customer. Typical discrimination attributes are as follows:

- ► Individuals
  - ► Date of birth (DOB)
  - ► Date of death
  - ► Gender
- ► Organizations
  - ► Date of incorporation/establishment
  - ► Date of closure

Discrimination attributes are often utilized in combination with identity attributes to reduce the probability of false positive matches. Typical situations in which discrimination attributes help include the following scenarios:

- ► Husband and wife or a parent and a child with the same first initial and last name, e.g., J. Smith can be John Smith or Jane Smith, or, using our Johnson family example, M. Johnson can be Mike or Mack Johnson.
- ► Similarly, J. Smith can represent two brothers partnering in business. Assuming they were not born on the same date, the DOB attributes will help.

Unlike identity attributes, discrimination attributes typically have a lower-level cardinality. From this perspective, Gender is a common discrimination attribute with a cardinality of 2. However, note that the cardinality of Gender is sometimes defined by a number greater than 2. There are local variations where, for example, a common discrimination attribute such as Gender can assume up to six distinct values. Although the cardinality of the Date of Birth (DOB) attribute is much higher, in a typical customer data store that covers 50 years of customer life span for active customers, and using 365 days a year, the cardinality of the DOB attribute is 18,250.

While this number may appear large, for a multimillion-customer file this translates into hundreds or even thousands of individuals with the same date of birth.

Additional characteristics of discrimination attributes that are also important in term of customer Identification include:

► Stability

    ► Unlike identification attributes, which are made up by people and can change over time, in real time, or in one mass change operation (for example, a group of customers from the same retirement plan was reassigned to a new plan with different account numbers), the discrimination attributes for individuals are much less volatile. Indeed, your first name and middle initial are normally given by your parents, and the last name can change as a result of marriage or some other events. The DOB attribute should never change. Even though gender can be changed by modern medical science, it is still a relatively rare event.

    ► Similarly, when we deal with the organizations, the Incorporation Date and Business Closure date do not change. This applies at least to formal organizations that are registered with the appropriate government agencies and assigned tax identifiers.

► Universality

    ► By their nature, every individual regardless of the country of residence, citizenship, occupation, and other characteristics has such attributes as Date of Birth and Gender, and they can be used for global identification. On the other hand, identification attributes such as social security numbers that are used as unique identifiers for individuals in the U.S. most likely cannot be used to identify individuals outside the United States. To make it even more interesting, there are some exceptions when U.S. residents do not have an SSN either.

► Availability

    ► Gender is one of the most easily available attributes. Most customers do not keep their gender secret.

    ► Date of Birth is more difficult to obtain than Gender but it is still easier to obtain than the social security number. Certain data privacy regulations discussed in Part III prohibit the disclosure and use of social security numbers for identification purposes.

► Ease of validation

    ► For Gender, the format maintenance is straightforward; for example, a typical rule allows for only "F" (Female), "M" (Male), and "U" (Unknown) values.

▶ Date validation formats are well known and date validation functions are widely available in multiple products including commonly used relational databases. It is important to note that common calendar and date formats are accepted and used globally. However, it is not easy to establish global validation rules for names and addresses. Indeed, multiple attempts to apply rules such as "Last Name must have more than one character" have been defeated. Even though such last names are infrequent, they do exist.

It is our recommendation to maintain the discrimination attributes in the best possible condition in terms of data quality. Best of all, discrimination attributes should be defined as mandatory fields that have assigned values. In other words, in terms of database technology, the discrimination attributes should be defined as NOT NULL if possible. If this is not possible, data profiling and data quality maintenance on these attributes should be a priority task for data stewards.

The attributes of "Date of Birth" and "Business Incorporation/Establishment Date" are particularly important and attractive from the identification perspective. Even though these attributes are considered to be discrimination attributes (this is how they are commonly perceived), they can be successfully used for identification purposes as well.

Record Qualification Attributes

The *record qualification attributes* are used to provide additional metadata about the records. This information helps the matching algorithm to determine which identification rules should be applied to the record. The following attributes are typically used as record type identifiers:

▶ Party Type

▶ Country Attribute and Domestic vs. International Identifiers

▶ Leading Relationship (if a customer has multiple relationships with the enterprise, the most important relationship from the enterprise perspective is referred to as a Leading Relationship)

The need for record qualification attributes reinforces the assertion that the quality of a CDI solution depends not only on the narrow set of identification and discrimination attributes but also on a wider set of attributes that are typically included in the data scope of MDM-CDI projects. Consequently, for many organizations MDM-CDI projects become drivers for enterprise-wide data quality improvement initiatives.

Party Type

Customer data that exists in different data stores within a firm, tends to be very heterogeneous. Consequently, from the matching perspective, it is important for the matching algorithm to qualify the record type to determine appropriate matching rules for that record type. The Party Type attribute characterizes the type of customer the record belongs to. The most common Party Types are Individual (retail customers) and Organization (wholesale, commercial, business, and institutional customers). Typical attributes for individuals are quite different from those for organizations. The most obvious example illustrating this distinction is the set of the name attributes. For an individual, first name, last name, and middle initial are typical while businesses are characterized by full business names.

Some attributes, e.g., Gender, provide information about a person but do not apply to businesses. Social Security numbers for living individuals are unique within the United States. Unfortunately, this uniqueness does not hold true if the matching record set includes both individuals and businesses. The Business Tax Identification Number can even be the same as an individual SSN. The list of examples illustrating the differences between individual and organizational records can be significantly extended. The bottom line here is that the matching algorithm needs the Party Type as an important record-qualifying attribute since different matching rules apply to different Party Types.

We have to point out that individual customers are somewhat easier to identify since in general, the individuals can be better "defined." For example, each individual is identified by his or her unique DNA. Even though the DNA data is not typically available for most CDI systems, this does not change the fact that conceptually the individuals are better defined for recognition than organizations are. The latter can frequently be viewed as subjects of fuzzy matching and identification. Indeed, the Party Type of "Organization" is often subcategorized, where subcategories depend on the industry segment in which the "Organization" operates. In financial services organizations, the subcategory list may include such party types as trust, fund, estate, annuity, association, etc. A party subcategory might be important in refining the rules on how the customer record should be processed by the matching algorithm.

Country Attribute and Domestic vs. International Identifiers

The country attribute is important for correct address recognition. As we discussed in Part I of the book, different rules apply to names with different ethnic backgrounds. Accordingly, advanced customer matching and recognition algorithms that use probabilistic models can take advantage of the country and geography information (e.g. state or province data) to improve the accuracy of matching. The address structure and ultimately the party recognition and identification depend on the way addresses are defined in a given country.

Therefore, it is important to determine the country type for each record that has to be matched. In many cases, when the country data is not reliable, it is important to differentiate between U.S. domestic addresses and international addresses. This distinction is important because domestic addresses are normally better defined and therefore can be processed in a more automated fashion while the international addresses require more manual intervention. Even if the CDI system is designed to access an external knowledge base from a "trusted" data provider such as Acxiom or Dun & Bradstreet, it is important to know that the commercially available U.S. domestic name and address information is more accurate and complete than international name and address data for most foreign countries.

Leading Relationship and Relationship Level

Another important piece of the record identification metadata is the information about the details of an individual's relationships with the firm. This information can be used by the CDI system to identify the most profitable low/high-risk customers and the relationship managers who are responsible for maintaining the corresponding customers' accounts. The Leading Relationship information is particularly important since it can help prioritize the way customer records have to be cleansed up and processed for identification.

Personal information about the customers is typically more complete and accurate than data about the prospects. It is a good practice to maintain a special attribute that indicates whether the party is a customer or a prospect. A person is considered to be a customer if he or she has at least one account with the firm. In the case of a customer, some minimum information is not just required but is in fact mandatory in order to open an account. For prospects that are only potential customers, minimum data requirements do not exist or can be much less restrictive. Consequently, the expected accuracy of matching for prospects is lower than that for the customers. Similarly, the expected accuracy for the primary customers is higher than that for the secondary customers (e.g., a spouse listed on the account as a beneficiary), third-party vendors, etc.

The identification accuracy of the most profitable customers is a business imperative that is aimed at increasing the customer's level of satisfaction, so it is not unusual to invoke a manual identification process to reduce the number of identification errors. In order to support a manual customer identification effort, it is critical to know who in the firm is primarily responsible for the relationship. Thus, a CDI solution must maintain the attributes that link customer information with the relationship owners. For example, a financial services firm would have to know and maintain information about customer relationship managers, financial advisors, agents, or account managers who manage the relationship with the customer.

Customer Identification, Matching Process, and Models

Let's take a closer look at customer identification processes and concerns.

Minimum Data Requirements

A prerequisite to effective customer identification and matching is the consideration of minimum data requirements for any record to be included as a matching candidate. This notion is reflected in Figure 12-4.

If the minimum data requirements are not met, the record may require additional manual processing, e.g. additional data must be collected, entered, or changed. Data change is required if an attribute value is determined to be invalid. Figure 12-4 shows six combinations of attributes. If a record does not meet any of the requirements specified here, the matching algorithm will exclude the record from the matching process and report it as a data quality exception.

Matching Modes

From a systemic perspective, the customer identification process consists of two high-level steps: *record match* and *record merge*.

Merge and split processing is discussed in some detail in Chapter 13. This chapter is focused on the implementation issues of record matching. The goal of the record match process is to create Match Groups. Each group contains one or more records that represent a party. Typically, once the Match Groups are identified, the goal is to eliminate duplicate records and create a unique "Golden copy" of each customer record. Depending on the business requirements, creation of a Golden copy may not be mandatory. Moreover, some CDI implementations require keeping multiple linked records without removing duplicates.

Match Group is used to systemically identify parties. This may or may not be identical to Party ID, which is the ultimate "Golden copy" identifier for a Party.

No	Full Name	Address	Home Phone	Date of Birth	SSN
1	+				+
2		+			+
3			+		+
4				+	+
5	+	+		+	
6	+		+	+	

Figure 12-4 *An example of a minimum requirements definition*

Record	Match Group
Customer record 1	
Customer record 2	
Customer record 3	
Customer record 4	
Customer record 5	
Customer record 6	
Customer record 7	

During the initial "unseeded" match process all Match Groups are assigned

Record	Match Group
Customer record 1	1
Customer record 2	2
Customer record 3	1
Customer record 4	2
Customer record 5	3
Customer record 6	3
Customer record 7	2

Figure 12-5 *Initial match process*

If an end-user input is required to assert the Match Group value, then the terms Party and Match Group may have different meaning. The Party identifier represents true single customer view created with a manual expert input while the Match Group identifier is the best the system could do to automatically identify the customer in order to assist the expert.

Operationally, we can distinguish between batch and online matching modes. *Batch matching* applies to a process in which a large number of records must be processed to cluster customer records and assign a unique Party ID to each Match Group. Note that the Party ID is a unique identifier for each cluster representing a single customer. During the initial "unseeded" match, all records are assigned to Match Groups (see Figure 12-5). It is not unusual for the batch-matching process to cover a complete multimillion-record customer database and to run for hours and possibly even days.

Online matching is part of daily ongoing activities when new party records are created, deleted, deactivated, or updated (see Figure 12-6). Online matching is a

Customer record 8 →

Record	Match Group
Customer record 1	1
Customer record 2	2
Customer record 3	1
Customer record 4	2
Customer record 5	3
Customer record 6	3
Customer record 7	2

A new record is matched against the existing customer base and assigned to Match Group 2

Record	Match Group
Customer record 1	1
Customer record 2	2
Customer record 3	1
Customer record 4	2
Customer record 5	3
Customer record 6	3
Customer record 7	2
Customer record 8	2

Figure 12-6 *Online, real-time, or near-real-time match*

"seeded" process, where each new record is matched against the existing records with assigned Match Groups identifiers and/or Party Ids.

In this example, the addition of a record does not cause any Match Group changes. However, this is not always true. As we will discuss later in this chapter, a new record can "chain" two or more other records, which results in changes of the Match Group assignment for the existing records.

Defining Matching Rules for Customer Records

This section lists typical steps used to define matching rules for customer records.

First, we need to identify the matching attributes. All attributes that should be used for matching need to be identified. This includes all types of the attributes previously discussed:

- ▶ Identity attributes
- ▶ Discrimination attributes
- ▶ Record qualification attributes

Defining Matching Rules at the Attribute or Attribute Group Level

This section discusses factors that need to be considered when two attributes are compared for matching, and how to quantify them.

Matching factors include a number of types:

- ▶ Exact match
    - ▶ Within this comparison model, two attributes are considered to be matched if they are represented by two equal attribute values, for example, character strings after removal of padding spaces, carriage return and other characters not meaningful for string comparison in the context of customer matching.
- ▶ Match with the use of "common sense" standardization rules
    - ▶ These standardization rules cover a number of "common sense" rules about individual names and addresses, e.g. match Steve to Steven, Ave. to Avenue, St. to Street, and names that sound similar (e.g., Stacy matches with Stacey).
- ▶ Match with the use of knowledge-base intelligence
    - ▶ This category of matching involves rules that can be implemented based only on the facts available in the knowledge databases and data libraries. For instance, a knowledge base can hold data about the streets available in each town, valid ranges for street addresses, vanity addresses, and the National Change of Address (NCOA) data.

▶   Probabilistic attribute match

    ▶   A Probabilistic Attribute Match algorithm utilizes frequency-based data analysis for attribute value distribution on the attributes in the customer database. For instance, a probabilistic approach will take into account that the first name "John" is much more frequent in the database than the first name "Dushan." From the probabilistic approach perspective, a match on a less frequent attribute value is statistically more significant than a match on an attribute value that is very frequent in the database. It should be pointed out that customer locality or geography can affect and even reverse the attribute frequency ratio. Indeed, the first name "Dushan" will be more frequent in the Balkans than the first name "John." This improves the accuracy of matching by 4–10 percent.

Nevertheless, in most situations, CDI projects focus on deploying a deterministic approach. The primary advantage of deterministic approaches is that the matching results are simpler to understand. Indeed, since the probabilistic match performs a significant portion of the analysis under the covers, the matching results are more difficult to interpret and therefore, to test and validate.

Matching Quantification   Once all factors driving a match decision are established, the model should also define how the attribute match will be quantified. The simplest case is a binary decision. The result of an attribute to attribute comparison can be presented as

$$\text{Match} = \text{True}$$

or

$$\text{Match} = \text{False}$$

More complex algorithms take into account various degrees of the confidence level of an attribute match. The confidence is at the maximum level for exact matches and decreases as the match becomes fuzzier. The confidence parameters need to be set and tuned in terms of the rules through which the match has been established. In cluster algorithms, the attribute match confidence is expressed through the "distance" between the two attribute values. The exact match would be characterized by the distance value of zero (distance = 0). As the match becomes less certain, the distance between the two values grows. There are several variations of these algorithms where, for example, different match weights are used to reflect different confidence levels.

Record-Level Match

Once the attribute-level match has been performed, it is time to evaluate the customer record match. There are a few ways to combine attribute-level matches and convert them into a record-level match.

Binary Rule for the Attribute Match and Binary Rule for the Record Match   In this scenario, based on the attribute match defined as binary, the record match is defined by a number of explicitly specified matching rules. These rules can be simply codified in the "M" of "N" model (M of the total attributes N match). Figure 12-7 illustrates this approach.

The match criteria shown in Figure 12-7 require a match of any three attributes or attribute groups (M = 3) out of the five (N = 5). The "M" of "N" model requires that in order for two records to be considered a match, M out of N attributes or groups of attributes should match. In the following example, there are five attribute groups or individual attributes:

- ▶ Full Name
- ▶ Address
- ▶ Phone
- ▶ Date of Birth
- ▶ SSN

Since three of them match within this rule, the two records match. Typically, a simple rule like "M" of "N" will not hold true from a match accuracy perspective. Given the complexity of enterprise data, the number of explicitly defined rules can easily reach hundreds. Also, in order to achieve the desired accuracy, the rules tend to be fairly complex and include conditional logic with dependencies on multiple attributes. The result of the computation is expressed in terms of a binary match/no match decision for the records. For instance, a rule may read: *If the social security numbers match and the last names match, then the records are determined to be a match unless two valid and different dates of birth are found in the records.*

Binary Rule for the Attribute Match and Score for Record Match   In this scenario, assuming that the Binary Attribute match is true, the record match is defined through a score. First, we define attribute match weights for each attribute. Then the overall record-to-record matching score is computed as a total over the field matching scores. Finally, the calculated record score is compared with the matching threshold. If the computed value exceeds the threshold, the two records are considered to be a match.

Full Name			Address				Phone		Date of Birth	SSN
First	M.	Last	Street	City	State	ZIP Code	Area Code	Phone #		
Tom	J	Jones	231 Main St	Blue Sky	XY	12345	512	123-1010	03/12/1961	111-22-3333
Tom	J	Jones	12 Mercer St	Blue Sky	XY	12345	512	123-1010	03/12/1961	
Match							Match		Match	

Figure 12-7 *A simple "M" of "N" attributes match scenario*

Scoring for Both the Attribute Match and Record Match   In this scenario, the scores obtained from the attribute-level calculations, optionally weighted by the relative attribute weights, are used to compute the record-level score. If the computed value exceeds the threshold, then the two records are considered to be a match.

It should be pointed out that one of the advantages of scoring methodologies is based on the fact that the matching requirements can be defined in a more compact form than the requirements defined explicitly in term of a great number of complex business rules. The scoring models allow for ease in defining matching iterations and testing procedures. This is particularly important since any matching process requires multiple iterations to reach the required level of accuracy.

Defining the Thresholds

As we discussed in the preceding section, the scoring models require a definition of match accuracy threshold. A higher threshold will make the matching more conservative, which means that the procedure will minimize false positive matches. A higher threshold will also result in a higher tolerance to false negatives. This is a disadvantage of any one-threshold model. A more flexible model should include two thresholds, as shown in Figure 12-8. In the figure, the scoring values are segmented into three areas: confident match, confident mismatch, and the "gray" area where additional information or human input is required to determine the match.

Effect of Chaining

It is important to understand the effect of chaining in matching. *Chaining* is a situation where two or more records are assigned to the same Match Groups even though they should not be matched by using the rules defined by a direct record-to-record match; instead, the records are "chained" by a third record that is directly matched to the first two records.

The accuracy of matching and performance may be impacted by how the matching algorithm handles chaining. A chaining scenario is illustrated by Figure 12-9.

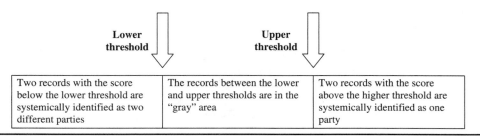

Figure 12-8 *Two thresholds segment the scoring values into three areas*

Full Name			Address				Phone		Date of Birth	SSN
First	M.	Last	Street	City	State	ZIP Code	Area Code	Phone #		
Tom	J	Jones	231 Main St	Blue Sky	XY	12345	512	123-1010	03/12/1961	111-22-3333
Tom	J	Jones	12 Mercer St	Blue Sky	XY	12345	512	123-1010	03/12/1961	
Tom	J	Jones	12 Mercer St	Blue Sky	XY	12345	512	123-1010		

Figure 12-9 *Effect of chaining for customer records*

In this example, we assume that the matching rule requires three attribute group matches for the records to be linked to the same party. The second record is linked to the first one on the Full Name, Phone, and Date of Birth. The third record is linked to the second one on the Full Name, Address, and Phone. Since three matching attributes are required to directly link records, the third record is not directly linked to the first one because only two attribute groups, Full Name and Phone, are matched for these records. Nevertheless, the first record and the third record are linked to each other indirectly through the second record.

In order to understand potential difficulties with chaining, we should note that the result of chaining depends on the order in which the records were processed. If Record 3 is processed after Record 1 but before Record 2, then Record 3 will not be linked to Record 1 and therefore will be assigned a different Party ID. When Record 2 is processed, it will be assigned its own Party ID. Consequently, three records will not be linked in the first pass. This may create matching accuracy and/or performance and scalability issues. Today, advances in developing matching algorithms allow CDI systems to achieve reliable scalability characteristics by aligning processing time with the number of matching records.

As we pointed out earlier, there are situations where a new record can cause a Match Group recalculation in other records. Figure 12-10 illustrates this point.

In this figure, Customer Record 8 is found to match a record from Match Group 2 and a record from Match Group 3. This results in the merge of Match Groups 2 and 3. From a business perspective, this means that an addition of a new record led the matching algorithm to a conclusion that Match Groups 2 and 3 represent the same customer.

Similarly, an update or a deletion of a customer record can cause changes in Match Group assignments of other records. For instance, if Customer Record 8 is deleted, the process in Figure 12-10 may be reversed and the three Match Groups may be created.

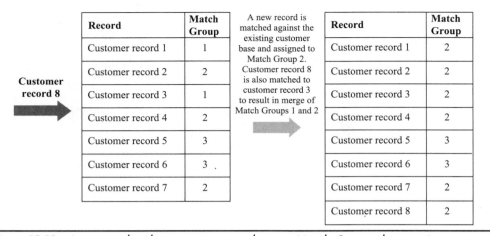

Record	Match Group		Record	Match Group
Customer record 1	1		Customer record 1	2
Customer record 2	2	A new record is matched against the existing customer base and assigned to Match Group 2. Customer record 8 is also matched to customer record 3 to result in merge of Match Groups 1 and 2	Customer record 2	2
Customer record 3	1		Customer record 3	2
Customer record 4	2		Customer record 4	2
Customer record 5	3		Customer record 5	3
Customer record 6	3 .		Customer record 6	3
Customer record 7	2		Customer record 7	2
			Customer record 8	2

Customer record 8 →

Figure 12-10 *An example where a new record cause Match Group changes in existing records*

Break Groups and Performance Considerations

In practice, performance concerns about matching records on a very large data set can be addressed if we apply a matching algorithm on smaller sets of records called *break groups*. There are other optimization techniques that allow CDI systems to achieve acceptable levels of performance and scalability. Many of these techniques are the subject of published and ongoing research, and are well beyond the scope of this book. Nevertheless, the performance of the matching process, in combination with its accuracy, is one of the topics presented by practically all CDI vendors as their competitive "differentiator." Many claims have been made that a particular proprietary technique can match hundreds of millions or even billions of records in practically near-real time. While we're not going to dispute these claims, we want to turn the reader's attention to a set of considerations designed to separate the reality of match scalability from the marketing hype. The discussion that follows describes an analytical approach to matching performance that is based on the concept of break groups.

When a matching algorithm runs against a dataset, in general, it has to evaluate match/no match conditions for all records in the dataset in a pairwise fashion. The total time spent on matching depends to a large degree on the time spent on the match/no match evaluation for the record pairs.

Using this as a base, let's consider a simple model where the dataset contains N records. Assume that M attributes are used for the match. Let t be the time required to evaluate matching conditions for a given attribute for a given pair of records. The number of pairs of records can be evaluated through the number of combinations of

N by 2, which yields $N \times (N - 1)/2$. The time required to perform the match/no match decisions for all record couples is

$$T = t \times M \times N \times (N - 1)/2$$

Given that $N \gg 1$, we arrive at

$$T \approx t \times M \times N^2/2$$

The value of t depends on a number of factors such as hardware, complexity of comparison, etc. For this evaluation we will use $t = 10^{-8}s$. For typical values of $M = 20$ and $N = 30,000,000$, the factor $M \times N^2/2$ evaluates to 10^{16}. With this number of comparison operations the time required to complete matching is $T = 10^8 s$, which is over three years. This indicates that it is practically impossible to get a reasonable matching performance on a very large dataset using the current state of the art in conventional computing platforms. The number of comparisons must be decreased by orders of magnitude to get meaningful performance results. This can be achieved by using break groups that segment the dataset into smaller sets of records so that record matches are possible only within the break groups and never across them.

Let's evaluate the change in the number of comparisons as a result of creating B break groups. For simplicity, let's assume that all break groups are equal and hence each of the groups contains N/B records. Then the time required to perform the match/no match decisions for all record pairs within each group is

$$T_B \approx t \times M \times N^2/(2 \times B^2)$$

If matching is performed in break groups sequentially, the total computation time is

$$T \approx t \times M \times N^2/(2 \times B)$$

We can conclude that the number of comparisons is inversely proportional to the number of break groups. Moreover, we can further improve total match time using parallel processing platforms and database systems. The break group algorithm supports software- and hardware-based parallelism since matching within each of the break groups does not depend upon matching in all other break groups.

Let's define the optimum configuration for the break groups. Let's assume that out of M critical attributes used for matching, some attributes are more important than others. From the matching-engine configuration perspective, this means that higher weights were assigned to these attributes than to other attributes. In this case, we can select a small subset of the most important attributes $K \ll M$ so that any two records cannot possibly match if none of the K attributes match. We will also assume that since the selected K attributes are so important, at least one of the K attributes must contain a value; otherwise, the record does not meet minimum data requirements and will be excluded from the matching process. We can define a break group on the K attributes as follows: Any two records belong to the same break group if and only if they have a match on at least one attribute of the K selected attributes. From the performance perspective, it is important to realize that the number of break groups defined this way is high, which is caused by high cardinality of the values in the selected K fields.

To illustrate these points, assume that $K = 3$ and the three selected attributes are the credit card number, full name, and the phone number. The data is loaded from multiple systems and not all of the three attribute values are available for each record. However, at least one of the three attributes must have a value to meet the minimum data requirements. The number of break groups B defined this way is very high, and the match engine should be able to perform the first pass of the match process to assign break group keys based on simplified matching conditions that include only the selected K fields. The second pass will be performed within a large number B of break groups.

We can now summarize the findings of this section as follows:

▶   For a multimillion-record dataset, a matching process can achieve a reasonably good performance if it can identify break groups with high cardinality, i.e. the number of break groups is high and the average number of records in each group is low.

▶   The matching engine should be selected with the break-group matching capability in mind.

▶   The matching engine should be able to support hardware- and software-based parallel processing to perform matching within break groups in parallel.

Similarity Libraries and Fuzzy Logic for Attribute Comparisons

Individuals use different names such as legal names, aliases, nicknames, etc. The matching algorithm should take into account the connections between names like "Bill" and "William" or "Larry" and "Lawrence." Name alias libraries that are based on human knowledge must be built and made available to the matching engine to link this type of string values. Such a library should maintain only commonly used names. Otherwise, if unusual aliases are in the library, the probability of overmatching increases. For instance, if John Michael Smith wants to use an alias JM, such an alias should not be placed in the library.

A similar problem exists for addresses. It is not unusual for multiple small towns to be served by one postal office. In this case the town names can be used interchangeably. The mail will be delivered anyway. From the CDI perspective this means that two town aliases can be used for a given address. A similar condition exists for street names. This situation is known as vanity addresses. For example, a 5th Avenue address in Manhattan sounds better than 86th Street, and Lincoln Center sounds more prestigious than West 66th Street, etc. Such vanity addresses are used as aliases for locations that are close but not exactly on the street, or locations that sound prestigious and expensive. As in the name libraries, address-alias libraries based on human knowledge must be built to link this type of string values. The National Change of Address (NCOA) database is a good example where additional libraries should be used to achieve good matching results.

Similarity libraries cannot resolve the matching problems when the names or addresses are misspelled. Phonetic conversion algorithms (many of them based on fuzzy logic) are used in this case. Typically, fuzzy logic is required when comparing names, addresses, and other textual attributes. This type of comparison is one of the greatest CDI challenges. The fuzzy logic algorithms provide inexact match comparisons. SOUNDEX is the most widely known phonetic algorithm, developed in the beginning of the twentieth century. There are many modifications of this algorithm. They convert character strings into digital codes in such a way that phonetically similar strings acquire the same code values. It is included in many libraries of standard string-comparison functions.

NYSIIS is another phonetic algorithm, which was developed in 1970. The acronym NYSIIS stands for "New York State Identification and Intelligence." This algorithm is said to improve SOUNDEX matching capabilities by 2.7 percent. For details please refer to the web site of the National Institute of Standards and Technology: http://www.nist.gov/dads/HTML/nysiis.html.

A more recent sophisticated inexact string comparison algorithm known as Bipartite Graph Matching (BGM) is based on mathematical modeling that simulates the human notion of similarity. We will touch on BGM in vendor products in Chapter 17 of this book again.

Summary of Data-Matching Requirements and Solutions

Let us summarize key considerations that should be used to evaluate data-matching solutions and engines. This summary can be also used as a decision-making check list for CDI designers and product evaluators. As a base we will use the list originally published by Initiate Systems (2004) in the white paper titled: "Initiate Customer Data Integration and Customer Data Matching: Achieving a 360-Degree Customer View" and make some changes and additions that come from our implementation experience.

- ▶ Accuracy and key characteristics of matching algorithm:
  - ▶ Support probabilistic and/or deterministic matching algorithms.
  - ▶ Support for history of attribute changes as they relate to matching.
  - ▶ Support for single and/or dual threshold capabilities.

- ▶ Support for a "human similarity" match that utilizes learning algorithms. Instead of defining matching rules explicitly, which sometimes is not easy, the end users do manual matching on a "training" set. The matching engine mines the rules and provides a "human similarity" match.
- ▶ Ability to use National Change of Address and other event-based matching capabilities.

- ▶ Batch load
  - ▶ Support for initial load with required performance
  - ▶ Implementation of chaining scenarios and how the scenarios affect performance
  - ▶ Scalability: time of processing as a function of the number of records
- ▶ Real time
  - ▶ Real-time processing for new customer records and record updates, merges, splits, etc.
  - ▶ Implementation of chaining scenarios in real time
- ▶ Architecture
  - ▶ Integration with web services and SOA
  - ▶ Data exchange solution architecture between the matching engine and the primary database
  - ▶ Platforms supported: operating systems and databases
  - ▶ Support for parallel processing
  - ▶ Openness of solution parameters for integration and iterative improvements
- ▶ Flexibility of configuration and customization
  - ▶ Matching parameters supported
  - ▶ Solution customization; languages supported, if any
- ▶ Merge and split (these points are discussed in more detail in Chapter 13)
  - ▶ Support for data merge data survivorship rules
  - ▶ Support for symmetric split
  - ▶ Support for asymmetric spit
- ▶ Solution change control
  - ▶ Solution change-control capabilities are important to support the history of configuration changes. It is important in some cases to review what configuration was used at some point in the past.

► Operational complexity

    ► Matching file preparation

    ► Match/merge configuration setup

    ► Creation of the matching dataset

► Reporting

    ► Change configuration reporting

    ► Reporting in support of operational processing

► Error processing

    ► Automatic error processing

    ► Support for manual entry to resolve errors and conditions when the algorithm cannot resolve matching

► Ability to work with country-specific plug-ins for data match including name and address aliases, phonetic and string similarity algorithms, transliteration problems, and differences in the character codes

    ► Two different competing approaches can be used here. The first approach assumes that name and address standardization is performed first. Then a match is executed against persistently stored standardized names and addresses and other attributes participating in the match process. This approach is most common. It generates standardized names and addresses that are beneficial for other purposes beyond matching. There is a second school of thought. It suggests that a higher match accuracy can be achieved if the record is matched as is with all fuzziness and library issues resolved dynamically in a holistic manner for all attributes participating in the matching process.

To sum up, this chapter discusses key issues and approaches associated with customer identification and matching. This topic is one of the core requirements and benefits of any MDM-CDI project and has profound implications for the way business processes and applications are affected by a new authoritative system of record created and managed by an MDM-CDI Data Hub.

Beyond Party Match: Merge, Split, Party Groups, and Relationships

IN THIS CHAPTER

Merge and Split

Relationships and Groups

Merge and Split

The previous chapter provided an in-depth discussion of how a CDI solution enables customer identification using various attribute- and record-level matching techniques. We continue this discussion by taking a closer look at the complementary operations of record merge and split.

Merge

Chapter 12 showed how to match records and link them into match groups or clusters of affinity. Figure 13-1 illustrates how a match and link process can uniquely identify a Match Group 100.

Matching and linking operations represent a critical step in customer identification, but as the example in Figure 13-1 illustrates, the records describing the individual contain some contradictions. For example, it is unclear what name, residential address, SSN etc. represent the "right" data about the individual. The CDI Data Hub has to solve this problem and decide what attributes should "survive" when the Hub *merges* records in the match group in order to create a single customer record that represents a 360-degree view of the individual, including a complete and accurate net-worth of the customer.

In general terms, a successful and flexible approach to merging match group records calls for the development and implementation of a hybrid automatic and manual, user-guided process. This process should allow the user to select the correct attribute values for the individual, where the "correctness" is typically determined by a human operator familiar with the individual, or a systemic, automated process that can make this determination based on additional information. Such information may include individual preferences captured via a service channel, or reference information acquired from a trusted external data provider, e.g., National Change of Address [NCOA]. In the latter case, a CDI system can assist the user to make the right decision by providing some default merge recommendations that can then be validated or overridden by the end user. The attribute survivorship decisions can be driven by simple rules or arbitrary complex business logic. For example,

Full Name	Address	SSN	Match Group
Thomas Wilson	67 Main Street. Ocean View, CA 19765	123-456-7890	100
Tom Wilson	61 Main St. Ocean View, CA 19765	123-456-7890	100

Figure 13-1   *Linked records—candidates for merge*

Entity Name	Field Name	Survivorship Rule
Individual	Individual Name	Is to be sourced from system "A" provided that the value in system "A" is not blank. Otherwise use the value from system "B"
Individual	Individual Date of Birth	Is to be sourced from system "A" if the individual is an active or former client. For prospective clients the attribute value should be sourced from system "C". If systems "A" and "C" do not provide valid attribute values or the values are blank, the attribute value should be sourced from system "B" or system "D". If both systems contain valid data, the latest assigned value should prevail.

Figure 13-2   *A template defining attribute survivorship rules*

survivorship of a particular attribute can be based on the source systems that hold the record, the value the record displays, the end user who entered the attribute value, and other factors. This indicates that the CDI Data Hub solution must maintain attribute-level data about the record's source, time stamp of creation and modification, and certain user information including user role and other identity attributes (often referred to as user credentials). Figure 13-2 shows a sample spreadsheet that can be used as a template for specifying default survivorship rules.

A pragmatic approach to developing merge capabilities for CDI Data Hub solutions states that each survivorship candidate attribute should be defined and uniquely identified in the Data Hub's logical data model. If the project requirements call for the creation of a persistent merge history, we can extend the Hub data model by creating a history entity as shown in Figure 13-3.

This model supports the notion of inheritance of records merged from the same system or multiple legacy sources.

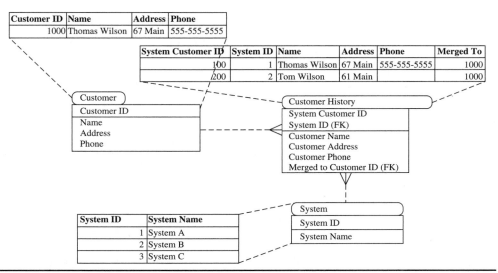

Figure 13-3   *A model supporting merge history*

If two records are merged, the new "golden" record is created. The "golden" record may or may not inherit CUSTOMER_ID from one of the existing records. The attribute MERGED_TO_CUSTOMER_ID in the Customer History table points to the record created as a result of the merge in the table Customer (where the MERGED_TO value is equal to 1000).

As we have noted before, creation and maintenance of a high-confidence "golden" party record requires user input. The technology organization supporting the CDI project should develop a user-friendly interface that allows end users to create customer record groupings, display the duplicates, and choose the attribute values for the "golden" record.

Merge operations can be rather complex and impact other systems that are using or are used by the Data Hub. The changes in the data content that result from performing a merge operation should be propagated to other systems in order to synchronize their data content with the Data Hub as the master record. Additional complexity of the merge may be caused by the need to merge relationships, agreements, and other documents that have been tied to two or more separate party records before the merge.

Split

A *split* is a CDI process that is functionally opposite to a merge. A split is required if information gathered from two or more parties has been mistakenly stored in a single party record. Figure 13-4 displays an example in which a record that was thought to represent one individual, Bill Johns, in reality represents two individuals, Bill Johns, Sr. and his son Bill Johns, Jr., with different dates of birth.

Party ID	Name	Address	Phone Number	Gender	Date of Birth
100	Bill Johns	467 Mercer Street. Ocean View, CA 19765	(818) 456-7890	M	Unknown

Split

Party ID	Name	Address	Phone Number	Gender	Date of Birth
100	Bill Johns, Sr	467 Mercer Street. Ocean View, CA 19765	(818) 456-7890	M	04/25/1954
110	Bill Johns, Jr	467 Mercer Street. Ocean View, CA 19765	(818) 456-7890	M	09/25/1992

Figure 13-4 *An example of a split*

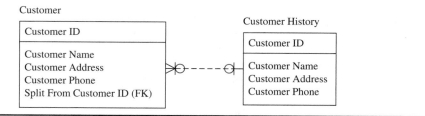

Figure 13-5 *A logical data model representing party split*

Procedurally, the split would reverse a merge operation provided that the appropriate information to perform the split becomes available after the merge is done.

In this example, as soon as the mistake of the merge decision has been discovered, a corrective action is taken. Typically, this is a manual action that requires input of additional information. In the example shown in Figure 13-4, Bill Johns, Sr. retains the Party ID (100) while a new Party ID (110) is created for Bill Johns, Jr. Project's technology team should plan on providing a user-friendly interface that allows the business user to perform the split process. Similarly, in order to merge, if the project requirements include split history support, we can further extend our CDI logical data model as shown in Figure 13-5. If documents, relationships, and other information had been tied to a party record before the split, all pieces of this information must be distributed between the records formed as a result of the split. This adds to the complexity of splits.

Implementation note: As described in the Merge and Split sections above, the project team should plan for an additional modeling effort if the business functional requirements include support for merge and split within a single model.

Relationships and Groups

While solving customer and party identification problems is key to creating any CDI solution, it is not the end of the road for a CDI project. Indeed, the newly created CDI Data Hub contains the superset of parties from multiple source systems. Some of the parties are current customers while others are still prospects or past customers who terminated their relationships with the firm for any number of reasons. Moreover, some of the parties may not be customers but are important to the organization since they are related to the current customers or provide some service to them. For example, a CDI Data Hub may contain information about spouses and children named as beneficiaries on customer accounts, trustees of the customer, or powerful and influential individuals who are designated as having power of attorney for some customers.

These relationships may represent a very attractive opportunity to the enterprise that is looking to increase its customer base and grow the share of its customers' wallets. In order to take advantage of this opportunity a CDI Data Hub has to support the notion of explicit and implied party relationships and party groups. Specific requirements to support these features as well as their implementation priorities depend on the industry, line of business, and specific needs of the business as defined in the business scope documentation for the project. Thus, we limit the discussion on these topics to a generic overview of the issues, concerns, and approaches to solve the party relationship and grouping challenge.

Direct Business Relationships with an Individual

We will use an example of financial services that include brokerage, banking, and insurance to explain the notion of direct relationships. In the case of financial services, a relationship with an individual begins when the individual becomes a prospect (potential customer). Depending on the channel used, a financial services enterprise would create a record for this individual that points to a new relationship between the enterprise and the individual. Depending on the architecture style of the CDI Data Hub, this party record for the individual is created either in the Hub or in one of the source systems. If the sales process was successful (for example, the individual decides to open one or more accounts with the firm), the prospect becomes a customer. Depending on the individual situation and set of preferences, this newly created customer may have different roles on his or her accounts. In the example shown in Figure 13-6, John S. Smith is in the role of "Primary" on account 4736922239.

The attribute "Date Closed" in the Account table is blank, which identifies John Smith as an active existing customer. When the account is closed, this attribute is updated with the event date. If this happens with all of John's accounts, he assumes the role of a "Former Customer."

Another type of direct relationship between an individual and organization is an agreement according to which the individual provides services to some of the customers or works with prospects. The individuals can be employees of the firm or work on a contractual basis (for example, consider external consultants that provide some very specialized services, such as jumbo insurance policies, to a small group of enterprise customers). The individuals responsible for servicing accounts or interacting directly with customers or prospects can also be customers or prospects of the same enterprise, which means that depending on the functions/services they perform, the individuals can have multiple roles and relationships with the enterprise.

Relationship Between Two Individuals

When dealing with individual customers and prospects, the enterprise needs to know the potential and actual "value" of the individual and his or her specific assets along with the roles the individual plays on the assets. To provide an effective personalized customer service, the enterprise needs to be able to recognize all of the individual's assets managed by the firm across lines of business. This goal can be achieved when the CDI Data Hub solves the party identification problem. As a result, the enterprise

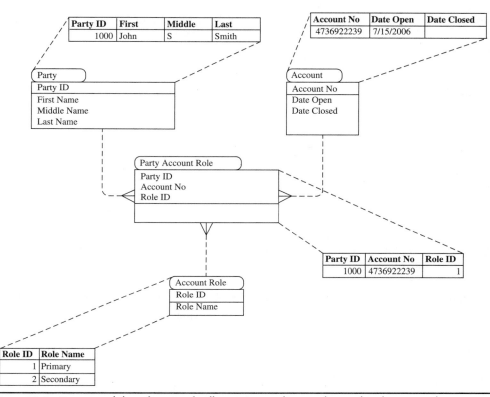

Figure 13-6 *Data model and example illustrating a direct relationship between the enterprise and individual*

gains a clear view of its direct customers. The missing component of the equation is to assess the relationships between customers, and particularly high-value customers. The fragment of a data model shown in Figure 13-7 represents a structure that can be used to support *symmetric* relationships between individuals, e.g. siblings, spouses, partners in business, etc.

Figure 13-7 illustrates the relationship between John Smith and Mary Smith. Relationship ID = 1 points to "Spouse" for the relationship between John and Mary with Party IDs equal to 1000 and 1100 respectively.

We can also use the example of John and Mary to illustrate *asymmetric* relationships. If, for example, Mary is a high-value customer and John has no accounts with the firm, the enterprise will be able to recognize John only as an "indirect" customer through his relationship with Mary. The relationships that can be supported by the data structure shown in Figure 13-7 are limited to symmetric relationships where the result will not change if the columns in the table "Individual to Individual Relationship" are swapped. Indeed, if "John is Mary's spouse" is a valid statement, the reverse statement is valid too: "Mary is John's spouse."

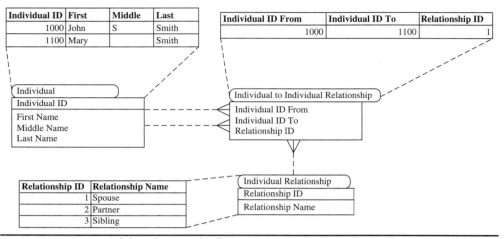

Individual ID	First	Middle	Last
1000	John	S	Smith
1100	Mary		Smith

Individual ID From	Individual ID To	Relationship ID
1000	1100	1

Individual
- Individual ID
- First Name
- Middle Name
- Last Name

Individual to Individual Relationship
- Individual ID From
- Individual ID To
- Relationship ID

Relationship ID	Relationship Name
1	Spouse
2	Partner
3	Sibling

Individual Relationship
- Relationship ID
- Relationship Name

Figure 13-7 *Data model and example illustrating a symmetric relationship between two individuals*

Such symmetry does not hold for other types of relationships, e.g. parent/child relationships or service provider/customer relationship. To support these relationship types, the two columns "Individual ID" in the table "Individual to Individual Relationship" should be changed to "Individual ID From" and "Individual ID To" to create an asymmetric relationship. This transformation is shown in Figure 13-8 where Larry Smith is John Smith's father and Tom Logan is John's accountant.

Households and Family Groups

CDI capabilities that support the discovery of customer relationships should include the ability to recognize customers' Households or Family Groups. Indeed, the members of these entities may or may not be direct customers at present, but certainly represent an opportunity for the enterprise to convert them into direct customers. The term *Family Group* is used to denote a group of individuals or business partners that should be considered as a Customer from the firm's relationship perspective. The term *Household* is typically limited to the family members residing at the same address. If the CDI Data Hub can recognize Households and Family Groups, the enterprise can offer customized products and services to the group's members proactively even before they are recognized as high-value individual customers. Understanding these relationships provides the enterprise with a competitive advantage and opportunity to improve overall customer experience, strengthen customer relationships, and reduce customer attrition.

Recognizing the totality of customer relationships allows organizations to create cross-sell and up-sell opportunities and increase the share of wallet within each Household and a Family Group. The association between individuals and households is

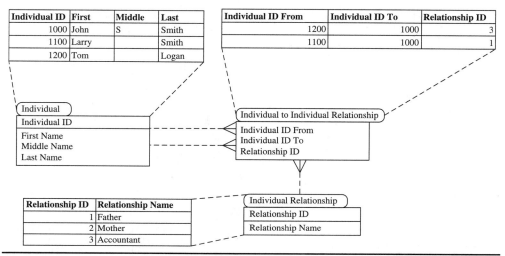

Individual ID	First	Middle	Last
1000	John	S	Smith
1100	Larry		Smith
1200	Tom		Logan

Individual ID From	Individual ID To	Relationship ID
1200	1000	3
1100	1000	1

Individual
Individual ID
First Name
Middle Name
Last Name

Individual to Individual Relationship
Individual ID From
Individual ID To
Relationship ID

Relationship ID	Relationship Name
1	Father
2	Mother
3	Accountant

Individual Relationship
Relationship ID
Relationship Name

Figure 13-8 *Data model and example illustrating an asymmetric relationship between two individuals*

depicted in Figure 13-9. The Household/Family Group structure shown in Figure 13-9 is limited in that one individual cannot cross Households/Family Groups.

Customer Groups

The notion of a *Customer Group* avoids the single-group limitation by defining a structure in which an individual can belong to multiple groups. For example, a group of individuals having a common interest can open an account and by doing so establishes a direct relationship with the enterprise, with the Customer Group playing the role of a customer. A Customer Group can be formal (i.e., includes businesses, organizations, legal entities, and associations that have a legal status and are recognized as legal entities), or informal. Figure 13-10 illustrates the notion of a Customer Group.

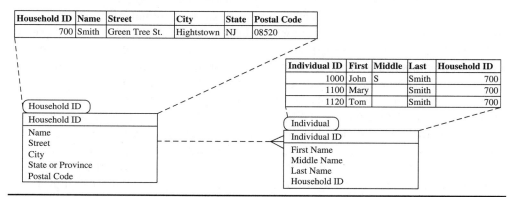

Household ID	Name	Street	City	State	Postal Code
700	Smith	Green Tree St.	Hightstown	NJ	08520

Individual ID	First	Middle	Last	Household ID
1000	John	S	Smith	700
1100	Mary		Smith	700
1120	Tom		Smith	700

Household ID
Household ID
Name
Street
City
State or Province
Postal Code

Individual
Individual ID
First Name
Middle Name
Last Name
Household ID

Figure 13-9 *Data model and example illustrating the concept of Household or Family Group*

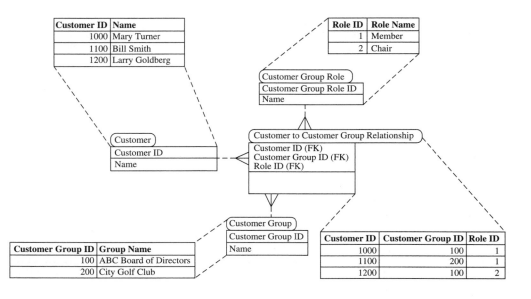

Figure 13-10 *Data model and example illustrating the concept of a Customer Group*

It follows from the example in Figure 13-10 that Mary Turner and Larry Goldberg serve on the "ABC Board of Directors," Larry as the "Chair" and Mary as a "Member."

Relationships Between Institutional Customers and Individuals

The Basel Committee and other regulatory bodies require that corporations, shareholders, signatories, and other decision-making individuals and groups in positions of power and control be identifiable with the required degree of reliability. These requirements have direct implications on how a Data Hub should recognize individuals who represent institutions and act on their behalf. The recognition challenge in this case is complicated by the fact that institutional customers may use the identification attributes provided to them by their institution. For example, a trader working for a major brokerage house may be identified by his or her exchange registration number rather than by name and social security number. When such an institutional customer interacts with the enterprise on his or her firm's behalf, the enterprise must recognize these types of relationships and the role the individual and the firm can assume in the relationships. This is a difficult problem that can be addressed differently depending on the set of business rules and allowed roles that vary from industry to industry and from one institution type to another. For example, the roles and rules may depend on whether the corporation represented by an individual is listed on a recognized stock exchange. In general, these complex relationships can be maintained by the structure shown in Figure 13-11.

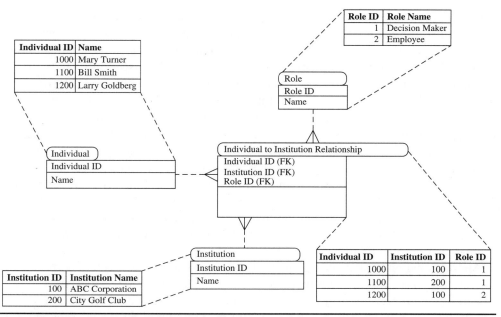

Figure 13-11   *Data model and example illustrating relationships between institutional customers and individuals*

In the preceding example, Mary Turner and Larry Goldberg work for ABC Corporation. Mary's role is "Decision Maker" (could be CEO, CFO, etc.) while Larry is an employee.

Relationships Between Institutional Customers

Dealing with institutional customers and their relationships is extremely challenging. In addition to the data quality and clerical issues common to both individual and institutional customers, there is frequently a lack of solid definition of what constitutes an institutional customer. This is particularly true in cases where a firm has multiple relationships with the institutions represented by various individuals. In this case, the firm may have multiple customers with the same customer tax identifier. This indicates that the tax identification number may not be granular enough to uniquely identify the customers. Separate customer relationships can exist with different customer corporations, lines of business, geographic locations, divisions, and departments. In this case, the notion of customer relationship can become very uncertain and depends on how the customer account managers wish to define the customer. Different units within the organization may have different granularity needs for customer relationship definition. Moreover, when dealing with large institutional customers CDI solutions face additional challenges that result from merger and acquisition activities. For example, corporations, their business units, and their lines of business may change names as a result of mergers and acquisitions, rebranding, internal reorganizations, etc. The relationships between parent companies and their subsidiaries are also unstable. The same applies to the organizational hierarchies of institutional customers and consequently, to their relationships with the enterprise. Institutional customers may require different customer definitions for the same customer depending on the line of business, a channel, or other conditions. For example, a business unit responsible for shipping is likely to identify customers by a mailing label that includes the name of organization and its address. From the sales organization's perspective, each customer relationship is identified through the relationship's contacts. As the result, institutional relationships require more complex and at the same time, more flexible data models than those built for the individual customers. Of course, we recognize that in general, the number of institutional customers is much smaller than the number of individual customers, and that fact helps Data Hub systems to effectively manage institutional relationships.

Another challenge presented by institutional customers is the need to correlate customer records in order to remediate customer hierarchy data. Often, data describing the hierarchy of institutional customers is perceived to be incorrect, incomplete, and unreliable. Incorrect institutional customer hierarchy data can negatively affect the enterprise in multiple ways. For financial services companies that deal with the institutional customer (e.g., investment banks), incorrect customer hierarchy data may cause failures in trading, erroneous financial reporting, lost marketing opportunities, failure in Anti-Money Laundering (AML) and Know Your Customer (KYC) processing, and other business and regulatory issues. This challenge is rapidly coming to the forefront of business concerns for any enterprise that supports institutional customers, and many MDM-CDI solutions are being developed or modified today to address this concern.

To illustrate the problem in its simplest form, consider an institutional hierarchy where each node is the root with no parents or a leaf that can have only one parent. Figure 13-12 illustrates this situation by showing two institutions, B and C, that are in fact the subsidiaries of institution A.

However, if we apply a customer-level matching process, it may identify B and C as likely to be the same institutional customer whose name was changed or misspelled. This happens because the institutional customer hierarchy and the associated relationship data represent a new piece of information never used by the matching process. In principle, this problem can be addressed in one of two ways: modifying the matching process to include hierarchy-based relationship data, or changing the relationship hierarchy traversal to leverage the results of the matching process.

In either situation, an MDM-CDI system should be extended to accommodate additional business rules and workflow semantics that can handle institutional

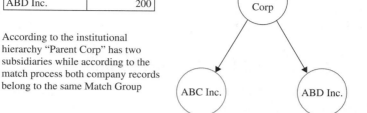

Institution Name	Match Group
ABC Inc.	200
ABD Inc.	200

According to the institutional hierarchy "Parent Corp" has two subsidiaries while according to the match process both company records belong to the same Match Group

Figure 13-12 *A simple institutional hierarchy that conflicts with institutional customer identification*

customer hierarchies. Then the modified MDM-CDI system will be able to identify, profile, quantify, and remediate errors in matching and institutional hierarchy data by mapping hierarchy nodes to integrated customer entities.

Need for Persistent Match Group Identifier

Match Groups may or may not have to be persisted. If a match engine is used to find potential matches to one or a few party records, it is not necessary to persist a match group even though such persistence may be beneficial from the search performance perspective. There are maintenance cost trade-offs in implementing this. As soon as we persist something that can change, we have to capture and manage the change, which is a complex task. Indeed, match groups can change if critical match attributes change. This can trigger a chain of events within and outside the matching process. What if legal documents have already been tagged by the match group identifiers? Can we allow a systemic change of the identifier? The answer is most likely negative.

Generally speaking, match group identifiers should be persisted and thoroughly managed when the records representing individuals and/or organizations are linked to other entities. Creation and maintenance of relationships and hierarchies are typical situations that require the match group identifier to be persisted.

There are scenarios where the match group identifiers do not need to be persisted. For instance, if a match process is used only to eliminate duplicates and create merged records that will be used for a stand-alone marketing campaign, the goal can be achieved without storing and therefore managing the match group identifiers. Another typical scenario occurs when the matching process is only used for computer-assisted manual data de-duping. In some situations with very conservative requirements for match and merge, only the end users can provide the ultimate match, link, and merge decisions. In these situations the Match Group identifier is not equal to the "golden copy" Party ID, but is treated as an intermediate attribute assisting the end user with customer identification key assignment.

Even though some specific needs may not require generation and storage of the match group identifiers, the general intent to create and maintain a single unique "golden copy" of the Party ID across the enterprise is a good idea that aligns the Data hub design with the strategic intent of Customer Data Integration.

Additional Considerations for Customer Identifiers

Whether you operate in an account-centric enterprise and are planning for a transition to a customer-centric enterprise, or a transition to a customer-centric business is already under way, the majority of data access requests still rely on the account numbers for inquiries, updates, deletes, and other operations. It probably makes no sense to try to get rid of account numbers as entity identifiers and a communication exchange vehicle that all participants are familiar with and clearly understand.

So what will happen when the migration to the customer-centric view is complete? Would it be a good idea to maintain account numbers and associated entities in the customer-centric world? So far, we presented the customer identifier solely as a technical artifact, a key generated, maintained, and used by the system with no exposure to the end user. Depending on a given project's requirements this may continue to be the case. Alternatively, the customer identifier may be exposed to end-user applications and users may be trained to use the customer identifier in addition to or in conjunction with the traditional account number in order to search for customer groups, family groups, relationships, customer agreements, and other related entities. If the business requirements specifically ask for customer identifiers to be exposed to end-user applications, then the project team needs to carefully plan and design the rules for generating and using customer identifiers prior to the first Data Hub deployment.

Here are some considerations related to the generation of customer identifiers:

▶ The key must be unique. This sounds obvious but we do not want to miss this critical requirement here.

▶ The key should have a check digit or other data integrity check rule so that the validity of the key can be confirmed.

▶ We do not recommend defining key ranges unless there are very compelling reasons such as established business processes and inflexible technology infrastructure.

▶ Generally speaking, use of intelligent keys is not a good practice because it limits the solution's flexibility and adaptability to changing business conditions.

▶ The key length should be sufficient to provide unique identification for all customer entities in the Customer Data Hub.

A customer identifier that conforms to the technical requirements in this list is referred to as a *well-formed identifier*, and is a primary vehicle that enables customer identification.

To reiterate, customer identification is one of the primary functional requirements for any CDI Data Hub solution. As the scope of customer data managed by the CDI Data Hub increases over time, the requirement to create and maintain well-formed identifiers may be extended to include relationships, family groups, and other attributes that are selected to act as enablers of the enterprise-wide customer-centric transformation.

CHAPTER

14

Data Governance, Standards, Information Quality, and Validation

IN THIS CHAPTER
Overview of Data Governance, Standards, and Information Quality

Information Quality

Overview of Data Governance, Standards, and Information Quality

Data governance is a process focused on managing the quality, consistency, usability, security, availability, and ownership of information. Government organizations and private sector businesses are strongly impacted by gaps in data governance. Over the last decade, recognition of the importance of enterprise data governance grew considerably. Indeed, information systems cannot be properly integrated, deployed, and managed without sound data governance solutions no matter what technology they use. Accordingly, Master Data Management and Customer Data Integration solutions cannot be implemented and operated correctly without having strong data governance strategy and processes.

The key objective of data governance is to create a framework aimed at continuous data quality measurement and improvement. This framework includes organizational structures, policies, processes, procedures, metadata management and administration, and business rules affecting data quality. As soon as the data governance framework is established, data stewards must assume accountability for corporate data and manage it as a most valuable corporate asset (we started the discussion of data governance and data stewardship in Chapter 6).

Data governance does not just happen, nor can it be delivered as an afterthought. It requires organizational structure and commitment. Specifically, an organization has to set up a dedicated group that would work in close cooperation with business, operations, and technology groups. To reflect the group's functional role in the data governance process we will call it an Enterprise Information Governance Group (EIGG), although different organizations may choose different names for such a group. The responsibility of the EIGG should be to establish, maintain, and oversee policies, procedures, and standards governing information management, quality, visibility, security, and availability of data within the enterprise. Policies and procedures developed by the EIGG must be reviewed frequently to ensure compliance with changing regulations. All changes to the policies and procedures must be reported and distributed to all stakeholders.

The EIGG must work closely with the technology organization in defining a service-level agreement that determines system performance, access controls, information latency, downtime window requirements, reference code definitions, etc. The EIGG should have a strong and holistic understanding of business operations and processes, especially the business processes that require improvements.

The discussion that follows is focused on providing a comprehensive description of the EIGG role and functions. This discussion is structured in the context of the data governance tasks that are critical to the success of any MDM-CDI project. The EIGG group is one of the key stakeholders of the CDI project, and therefore should take a lead in addressing certain data integration concerns. The EIGG engagement model should include both direct task ownership and joint responsibility on the tasks that are led by the technology organization.

One of the data governance responsibilities is the need to define information management standards. This activity should be performed in close collaboration with the technology team, and its output should be closely aligned with the technical standards that are adopted by the enterprise. The data governance standards must be established either before the project start or early in the CDI project life cycle. The EIGG team should have a clear understanding of the following domains of standards:

▶ Naming conventions for files, database and XML schemas, entities, attributes, tables, fields, message formats, etc.

▶ Messaging protocols and SOA-specific standards including business- and technical-level service definitions

▶ Standards for developing data models, process models, class models, etc. (UML, EMF, and others)

▶ Data access standards (SQL, JDBC, ODBC, etc.)

▶ Transactional integrity standards, e.g., XA protocol for distributed transaction processing

▶ Standards for application forms

EIGG should own or oversee the policies around standards that are to be used for Master Data Management implementation including the following:

▶ Established or emerging international and national standards, e.g., World Wide Web Consortium (W3C) standards and Organization for the Advancement of Structures Information Systems (OASIS) standards including XCRL for customer relationship data.

▶ Established or emerging industry-specific standards, e.g., Health Level Seven (HL7) for the health care industry; AMQ (open source messaging standard for the financial industry), ACORD, eEG7 (Europe), IAA XML, CSIO XML, Polaris, Instep (UK) for Insurance; XBRL for financial reporting, MDDL for market data definitions, RIXML for investment and financial research; FpML for financial derivatives; OTA and HTNG standards, which are used by the hospitality industry; and other standards relevant to the core business of the enterprise.

▶ Internal enterprise standards; ideally, internal standards should fill the gaps left by the national, international, or de-facto industry standards, but should be closely aligned with those standards for obvious reasons. Exceptions to this approach should be kept to a bare minimum, and the reasons for this deviation from standards directions should be documented and the implications of these decisions must be clearly understood by the project team.

Code semantics for reference data, also known as *indicative data*, is another important area that must be clearly and proactively defined by the EIGG. The gender codes represent a well-known and frequently cited example illustrating the code semantics issue. System A uses numeric gender codes 1 for Male and 2 for Female while system B utilizes codes "M" and "F" respectively. Inconsistent codes for departments, branches, or divisions also exemplify codes that are frequently inconsistent across the enterprise. This inconsistency may have been accumulated over the decades of multiple generations of technology development, as well as the result of several mergers and acquisitions of companies with different and highly heterogeneous technology solutions.

Regardless of the source of this semantic inconsistency, the EIGG should define and establish enterprise-wide standards for code semantics. The data structure that can be used to maintain consistent code semantics is shown in Figure 14-1.

A part of the semantic inconsistency problem lies in the different degrees of granularity of the code that is defined in different systems. To address this issue, we introduce a new attribute called SEQUENCE_NO that can support a scenario where the granularity of the system code is higher than that defined by the enterprise. Generally speaking, if the enterprise translation codes are defined at the most granular level that accommodates all systems in scope, the issue is resolved.

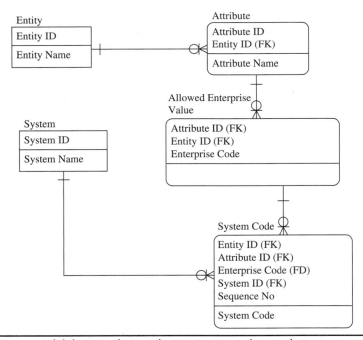

Figure 14-1 *Data model that can be used to maintain code translations*

On the other hand, if a system ABC utilizes codes that are more granular than those defined at the enterprise level, a single code at the enterprise level corresponds to multiple codes in system ABC. For example, location codes for the enterprise may be defined at the state level while the system ABC's location codes are defined at the town or city level. In this case, the data can be easily transformed to the enterprise coding level (Baltimore, MD becomes MD). But the reverse translation becomes a problem. If the location changed from MD to NY, the town or city information would be unknown and there will be a problem with propagating this change to the source system. It is the responsibility of the EIGG to address the issue of incompatible levels of code granularity. Working jointly with the technology organization, EIGG can help define a set of Code Translation services that encapsulate and translate internal reference codes into the enterprise standard code for data interchange with other enterprise systems.

As the keeper of the data governance strategy, the EIGG should own and/or co-own the following areas:

▶ Creation and review of information quality metrics, standards, and procedures that support data stewardship and measurement, enforcement, and resolution of information quality issues.

▶ Definition and maintenance of the logical data model of the MDM-CDI solution.

▶ Definition, maintenance, and proper documentation of source systems, data elements, and other conditions in scope for the MDM-CDI project.

▶ Proper distribution of data governance documentation.

▶ Establishment of procedures that would allow all stakeholders to actively participate in data governance processes and agree or disagree with particular approaches and directions.

▶ Definition of acceptable levels of granularity and rules around CDI Data Hub's data aggregation including merge, split, and customer grouping.

▶ A strategy for well-formed customer identification (see discussion on this topic in Chapter 13).

▶ Rules defining what changes to the customer data can be made systemically as part of data cleansing and customer record de-duping. Specifically, the EIGG should determine conditions under which the CDI system should automatically change, merge, or possibly split customer records. As a practical rule of thumb, we can state that if customer data is used for legal and financial purposes, then using an automated approach to data changes, merges, and splits may force too many data synchronization and reconciliation activities. A risk mitigation strategy for data change management would be to limit systemic updates to a bare minimum.

▶ Definition of survivorship rules for data attributes. These rules should take into accounts such factors as the timing of data availability and trust across multiple systems. The term *racing conditions* is sometimes used to describe the timing perspective of attribute change. A racing condition may occur when changes to a given data attribute happen or become visible within a predefined time threshold in a source system and the Data Hub. In that case, the Hub should act as an arbiter to decide which change takes precedence and what changed content should survive in the persistent data store.

▶ Requirements for Data History and Change Log. This is a typical requirement for a CDI solution, and it may include a configurable change log facility that maintains a series of *before* and *after* images or just net changes to every record and possibly to every attribute, with an indication of what system or application the change came from and its time stamp. The history time interval should be a configurable feature of the Data Hub.

▶ Definition of data entry templates and data validation standards. EIGG should work with the technology team to define how to efficiently support data entry processes that can enforce certain domain constraints (e.g., ranges of allowed values). EIGG should help define data entry procedures that can automate both data entry and the exception processing.

▶ Definition of administrative interfaces and metadata structures. The EIGG should define user interface requirements that will be used to administer data-driven rules and parameters.

▶ Glossary of terms that are accepted by all participants.

▶ Sometimes EIGG should act as a super-user to define and modify data visibility rules. These rules specify which users can have access to what data records or data attributes, and under what conditions this access is allowed (please see Chapter 10 for an in-depth discussion on this subject). A typical example of a situation where rules of visibility have to be defined and enforced would be financial services companies, where access to some parts of the customer information depends on the role and other credentials of the users (such as brokers, financial advisors, benefit plan administrators, customer service representatives, insurance agents, etc.).

Of course, EIGG can be successful in handling these tasks only if its staff is well-trained and experienced in all of the aforementioned areas. That also implies that EIGG has a sufficient number of qualified resources to handle the multitude of tasks associated with large information management projects of the MDM-CDI class. Experience shows that not having a competent and actively participating data governance group (i.e., EIGG) often impacts CDI projects in a profoundly negative way.

Information Quality

Information quality is often considered synonymous with data quality; thus, we will use these two terms interchangeably.

Information quality issues exist in practically any enterprise even though some companies would not admit that they have data quality issues for fear of creating a negative public or customer perception and thus increasing reputation risk for the company.

The very first EIGG responsibility listed in the preceding section is its role in addressing information quality issues. As recommended by Larry English, it is important to create a "non-blame, non-judgment atmosphere" to facilitate candid information quality discussion and assessment, and this is clearly a major part of the EIGG mission.

According to Forrester Research, Inc., the information quality market is growing 17 percent annually and is expected to exceed $1B in 2008. It is not unusual to see data quality discussions on the agenda of board of directors and executive committee meetings. A decade ago, data quality was primarily the responsibility of information technology departments. Today, this responsibility is moving to data stewards and data governance groups—a clear indication of growing corporate recognition of the importance of information quality. The cost of not having standardized high-quality data may impact executive management strategy and performance, business operations, IT operations, and compliance. Poor information quality is one of the most common implementation risk factors that cause many corporate initiatives to fail. Master Data Management has further elevated the importance of information quality, and it is not unusual to see how new data quality activities come to life under the umbrella of an MDM-CDI project and then get expanded to include other enterprise initiatives. This growing need for better data quality has been recognized by the vendor community, which is delivering a variety of sophisticated stand-alone and integrated data quality tools (we discuss some of these tools in Chapter 17).

Information Quality in Master Data Management vs. Data Warehousing

When we discuss information quality in the context of Master Data Management and Customer Data Integration, we need to point out the difference between the scope of information quality in CDI systems and data warehousing environments. In data warehousing, the data is normally cleansed in the course of the extract, transform, and load (ETL) process, which sources data to build a well-defined data subject area or a data domain to serve a particular set of applications (e.g., a data warehouse of sales information, financial data warehouse, product data warehouse, etc). Master Data Management and Customer Data Integration, on the other hand, are focused on solving data quality concerns in an integrated fashion across the entire enterprise, and thus need to address data quality not just during data load activity but also in the process of matching and linking, identification and aggregation, and data synchronization and reconciliation.

For example, when the Data Hub is designed to be a "thin" layer that provides pointers to the source systems at the record and attribute level, the data quality issue is focused on maintaining accurate references as opposed to the actual data content.

Another difference in data quality processing between these two environments is in the way different input formats are reconciled by the target system (a Data Hub and a data warehouse). We illustrate these points in Figures 14-2 and 14-3, which show how the difference in data formats is handled by a data warehouse and a CDI system.

In Figure 14-2, the data warehouse is loaded from three legacy sources. Each of the data sources contains the attribute "Last Name." The data formats used in these systems specify field lengths of 30, 40, and 50 characters respectively. In the data warehousing solution, it is sufficient to have the length of the target attribute "Last Name" equal to 50 since the data flow is one-directional (from sources to the data warehouse as target). A Data Hub master scenario, shown in Figure 14-3, needs to support bidirectional data flows. The data created in the Data Hub should be propagated to other systems.

This will require that attribute properties such as length are consistently defined across all interconnected systems defined in the scope of the CDI project. Generalizing this example, we can conclude that MDM-CDI solutions that implement bidirectional data flows will require consistent data governance and data quality standards that span a large portion of the entire enterprise.

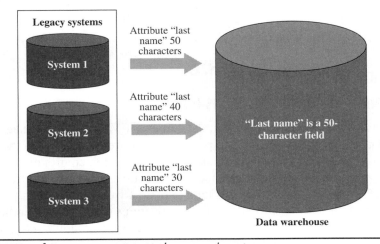

Figure 14-2 *Data format conversion in data warehousing*

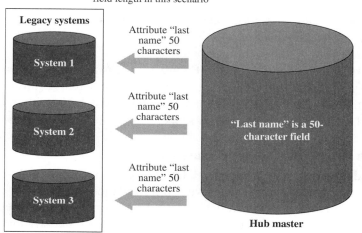

Figure 14-3 *Data type synchronization in CDI Hub Master scenario*

MDM-CDI implementations tend to enforce information quality rules as close to the point of data entering the Data Hub as technically possible. In the most simplistic case, this enforcement can be implemented by creating data entry validation at the user-interface and business-logic levels of data entry applications. This, of course, is not new, and such an approach is often used in any data entry situation, not just in CDI systems. This approach will not work at all if for a variety of business reasons some data quality controls can be overridden by a user; for example, if the user needs to enter a customer's telephone number as a mandatory field but the number is not available, the user then can bypass the data quality check by leaving the field empty or by entering some obviously invalid data such as 123-456-7890.

More sophisticated approaches rely on a metadata repository for data quality definitions, and on a variety of data quality measurement and improvement techniques that can analyze and correct missing, incorrect, and inconsistent data for a large number of specific data domains such as names, addresses, social security numbers, geographical or scientific references, etc. The biggest challenge in assessing and improving data quality problems is the challenge of semantic inconsistency. This is where the role of data governance and data quality standards that are overseen and enforced by qualified data stewards becomes a critical success factor in delivering high-quality, reliable master data for the enterprise.

Information Quality Loop and Interaction with the Match Process

One of the tasks of the EIGG is to provide guidance for defining the rules for the matching and linking process. Defining matching rules is a highly iterative process that requires continuous adjustments, tuning, testing, and evaluation of the results. As soon as the initial set of matching rules is defined, the technology team can implement the rules by configuring and/or customizing the matching tool of choice for the project. The data quality loop shown in Figure 14-4 describes the process in more detail.

An important term that we show in Figure 14-4 is *Data On-Boarding*. Data On-Boarding and System On-Boarding are a set of standards, requirements, and procedures that any external data and/or systems should comply with to be included in the MDM-CDI Data Hub integration scope.

Information Quality Deterioration Concerns

As we stated previously, the EIGG must define information quality metrics and control their changes over time. Otherwise, if information quality is not continually monitored and maintained, it will deteriorate. The deterioration rate depends on specifics of the industry and a given company's business processes and technology maturity, but a generally estimated deterioration rate of 2 percent per month is quite typical.

For systematic analysis of information quality as it relates to Master Data Management and Customer Data Integration, we recommend using some of the information quality characteristics defined in "IQ 101: Information Quality Principles & Processes: Foundations for Sustainable IQ" by Larry English:

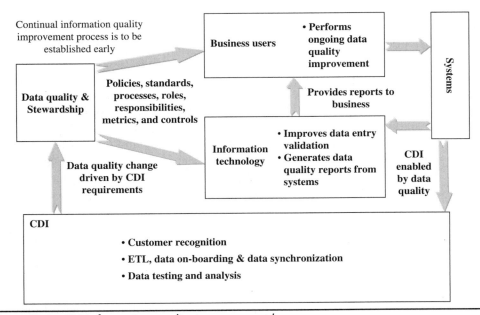

Figure 14-4 *CDI information quality improvement loop*

▶ **Completeness** Data profiling is an important step aimed at gaining understanding of completeness and other information quality statistics. This information is of particular importance for attributes that are going to be used as critical attributes for matching (see Chapter 12). Profiling is not a one-time exercise, and it should be performed on a regular basis. A data quality team or the EIGG should develop an attribute-sampling plan that defines profiling frequency, the attributes in scope of profiling, and possibly conditions that are to be profiled for each attribute. Depending on the role a given attribute plays in the matching process, the attribute sampling plan may define attribute-grain-level steps and tasks to ensure more frequent and complete sampling for most important attributes.

▶ **Validity** We will focus on data validation in the next section. This is another area where information quality approach must be carefully thought out.

▶ **Accuracy** It is difficult to provide specific recommendations on how to improve and maintain data accuracy. The methodology depends on business specifics and often includes interactions with customers and data domain subject matter experts to verify the accuracy of data.

▶ **Consistency** When the data is redundant and distributed across multiple systems, the data may become inconsistent. Data consistency checks should be included in the scope of profiling activity.

▶ **Nonduplication** This principle, if applied to a CDI Data Hub, would require a single record for each individual. As a rule, it is a valid principle and the right approach. However, there are a few situations where a company's business practices do not allow sharing of individual customers among different customer relationship managers. For example, this situation occurs when a customer opens two accounts with two different agents who are not allowed to see each other's books of business. In this case, the Data Hub would maintain two customer records, but each of these records would reflect a customer view known or visible to the specific agent; so technically speaking, the records are not equal, and the duplication rule is not violated.

▶ **Timeliness** Timeliness is one of the reasons why data can be inconsistent. The timeliness/latency requirements must be defined by the business. Based on these requirements the technology organization will develop appropriate synchronization solutions. Synchronization is discussed in Chapter 15.

The EIGG should take the lead in defining other information quality metrics, reports, and alerts. The information quality reports and alerts are the primary communication vehicle that should be made available to all responsible parties in business, technology, operations, and data governance groups when information quality anomalies are found. Once the root cause of the data quality problem is established, the data can be changed to correct the problem. However, as we already stated, data changes can trigger a rematch of customer records, which in turn can lead to discovery of new data quality anomalies. This data quality loop is a permanent process that enables and at the same time, requires continuous data quality improvement.

Data Validation

Data validation and verification are powerful methods in information quality control. Proper validation and verification requirements are some of the key areas that have to be addressed by the EIGG in collaboration with other CDI project teams.

Data validation can be defined as a process that ensures that the data under evaluation matches its intended expression and use. In that context, data validation is different from data accuracy. For example, if a data attribute for customer age contains a value of 50, it will most likely pass the validation check but may fail the accuracy test since the actual customer age could be 58. At the same time, if the value of the Age attribute is 500, then the data validation routine should flag it as erroneous because the valid range of Age values, defined in the appropriate area of the Data Hub metadata repository, is probably between 1 and 120.

Attribute validation is an important step that should be performed before the matching process takes place. Indeed, it does not make much sense to use invalid data for identification.

Validation rules can range from quite simple rules, such as data type, distinct value list, or value range, to fairly complex validation rules that incorporate attribute value rules for credit card numbers, social security numbers, etc. Typical types of data validation address the following concerns:

▶ **Data type validation** The system validates the entered data type differentiating between Date/Time, Number (multiple data subtypes can be enforced within this data type), or text. For the "text" data type, the system enforces the maximum attribute length. Text or string is the most flexible data format that can be used to display all other data types. For instance, an integer such as 123 can also be displayed by the string data type. Naturally, the string data type should be used to represent names and addresses. Numeric data types should be used, for instance, to store account value or customer age. Classic examples of the date data type are Date of Birth, Date of Death, and the date when the account was opened or closed.

▶ **Optionality** This requirement defines whether an attribute is mandatory or optional. If the attribute is mandatory, it is not allowed to be null or blank.

▶ **Uniqueness** An attribute or a combination of attributes can be defined as unique. The system will enforce the uniqueness of the attribute values across the universe of all values for this attribute or attributes found in all Data Hub records.

▶ **Range**   Any of the data types can have additional constraints on the allowed continuous ranges of values.

▶ **Data length**   For text attributes this requirement determines the allowed maximum number of characters.

▶ **List of allowed values**   Some attributes allow only some discrete values. For instance, allowed values for gender can be "M" for male, "F" for female, and "U" for unknown. A list of discrete values is typically enforced through a database lookup, a check constraint set in the database, or a distinct value list defined through the application interface.

▶ **Check digit/check sum**   For some attributes, one or more digits are reserved to validate the validity and integrity of all other digits. This is used for attributes such as credit card numbers, universal book identifiers such as ISBN, and other "intelligent" attributes. Sometimes the attribute semantics require more complex rules that go beyond the check digit rules (e.g., a social security number).

Figure 14-5 shows a template that can be used to document validation requirements.

No	Attribute	Data Type	Length	Mandatory	Additional Rules	If Invalid
1	First Name	String	30	Yes	Only characters A-Z and space allowed	Do not load the record and process as exception
2	Middle Name	String	30	No	Only characters A-Z and space allowed	Replace with "Unknown" if Length > 30
3	Last Name	String	30	Yes	Only characters A-Z and space allowed	Do not load the record and process as exception
4	Address Ln 1	String	100	Yes	None	Truncate to 100 characters if Length > 100; process as exception if blank
5	Address Ln 2	String	50	No	None	Truncate to 50 characters if Length > 50
6	City	String	50	Yes	Only characters A-Z and space allowed	Replace with "Invalid"
7	State Code	String	12	Yes	If country is U.S., only known state codes are allowed. Similarly, allowed state/province codes can be specified for other countries	Replace with "Invalid"
8	Postal Code	String	10	No	If country is U.S., postal code is to be represented by 5-digit ZIP code.	Replace with "Invalid"

Figure 14-5 *Sample illustrating validation rules*

The Structure of Social Security Numbers

A social security number (SSN) is a very important attribute for a CDI solution that supports U.S. domestic populations. If this attribute is available and contains valid values, it is often used as the primary attribute for customer identification. Indeed, the social security number was originally introduced for the explicit purpose of identifying individuals. Thus, if the correct social security number is available, it alone uniquely identifies the individual. There are several approaches designed to guarantee the correctness of an SSN. The first and most simple approach is to validate the social security numbers to exclude invalid values such as "111-11-1111" or "999-99-9999."

This approach would invalidate obvious invalid values. However, this is clearly not enough, and we need to find a way to validate a social security number that "looks" valid. Since a social security number contains nine nonrandom digits that are chosen according to well-defined SSN composition rules, the SSN validation can be performed either by applying SSN rules to the SSN attribute value, or by subscribing to or invoking an external service that can validate the value of the SSN attribute. A brief description of the SSN validation rules is offered below. Those readers who are interested in finding out more details about these rule can visit a special web site that describes these validation rules (http://www .usrecordsearch.com/ssn.htm).

The SSN structure does not contain any check digits, and the SSN rules have to be applied in order to validate SSN values. According to the published SSN rules (please see the web site reference above), each SSN consists of nine digits, commonly written as three groups of digits separated by hyphens: AAA-GG-SSSS. The first, three-digit group is called the "area number." The central, two-digit group is called the "group number." The final, four-digit group is called the "serial number." The group contains a combination of digits that is *not* random: each group of the SSN structure should adhere to certain rules that make the SSN an identifier with embedded intelligence.

The description that follows below is based on the official definition of the SSN rules and their history, and is offered here as an illustration of data validation approaches. We start with the area numbers. They are not random, and are assigned by geographic locations. Before 1972, the location of the Social Security Administration office determined the SSN area number. Since 1972, the residential address has been used to determine the area number as follows: the area numbers are assigned in east-to-west order, in many respects similar to the order used for U.S. postal zip codes. An exception to this principle was the range 700–728, which was assigned to railroad workers regardless of location (this practice was discontinued in 1964 and this range has not been used ever since). Based on range assignment logic, we can derive the following SSN validation rule: If the date of birth of an individual is greater than 1963 and his or her SSN falls within the 700–728 range, the SSN is invalid or the date of birth is incorrect. There are other area numbers that are unassigned and therefore, any SSN containing these areas numbers is also invalid. Table 14-1 shows the SSN area numbers by the locations (state codes).

001–003 NH	400–407 KY	530 NV
004–007 ME	408–415 TN	531–539 WA
008–009 VT	416–424 AL	540–544 OR
010–034 MA	425–428 MS	545–573 CA
035–039 RI	429–432 AR	574 AK
040–049 CT	433–439 LA	575–576 HI
050–134 NY	440–448 OK	577–579 DC
135–158 NJ	449–467 TX	580 VI (Virgin Islands)
159–211 PA	468–477 MN	581–584 PR (Puerto Rico)
212–220 MD	478–485 IA	585 NM
221–222 DE	486–500 MO	586 PI (Pacific Islands*)
223–231 VA	501–502 ND	587–588 MS
232–236 WV	503–504 SD	589–595 FL
237–246 NC	505–508 NE	596–599 PR (Puerto Rico)
247–251 SC	509–515 KS	600–601 AZ
252–260 GA	516–517 MT	602–626 CA
261–267 FL	518–519 ID	627–645 TX
268–302 OH	520 WY	646–647 UT
303–317 IN	521–524 CO	648–649 NM
318–361 IL	525 NM	*Guam, American Samoa, Philippine Islands, Northern Mariana Islands
362–386 MI	526–527 AZ	
387–399 WI	528–529 UT	
650–699 Unassigned, for future use 700–728 Railroad workers through 1963, then discontinued 729–799 Unassigned, for future use 800–999 Not valid SSNs		

Source: U.S. Record Search Web Site, http://www.usrecordsearch.com/ssn.htm

Table 14-1 *Social Security Numbers Assigned to States*

The group number (the fourth and fifth digit) has a chronological significance. The Social Security Administration (SSA) uses the following release order for the group numbers:

► Odd numbers, 01 to 09

► Even numbers, 10 to 98

► Even numbers, 02 to 08

► Odd numbers, 11 to 99

Group codes 00 are not used. SSA publishes newly released ranges on a monthly basis. If this information is used for the SSN validation, then the validation rules, strictly speaking, should be adjusted on a monthly basis. The significance of the group number release sequence is that if, for example, the latest released code was 90, then the code value 04 could not have been released yet and therefore is invalid.

Serial numbers are typically assigned in chronological order within each area and group number as the applications are processed with possibly some rare exceptions. It is unlikely that any validation logic can be applied to the serial number part of the SSN except serial number "0000," which is never used.

A CDI system can take advantage of a commercially available government service that performs SSN data validation. The ranges are updated on a monthly basis. This service is often bundled with packages provided by leading information quality vendors.

In addition to social security and tax identification numbers, a number of information quality vendors provide functional components aimed at validating credit card numbers, domestic and some international tax identification numbers, phone numbers, IP addresses, ISBN numbers, and other critical MDM-CDI attributes. Some of these validations are based on mathematical formula applied to the attributes when they are created, and the validation is quite straightforward. An example of such formula-based validation is check-digit validation of the ISBN number (for the easy-to-read details on the ISBN rules, please see the Wikipedia web site: http://en.wikipedia.org/wiki/International_Standard_Book_Number).

Some International Analogs of SSN   Each child born in the UK is issued a National Health Service Number (NHSN), structured as NNN-NNN-NNNN, for example, 122-762-9255. The last character of the number is a check digit, and it can and should be used for the validation of NHSN. However, National Health Service Numbers often change when individuals are moving to a different part of the country and having to change general practitioners, so these identifiers are not necessarily one person–one number constructs, which is a significant disadvantage of this identifier from the CDI perspective.

There are countries that have defined a unique national identifier that is both well formed and can be validated using a check digit procedure. For instance, New Zealand's National Health Index (NHI) is a unique identifier similar to the SSN. Its validation routine can effectively prevent or at least greatly minimize the likelihood of typing errors or attempts to enter some invalid numbers. The description of validation rules is available on the New Zealand Health Information Service web site: http://www.nzhis.govt.nz/nhi/validation.html.

The NHI number is a unique seven-character identifier (three alpha characters followed by four numeric characters) assigned to a health care user by the NHI. The first three characters of an NHI number must be alphabetic, but not "I" or "O," to avoid confusion with the digits one and zero. The fourth to sixth characters must be numeric. The seventh character is also numeric, and is a check digit that is based on modulus 11.

Even though New Zealand is a small country, we feel that NHI is a good example of how to define national identifiers that can greatly simplify the architecture and implementation of CDI systems designed to deliver single-customer views.

To sum up, when you're planning on starting an MDM-CDI project, you need to pay special attention to the issues of data governance, standards, and information quality. We showed that without a well-defined data governance strategy, organizational commitment, and dedicated resources, any project of MDM-CDI caliber will be at risk. Lack of data governance and data quality standards makes it extremely difficult and expensive to maintain the integrity of a CDI solution and the viability of key CDI features of identification, recognition, matching, and linking of party records. We also showed the practical approaches and implications of planning and implementing active validation processes and techniques that continue to ensure acceptable data quality.

CHAPTER
15

Data Synchronization

IN THIS CHAPTER

Goals of Data Synchronization

Technology Approach to Use Case Realization

Other Considerations

T his chapter deals with one of the most complex problems facing MDM-CDI designers—data synchronization. This chapter discusses both batch and real-time synchronization issues, concerns, and approaches.

Goals of Data Synchronization

Data synchronization is one of the most difficult and frequently underestimated areas of Master Data Management and Customer Data Integration. The purpose of this chapter is to describe a typical implementation of a synchronization solution in the context of the following use case.

Use Case: Delivering Customer Information to the Touch Point in Real Time

ABC Company has multiple applications and systems used across multiple lines of business to provide services to customers. The company faces a significant challenge—its inability to integrate information about customers and their relationships across different lines of business in a timely manner. Due to the heterogeneous and disconnected nature of these legacy systems, an integrated customer view can only be delivered using the existing customer data warehouse. Unfortunately, the data warehouse is updated only once a day using overnight batch processing. The resulting latency of customer information seriously impacts the company's ability to gain better insight into customer behavior including propensity to buy products and services, probability of default (e.g., on a loan), and other traits available through the use of customer analytics. At the same time, senior management wants to preserve the existing applications while making customer information available in real time to all applications and all customer touch points.

Technology Approach to Use Case Realization

When a customer initiates a contact with the ABC Company, the customer has to provide some pieces of identification information. Depending on the customer service channels supported by the ABC Company, the identification information may vary (from officially issued credentials such as SSN, driver license, or passport to authentication credentials the user has to possess in order to access the web site or a customer service call center). Regardless of the authentication method, the CDI

Data Hub would have to map user credentials to the identification attributes that are required to perform user identification and matching (see Chapter 12 for details). The Data Hub services are capable of recognizing the user as an existing or a new customer. ABC Company business requirements specify that for existing customers, all relevant customer information and recent contact history is displayed, subject to constraints imposed by the data visibility and security policy. Transactional information at each point of contact is captured in the legacy systems while all updates and new pieces of identity information for the existing customers are captured and stored in the CDI Data Hub. At the same time, new customers will be recognized by the appropriate Data Hub service and all relevant information will also be captured and stored in the CDI Data Hub using the transformation rules defined in the customer metadata repository.

Given this overall process view, we will discuss the technology approach to developing a CDI solution in the context of the various CDI Data Hub architecture styles discussed in the beginning of Part IV. Let's start with the Identity Hub, and then look at the additional considerations relevant to a more complex Data Hub style known as the Transaction Hub. As we discussed earlier in this part of the book, a CDI Data Hub system can act as a pass-through "slave" of the legacy systems, or be a master of some or all of customer profile data. The Transaction Hub style is a natural platform for the Data Hub to be a master of customer information, a facility that manages a new complete authoritative system of record. To be the master, the CDI Data Hub has to capture and apply the updates to the Hub and synchronize the data with the data sources and consuming applications on a continuous basis. We should contrast that behavior with the slave-style Data Hub that is the point of integration of legacy source systems of record, each of the systems being a system of record for a given set of attributes. In this scenario, continuous updates occur in the legacy systems of record, while the Data Hub content and the metadata defining it are updated infrequently.

Identity Hub with Multiple Points of Entry for Customer Information

Let's assume that a customer can interact with the ABC Company across a variety of different channels including web self-service, Interactive Voice Response (IVR) telephone system, customer service representative access via telephone or in-person, in-branch interactions, etc.

ABC Company's stated goal of the CDI project is to enable and ensure a consistent customer experience regardless of the channel or the interaction mode, and this experience should be achieved by creating a unified, holistic view of the customer and all of his or her relationships. Further, this holistic view has to be available on demand, in real time, to all channels supported by the ABC Company.

Let's start with the Identity Hub design approach. This architecture style positions the Data Hub as a "slave" of the existing data sources and applications.

With this background, consider specific process steps and Data Hub components that are involved when a customer interacts with one of the ABC Company's customer touch points: Figure 15-1 illustrates the key logical steps of the integrated solution.

1. At the point of contact, the customer provides his or her identification information, e.g., name and address, or a credit card number. The information is scanned or entered using a customer identification application interface that should be designed to enforce data entry formats and attribute values whenever possible. In the case of a self-service channel, the information is entered by the customer; otherwise, it is done by an authorized employee of the ABC Company. The identification application uses one of the published Data Hub services to initiate a check to verify whether the customer record exists in the Data Hub. The service forms a message with the received identification information using a standard matching message format.

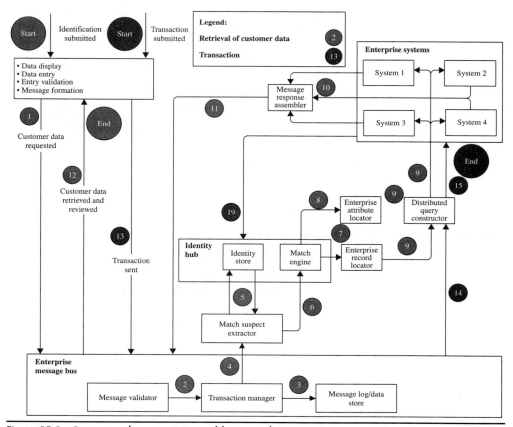

Figure 15-1 *Data synchronization and key synchronization components*

The message is published to the Enterprise Message Bus (EMB)—a middleware technology that is often presented as a component of the Service-Oriented Architecture known as the Enterprise Service Bus (ESB). Specifically, the first functional component to receive the message is the EMB Message Validator, which analyzes the message and confirms the correctness of the format. It also validates that the message context meets minimum data requirements. For flexibility and manageability, the CDI Data Hub system provides a management facility that allows users to configure minimum data requirements based on the appropriate metadata definitions.

2. The message is forwarded to the EMB Transaction Manager. The message gets assigned a unique transaction ID by the EMB Transaction Manager's Key Generator.

3. Transaction Manager can optionally log transaction information including the transaction type, transaction originator, time of origination, and possibly some other information about the transaction.

4. Transaction Manager forwards the message to the Match Suspect Extractor.

5. Match Suspect Extractor reads the identification parameters in the message and creates a Data Hub extract with suspect matches. Typically, this extract contains all records where at least one of the identifiers matches. It can also contain records that were selected using various fuzzy matching algorithms.

6. The Match Extractor sends the extract message to the Match Engine. The Match Engine is a CDI Data Hub component that performs the match. It can return zero, one, or multiple matches. The engine computes the confidence level for the matched records. We assume that the matching engine is configured for two thresholds $T1 < T2$ (the two-threshold model is discussed in Chapter 12).

   a. If the confidence level is above $T2$ and only one match is found, then the matching engine returns a unique customer ID along with additional data obtained from the Data Hub and/or external vendor knowledge bases. To improve the confidence of the match process, our ABC Company can choose to purchase and integrate an external information file (a knowledge base) that contains "trusted" information about the customer.

   b. If the match confidence level is between $T1$ and $T2$ and multiple suspect matches are found, the identification application may prompt the user for additional identification information, or alternatively, can ask the user to select the right customer record from the returned suspect match list. This latter can trigger another identification loop (see Chapter 14 for the discussion on the identification loops).

   c. If the match confidence is below $T1$, the match service returns a notification that the customer record is not found. The user may choose to modify identification information and resubmit the modified record for identification.

7. Transaction Manager orchestrates other Data Hub services to gather additional information about the identified customer. The customer identifier is sent to the Enterprise Record Locator, which contains a cross-reference facility with linkage information between the Data Hub keys and source system keys. The source system keys are returned to the Transaction Manager.

8. Transaction Manager invokes the Enterprise Attribute Locator service to identify the best sources of data for each attribute in the enterprise data model.

9. Transaction Manager sends inquiry messages to source systems through the EMB, where it invokes the Distributed Query Constructor service, which generates a distributed query against multiple systems.

10. The source systems process the query request messages and send the messages to the Response Assembler. The Response Assembler assembles the messages received from the Data Hub and source systems into the Response Message.

11. The assembled message is published to the EMB. Transaction Manager recognizes the message as part of the transaction that was initiated by the request in Step 2. Transaction Manager returns the message to the requestor and marks the transaction complete.

12. The ABC Company customer service employee who initiated this transaction in the first place can review the returned message and take advantage of the accurate and complete information about the customer and his or her transactions, which gives the customer service employee the required intelligence. Since the customer is identified with the appropriate degree of confidence, the customer service employee can initiate a business transaction to serve a customer request. For example, this could be a transaction that involves data changes to the customer information. Changes generated by the transaction are sent to the corresponding legacy system, while the customer identification information message is sent to the Data Hub via the EMB.

13. The Data Hub initiates a change transaction by sending a transaction message to the EMB. The transaction may result in changes to the critical attributes used for matches. As we discussed in previous chapters, this in turn can trigger merges and splits in the Data Hub. Splits can cause the creation of new customer IDs, while merges result in deletion of some customer records.

    a. Every time the customer keys stored in the Data Hub change, the corresponding changes in the Source System Record Locator (also referred to as the Cross-Reference Record Locator) must be applied as a single transaction.

    b. When the Data Hub and the Cross-Reference Record Locator are updated, the ABC Company's auditors may request a detailed record of these changes. A good practice is to design the CDI Data Hub to preserve the history and the change activity of all updates to the Data Hub. Thus, a good Data Hub design should provide for configurable archival and purge components and services. Typically, operational needs for archival and logging are relatively short-term and limited to a few days or a few weeks maximum. Audit requirements are driven by regulatory compliance and legal requirements and typically specify relatively long data retention terms that can cover a span of several years. Active access, retention, archival, and purge requirements must be defined based on the needs of all stakeholder groups.

14. The EMB invokes the Distributed Query Constructor service to generate distributed changes in the source systems. Since customer identity updates can come from multiple systems, the project design team must establish a set of rules that can resolve data synchronization conflicts for each attribute. Typically, the source and the date/time of the change at the attribute level are the most important factors that must be taken into account.

15. The Distributed Query Constructor sends updates to the systems. The data is updated in the source systems.

Considerations for the Transaction Hub Master Model

If our ABC Company plans to transition the CDI solution from the Hub Slave model to the Hub Master model, the resulting impact on the information flows and processes can be quite profound. In the Hub Master scenario, all customer profile data (whatever attributes are determined to constitute the customer profile) is entered through a new Customer Profile Management application pointed directly to the Data Hub. Customer profile attributes that were previously editable through multiple legacy applications should be protected from changes through these applications and should become read-only attributes. A typical scenario implementing this approach may be as follows:

▶ The end users can search for a customer using identity attributes.

▶ As soon as a customer is found and selected by the end user, all customer profile information may be retrieved from the Data Hub and displayed in the legacy application screen.

▶ With a single point of entry into the Data Hub, data synchronization in the Hub Master scenario is much easier.

Still, overall Hub master implementations are quite difficult, particularly in organizations with a large legacy environment, multiple generations of legacy systems, and complex delta processing and synchronization that involves many legacy systems. In practice, legacy-rich organizations should start implementing a CDI solution as a Hub "slave" style, with the Data Hub providing identification services as discussed in the previous section. Conversely, for new organizations (e.g., a newly created bank), the legacy is not as big an issue, and a Transaction Hub (Hub Master) might be a viable option. Serious analysis is required to determine the right end-state of the CDI solution and the actionable implementation road map.

Real-Time/Near-Real-Time Synchronization Components

The use case of the ABC Company that we described in the previous sections is useful to show not only the synchronization data flows but also Data Hub components and services that should be in place to implement an enterprise-scale data synchronization solution. Let's take a closer look at these components and services.

Legacy System Data Entry Validation Component   This component serves as the first barrier preventing erroneous data entry into the system. As we discussed in Chapter 14, it is important to bring data validation upstream as close to the point of data entry as possible. Data validation components restrict the formats and set of values entered on the user interface screen for a data entry application (e.g., an account opening or user registration applications). Ideally, the Data Hub designers should strive to make data entry validation in the legacy systems consistent with the Data Hub validation requirements.

Legacy System Message Creation and Canonical Message Format Component   Each legacy system that needs to be integrated into the real-time synchronization framework must have components responsible for creating and publishing the message to the Enterprise Message Bus. The message must conform to the canonical message format, i.e., an enterprise standard message used for application-independent data exchange (the canonical data model and formats are discussed in Chapter 11). Canonical message format and the canonical data model are the foundational components that enable data synchronization.

Legacy System Message-Processing Components   Each legacy system should be able to receive and process messages in a canonical format. The processing includes message interpretation and orchestration in terms of native legacy system functions and procedures.

Message Validation and Translations   Message validation components must be able to validate the message structure and message content (payload). These components should also be code-translation-aware in order to translate system-specific reference code semantics into enterprise values, and vice versa.

Transaction Manager and Transaction Metadata Store   As the name implies, the Transaction Manager is responsible for the execution and control of each transaction. The Transaction Manager registers each transaction by assigning a transaction identifier (transaction ID).

All transactions in the transaction life cycle are recorded in the Transaction Metadata Store regardless of whether they are successful or not. Transaction Manager orchestrates and coordinates transaction processing of composite, complex transactions, and interfaces with the exception-processing and compensation transaction management components and services if a transaction fails for any reason.

Match Suspect Extractor   When a new piece of customer information arrives (new customer record, change in the existing customer record, or deletion of an existing record), the matching engine needs to receive an extract with suspected records for which the match groups must be recalculated. It is a challenge to construct this extract to be small enough to support real-time or near-real-time match calculation and at the same time to capture all impacted records. Since the match rules and the attributes used for matching have a tendency to evolve over time, it is a good practice to make the Match Suspect Extractor a configurable component that uses metadata definitions provided and maintained through an administrative application interface.

Identity Store   The Identity Store maintains the customer data with the superset of records that includes all participating systems in scope. The attributes are limited to the critical attributes needed for matching (see Chapter 12 for detailed discussion on critical data attributes). Also, the Identity Store includes the match group keys. In a typical CDI system for a large enterprise, the Identity Store may have hundreds of millions of records. A lot of computer power and performance optimization techniques are required to enable high throughput for both reads and updates. In addition, the Identity Store holds some amount of historical information. Typically, it is limited to recent history that enables error recovery and resolution of operational issues.

Change Capture   This component is responsible for capturing the record or records that have been changed, added, or deleted. Pointers to these records are the entry information required by the Match Suspect Extractor to begin match processing.

Purge, Archival, and Audit Support   Purge and archival components are responsible for purging records to get rid of history records that exceeded the predefined retention threshold. The audit features allow CDI Data Hub solutions to archive purged records for potential audit or investigation processing. More importantly, though, audit features are a required functionality to comply with regulatory requirements such as those of GLBA, the Sarbanes-Oxley Act, and many others. We recommend using a separate data store to maintain audit records and to support audit reporting.

Enterprise Record Locator Metadata   The Enterprise Record Locator contains metadata information about all system source keys and the Identity Store keys. The Enterprise Record Locator is the key component that stores cross-system reference information to maintain the integrity of the customer records. The Enterprise Record Locator should support many-to-many relationships between source system keys. Services built around this component should cross-reference keys from all involved systems including the Data Hub, and deliver this service with high throughput, low latency, and high concurrency.

Enterprise Attribute Locator Metadata   This component enables the data governance group to specify the best trusted source of data for each attribute in the canonical data model. The Enterprise Attribute Locator stores pointers to the best source of data. An administrative interface is required to maintain these pointers. The Enterprise Attribute Locator can be defined at different granularity levels:

▶ System-level trust, when a certain system is selected as the trusted source for all profile data.

▶ Attribute-level trust, when a single trusted source is defined for each attribute in the canonical data model.

▶ Trust at the level of attributes and record types, when a single trusted source is defined for each attribute in the canonical data model with additional dependencies on the record type, account type, etc.

▶ Trust at the level of attributes, record types, and time stamps is similar to the trust level defined in the previous bullet except that it includes the time stamp of when the attribute was changed. This time-stamp attribute is an additional factor that can impact the best source rules.

Race Condition Controller   The Race Condition Controller is responsible for defining what change must prevail and survive when two or more changes conflict with each other. This component should resolve the conflicts based on the evaluation of business rules that consider, among other factors, the source of change by attribute and the time stamp at the attribute level. This component should be configurable, metadata-driven, and have an administrative application interface for ease of administration.

Distributed or Federated Query Constructor   When the customer data is distributed or federated across multiple data stores, this component should be able to parse a message and transform it into a number of queries or messages against legacy systems.

Message Response Assembler   Once each of the source systems participating in creating a response generated its portion of the response message, the complete response message must be assembled for return. This is the job that the Message Response Assembler is responsible for.

Error Processing, Transactional Integrity, and Compensating Transactions   At a high level, there are two ways to handle errors. The conservative approach enforces all-or-nothing transactional semantics of atomicity, consistency, isolation, and durability (ACID properties) and requires the entire distributed transaction to complete without any errors in order to succeed. If any step in this transaction fails, the entire transaction fails and all its uncommitted changes are rolled back to the pre-transaction state. The other transaction mode is to support a complex multistep transaction in such a way that even though some steps may fail, the entire transaction may continue depending on the transactional context and the applicable business rules. Typically, these are long-running complex business transactions that are more difficult to design and manage. The integrity of these transactions is not ensured via an automatic rollback and usually requires a design of what is known as compensating transactions.

Hub Master Components   In the case of the Hub Master, such as Transaction Hub, all attributes that are maintained in the Hub Master must be protected from the changes in the source systems. In this scenario, the Data Hub becomes the authoritative source and the system of record for customer data it manages. The CDI Master Data Hub should include a set of services, components, and interfaces designed to maintain the Master Hub attributes centrally. All other applications and systems in the scope of the CDI project should access customer data from the Data Hub. The Hub Master will typically require the maintenance of relationships, groups of customers, and other associations and aggregations (these topics are discussed in Chapter 13).

Batch Processing

In the previous section, we were concentrating on the discussion of a real-time data synchronization solution that works for both the slave and the master models of the CDI Data Hub. Let's consider the question of whether the CDI system still needs a batch data synchronization facility that may use Extract, Transformation, and Load (ETL) processes and components. One way to think about this question is to decide whether the real-time messaging infrastructure and the appropriate Hub services can be used to process large sets of data synchronization messages as a single large batch.

The answer to this question consists of at least two parts.

The first part of the answer is based on the fact that almost any established enterprise maintains reliable, mission-critical batch processes that are aligned with the business models of the industry the enterprise operates in (e.g., nightly updates of inventory levels, trade settlements, insurance claim processing, etc.). This means that there will continue to be the need to process some aspects of master data management in batch mode.

The second part of the answer is that in cases where the Data Hub has to process millions of data changes at a time, batch processing is the right operational and technical approach, although the process itself has to be carefully designed and optimized to fit the available batch window. The latter point can be addressed effectively and efficiently by using mature technology such as ETL.

Indeed, the primary goal of ETL is to support large-scale batch transformations from one form of input data (e.g., account-centric structure) to another, potentially higher level of the output or target data (e.g., a customer-centric structure). Contemporary ETL technologies can parallelize the majority of transform and load operations and thus can achieve very high throughput and performance that can far outpace the capabilities of message-based processing. This is particularly important for initial data load processing and for rapidly bringing additional data sources into the Data Hub. Very large batches are required not only to seed the Data Hub initially. Mergers and acquisitions, changes in branch office hierarchies, new lines of business that have to be included in the scope of Data Hub, and other events may result in creating very large data files that have to be cleansed, transformed, and loaded into the Data Hub. In other words, ETL-style batch data processing including data load and by extension, data synchronization, are required for any enterprise-scale CDI implementation. We discussed the architectural approach to data loading in Part II, Chapter 6 of the book where we introduced the Data Zone architecture approach to data management (see Figure 6-2). A simplified high-level view of the ETL processing from the data sources through the loading and staging areas to the Data Hub is shown in Figure 15-2.

The process begins with file extraction from legacy systems. The file extracts are placed in the Loading Area and loaded into tables. The purpose of this area is to bring all the data onto a common platform. The Loading Area preserves the data in its original structure (in our example, account-centric). The following types of transformations occur when the data is loaded into the staging area:

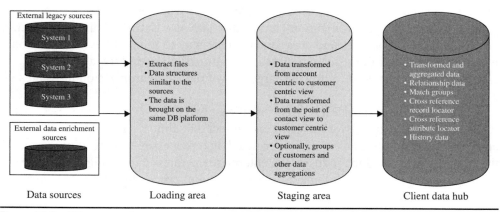

Figure 15-2 *ETL processing*

▶ Core transformations to the customer-centric view occur when the data is loaded in the staging area.

▶ Reference code translations are used to bring the codes into the Data Hub-specific format.

▶ The staging area must preserve legacy system keys. They will be used to build the cross-reference record locator service.

▶ Data validation and beginning of exception processing for records that do not comply with established standards. The records enter the exception processing framework from the staging area.

▶ Declaration of data defaults.

▶ If data enrichment processing from an external vendor or vendors is in scope, it can optionally be done in the staging area. Otherwise, data enrichment occurs in the Data Hub.

From the staging area the data is loaded into the Data Hub. The Data Hub data load performance has to be compatible with the processing throughput maintained by ETL. The Data Hub should support the following data transformations and manipulation functions:

▶ One of the most significant functions is the cross-reference record locator. This component consists of the cross-reference data store and services that manage the linkages between the customer keys stored in the Data Hub and legacy systems in scope. In the batch-processing mode, this component must be able to generate the Data Hub keys, cross-reference them with the legacy keys stored in the staging area, and persist the cross-reference information in the Data Hub.

▶ The Match Suspect Extractor component must be able to work in batch mode. Besides this requirement, this component is quite similar to the match extract component described in the real-time processing section. The main functional difference between the two component types is that for real-time processing, the Match Suspect Extractor generates an extract based on a single record change, while the batch version of the Match Extractor operates on multiple records affected by the batch.

▶ Matching is one of the core functions of the Data Hub. This function should be available in real-time and batch modes, and it should support batch mode for the initial data load and delta processing.

▶ As we mentioned earlier, if data enrichment processing from an external vendor or vendors is in scope, data enrichment is typically performed in the Data Hub. Initial data load and batch delta processing have to support processing of the enriched customer records.

▶ Batch processing has to be able to resolve race conditions (these were discussed in Chapter 14).

▶ The Data Hub also provides support for data aggregation, merge of matching records, and other data consolidation activities including processing of customer groups and relationships.

The distribution of CDI data manipulation functions and components between the staging area and the Data Hub often depends on the business requirements, legacy data landscape, and infrastructure requirements. The demarcation line is, therefore, flexible, and it can be moved.

A significant practical consideration for designing and deploying these components is the type of vendor solutions that the project team selected. The choice is usually between an ETL and a CDI vendor's products. Some CDI vendors offer functionality that traditionally belongs to the ETL and/or messaging vendor space. For instance, some CDI vendors offer their own staging area implementation and the corresponding procedures. A question that has to be answered is whether it is a good idea to bundle ETL transformation inside the CDI vendor solution. What follows is the list of considerations that have to be taken into account when answering this question.

Pros:

▶ Some CDI vendors provide a common framework, metadata, and component reuse capabilities for both ETL and real-time components. In general, however, ETL vendor products complement but do not replace real-time data transformation vendor products. Therefore, we can recommend that data validation components, match extractors, race condition components, and others must be evaluated, designed, and developed for both real-time and batch modes.

▶ This common synchronization framework offers a shared standard exception processing facility.

Cons:

▶ Most of the CDI vendors are relatively young companies and the Data Hub solution space has lots of room to mature. It is not unreasonable to assume that even if the organization is building a CDI solution today, it may decide to replace it tomorrow. Given this level of uncertainty, we believe it'll be preferable to use an ETL vendor solution to handle the functions that are native to ETL.

▶ It is reasonable to assume that the performance of ETL tools and real-time components will not be equal, leading to a decision to use these tools and techniques separately to satisfy specific business and operational requirements.

Other Considerations

Real-life operational data processing often encounters conditions different from the expected mainstream processing rules. These conditions can be caused by unexpected data values, violations of referential integrity, violations of sequence of record processing, access problems, system or object availability problems, etc. These conditions are known as *exceptions*. Exceptions can impact and even disrupt operations. Thus, CDI Data Hub architecture should include exception capture, management, and root-cause impact analysis and reporting.

Having a common standard framework for exception processing is a great idea. In its absence, different development groups may create their own disparate exception-processing solutions. A systematic approach to exception processing that will include batch and real-time operations will pay off multiple times. This framework should be able to create and maintain an exception-processing flow by orchestrating exception-processing scenarios. The exception-processing framework has to be metadata-driven. At a minimum, the framework defines a number of steps that should be performed for each exception or error capture. In addition, it defines a common format for the exception messages:

▶ The process (real time or ETL)

▶ Transaction identifier

▶ Module where the error occurred (e.g., staging area, matching engine, Data Validator)

▶ Error message

Once the exceptions are captured they have to be presented to the appropriate users and applications designed for exception handling and resolution. Exception handling and resolution may require separate administrative applications and exception-processing workflows.

An interesting concern about the exception-processing framework and its boundaries has to do with the scope of the exceptions (e.g., should the exception framework go beyond the synchronization components?). We believe that it should. For example, consider exceptions caused by unauthorized users or invalid requests.

It is true that data visibility and security (discussed in detail in Part III of the book) can significantly impact the processes surrounding a CDI Data Hub by applying additional constraints to the already complicated Data Hub services, ad-hoc queries, and predefined access routines. To state it differently, many data exceptions are caused by data security controls. In this case, exception processing needs to capture all relevant information about the user identity, content of the request, and statement of the security policies and rules that the system has to follow to process the request. The result of this analysis could indicate not a technology failure but rather an attempt at the unauthorized request or incorrect, incomplete, or contradictory set of policies and rules.

The variety of exception types causes a variety of exception-processing workflows and organizational roles that are to be involved in exception handling. Therefore exception processing requires robust and configurable mechanism distributing and routing the exceptions to the right organizational roles. Data exceptions may also contain sensitive information requiring visibility and security constraints to be imposed on the access to exception processing data.

As we discussed in Chapter 12, the CDI Data Hub supports many attributes that the Hub can use to identify an individual and/or organization. From the synchronization perspective, a decision must be made as to when an identity of the party must be reevaluated. For example, if a name, phone number, address, and credit card number are used for identification, should we recompute the match group every time when one of these attributes changes? If a phone number change occurs because the phone number was initially incorrect, then this may be a reason for the match group recomputation. On the other hand, if a correction has been made because a well-known customer changes his or her phone number, there is no need to trigger the match group recomputation. A good practice in this case is to make sure that attribute changes are tagged with the reason for the change, time stamp of the change, and other decision-driving attributes. These attributes should be used by the Data Hub to help make a decision about whether the change should trigger the match process. Typically, as soon as a customer record is identified with a sufficient level of confidence, it should not change the associated identity. This simplifies data synchronization considerably.

Given that large companies have many systems that are to be integrated within a CDI framework, a significant milestone from the data synchronization perspective would be a detailed definition of system on-boarding. This term refers to a set of standards that determine what applications and attributes each system should comply with as a prerequisite to being integrated into the enterprise CDI solution. These standards and procedures should typically cover multiple scenarios, e.g., real-time vs. batch integration, service integration using SOA principles vs. native APIs, integration in a pure "slave" scenario, master for certain attributes, etc.

Granularity of the standard message must also be considered. A standard message is typically defined at the customer level. This message is represented by multiple data model entities that may include customer, address, and many other entities and attributes comprising the customer profile. If some entity or entities within the customer profile are updated much more often than others, it may be a good idea to consider a separate message that affects only the frequently changing entities.

It is always a trade-off between the simplicity of having a single standard message and enterprise CDI system performance considerations. For example, if changes in the phone number or address are much more frequent than changes in other attributes of the profile, a dedicated standard message can target the frequently updated attributes. In some cases, more complex hierarchies of standard synchronization messages may be required.

To sum up, this chapter discussed practical implementation concerns and approaches for implementing and managing data synchronization of a CDI Data Hub with other systems across the enterprise. We discussed these concerns in the example of a use case that defined the need for real-time data synchronization across various customer touch points. The use case helped us to illustrate typical components that system designers should be considering when developing a CDI data synchronization solution. We leveraged the MDM-CDI architecture concepts and principles discussed in Part II of the book to look at the implementation aspects of the CDI synchronization components and their integration requirements. This chapter concluded with a brief discussion on the principal differences between batch and real-time data synchronization while emphasizing that there is a place for each of these approaches and technologies within a typical MDM-CDI project.

CHAPTER 16

Additional Implementation Considerations

IN THIS CHAPTER

Considerations on the CDI Presentation Layer

Testing Considerations

Additional Technical and Operational Concerns

I n this chapter, we will present a number of additional considerations important enough to be discussed in this book, including implementation, testing,
and technical and operational concerns. The discussion points covered here
are either MDM-CDI-specific or generic issues that frequently cause problems
from the Master Data Management and especially Customer Data Integration
implementation perspective.

Considerations on the CDI Presentation Layer

Let's briefly look at the presentation layer components that are often involved in
implementing applications that consume the data and services of a CDI Data Hub.
These applications include new customer-centric applications (e.g., customer/prospect
on-boarding and account opening), reporting applications, and administrative
applications.

Customer-Centric Applications

Different CDI Data Hub styles enable customer-centric application functionality in
different ways. In the case of a Registry-style approach, the CDI Hub maintains an
integrated registry of links to the customer records that reside in existing applications
and data stores. Consequently, both old (existing legacy) and new applications can
retrieve and use the centrally maintained customer profile data while preserving
most key application features. The existing applications and data stores continue to
remain the systems of record for customer information.

As we move toward the Transaction Hub, which stores and manages not
just links and pointer references but also the actual customer data, the need for
new, customer-centric applications becomes especially clear. In a Transaction
Hub solution, a new customer-centric application should be able to create, read,
update, and delete (CRUD) records in the Data Hub at the account *and* customer
levels. Transaction Hub should allow the end users to eliminate duplicate records
if this has not been achieved systemically. Transaction Hub should enable new
customer-centric features such as creation of customer groups and maintenance of
corporate hierarchies for institutional customers, and should support other types of
associations and aggregations inside the Data Hub.

In general, a CDI Data Hub enables new customer-centric applications to search
and access information not just via an account number, invoice number, confirmation
number, etc., but rather via relevant customer keys. As we discussed in Part II of the
book, these customer keys are often industry-segment-specific in order to recognize the
entities that we generally call "customers." Indeed, a retail banking customer differs
from a medical service provider (e.g., a doctor) or from an institutional customer

(e.g., a broker-dealer), etc. As the result, the customer recognition and identification capabilities of the CDI Data Hub have to be adaptable to the business model, rules, and semantics of a given industry vertical. This difference not only affects the way the customers are recognized, but naturally it also impacts the way new customer-centric applications and processes are designed and deployed throughout the enterprise.

Reporting

MDM-CDI solutions tend to be optimized for real-time/near-real-time operations but not necessarily for batch reporting. Experience in implementing large data warehouses and business intelligence applications proves that running complex queries against very large databases (and of course, a CDI solution usually ends up having to support a very large data store known as a Data Hub) may have serious performance and throughput implications on the technical infrastructure and end-user application response times.

If the CDI project specifies the need for extensive customer-centric reporting, the project architects may consider implementing a separate reporting environment that loads a performance-optimized reporting data mart from the Data Hub and makes its data available to the end-user BI and reporting application suite. We touched on this point in Chapter 11 and showed a conceptual design diagram for the Transaction-style Data Hub in Figure 11-5, but the approach is valid for any CDI Data Hub architecture style since Data Hub design is rarely optimized for data-warehousing type queries.

These considerations apply to end-user BI-style reporting. Of course, there are other types of reports that need to be developed to support Data Hub and application testing and operations. In fact, testing relies heavily on reporting. The good news is that the majority of the reports developed for testing can be leveraged and sometimes reused for operational controls when the CDI system is deployed in production.

Administrative Applications

In addition to the end-user BI reporting applications and applications designed for operational and production support, an MDM-CDI Data Hub system has to support various administrative applications. These applications are designed to manage the configuration complexity of the Data Hub environment by making Hub operational parameters data-driven. Some of these applications are shown in the following list:

- ▶ **Reference code maintenance application**   This application maintains allowed code values in the CDI Data Hub.

- ▶ **Default management application**   This application allows the users to define and maintain default values.

▶ **Maintenance of critical matching data attributes**   This application defines what attributes are used as critical data attributes. The extract for the matching engine is generated based on the entries from this application.

▶ **Exception-processing metadata support**   This application should be able to define new error types and exception-processing flows.

Testing Considerations

Testing is a critical work stream that is often (in fact, almost always!) underestimated, especially in the context of a CDI Data Hub. When we discuss the topic of testing, we include several testing categories and dimensions. On the one hand, testing should include functional testing, data testing, and nonfunctional testing (the latter includes performance, scalability, throughput, manageability, resilience to failure, interface compliance, etc.). On the other hand, testing is an iterative process that should be defined and implemented as a sequence of iterative steps that may include unit test, system test, integration test, QA test, and user acceptance test (UAT). When embarking on a CDI project, the project team has to make sure that the scope of testing is clearly defined and mapped to the business requirements for traceability, and to the project acceptance criteria for project management and stakeholder buy-in.

We further suggest that regression testing should be performed for each testing type. Testing activities should begin very early in the project's life cycle. The testing team should develop a comprehensive test strategy as soon as the business requirements are defined and some initial technical elaboration is complete. Best practices suggest that the test cases should be developed in parallel with the software requirement and design specifications. For example, when the team uses Rational Unified Process and defines use cases to articulate software requirements, the test cases can be (and should be) developed at the same time as the use cases. MDM-CDI technologies and CDI use cases introduce additional complexities to the test strategy. In order to illustrate this complexity, let us consider the following categories of test-related issues:

▶ CDI testing of data and services
▶ Match group testing
▶ Creation and protection of test data

Testing of CDI Data and Services

The high-level approach to testing CDI data and services has to follow standard testing methodology that defines the following test levels:

▶ **Unit testing**   This testing is performed by developers, who verify and certify their own work. They have to come up with their own test cases. Typically, these test cases are executed automatically. Some manual testing may also be involved. Unit testing is limited in scope and often tests only individual components rather than the end-to-end solution. Unit testing also addresses the validity of internal components that may not be included in other test groups, e.g., internally called functions, procedures, and services.

▶ **System testing, also known as integration testing**   This process tests multiple components of a system in an integrated fashion, with the test cases defining initial conditions, test sequences, and expected outcome from executing all components required to implement a complete business function or a service. Integration testing provides an insight into overall system behavior as well as performance and throughput characteristics.

▶ **Quality assurance testing**   This level of testing provides the technology organization and the business community with the assessment and measurement of the quality of the developed system. QA testing can be further broken down into Technical QA and Business QA. These tests are executed independently from each other, and by different groups:

  ▶ Technical QA is performed by a Technology QA group that uses independently developed test cases. The goal of the Technical QA is to certify that the solution is developed in compliance with approved technical requirements. Technical QA testing is focused primarily on the technical behavior of the system under test, and does not test technical features and functions at the same level as unit testing. The intent of Technical QA is to test end-to-end applications and systems in accordance with the technical software requirements documentation and based on their interpretation of the requirements. The Technology QA group interacts closely with the development organization in order to resolve issues discovered during testing. From the process point of view, defects identified by the Technology QA group should be formally logged into the dedicated system used for defect resolution. If defects are found and fixed by the development group, regression testing may be required to validate the corrected code. On completion of regression testing the results are documented and certified by Technology QA.

  ▶ Business QA tests are performed by a dedicated Business QA team. The Business QA team executes end-to-end test cases and compares the results with the business requirements as well as with specific examples derived from running real-life production applications. In addition to validating test results against business requirements, the Business QA team works closely with the Technology QA team and business stakeholders to refine both the business requirements and their technical interpretation. The resulting changes have to be retested, which, in turn, may require a cycle of regression testing at the Unit, System, and QA levels.

A joint Technical QA/Business QA testing is especially important when testing the CDI Data Hub data security and visibility implementation (see detailed discussion on data security and visibility in Chapter 10). The project team has to work closely with the enterprise security organization and the policy administration team to make sure that access controls are implemented and enforced according to the policy statements and users' roles and entitlements, and that every authorization decision can be traced back to the appropriate policy. In addition, when developing testing scenarios for data visibility, the team has to make sure that these scenarios include both necessary and sufficient conditions. To state it differently, when a visibility engine allows access to a particular set of Data Hub data, the QA teams have to make sure that all data that was supposed to be accessed based on the policy is granted such an access, and that there are no records or attributes access to which was not allowed by mistake.

MDM-CDI solutions put additional emphasis on testing not only services and components, but often the data itself. Not surprisingly, one of the key testing targets of a CDI system is data quality. If the data quality of the source system is a part of the testing process, it should include definition, measurement, and defect-resolution steps. The entire test suite should include clearly defined assumptions, pre- and post-conditions, defect-tracking tools and procedures, and acceptance criteria. At a minimum, testing deliverables should include test cases, reports used for testing, test scripts, test execution results, traceability matrices, and defect-management logs.

Typically, data testing is performed using either or both of the following approaches:

▶ **Bulk statistical analysis executed against all data**   The fact that all data is covered by the analysis contributes to its strength. A common weakness is that it is not easy to resolve abnormalities if and when they are found.

▶ **Scenario-based testing performed on a small subset of records**   It is always a question of how many records need to be tested and how to select the subset optimally to cover a representative set of scenarios. Since we are dealing with projects where the number of records is typically in excess of seven digits, manual processing is not an option and automation is not always feasible either.

When we perform data testing in the CDI environment, we have to select the source and the target data files for testing. Let's use a typical data transformation sequence that the data undergoes during the initial load process into the Data Hub. We discussed this topic in Chapter 15, and Figure 15-2 illustrates the process. An important choice facing the CDI designers is whether the testing routines should be performed on each data migration step, e.g., loading area, staging area, record locator metadata store, etc. If the decision is negative, then all test cases should compare the initial source (the legacy source systems) with the content of the ultimate, post-transformation target (the CDI Data Hub). This amounts to the end-to-end testing that is typically a province of Technical and/or Business QA.

However, end-to-end data testing is somewhat different from functional testing in that it requires a low level of detail in order to discover data defects and trace their origins. This can be a very complex task given the variety and scope of various data transformation steps. Therefore, an effective approach to Technical QA and Business QA testing is to implement it as a stepwise process, where testing of some steps could be quite complex.

Bulk Statistical Testing Challenges

Let's consider a "simple" example of testing one-step data transformations between the loading and staging areas of the Data Hub, using bulk statistical testing to confirm the number of records where a certain attribute is blank (see Figures 16-1 and 16-2). The goal is to reconcile the number of records where the ZIP Code is blank (NULL). The account-centric structure shown in Figure 16-1 (the source) contains three customer records and two different account numbers.

The customer-reporting application would show three customer records: Mary Turner, Mary L. Turner, and Paul Turner, with three addresses, two of them having ZIP Code NULL (we assume that two records for Mary Turner belong to the same individual).

In contrast, the customer/account data in the customer-centric structure, shown in Figure 16-2, has a single address that belongs to the aggregated customer.

As a result of the transformation to a customer-centric model and customer and address de-duping, the two records indicate that one person (Mary Turner) and the

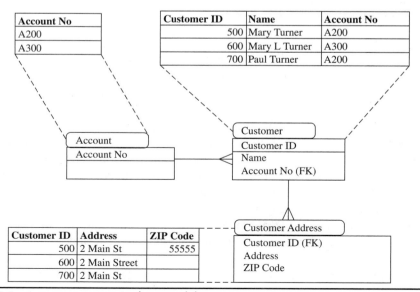

Figure 16-1 *An account-centric data model*

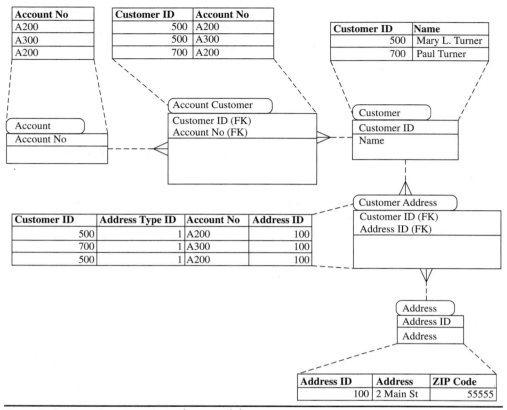

Figure 16-2 *A customer-centric data model*

three addresses are recognized as one. In the customer-centric structure there are no records with ZIP Code equal to NULL. Therefore, a direct comparison of NULL counts in the two data structures would not provide meaningful testing results.

Records that are rejected during the transformation operation drive additional complexity into the process of bulk statistical testing. In order to reconcile record counts where a certain attribute is blank (NULL), the source should be compared with the target corrected by the rejected records. A combination of data transformation, data cleansing, de-duping, and record rejection makes bulk comparison difficult. We are not trying to discourage the reader from using this approach, but rather want to make sure that the difficulties of bulk testing are correctly understood.

Looking at the problem of attribute testing in more general terms, we suggest the following attribute transformation categories that have to be tested:

▶   Attributes that are expected to be unchanged after the transformation

▶   Attributes that changed only due to the code translation

▶ Attributes that change after applying complex business rules

▶ Attributes created in new entities due to new levels of aggregation

Testing should cover both real-time/near-real-time processing and batch processing.

Scenario-Based Testing   This approach requires very tedious analysis and specification for all transformation scenarios. In a typical CDI environment, there are hundreds or even thousands of scenarios that have to be tested. In some cases, if there is no data in the test data set to support certain test conditions, these conditions and the corresponding test data have to be created.

Testing CDI Services   CDI testing is not limited to data testing. Since a Customer Data Hub is built on the foundation of a service-oriented architecture (SOA), testers must be able to test Data Hub services, especially Web Services. Testing Web Services is a challenge since the testing processes, procedures, and test cases should take into account the disconnected nature of the services, protocols used to publish and consume services, and many other concerns. Among these concerns are

▶ Testing SOAP messages

▶ Testing WSDL files and using them for test plan generation

▶ Web Service consumer and producer emulation

▶ Testing the publish, find, and bind capabilities of an SOA-based solution

▶ Testing the asynchronous capabilities of Web Services

▶ Testing dynamic run-time capabilities of Web Services

▶ Web Services orchestration testing

▶ Web Services versioning testing

Considering these and other challenges of testing CDI solutions, components, data, and services, we have to conclude that the skill set that the Technical QA team should possess is quite diverse and hard to come by. The Technical QA team skill set should include the following:

▶ Test-strategy development skills that cover both data-testing capabilities and testing of services.

▶ Ability to develop test cases that require strong data analysis skills. This includes batch processing and real-time/near-real-time data flows.

▶ Reporting and query-building skills that require experience with reporting and business intelligence tools.

▶ Application and process testing for new customer-centric applications.

These testing qualifications are difficult to find. Usually, the variety of skills required for testing leads to very little overlap in experience among the Technical QA team members, which in turn leads to a necessarily large Technical QA team. The rule of thumb for CDI projects is that the number of testing resources should be about 75% of the number of developers.

Match Group Testing

Another CDI-specific functional area of testing is the verification of Match Group assignments. As we discussed earlier in Chapter 12, the Match Groups are created to identify and link the records that belong to one party, i.e., an individual or an organization. The process of creating and testing match groups is critical for any CDI project. Since the matching algorithm is iteratively tuned throughout the testing cycles in order to optimize matching accuracy and performance, it is very important to have a process that verifies the results of matching and discovers errors and issues.

Let us suggest a simple process successfully used by the authors on multiple projects. Assume that the Match Groups have been computed as a result of the matching process and the Match Group Identifier has been assigned to each record in the Data Hub.

- ▶ The process begins with a search for false positives. In order to do that, the match results are sorted by the Match Group. If the match is based on scoring, the match score should be displayed next to the match group ID. In this case, the correctness of the score could be verified for each combination of attributes that should be treated as a test case. Similarly, if the match is based on business rules defined as conditional statements, the match results should also be tested for each scenario. From the testing perspective, the use of scoring systems for matching is more convenient and enables faster test processing.

- ▶ False negatives are tested as soon as the analysis of false positives is complete. Assume that there are few attributes such that at least one of them must match in order for two records to acquire the same match identifier. If fuzzy logic is used for attribute comparison, the index generated by fuzzy logic should be used instead of the attribute value. Let's assume that there are three most critical attributes: credit card number, phone number, and address.

  - ▶ Only records for which the credit card number is the same but match group identifiers are different are included. The results are sorted by credit card number and analyzed.

  - ▶ Only records for which the phone number is the same but match group identifiers are different are included. The results are sorted by phone number and analyzed.

  - ▶ Only records for which the address is the same but match group identifiers are different are included. The results are sorted by address and analyzed.

In order to come up with conclusive results on match testing, the test must cover a representative set of scenarios. Scenarios should be defined on a case-by-case basis. Unlike transformation test processing where most scenarios are at the record level, match-testing scenarios, by their nature, include multiple records, which may result in an unmanageably high number of scenarios. If matching requirements are clearly defined, they can be used to construct appropriate test scenarios. A report representing the results of match testing should include an analysis of what attributes and matching conditions have been covered within the test data set.

Some vendors and CDI practitioners question the value of the detailed scenario-level or attribute-level requirements. We recommend that business users should identify matching requirements and guidelines at a high level, and leave the matching details to the implementation team. Once the matching design is completed and the tool is selected and/or configured, a match audit process should be invoked to assess the accuracy of the match. This match audit process usually involves an independent, often external, match audit provider. Responsibilities of a match audit provider include the following:

- ▶ Perform an independent match and identify the match groups
- ▶ Compare the results with the results obtained by the match process under audit
- ▶ Recommend improvements in business rules, data quality, profiling by attributes, etc.

Creation and Protection of Test Data

Today, companies have to comply with numerous global and local data privacy and confidentiality rules and regulations. Many organizations treat the need to protect sensitive data such as financial data and customer data very seriously. These organizations develop information security strategy and implement appropriate auditable security controls as required by regulations such as the Sarbanes-Oxley Act and the Gramm-Leach-Bliley Act. These steps are designed to protect sensitive data from external attacks. However, a slew of recent security breaches shows that the threat to data privacy and confidentiality comes from outside the corporation as well as from internal users (disgruntled employees, lack of security awareness, improper sharing of access privileges, etc.). What makes this data security problem even more alarming is a large number of incidents where a security-aware organization that is focused on protecting sensitive production data allows copies of that data to be used for testing of new systems and applications even though it is a known fact that test environments are rarely protected as strongly as the ones used for production. Regulations such as OCC Regulation 2001-47 have been developed specifically to address the issue of third-party data sharing, since many companies are outsourcing large-data-volume system testing to third-party service or solution providers.

All these concerns apply directly to MDM-CDI solutions: CDI test data tend to "look" almost like production data in its content and volumes. To avoid the data security exposure discussed earlier, a CDI project team has to recognize test data security issues at the beginning of the project, and develop approaches to protect not just production data but also test data. These approaches usually fall into two major categories: protecting or hardening the test environment, and protecting or sufficiently modifying test data content to avoid security compromise.

Let's look at the latter since it deals with the data content and thus may affect the way the CDI testing is performed. Test data protection can be achieved by anonymizing (obfuscating or cloaking) data at the file, record, or attribute level. The level of obfuscating is determined by the company's security and privacy policy and the nature of the data. In the case of customer data protection, the goal is to protect those attributes that can directly or indirectly identify individuals (i.e., social security numbers, credit card numbers, bank account numbers, medical information, and other personal information). From the regulatory compliance point of view, companies should be aware that if such nonpublic personal information (NPI) is compromised even outside the company walls (for example, the data security is breached at the outsourced third-party vendor site), the company is still responsible for data confidentiality protection. But because the security violation happened outside the company walls, the risk to the company's reputation is even greater.

The key challenges in using data anonymization techniques include:

▶ The ability to preserve logic potentially embedded in data structure and attributes to ensure that application logic continues to function.

▶ The ability to provide a consistent transformation outcome for the same data. In other words, many obfuscation techniques transform a particular attribute value into a different but predictable value consistently (e.g., "Alex" always gets converted into "Larry").

   ▶ There are some situations where the data sensitivity is so high that the transformations are designed to provide random, nonrepeatable values.

▶ Support for enterprise-scale data sets at the required levels of performance, scalability, and throughput.

Most popular anonymization techniques include the following:

▶ **Nullification**   All attribute values are replaced with NULL. The solution is simple and easily implementable. The primary disadvantage is that the data is lost and cannot be tested.

▶ **Masking data**   All attribute values are replaced with masking characters. The solution is also simple and easily implementable. Only limited testing is possible, for instance, on the number of characters. The primary disadvantage is that the logic embedded in the data is lost, and thus application or functional testing may be infeasible.

▶ **Substitution**   Replace the data values with similar-looking data created in separate stand-alone tables. For instance, if last names must be anonymized, all last names will be replaced with different last names in a cross-reference table. The algorithm is reasonably fast and preserves consistency across records, e.g., if the last name Smith is replaced with the last name Johns, this replacement will occur consistently for all records with the last name Smith. The last name lookup table serves as the key and must be protected. This approach allows for testing of entity matching, although fuzzy matching may require additional in-depth analysis of the testing outcome.

▶ **Shuffling records**   This method is similar to substitution, but unlike the Substitution method where the lookup table stores the cross-reference values, the record-shuffling method stores cross-reference pointers that randomly point to the records in the table that contains the anonymized data.

▶ **Number variance**   The algorithm multiplies each value by a random number.

▶ **Gibberish generation**   Random substitution of characters. The length of the data will be preserved. One-to-one relationships between the original code values and the anonymized code values can be preserved.

▶ **Encryption/decryption**   This is a classical approach, and many vendor solutions that perform encryption/decryption of data are available. The biggest challenge of this approach is related to the performance and key manageability of the algorithm. Indeed, if the encryption/decryption key pairs get lost or destroyed, the data may not be useable at all.

Many organizations decide to implement a combination of various techniques in order to meet all anonymization requirements.

Additional Technical and Operational Concerns

In addition to the issues discussed in the previous sections, we have to mention a few technical considerations that CDI projects need to take into account when building Data Hub systems.

Environment and Infrastructure Considerations

In general, building and deploying a CDI Data Hub platform should be done using the same approaches, processes, and procedures that are common in any large enterprise initiative. For example:

▶ Enterprise Database Administrator (DBA) and the infrastructure team should be adequately staffed. DBAs and infrastructure architects should work proactively to gather, understand, document, and integrate requirements from all work streams participating in the CDI project (the list of typical work streams is discussed in Chapter 11).

▶ Given the number of work streams, diversity of software, requirements for parallel processing, and need to support multiple system environments (e.g., test, QA, production), each of which should be able to store possibly terabytes of data, the success of the CDI project would depend on the availability of a dedicated and appropriately resourced infrastructure and architecture work stream.

▶ At a minimum, the following infrastructure environments have to be set up:

  ▶ Development

  ▶ Unit testing

  ▶ Integration testing

  ▶ Technology QA

  ▶ Business QA

  ▶ Performance testing

  ▶ Production

Typically, one or two additional environments are required specifically for data testing. These environments support snapshots of data and provide basic data management capabilities but may not include all CDI services and application components.

The following logical components must be acquired, installed, and configured as a part of the CDI technical architecture definition step (these logical components may be represented by a different number of physical infrastructure components):

▶ **Database servers**   These servers support the relational database management systems used by the CDI project (for example, an enterprise may decide to use Oracle DBMS for the Data Hub, and SQL Server for the loading and staging areas of the data architecture). Regardless of the DBMS technology, these servers should be able to support operations and recovery of very large volumes of data.

▶ **Message server (Enterprise Message Bus)**   This server supports real-time or near-real-time messaging and data synchronization requirements.

▶ **ETL servers**   These servers are focused on supporting batch data load processing.

▶ **Core CDI Data Hub and entity-matching server**   This server supports core CDI services including record matching.

- ▶ **Web servers**

- ▶ **Test Management server** This server is used for test planning, execution, and defect management.

- ▶ **Reporting server**

- ▶ **Change Management server**

- ▶ **Knowledge Management server** This server would support a project documentation and a searchable shared knowledge library for the project (e.g., an internal WiKi server).

Deployment

As we have stated repeatedly throughout the book, Master Data Management and Customer Data Integration are enterprise-wide initiatives that may have a profound impact on how an enterprise manages its core data. Deployment of any enterprise-wide structural change that impacts established business processes is a significant technical, organizational, and political challenge. The deployment complexity grows as the CDI solution evolves from the Registry Hub to the Transaction Hub. Indeed, we have shown in the previous chapters that Transaction Hub requires more invasive modifications of the data structures and radical changes to established business processes. Managing change and managing expectations of a CDI project should go hand in hand. Thus, the CDI project team should consider these typical deployment options:

- ▶ The "Big Bang" scenario includes CDI and new applications deployment across the entire enterprise in a single system release.

    - ▶ Pros: The enterprise-wide change avoids potential inconsistencies that are inevitable if only some of the processes and systems are migrated to the new customer-centric world.

    - ▶ Cons: High implementation risk of changing the entire organization at once. If the transition to customer centricity runs into any kind of problem (organizational, technical, budgetary, etc.), the resulting risk of project failure will be high.

- ▶ Deployment by line of business or geography

    - ▶ Pros: This deployment strategy makes sense if the entire customer base can be partitioned, and if the new applications can process smaller segments of data independently from each other. Partitioning the data files allows for more manageable chunks of data to be handled by new applications. Moreover, smaller data set partitions allow for smaller groups of users to be trained on their familiar data segments in parallel.

▶ Cons: During the deployment rollout, some parts of the enterprise will be transitioned onto a new CDI platform while others may still be using legacy systems. If not planned and carefully coordinated, this coexistence of the two modes of operations can cause significant problems. Multiple releases may be required to complete the enterprise-wide transition.

▶ Deployment for new transactions only

▶ Pros: This deployment strategy involves the entire enterprise and completes transition in a single release.

▶ Cons: This deployment strategy has similar implementation and management issues as the LOB and geography deployment options discussed earlier. The main concern is the necessity to manage both new and old environments and transactions concurrently until the migration to new systems is completed.

Considerations for the CDI Data Hub Data Model and Services

An important consideration in evaluating CDI Data Hub products deals with the Data Hub data model. A business-domain-specific, proven data model should be at the top of the CDI Data Hub selection criteria list. Is that always the right approach?

There are two competing CDI Data Hub product approaches as they relate to the Data Hub data model:

▶ The first one is based on a vendor-developed, out-of-the-box data model. It is very attractive for most firms to have the "right" data model. The "correctness" of the data model is a point-in-time decision since data models tend to evolve over time. The majority of CDI solutions available in the marketplace today provide a mechanism by which the model can be customized, but these customizations may be quite complex, and the resulting data model may have to be tuned and customized again and again until all business and technical requirements are met. This is particularly true if the core CDI data model includes hundreds or even thousands of entities, while only 10 to 30 entities (i.e., tables) are required to support CDI implementation that is based on the enterprise canonical data model.

▶ The second approach is data-model-agnostic. A chosen CDI product can instantiate any data model that better fits the organization. When the data model is instantiated, the CDI Data Hub automatically generates prerequisite core Hub services. Such products provide a higher level of flexibility but the data model needs to be defined separately. Also, the set of services generated automatically is often limited to low-level services. More complex composite services have to be developed by the project team and the enterprise application developers where appropriate. These data-model-agnostic products are in fact tools designed for accelerated MDM-CDI development. Figure 16-3 illustrates the idea of the data model for the Data Hub data-model-agnostic solution architecture.

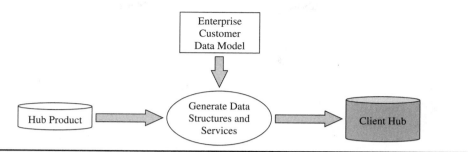

Figure 16-3 *Data-model-agnostic solution architecture*

We discuss various categories and types of the CDI Data Hub products in Part V of the book.

To sum up, this chapter offered a brief discussion of several implementation considerations for MDM-CDI solutions. These considerations include issues related to building customer-centric applications, reporting, testing, and other operational and deployment concerns. Even though these concerns may not be viewed as the core of CDI Data Hub solutions, they are extremely important from the CDI implementation perspective. If underestimated, these areas of concern can represent significant project risks and can ultimately cause a project to fail. We discuss some of the key reasons for MDM-CDI project failures in Chapter 18.

Master Data Management:
Markets, Trends, and Directions

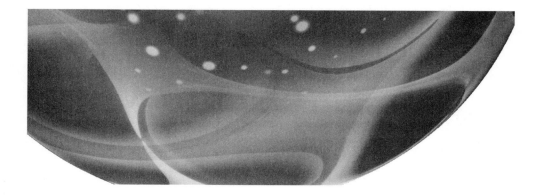

I n the previous parts of the book we described the goals, principles, benefits, architecture, design, and implementation concerns of MDM-CDI solutions in a way that was independent of specific vendors and their products. This independence from vendors and products allowed us to concentrate on defining Master Data Management and how it should be designed and implemented.

This part of the book addresses two topics and is organized into two chapters. Chapter 17 offers an overview of CDI vendors and their products, while Chapter 18 provides a recap of what we discussed so far. As part of this recap, Chapter 18 focuses on the major reasons why MDM and CDI projects fail. It takes a close look at the key reasons for CDI project failures, and concludes with a discussion on the market and technical trends and directions of Master Data Management and Customer Data Integration. This discussion is aimed at providing the readers with the authors' insight into what may lie ahead for us on this long and winding road to creating, managing, and effectively using information assets in a global enterprise.

CHAPTER 17

MDM-CDI Vendors and Products Landscape

IN THIS CHAPTER

Data Hub Products

Information Quality Products

Data Providers

Delivery Accelerators

I n Parts I through IV we described the architecture, design, and implementation approaches of MDM-CDI solutions, trying to avoid references to specific vendors. This was done in order to have a better focus on the essence of MDM-CDI projects and to cover common domain areas, issues, and risks. On the other hand, decisions on buy vs. build, what vendor to partner with, in which area and how, are extremely important for any MDM-CDI project. In other words, we need to know what features and functions are available today from what vendor, what is the vendor product road map, what pitfalls to look for when planning to establish a partnership with a particular vendor, and a host of other very relevant questions. Therefore, this book would be incomplete without an overview of the primary CDI vendors and their products.

The purpose of this chapter is twofold:

▶   First, to discuss the categories of vendors that should be considered in conjunction with MDM-CDI design, implementation, and deployment. Even though the vendor landscape in the MDM-CDI area is changing quickly, we believe that this discussion about the categories of relevant vendors will remain valid for some time.

▶   Second, to discuss specific vendors and their major products. We structured this part of the discussion as a point-in-time view of how various market-leading vendors are positioned today to help their customers to implement MDM-CDI solutions successfully, on time and on budget.

As we stated throughout the book, Master Data Management and Customer Data Integration are complex, multicomponent integrated platforms that involve numerous technical, organizational, and business process areas of concerns (please refer to Figure 11-1 showing the CDI "ecosystem"). Like any large and complex computer systems, MDM-CDI solutions represent an attractive and lucrative target to large and small vendors, some of whom attempt to develop integrated product suites that are designed to provide a "CDI in the box," while others concentrate on particular aspects of the MDM-CDI challenge or focus on providing supporting or enabling functionality. Clearly, discussing all vendors that offer CDI-related products is well beyond the scope of this book. Therefore, the sections that follow discuss leading vendors and their products that offer solutions in the following key MDM-CDI categories:

▶   Data Hub products
▶   Information quality tools
▶   Data providers
▶   Delivery accelerators

Of course, this categorization leaves a lot of ground uncovered. For example, in preceding chapters we showed the key role that metadata management and metadata repository can play in developing MDM-CDI solutions. However, since metadata management is a relatively mature category, and products providing metadata management capabilities are not an exclusive province of MDM-CDI, we'll leave the analysis of metadata solution providers out of this chapter. There are numerous publicly available references and information sources that discuss metadata-related issues in depth.

Another extremely important area of MDM-CDI functionality is concerned with protecting data from unauthorized access, and with achieving and maintaining compliance with numerous governmental and industry regulations. We believe that this area of concern has profound implications for the viability and usefulness of MDM-CDI solutions. In fact, we dedicated Part III of the book to discussing the issues of information security, compliance, and data visibility. Many vendors provide data security, access control, and visibility solutions, and the majority of these solutions are not MDM-CDI-specific. Moreover, in many cases, CDI Data Hub products do not provide integrated data security and visibility capabilities, and the MDM-CDI designers focus on integrating Data Hub systems with the existing enterprise security framework. We discussed security integration approaches in Chapter 10, but did not include the category of data security vendors in the discussion on CDI vendor landscape.

There are other vendor categories that are not discussed in this chapter, either because their involvement in MDM-CDI is peripheral (e.g., Enterprise Information Integration [EII]), or because of their maturity and general knowledge of their capabilities (e.g., pure-play ETL vendors).

NOTE ON THE STRUCTURE AND CONTENT OF THIS CHAPTER

We recognize that the information about specific vendors and their products is extremely volatile, and most of it may become quickly outdated. We also recognize that the list of vendors discussed in this chapter is far from complete. We focused on several key players that were either leading or gaining market share at the time of this writing. Nevertheless, we believe that the choice of vendors discussed here provides a good snapshot of the current MDM-CDI market landscape.

The information presented in this chapter has been synthesized from various sources including vendor briefings, analysis of publicly available research reports, and the authors' practical experience implementing MDM-CDI solutions using a number of mature and new vendor products. We used this synthesized information to describe the key features of a given product. However, the goal of this chapter is not to provide a comprehensive competitive analysis or a side-by-side comparison of the MDM-CDI vendors and their products. That information is available in research reports provided by industry research firms such as the Gartner Group, Forester Research, and others.

Data Hub Products

CDI Data Hub products are packaged solutions that provide multiple pieces of functionality enabling MDM-CDI implementations. This area is still young but it is maturing rapidly. According to "The Magic Quadrant for Customer Data Integration Hubs, 2Q2006" by John Radcliffe (Gartner Group, May 2006), the CDI Data Hub software market size will achieve an estimated $400 million by 2010. The same research shows that an estimated 50 percent of large organizations will engage in CDI implementations.

In general, Data Hub products are designed to provide support for data, content, structure, and services and they strive to offer a comprehensive set of data management, information quality, and data synchronization capabilities. Naturally, the leading Data Hub vendor products differ significantly from each other. The choice of the Data Hub product depends on many technical, political, economical, licensing, and even organizational factors (we covered this topic in the previous chapters of this book).

IBM WCC

After the acquisition of DWL by IBM, the original CDI product called DWL Customer received a new name, IBM WebSphere Customer Center (WCC). Gartner Group's "The Magic Quadrant for Customer Data Integration Hubs, 2Q2006" singles out WCC as the emerging leader in the Data Hub space. The base product was developed as a J2EE application supported and controlled by a J2EE-compliant application server. The product includes customer-centric customizable data structures and a few hundred basic business Web Services. These services support real-time transactions such as managing core customer data, address and contact information, customer grouping and aggregation, financial information, customer roles and relationships, alerts, matching, and duplicate suspect processing. More complex services known as composite transactions can be built using the basic Web Services.

The WCC solution includes several levels of services and components to support the flexibility of the business service model:

► Coarse-grained business services

► Fine-grained business services

► Business Object Model

► Database

The solution offers multiple access methods such as Web Services, EAI publish-subscribe interfaces, and object-level interfaces. The ability to build composite transactions by calling coarse-grained, fine-grained, and business object components at run time makes the solution even more flexible.

WCC provides some data visibility functionality using its Rules of Visibility engine (RoV). Batch Framework is available to support batch processing when real-time synchronization is not required or not feasible. The EverGreen module supports matching, management of suspect duplicates, and alert and notification capabilities. The WebSphere Portal provides business and operational reporting capabilities.

The product formerly known as DWL Customer was originally developed for the insurance industry and therefore its out-of-the-box components are optimized for this industry. The product is used in financial services and other industries.

Siperian

The Siperian solution is considered "visionary" by Gartner Group's "The Magic Quadrant for Customer Data Integration Hubs, 2Q2006." The Siperian Hub is designed as a metadata-driven J2EE application that can work with any data model. This flexibility positions Siperian not only as a CDI solution but also as a platform applicable to a wider MDM area. The version of the Data Hub known as Siperian Hub XT includes the following high-level components:

- ▶ Master Reference Manager (MRM) creates and manages record location metadata to support data synchronization in batch and real-time modes.

- ▶ Hierarchy Manager (HM) manages relationship hierarchies.

- ▶ Activity Manager (AM) manages a unified view of transaction and reference data across systems. It is used to continually monitor and evaluate data and act on data events.

Siperian Hub XT has its own cleanse and match capabilities. Alternatively, external engines can be used to cleanse and standardize the data, e.g. Business Objects/First Logic or Trillium. Typically, Business Objects/First Logic or Trillium cleanses and standardizes the data while Siperian hub performs matching and linking. Siperian licenses MetaMatrix Data Services Solution, which supports on-demand access to associated customer activity data not stored in the customer master. MetaMatrix provides Siperian with additional capabilities to implement the Registry-style solution even though initially the Siperian Hub was developed with the Transaction-style Hub in mind.

The Siperian Hub was originally adopted in the pharmaceutical industry and is increasing its presence in other industries including financial services.

Initiate Systems

Initiate is rated as "visionary" by the Gartner Group's "The Magic Quadrant for Customer Data Integration Hubs, 2Q2006." Initiate provides a sound solution for the Reference-style Hub. The solution integrates multiple systems and databases by providing a metadata-driven view that federates distributed data stores in real time. Initiate provides strong matching capabilities that enable its clients to create a single trusted view of the client profile data. Initiate supports management of organizational hierarchies for institutional customers. Initiate provides a set of APIs and Web Services that can effectively support application integration. The Initiate Identity Hub engine and its flow-invocation service are used for processing, linking, and retrieval of the federated data. The solution can federate data from multiple sources including primary relational databases, files, messaging systems, etc. The main components of the Initiate solution include:

► Initiate Enterprise Viewer enables the users to view linked records across lines of business and systems.

► Initiate Auditor is used to resolve data quality issues.

► Initiate Reporting Database provides on-demand access to all information in the Initiate Identity Hub database.

Initiate started as a solution integrating medical records and is currently expanding in other industries, most notably, financial services.

Siebel/Oracle

Siebel is known as the leader in the CRM space. Recently acquired by Oracle, the company was identified as a "visionary" player in the CDI area by Gartner Group's "The Magic Quadrant for Customer Data Integration Hubs, 2Q2006." Siebel has well-developed customer-centric data structures and modules for a number of industries. Siebel's CDI solution consists of three modules:

► Universal Application Network (UAN) enables organizations to deploy business processes. UAN includes UAN Integration Processes, UAN Common Objects, and UAN Transformations.

► The Data Quality module provides matching capabilities in real-time and batch modes. It supports integration with other data-cleansing tools. These capabilities are available for multiple countries, languages, and character sets.

► Universal Customer Master is a customer Data Hub that provides prebuilt components that integrate customer data from multiple systems.

Oracle

Oracle Corporation positions its Data Hub products as part of its open architecture middleware family of products. Each of the Oracle Data Hub products operates as a Transaction Hub with appropriate data structures and services customized and configured to support particular data domains.

▶ Oracle Customer Data Hub assembles a broad set of components including data quality, matching, customer key management, data enrichment, data synchronization, and analytics.

▶ Oracle Financial Consolidation Hub integrates financial data from multiple sources.

▶ Oracle Product Information Management Data Hub integrates product data by creating a centralized product database.

After acquisition of Siebel, Oracle added Siebel Universal Customer Master to its CDI offerings. With a variety of CDI products in its portfolio, Oracle has the potential of becoming one of the leaders in the CDI Data Hub space. Oracle's advances in the MDM-CDI area are aligned with the overall company strategy and market acceptance of the Oracle Fusion Middleware program.

Purisma

Purisma Customer Registry is a "thin" Registry-style customer Data Hub solution that enables the company to align multiple applications from the perspectives of customer data accuracy and data quality. The product offers strong matching capabilities and supports complex hierarchical relationships between customers with a focus on institutional entities. The support for hierarchical relationships includes systemic relationship correlation capabilities. Purisma stores relevant data in the module known as Master Customer Identity Index. The product consists of the following three tightly integrated components:

▶ Purisma Correlation Engine is at the core of the solution. This component manages matching and association metadata, and ultimately maintains customer identity.

▶ Purisma Data Stewardship Engine provides views and user interfaces that allow the user to analyze the data, manage exceptions, and perform audit, hierarchy management, and other manual control functions.

▶ Purisma Integration Services provides Web Services–based utilities for third-party integration.

Purisma supports Transaction Hub capabilities that enable enterprises to use the Purisma Hub as the master hub that provides bidirectional synchronization with multiple systems.

Sun Microsystems

After the acquisition of SeeBeyond in August 2005, Sun Microsystems entered the customer Data Hub market. Sun's Single Customer View solution consists of the following components developed on the J2EE platform:

- ▶ eView Studio provides cleansing and matching capabilities.

- ▶ eInsight Business Process Manager orchestrates business processes.

- ▶ eGate Integrator provides Web Services–based data synchronization capabilities including data transformation, guaranteed transactions, and messaging.

- ▶ eVision Studio enables the enterprise to build web-based presentation layers.

- ▶ ePortal Composer personalizes applications and manages end-user access to the data stored in the Data Hub.

As you can see, this product suite provides a variety of technical capabilities that are required for MDM-CDI implementations.

GoldenSource

GoldenSource is a Master Data Management solution developed specifically for the financial services industry. GoldenSource creates and manages master data environments that include all financial instruments, business entities, consolidated transactions, and positions. As such, GoldenSource's scope is broader than just Customer Data Integration. There are a number of modules supported by GoldenSource:

- ▶ GoldenSource Securities & Products operates as the global security master hub that enables a financial institution to process financial information from multiple internal and external sources and to maintain it in a single data store. The product creates, maintains, and publishes standardized reference data to other financial tools and applications.

- ▶ GoldenSource Customers and Counterparties modules provide core CDI functionality. These components create, maintain, and publish standardized customer profile data. The product supports multiple party types out of the box, organizational hierarchy data, credit and operational information, and can use external data for risk and exposure management.

▶ GoldenSource Positions provides access to positions and balances for the customer accounts. This information can be aggregated at various levels to assist business users in making operational decisions.

▶ GoldenSource Transactions provides real-time data synchronization and integration capabilities by standardizing, enriching, and linking data from disparate data sources.

SAP

SAP started out as a premier vendor in the Enterprise Resource Planning (ERP) market. It has rapidly evolved into a major player in Master Data Management. SAP offers a well-known and widely deployed suite of business applications. One of them, MySAP Customer Relationship Management, is designed for customer-centric solutions. SAP is optimized for transaction-style implementations, including its own version of the Data Hub. SAP solutions provide an integrated set of information management capabilities including catalog and content management as well as product life-cycle management (PLM) with a particular focus on marketing, merchandising, and promotions (these features came from the acquisition of A2i in 2004). SAP is known for its ability to optimize processes for transaction-style implementations.

SAP CDI solutions are based on NetWeaver technology, which provides a service-oriented architecture approach to integrating business processes, software components, information, and organizational entities. NetWeaver is designed to be platform-agnostic and thus can interoperate with Microsoft .NET and IBM WebSphere (J2EE). The power and flexibility of the NetWeaver platform and the size and influence of SAP as a leader in ERP solutions help position SAP to become one of the leaders in the MDM-CDI space. In fact, according to the Gartner Group's 2006 "CDI Magic Quadrant" report, SAP is predicted to become one of the market leaders by 2010 and along with Oracle, IBM, and Microsoft is projected to collect over 50 percent of the CDI software license revenue.

DataFlux Data Hub Product

DataFlux is a division of SAS. DataFlux complements SAS core competencies in business intelligence software and services by providing solutions aimed at information quality and data profiling. Its focus on information quality and related areas allows DataFlux to enter the CDI Data Hub space by defining a very important niche and naming its product the Data Quality Hub. DataFlux's Data Quality Hub product includes the following components:

▶ Master Customer Reference Database stores customer information.

▶ dfPowerStudio enables data stewards and data governance professionals to monitor and profile data enterprise-wide, analyze the data quality, and take corrective actions using a single interface. Data quality features are based on libraries that enable address standardization and enrichment in line with U.S. Postal Service standards, party-type recognition (individual vs. organization), gender recognition, and other critical CDI data quality functions. Data integration features allow the users to match, link, and merge records across systems.

► DataFlux Integration Server provides a single mechanism for batch and real-time data synchronization. It reads the business rules from the metadata created by dfPowerStudio and enforces the rules for data synchronization, taking advantage of parallel processing to support higher throughput. The product is capable of running batch jobs and exposes interfaces to its data quality functions and algorithms, which can be called from many languages. Otherwise, the functions and algorithms can be called as Web Services.

Being part of SAS, the DataFlux products are well positioned to leverage their data quality and CDI strengths with SAS's capabilities in the business intelligence and marketing analytics areas.

VisionWare MultiVue

Unlike many Data Hub products that are built on the Java platform, VisionWare MultiVue is developed using Microsoft .NET technology. Its core product, MultiVue Identification Server, is designed to support customer identity and address management as well as data cleansing, matching, and indexing functionality—key CDI capabilities that support the creation of a single aggregated customer view from data collected from disparate systems. The solution has a robust probabilistic match engine. For its data load and some other data management needs, it relies on Microsoft SQL Server and its utilities.

On September 7, 2006 Visionware announced that MultiVue had been selected by Microsoft as a priority solution partner for the public sector. Eventually this can significantly strengthen the company's position in the CDI space, particularly with Microsoft's introduction of its Advisor Platform aimed at helping financial advisors take a centralized view of customers, investment products, and services.

ObjectRiver

ObjectRiver offers a product called ObjectRiver MDM that enables an enterprise to generate an MDM solution based on any canonical data model defined by the enterprise. The product is model-driven and automatically generates the required data structures; builds coarse-grained business objects, functional (CRUD) data access interfaces and Web Services, the presentation layer; and ultimately creates an MDM Web portal. In other words, ObjectRiver MDM provides a rapid MDM SOA development and maintenance environment that enables an enterprise to build real-time transaction Data Hub systems quickly. The product includes:

► Integration with Computer Associates' AllFusion ERwin Data Modeler, which is used to generate relational tables, stored procedures, and XML schemas for Web Services, and a Java data access layer for developers.

► Model Compiler, which reads the model and generates a complete database infrastructure for the master database.

► An out-of-the-box audit for all changes to business objects.

► Business Event Factory, which allows an enterprise to define, process, and deliver well-defined messages and data changes triggered by business events. ObjectRiver MDM integrates with several Enterprise Message Bus middleware products including Oracle Fusion ESB, IBM MQSeries, and TIBCO, and supports a message subscription and routing mechanism to manage data flows.

Information Quality Products

As we discussed earlier, information quality is a very complex and at the same time an absolutely critical part of any MDM-CDI solution. Data Hub solutions are often enhanced by integrating them with data quality products specialized in data profiling, cleansing, standardization, and matching.

Information quality is a $300-million market in license revenue annually and is growing, according to Gartner Group's "Magic Quadrant for Data Quality Tools" by Ted Friedman and Andreas Bitter (April 2006). And according to "Forrester's Market Overview" by Lou Agosta, Philip Russom, Elana Anderson, and Colin Teubner, the total size of the information quality market is expected to reach $1 billion. This estimate includes software licenses, professional services, and data enhancement segments.

Business Objects (First Logic)

Acquired by Business Objects in April 2006, First Logic is a specialist data quality product vendor. Its solution is designed to integrate with most leading Data Hub vendors. The capabilities commonly used for CDI implementations include data cleansing and standardization for names and addresses, and entity match and merge (consolidate). Version 7 of the product includes a number of modules such as

► MCD 7 used for match and consolidate

► RAPID APIs used for batch and real-time online integration with the match engine

▶ ACE (Address Correction and Encoding)

▶ DataRight, which parses names to identify name elements for individuals and companies. It also provides a variety of validation features, e.g., Tax Identification number (TIN) validation.

IQ8 (DQXI) is a new version of the data quality product re-engineered on a .NET Web Services platform. The product includes all the data quality features of version 7 and significantly extends and integrates them. With the introduction of version 8, the product significantly enhanced its throughput and improved real-time data standardization and matching.

Trillium

Trillium is one of the leading vendors in the data quality space. It integrates with most data hub vendors and demonstrates high performance for data quality operations. Trillium has developed an end-to-end solution referred to as Total Data Quality. This solution includes two major components:

▶ TS Discovery discovers and analyzes enterprise data to reveal data anomalies and violations of established business rules, relationships, and other data irregularities. The product automates data profiling process and significantly increases its accuracy and efficiency. The product creates a repository of metadata, and actual data content. It detects irregularities and provides metrics on frequencies for data anomalies. The irregularities can be continually monitored to assess changes in data quality for the existing data and to evaluate the impact of new data. TS Discovery provides drill-down views that allow the users to perform comparisons of the data quality results before and after data cleansing, consolidation, or any other improvement.

▶ TS Quality provides data standardization capabilities that enrich data with geographical, census, and other third-party information. The data match engine identifies individual and business records, households, and other relationships. The product provides address validation functions based on postal authority files, name and address verification, correction, standardization, and other data enrichment capabilities including Unicode format for international and global CDI solutions.

DataFlux Information Quality Product

DataFlux has been reviewed earlier in this chapter when we discussed Data Hub products. We mention DataFlux in this section as recognition of the product's strength as one of the leading data quality tools.

IBM Product Suite

After the acquisition of Ascential Software Corp in 2005, the IBM family of data quality products includes WebSphere ProfileStage and WebSphere QualityStage.

▶ WebSphere ProfileStage should be used first in the early stages of a CDI project and then on an ongoing basis to monitor data profiling changes. The product performs data profiling and produces detail reports at multiple levels: column, table, and across tables. Column analysis helps with understanding the data content and quality, value frequency, uniqueness measurements, null-value measurements, etc. The table-level analysis provides insights into the primary key structures and issues. The cross-table analysis enables the users to infer foreign keys and identify redundancies and other cross-table data issues. ProfileStage together with a companion product called AuditStage can validate business rules and discover hidden information in the data.

▶ WebSphere QualityStage provides a high-performance solution for data standardization and matching. Name recognition includes intelligent algorithms capable of parsing a free-form name to recognize first and last names, initials, name prefixes, titles, generational suffixes, and separate them from "noise" constructs such as "Attn," "C/O," "and," and other frequently used constructs. The product applies postal standards to addresses. The matching algorithm can use fuzzy probabilistic match and consolidate data utilizing configurable survivorship rules. The product supports postal verification (WAVES—worldwide) and postal certification (CASS—U.S., SERP—Canada, DPID—Australia).

Both ProfileStage and QualityStage products are built to comply with industry standards (XML, EDI, JMS, JCA). These products are components of an integrated suite, and as such they integrate with each other and with the WebSphere DataStage (an ETL tool), MetaStage (Metadata Management tool), and numerous external products. As IBM evolves and integrates these products, the next major release of the suite may integrate all WebSphere products including the Data Hub product WCC, thus creating a full-function CDI platform.

Group 1 Software

Group 1 Software provides a number of products that can be used on MDM-CDI implementations. The products and capabilities include the following:

▶ Strong address and postal code validation, verification, and standardization worldwide is provided by the Address Now and CODE-1 Plus suite for U.S., Canadian, and international addresses.

> ▶ FineTune Data helps organizations parse and correct customer names and addresses. In addition to correcting personal names, addresses, and personal titles, etc., the product identifies atypical names and name suffixes. The product is capable of identifying the newest address for an individual or business (using the VeriMove component).

Informatica

Informatica is one of the leaders in the ETL market. With the acquisition of Similarity Systems in January of 2006, Informatica took a significant step toward getting a leadership position in data quality as it relates to the MDM-CDI domain. Similarity Systems expands traditional Informatica's offering in the ETL and data integration spaces by bringing strong data profiling, data standardization, and matching capabilities.

Informatica Data Quality Suite is built on Similarity Systems' ATHANOR product and delivers data standardization, data matching, and data quality monitoring capabilities to its users.

Informatica Data Quality Suite enables enterprise data stewards and data governance officers to establish and maintain data quality rules. These rules and associated capabilities cover name and address parsing and validation for all countries, and data validation and corrections for various business domains such as Product, Inventory, Assets, etc. The product provides robust matching and householding capabilities. In addition, Informatica Data Quality Suite offers industry-specific libraries of data quality content for financial services and consumer packaged goods (CPG) companies. The suite provides Unicode-compliant technologies important for global projects since Unicode allows all writing systems and languages of the world to be represented and handled consistently.

Informatica Data Quality Suite uses an integrated data repository shared by the following components:

> ▶ Informatica Data Quality's Designer provides an interface used to build information quality rules and plans.

> ▶ Informatica Data Quality Server provides the platform for the development, testing, and execution of the information quality rules and plans.

> ▶ Informatica Data Quality's Runtime enables the enterprise to schedule and run data analysis, profiling, and other information quality processes.

> ▶ Informatica Data Quality's RealtimeSDK provides real-time capabilities for information quality processes such as data validation, corrections, standardization, and enrichment.

> ▶ A library of reference data is a section of the repository that maintains synonyms, aliases, and other data required to support the tool's navigational capabilities.

Innovative Systems

Innovative Systems has developed its i/Lytics suite of products, which enable the enterprise to profile, cleanse, and standardize its data and resolve other data quality issues. The suite consists of the following products:

- ▶ i/Lytics Data Profiler provides automated data profiling capabilities

- ▶ i/Lytics Data Quality provides integrated capabilities for data cleansing, standardization, matching, and householding. The product can process name and address data and validate TINs, e-mail addresses, and other customer and account information. When integrated with customer profile management applications, these capabilities can be used to collapse and maintain single customer profiles.

- ▶ i/Lytics GLOBAL provides address verification and correction capabilities for domestic and international addresses. The product supports both batch and real-time capabilities. The product is compliant with USPS standards.

- ▶ i/Lytics SECURE provides matching capabilities in the context of fraud detection and regulatory compliance. This product matches customers against any database or lists of criminals, terrorists, suspects, or other identified individuals and organizations that are published by U.S. and international government agencies, industry groups, and internal enterprise risk management and compliance groups.

Data Providers

The vendors in this category maintain databases with customer profile information. In addition to more traditional cleansing, standardization, and matching capabilities, these vendors provide their Knowledge Bases with customer profiles that can be used for customer identification, marketing campaigns, analysis and research, and other applications. CDI Data Hub systems can use these Knowledge Bases in order to cross-reference, verify, and enrich the enterprise customer data. It is not uncommon that only a particular Knowledge Base can match customers at different addresses, customers that change names, vanity addresses, and other conditions that require specific knowledge.

Acxiom

Acxiom's primary focus is customer information management and customer data integration. Acxiom's Knowledge Base contains records of customer information collected from and verified by multiple sources. Acxiom's Command Center supports over 850 terabytes of storage space. Acxiom provides a very broad coverage of individuals residing in the United States. Acxiom licenses United States Postal Service information, in particular, its National Change of Address (NCOA) file. This enables the company to store and maintain up-to-date name and address information. Therefore, if one is going to implement an MDM-CDI solution that needs to use name and address to match its corporate customer data, a partnership with Acxiom can provide significant benefits to data quality and confidence of the match process. Some of the Acxiom products frequently used on CDI projects are as follows:

▶ AbiliTec is a product that provides batch and near-real-time matching and data enrichment information. AbiliTec receives an information request for customer name and address and returns the AbiliTec links that represent the event of matching this name and address data against Acxiom's Knowledge Base. Specifically, if the match has been found, the link type is referred to as "maintained"; otherwise, a "derived" AbiliTec link is returned. The product supports individual and business links for the U.S., the UK, and Australia.

▶ AddressAbility is a product that verifies, corrects, and standardizes addresses to USPS specifications, which includes Zip codes, city names and state abbreviations, resolution of vanity addresses, etc.

▶ DSF^2 is a product that stores all valid addresses recognized by USPS. The product can also differentiate between residential and business addresses. This product can assist in party type identification. We discussed the importance of party identification in Chapter 12.

▶ NCOA^{Link} provides change of address information. From the CDI perspective, this information can be used to bring two individual records at different addresses, recognizing them as one individual.

▶ LACS^{Link} provides information about permanent address conversions resulting from renumbering, street or city name changes, etc. This is a critical piece of information that helps in matching customer records.

Dun and Bradstreet

Dun & Bradstreet (D&B) assists companies and government organizations in implementing MDM and CDI projects. The company's global commercial database contains over 100 million customer records. It provides valuable information about businesses worldwide. A partnership with D&B can make a difference for MDM-CDI projects focusing on commercial customers. Such a partnership can be particularly helpful for sales and marketing, credit management, and managing the company's suppliers. The D&B data contains global business profile information. The information includes company name, headquarters address, phone and fax, primary office or site locations, corporate executives, stock index, parent company information, year of establishment, approximate or reported net worth, current financial information, credit risk information, lawsuits against the company, history of slow payments, and many other data attributes. D&B creates and maintains a unique D&B DUNS number for each entity (company) that it recognizes and maintains information on. DUNS numbers are useful attributes that can enhance accuracy of matching applications. D&B also maintains the company's credit ratings and D&B PAYDEX scores.

D&B provides a wide variety of products and services that include the following:

▶ D&B Data maintains profile information for businesses.

▶ Alert services generate automated alerts on a selected set of data attributes when one of them changes as defined by a specified business rule.

▶ Market Spectrum Web supports market analysis to identify potentially most-profitable customers and promising prospects.

▶ Predictive Indicators help in analyzing the behavior for institutional customers to predict potential buyers for a given product.

▶ Reports provide key financial information: Report types include Business Information Report (BIR) and Comprehensive Report.

▶ DUNSRight Quality Process transforms the data to make it consistent with the formats and standards required for data retrieval and analysis.

D&B offers a number of packaged solutions including Risk Management Solutions, which assists in mitigating project risks; Sales and Marketing Solutions; E-Business Solutions, which help in market research; and Supply Chain Management Solutions.

D&B announced a Product and Technology Outsourcing Agreement with Acxiom on August 2, 2006. The agreement is aimed at increasing data processing capacity and matching rates by using Acxiom technology.

Experian

Experian has developed its Truvue CDI technology aimed at easy integration with sales and marketing applications worldwide. Truvue uses variety of sources to bring, store, and maintain standardized customer information. This includes both individual (consumer) and business customer data. Truvue provides a standard real-time XML interface to its service, which allows companies to process and match customer information at the point of contact. The Flexible Links functionality allows companies to create their own data enrichment rules by combining party information.

Experian data stores maintain name, address, life-style data, and other attributes that can be beneficial to marketing campaigns. Truvue keeps track of address and name changes, marriages, and other life events from the customer identification and marketing perspective. Experian helps companies improve their real-time customer authentication and identity management capabilities, which allows the companies to minimize fraud. In addition, Experian has developed predictive modeling capabilities that are based on the demographics data. These capabilities can be used in marketing campaigns, to screen for most profitable customers and best prospects.

Delivery Accelerators

Data Hub vendors are at the core of MDM-CDI projects. Their products work in concert with data quality products that are also critically important for the projects' success. In addition to these product categories, other products can also significantly accelerate MDM-CDI projects and improve the desired results. We discuss some of these products in the following section.

DataDelta

As we discussed in Chapter 15, match optimization is an iterative process that typically requires multiple cycles. When the number of records is high, the records are highly heterogeneous, and the number of parameters in the matching algorithm is high, it is quite common that iterations may take long time to complete. Even after months of running iteration cycles, it may still be unclear whether the engine has achieved required match accuracy. DataDelta helps accelerate tuning of match engines for maximum accuracy. DataDelta achieves this goal by generating reports (change metrics) that quantify changes in match results and enable the user to quickly compare two sets of match results. This makes it possible to evaluate the effect of changes in business rules and parameters rapidly and optimize changes for the next iteration to meet business objectives. In addition to providing summary reports that reflect the trends, changes, and impacts caused by business rule change, DataDelta provides a "fit" metric for each record that can be joined for record-level impact analysis.

The product can be used at early stages of the project to assist in the evaluation of the quality of match operations. This provides valuable information helping users to assess the significance of the existing match problems and their potential impact on the business. This information can be useful in formulating CDI value propositions and justifying the investments.

Netrics

Netrics provides unique matching capabilities based on graph theory, specifically on the *Bipartite Graph Matching (BGM)* algorithm. This algorithm makes it possible to incorporate a human-like intelligence in the matching process.

These matching capabilities significantly exceed the capabilities provided by more traditional fuzzy algorithms such as SOUNDEX and NYSIIS. The algorithm scales as $N*logN$, where N is the number of records in the matching record set. Also, the algorithm works well with sparse data. Sparse data is a common problem when matching heterogeneous records sourced from multiple systems and lines of business. Most traditional algorithms are not optimized to handle this problem.

Netrics can utilize a learning algorithm that can accept manual user input to refine the matching rules. This empowers the user to change match groups for a small sample data set manually and use the learning algorithm. The learning algorithm will automatically interpret the manual input and define it internally as a generic rule that it will apply on the next matching iteration.

Identity Systems

Identity Systems, a Nokia Company, is focused primarily on customer search and matching. Its matching solution handles variations of name and address such as spelling errors and phonetic errors. It supports match on formal names to nicknames, missing words, word sequence differences, inconsistent abbreviations, titles, and suffixes.

Identity Search Server provides high quality and accuracy in search, matching, and relationship linking and index building. The algorithm can deal with unformatted names and addresses. It provides high-accuracy searches and matches without having to standardize the data before the match. The algorithm is customizable and scalable. The company has developed significant intellectual property embedded in its match algorithm, and offers a variety of reusable components for match and search projects. This includes global implementations where the match engine has to deal with languages other than English, including Unicode-based environments. The product can standardize data that includes CASS-certified Global Address standardization.

Exeros

Data mapping is one of the most tedious, time-consuming, and labor-intensive tasks that MDM-CDI project teams have to deal with. Exeros provides the metadata facility and user interfaces that can significantly speed up the mapping process and improve its accuracy. The mapping metadata is compliant with open standards, supports strong reporting capabilities, and can be used by multiple consuming applications and systems such as ETL, messaging middleware, and other systems and processes that require and consume data mapping metadata information.

Exeros DataMapper with its DataBot technology offers an innovative approach to data mapping that performs data analysis to determine data relationships and business rules. The tool analyzes the content of the source systems column by column and infers which columns should be mapped to each other and how.

The product utilizes an automated semantic reconciliation process to generate mapping rules. The product automatically generates rules, and the users can correct and refine the rules manually. This approach can provide significant benefits over a traditional methodology when mapping is performed based on attribute names.

In conclusion, we would like to reemphasize how the content of this chapter was collected and organized. The information presented in this chapter has been synthesized from various sources including vendor briefings, analysis of publicly available research reports, and the authors' practical experience implementing MDM-CDI Data Hubs using a number of market-leading vendor products. However, the goal of this chapter was not to provide a comprehensive competitive analysis or side-by-side comparison of MDM-CDI vendors and their products. This information is available in research reports provided by industry research firms such as the Gartner Group, Forester Research, and others. We referred to some published research information only to illustrate the product's capabilities and the analysts' opinion about a given vendor's positioning in the marketplace.

CHAPTER
18

Where Do We Go from Here?

IN THIS CHAPTER

Master Data Management and Customer Data Integration Today

Master Data Management and Customer Data Integration: Trends and Directions

367

Master Data Management and Customer Data Integration Today

We have arrived at the point in the book that allows us to talk about the future of Master Data Management and Customer Data Integration. Throughout the book, we have used various ways to define MDM and CDI and to articulate the business drivers and technical challenges of implementing these types of initiatives. We showed the complexities surrounding MDM and CDI architecture, paid close attention to often-overlooked issues of data security and visibility, and shared the authors' personal experiences in addressing implementation concerns on a number of MDM and CDI projects across several industries.

Here is a brief summary of the key points we covered in the preceding chapters:

▶ The key terms used in the area of Customer Data Integration, specifically, the terms "customer" and "party," mean much more than just simply a single individual that an enterprise considers a customer. In fact, these are somewhat generic and abstract terms that include individual customers, prospects, or business entities that are the "customers" of an enterprise's line of business (for example, small businesses can be customers of a retirement plan service provider, with their employees representing an additional level of customer details). Therefore, the term Customer can and usually is replaced by industry-specific or line-of-business–specific terms such as: Client, Contact, Party, Counterparty, Patient, Subscriber, Supplier, Prospect, Service Provider, Citizen, Guest, Legal Entity, Trust, Business Entity, and other terms.

▶ The ability to recognize individual entities as members of arbitrary complex groups (e.g., households and extended families for individuals, holding companies, and other organizational hierarchies for business entities such as corporations) is one of the key properties of Master Data Management, and applies equally well to Customer Data Integration solutions, Reference Data Management, Product Master Hubs, etc., with the complexity of the associations and grouping depending in large part on the completeness and accuracy of data and the business rules driving the resolution of conflicting or undetermined links.

▶ Master Data Management is a horizontal technology that applies equally well to all industries and markets and is global in nature. The latter point has two equally important aspects:

    ▶ MDM and its customer-centric version known as Customer Data Integration are especially effective in modernizing a global enterprise.

    ▶ The need for an authoritative, accurate, timely, and secure "single version of the truth" is pervasive and is not particular to a specific country or geography.

▶ Customer Data Integration, while evolutionary from the pure technological point of view, is revolutionary in its potential business impact of transforming the enterprise into a customer-centric model. In that, CDI represents a particularly interesting opportunity to any customer or citizen facing organizations including commercial businesses and government agencies alike.

▶ Master Data Management and Customer Data Integration can enable an enterprise to achieve sustainable competitive advantage by improving levels of customer service and overall customer experience, reducing the attrition rates, growing customer-based revenue as a share of their wallet by understanding and leveraging the totality of customer relationships with the enterprise, and helping the enterprise to be in a better position to achieve regulatory compliance, to name just a few.

▶ MDM-CDI can be extremely beneficial to various government agencies and businesses not only from a customer service point of view but also in helping law enforcement agencies in threat detection and prevention.

▶ MDM and CDI technical approaches and challenges include:

  ▶ Building an MDM-CDI solution as an instance of a Service-Oriented Architecture (SOA)

  ▶ Building CDI solutions to utilize Web Services as the insulation vehicle between new master data, legacy data stores, business processes, and applications

  ▶ Addressing data governance and data quality issues

  ▶ Defining and applying accurate matching algorithms for batch and real-time processing

  ▶ Defining and applying survivorship rules for the "single version of truth" record

  ▶ Solving complex data synchronization and reconciliation issues

  ▶ Considering the complexity of new, CDI-enabled business transactions that span systems and applications not only within the enterprise but also across system domains of its business partners

  ▶ Addressing the scalability challenges of data volumes, transactional throughput, and structured and unstructured data types

  ▶ Enabling robust process controls to support audit and compliance reporting

  ▶ Designing effective approaches to protecting access to the integrated data as well as to the services and applications that can access that data—fine-grained access controls and policy- and entitlements-driven data visibility and security

> ► There are many CDI implementation challenges, and a typical CDI project may start small but inevitably grows into a large, multidisciplinary, enterprise-wide, complex, time-consuming initiative that requires a significant investment of time, resources, and money, and therefore, a senior, often executive-level organizational commitment, and obtaining such a commitment is not an easy task.

We also learned that addressing the points in the preceding list does not guarantee that a CDI or MDM project will be a success. Today, we know of several predominant reasons why CDI initiatives fail.

Main Reasons CDI Projects Fail

Master Data Management in general, and Customer Data Integration projects in particular, represent significant enterprise-wide undertakings that rely on and impact four pillars of successful CDI initiatives: business processes, people, organizational structure, and technology. These four pillars of CDI are needed to maintain the balance—break one pillar, and the entire CDI "house" may fall! Let's review some of the key reasons why CDI projects may fail:

► **Lack of executive support and budgetary commitment** As we mentioned several times, CDI initiatives can succeed only if there is executive-level support. This is the key since many CDI projects tend to become very large very quickly and last longer than a few months. Even though signing checks is critical, senior management commitment must go beyond that. Senior management must understand the key benefits, dependencies, release scope and timing, high-level risks, and trade-offs the project is facing.

► **Lack of coordination and cooperation between business and technology organizations** The complexity, size, and the implementation risk of CDI initiatives require close coordination and cooperation between business and technology organizations involved in the CDI initiative not only in order to achieve the goals of the project but also to reach an agreement that these goals have been met. All too often a business unit defines the high-level business requirements for a CDI solution and passes them on to the technology team to implement. The technology team analyzes the requirements and their technical feasibility, and defines the plan, the approach, the architecture, infrastructure, and tools required to deliver what has been requested by the business. However, sometimes the requirements are expressed in such high-level terms that their technical implications are not apparent to the business and technology organizations. Without a continuous joint effort to address the potential ambiguity of the requirements, the technology team may create a project plan that, from the business-unit point of view, is too long, too expensive, and does not deliver what the business sees as a timely value proposition. Without proper cooperation and coordination, this disconnect may be "discovered" several months into the project with the money already spent and no recognizable return on investment. A potential outcome might be the withdrawal of business support and funding that would lead to cancellation of the project for failure to deliver.

▶ **Lack of consuming applications** The old adage "if we build it they will come" does not always work in the case of Master Data Management and Customer Data Integration. MDM and CDI projects are often positioned as infrastructure projects, and here lies the danger. Typically, an infrastructure initiative becomes "visible" only when the organization experiences an infrastructure-type problem, for example, the enterprise network is not available and a major application or web server is down, etc. Successful infrastructure projects keep enterprises "alive" but are rarely appreciated unless a problem occurs. MDM and CDI projects hold a promise of significant business benefits and thus should not be invisible. To put it another way, it is very difficult to demonstrate the value and the benefits of a CDI solution if there are no applications and no end users that can take advantage of these new capabilities. Inability to demonstrate value may result in a negative perception of a project as a failure, with the project stakeholders withdrawing their support and looking for alternative solutions. For example, bundling CDI with customer on-boarding and account opening process can clearly demonstrate significant value and at the same time improve quality of CDI-enabled applications and processes. In this case, the added value becomes clear since the business community obtains a new, more efficient, and highly-visible account opening application. The increase in quality is driven by a single source customer profile data that is used during account opening, which results in improved data quality and reduced data redundancy.

▶ **Lack of user adoption** This reason is closely related to the preceding one. One of the impacts of a CDI project is the ability to view, use, and manage critical enterprise data differently, possibly using different applications and business processes. That requires not only the availability of new consuming applications that can take advantage of the CDI solution, but also an educated and trained end-user community. End-user education should start as soon as the project is approved. Training is another critical area of user adoption. Training performed too early is not effective since the end users may forget what they learned by the time the system is in production. In addition, training should be flexible enough to accommodate users with different levels of computer literacy, from novices to "power" users.

▶ **Underestimating or not considering impact of legacy** Many CDI implementations have to be developed and deployed into already-established enterprise system environments, and therefore have to deal with existing data sources and applications. While the need for an accurate, timely, and authoritative system of record is understood and shared by both business and technical teams, it is often the case that an application area in charge of an existing customer data store such as a data warehouse, CIF, or specialized customer file would consider extending existing customer data stores and consuming applications as well as attempting to improve data quality in a tactical fashion by focusing on the local data stores. In addition, the legacy system owners may put forward an argument that since their legacy solution is already in place, there is no need for additional system integration between the customer files and downstream systems. In short, a legacy extension and modernization approach may present a tactical alternative to a CDI solution that can be perceived by the management as a lower-risk approach. The CDI project team needs to assess the impact of the incremental system integration effort required to deploy a new CDI platform into the existing system environment, understand the potential shortcomings of legacy-based tactical solutions, and develop a CDI business case that would create compelling strategic arguments for a CDI solution.

▶ **Failing to socialize CDI throughout the enterprise**   CDI projects can affect practically every department in an enterprise. Therefore, CDI project owners must be also CDI evangelists and social champions who continuously work toward obtaining and maintaining enterprise-wide support, making sure that the project plan is built using realistic timelines and appropriate resources and budget. Effectively socializing the project's goals and benefits would ensure the proper level of stakeholder involvement from awareness to understanding and ownership.

▶ **Lack of a comprehensive, service-oriented CDI architecture**   As CDI projects grow up from their initial pilot implementations, they need to be architected to be easily integrated with the enterprise architecture. This requirement is easy to understand if you consider that the goal of any CDI project is to create an authoritative, accurate, and most importantly, enterprise-wide system of record. So, leveraging enterprise legacy infrastructure and applications, interoperability, performance, scalability, and security are only a few aspects that have to be addressed. Using a comprehensive architecture framework to build service-oriented CDI solution helps decouple end-user business applications from the structure and physical location of the customer data stores and thus helps reduce data and functional redundancy and provides the flexibility, scalability, and adaptability of the CDI solution.

▶ **Choosing the CDI data model poorly**   A choice between a vendor-provided data model and the custom data model developed in-house could spell the difference between success and failure of the project. This choice has to be made carefully and in the context of the enterprise business strategy and capability requirements.

▶ **Lack of the data governance strategy that includes well-defined data stewardship and formally managed data quality program** This reason is practically self-explanatory; without proper measurable data quality the CDI solution would be an integration point of inaccurate or incomplete data, which makes its usefulness questionable.

▶ **Project staffing** The complexity and multidisciplinary nature of Master Data Management and Customer Data Integration initiatives requires availability of a properly trained, knowledgeable cross-functional project team that has the appropriate number and the correct mix of subject matter experts, managers, planners, application developers, data analysts, database administrators, infrastructure designers, testers, and representatives of the business teams. Such a complex undertaking can be successful only if the project team has a respected, strong project leader who can also act as a visionary and evangelist who continues to reinforce the business value messages and to maintain effective collaboration and socialization among the team members.

Master Data Management and Customer Data Integration: Trends and Directions

Master Data Management and Customer Data Integration solutions are still relatively new, and the road ahead has unexpected turns, peaks, and valleys. At the present time, the market for MDM and CDI solutions appears to be growing fast, and there are numerous research reports and surveys indicating current and future market size in term of total expenditure and vendor revenue. However, the financial side does not necessarily indicate the direction that MDM-CDI would take going into the future.

It is hard to predict the future, and this is certainly true in the case of Master Data Management and Customer Data Integration. Nevertheless, there are a number of research reports from various industry analysts that attempt to define market trends with various degrees of accuracy. One of the better sources of such information is the CDI Institute's 2007 Strategic Planning Assumptions report titled "2007-2008 MDM Milestones". While reports like the one from the CDI Institute offer interesting insights into the MDM-CDI market trends, we would like to offer a slightly different view of these trends based on authors' experience and analysis of where the relevant MDM-CDI technologies, market practitioners, and vendors are headed.

▶ MDM-CDI Market Trends

　　▶ Companies will concentrate their CDI activities on the enterprise transformation toward customer-centricity not just by implementing a CDI Data Hub but also by starting business process and applications re-engineering and by developing new, more customer-centric, and user-friendly processes and applications.

▶ External reference data providers and their "trusted" data sources and services will play a more prominent role in MDM and CDI implementations. Companies such as Dun & Bradstreet, Acxiom, Lexus-Nexus, Transunion, and Experian are a few examples of these data providers. Although these companies may not offer complete CDI solutions, they will certainly be positioned to become key players in the data cleansing, rationalization, enrichment, and linking and matching space.

▶ Customer Data Integration solutions will proliferate throughout various industry segments but will maintain an industry-specific implementation and technology flavor; for example, financial services companies will focus on achieving a near-real-time complete customer view while life sciences/ pharmaceutical companies may find a batch-oriented approach more acceptable when dealing with a master file of pharmaceutical company customers—physicians and other health care providers.

▶ Vendor solutions will evolve to support specific domains, for example, delivering solutions such as Product Data Hub, Reference Data Hub, Account Data Hub, Privacy Data Hub, and others.

▶ Enterprises adopting an MDM-CDI strategy will focus on solving customer identity problems to achieve service-level improvements, to meet compliance requirements, and to enable or support initiatives such as national identifiers.

▶ The MDM-CDI vendor marketplace will continue to consolidate aggressively with large system vendors acquiring smaller MDM-CDI specialty vendors. Given the typical size and complexity of CDI initiatives, the willingness of companies to partner with a larger vendor is part and parcel of the implementation risk mitigation strategy.

▶ MDM-CDI Technical Capabilities Trends

    ▶ MDM and CDI solutions and vendor products will continue to extend master data capabilities along at least two dimensions: (1) "organically" by evolving core functionality within the MDM-CDI engine, and (2) through integration with new complementary technologies such as advanced data quality and matching solutions, as well as new approaches to building function-rich, extensible applications (for example, using AJAX). Indeed, we believe that techniques such as AJAX would help MDM-CDI developers to rapidly build and deploy function-rich web-based applications that can access, search, and navigate master data managed inside MDM-CDI Data Hub platforms.

    ▶ Support for institutional hierarchies in MDM and CDI solutions will rapidly mature from its current state to make sophisticated institutional hierarchy traversal one of the core MDM capabilities that could operate in a global enterprise. This will coincide with the development and adoption of relevant hierarchy identification standards.

▶ MDM and CDI implementations offer significant benefits to the organizations, but also represent certain risks. While enterprises are focused today on addressing the implementation and operational risk of deploying a CDI solution, they are beginning to recognize the risks associated with CDI's ability to integrate all data about customers or business entities in one place. This data must be protected not only from unauthorized, fraudulent use, but also from any attempt to access it that is against corporate business and security policy. The last point refers to what is known as data visibility. As the MDM-CDI market continues to mature, enterprises and vendors alike will be developing standards-based policy enforcement mechanisms that can protect data and preserve existing business processes, at the same time positioning the enterprise to be ready for verifiable, auditable compliance with government and industry regulations and laws concerning data security, visibility, confidentiality, and privacy protection.

▶ One of the key applications of a CDI solution will be a platform that would allow an enterprise to centrally manage privacy policies and thus to help enforce trusted relationships between the enterprise and its customers.

▶ MDM and CDI matching and linking technology will become much more sophisticated and powerful, and would support data matching for both structured and unstructured content.

▶ MDM and CDI ability to match and link data records from disparate sources based on certain criteria would create an opportunity to leverage robust search technologies to supplement or enhance traditional approaches to matching and linking, thus creating "virtualized" MDM-CDI platforms.

▶ Business demands and vendor consolidation will result in availability of integrated MDM and CDI solutions that would include sophisticated data quality components, flexible rules engines, metadata repositories, reporting and business intelligence tools, and even audit and compliance-monitoring capabilities in componentized service-based product suites.

AJAX

AJAX stands for Asynchronous JavaScript and XML, and is a web development technique for creating interactive web applications that can significantly enhance user experiences on the web. For example, AJAX allows developers to create a single web page that supports rich user interfaces and dynamic content over standard protocols. Moreover, such a single web page application can process requests to the MDM-CDI data store and update data without the need to load a new page. This efficiency and seamless operation is one of the factors affecting user experience.

One of the advantages of AJAX is the way it accelerates web page loading by generating the HTML locally within the browser, thus loading a more compact payload that contains only JavaScript calls and the actual data. This feature is extremely useful for data access applications that can quickly load and browse a multipage large data set that could be a result of data retrieval from the Data Hub.

Of course, this is far from a complete list of MDM and CDI trends. There are others, some more tactical and some that may be viewed as too radical or strange. Let's consider the following example:

▶ Current thinking in the MDM and CDI world is to build these integration solutions as Data Hubs. But we know from networking technologies that there are better, more efficient topologies than hub and spokes. Would it be possible to build the next generation of MDM-CDI solution as a "switch" or as a "data grid"?

We may not be able to answer questions like this today, but we're confident that collectively we will be able to see the answer emerging from the mist of the not-so-distant future. And then we can even find an answer to the *big* question: What is the next "disruptive" thing after MDM-CDI?

List of Acronyms

ACL   Access Control List

AJAX   Asynchronous JavaScript and XML

AML   Anti-Money Laundering

B2B   Business-to-Business

B2C   Business-to-Consumer

BGM   Bipartite Graph Matching algorithm

BI   Business Intelligence

CDI   Customer Data Integration

CFR   Code of Federal Regulation

CIF   Customer Information File

CPNI   Consumer Proprietary Network Information

CRM   Customer Relationship Management

CRUD   Create, Read, Update, Delete operations

CSIO XML   The Centre for Study of Insurance Operations standard XML

DNC   Do Not Call

DQ   Data Quality

ebXML   Electronic Business using eXtensible Markup Language

EDI   Electronic Data Interchange

EDW   Enterprise Data Warehouse

EIGG   Enterprise Information Governance Group

EII   Enterprise Information Integration

EIM   Enterprise Information Management

EMB   Enterprise Message Bus

EMF   Extensible Message Format

ETL   Extract, Transform, and Load

FDA   U.S. Food and Drug Administration

FDIC   Federal Deposit Insurance Corporation

FFIEC   Federal Financial Institutions Examination Council

FixML   Financial Information Exchange Markup Language

FpML   Financial Product Markup Language

FSI   Financial Services Institution

G2B   Government-to-Business

G2C   Government-to-Customer

GLBA   Gramm-Leach-Bliley Act

HHS   Health and Human Services

HIPAA   Health Insurance Profitability and Accountability Act

HL7   Health Level Seven

HTNG   Hotel Technology Next Generation standard

IAA XML   Insurance Application Architecture XML

ISO   International Standards Organization

IT   Information Technology

JAAS   Java Authentication and Authorization Service

JCA   J2EE Connector Architecture

JDBC   Java Database Connectivity

JMS   Java Message Service

KYC   Know Your Customer

LOB   Line of Business

MDDL   Market Data Definition Language

MDM   Master Data Management

NASD   National Association of Securities Dealers

NHI   National Health Index (New Zealand)

NYSIIS   New York State Identification and Intelligence algorithm

OASIS   Organization for the Advancement of Structured Information Standards

OCC   Office of the Comptroller of the Currency

ODBC   Open Database Connectivity

ODS   Operational Data Store

OFAC   Office of Foreign Asset Control

OIG   Office of Inspector General

OTA   OpenTravel Alliance standard

PAP   Policy Administration Point

PDP   Policy Decision Point

PEP   Policy Enforcement Point

QA   Quality Assurance

RBAC   Roles-Based Access Control

RFID   Radio Frequency Identification

RIXML   Research Information Markup Language

RUP   Rational Unified Process

SAML   Security Assertion Markup Language

SB 1386   California Database Security Breach Notification Act

SDN   Specially Designated Nationals

SEC   Security and Exchange Commission

SOA   Service-Oriented Architecture

SOX   Sarbanes-Oxley Act
SQL   Structured Query Language
SSN   Social Security Number
STP   Straight Through Processing
TIN   Tax Identification Number
UML   Unified Modeling Language
W3C   World Wide Web Consortium
WCC   WebSphere Customer Center
XACML   eXtensible Access Control Markup Language
XBRL   eXtensible Business Reporting Language
XCRL   eXtensible Customer Relationships Language
XRI   eXtensible Resource Identifier

B

Glossary

account-centric view   A physical or virtual representation of customer information that is limited only to the data affiliated with a particular customer account.

AJAX (Asynchronous JavaScript and XML)   A web development technique for creating interactive web applications.

authentication   A process designed to verify that an individual or a party are who they claim they are.

authorization   A process of determining what information and computing resources the authenticated party is allowed to access.

business rule   A statement that defines or constrains some aspect of the business. It is intended to assert business structure or to control or influence the behavior of the business.

Business Rules Engine (BRE)   A software application or a system that is designed to manage and enforce business rules based on a specified stimulus, for example, an event such as a change of an attribute value. Business rules engines are usually architected as pluggable software components that separate the business rules from the application code.

Coexistence-style Hub   The hub style that combines features of the Registry Hub and Transaction Hub. For some data attributes the Coexistence Hub maintains the system of record data; some other data attributes are managed by the metadata that points to data attributes in external systems.

compliance risk   Risk resulting from having inaccurate or untimely data related to consumer compliance disclosures, or unauthorized disclosure of confidential customer information.

confidentiality   In information security, a business requirement that defines the rules and processes that can protect certain information from unauthorized use.

counterparty   Each party to a (financial) transaction.

cryptography   The process of converting data into an unreadable form via an encryption algorithm. Cryptography enables information to be sent across communication networks that are assumed to be insecure, without losing confidentiality or integrity of information being sent.

cryptanalysis   The study of mathematical techniques designed to defeat cryptographic techniques. Collectively, a branch of science that deals with cryptography and cryptanalysis is called cryptology.

Customer   In the context of this book, "Customer" is used as a generic term that indicates an entity that requires and consumes an organization's products and services. The term "customer" can be replaced by industry- or line-of-business–specific terms such as: Client, Contact, Party, Counterparty, Patient, Subscriber, Supplier, Prospect, Service Provider, Citizen, Guest, Legal Entity, Trust, Business Entity, and other terms.

customer-centric view   An aggregated physical or virtual record of customer information spanning all customer accounts and anchored around customer identity.

Customer Data Integration (CDI)   A comprehensive set of technology components, services, and business processes that create, maintain, and make available an accurate, timely, integrated, and complete view of a customer across lines of business, channels, and business partners. Customer Data Integration is a customer-focused variant of Master Data Management.

Customer Relationship Management (CRM)   A set of technologies and business processes designed to understand a customer, improve customer experience, and optimize customer-facing business processes across marketing, sales, and servicing channels.

Data Hub   A common approach for a technical implementation of a service-oriented MDM-CDI solution. Data Hubs store and manage some data attributes and the metadata containing the location of data attributes in external systems in order to create a single physical or federated trusted source of information about customers, products, etc.

data governance   A process focused on managing the quality, consistency, usability, security, and availability of information.

data profiling   A process focused on generating data metrics and measuring data quality. The data metrics can be collected at the column level, e.g., value frequency, nullity measurements, and uniqueness/match quality measurements; at the table level, e.g., primary key violations; or cross-table relationships, e.g., foreign key violations.

data quality (DQ)   A set of measurable characteristics of data that define how well data represents the real-world construct to which it refers.

data security   An area of information security focused on the protection of data from either accidental or unauthorized intentional viewing, modification, destruction, duplication, or disclosure during input, processing, storage, transmission, or output operations. Data security deals with data that exists in two modes: data-in-transit and data-at -rest.

data-in-transit   Any data moving between systems over network connections as well as data transferred between applications using file transfer mechanisms, messaging and queuing mechanisms, and/or ETL tools.

data-at-rest   Data residing in locally attached or networked data stores as well as data in archives (e.g., tape backup).

data warehouse   "A data warehouse is a subject-oriented, integrated, time-variant, nonvolatile collection of data in support of management decisions." W. H. Inmon.

encryption algorithm   A process that transforms plain text into a coded equivalent, known as the cipher text, for transmission or storage.

Enterprise Architecture Framework   Pioneered by John Zachman, an Enterprise Architecture Framework is an abstraction that helps to solve the complexity of the enterprise architecture by decomposing the problem into two main dimensions each of which consists of multiple subcategories. The first dimension defines the various levels of abstraction that represent business scope, business, systems, and technology models. The second dimension consists of key decision-driving questions: *what, how, where, who, when,* and *why.*

Enterprise Rights Management (ERM)   A set of technologies designed to manage and enforce information access policies and use rights of electronic documents within an enterprise. ERM enables protection of intellectual property embedded in the electronic documents, and provides protection persistence that enforces information access policies to allow an organization to control access to information that needs to be secured for privacy, competitive, or compliance reasons, and prevents users and even administrators from disabling the protection mechanisms.

Enterprise Service Bus (ESB)   A middleware software architecture construct that provides foundational services for more complex architectures via an event-driven and standards-based messaging engine (the bus). An ESB generally provides an abstraction layer on top of an implementation of an enterprise messaging system.

entitlement   An expression meaning that a party has permission to do something with respect to some entity or an object.

Identity Hub   A hub style that stores the data attributes used for identification and matching. The primary purpose of an Identity Hub is to resolve customer identity.

identity management   An organizing principle, a framework, and a set of technologies designed to manage the flow, consumption, security, integrity, and privacy of identity and business data across the enterprise in line with business demands.

integrity   In information security, integrity is a business requirement that data in a file or a message traversing the network remains unchanged or that any data received matches exactly what was sent; data integrity deals with the prevention of accidental or malicious changes to data or message content.

intrusion detection   The process of monitoring the events occurring in a computer system or network and analyzing them for signs of intrusion.

Java Authentication and Authorization Service (JAAS)   A Java security facility that defines a pluggable, stacked authentication scheme. Different authentication schemes can be plugged in without having to modify or recompile existing applications.

Loss Data Warehouse (LDW)   In the context of the Basel II Capital Accord, LDW is a primary vehicle to provide accurate, up-to-date analysis of capital adequacy requirements, and is also a source of disclosure reporting.

loose coupling   An architecture and design principle that avoids rigid, tightly coupled structures in which changes to one component force that change to be propagated throughout the system, and where failure or poor performance of one component may bring the entire system down. Service-oriented architectures and Web Services support and promote loose coupling.

Master Data Management (MDM)   The framework of processes and technologies aimed at creating and maintaining an authoritative, reliable, sustainable, accurate, and secure data environment that represents a "single version of truth," an accepted system of record used both intra- and interenterprise across a diverse set of application systems, lines of business, and user communities.

matching   A highly specialized set of technologies that allows users to derive a high-confidence value of the party identification that can be used to construct a total view of a party from multiple party records.

matching algorithm   An algorithm that creates match groups from a set of detail-level records.

match group   In CDI, a group of customer records determined to belong to a single customer. The determination can be done systemically through the use of a matching algorithm or manually by end-user input.

merge   An event of creation of a single customer record from two or more customer records.

network security   A security discipline that deals with authenticating network users, authorizing access to the network resources, and protecting the information that flows over the network.

nonpublic personal information (NPI)   Personally identifiable legal and financial information that is provided by a customer to the enterprise; derived from any transaction with the customer, or any service performed for the customer; or obtained by the enterprise via other means.

nonrepudiation   In information security, the ability to confirm the fact that an action in question was undertaken by a party in question, and that the party in question cannot legally dispute or deny the fact of the action.

obligations   In defining and evaluating XACML policies, obligations refer to actions that must be performed as part of handling an access request.

opt-in   A privacy option that prohibits the sharing or sale of customer data *unless* the customer explicitly agreed to allow such actions.

opt-out   This privacy option means that *unless and until* the customers inform their financial institution that the customer does not want them to share or sell customer data to other companies, the company is free to do so. The implication of this law is that the initial burden of privacy protection is on the customer, not on the company.

party   A uniquely identified collection or cluster of individual detail-level records; the notion of the party supports multiple types including organizations, customers, prospects, etc.

perimeter security   This security discipline deals with security threats that arrive at the enterprise boundary via a network.

policy   The encoding of rules particular to a business domain, its data content, and the application systems designed to operate in this domain on this set of data.

provisioning   A set of management activities, business processes, and technologies governing the creation, modification, and deletion of user credentials and entitlements. It provides assured delivery and removal (deprovisioning) of the identity and entitlement data from all affected applications and systems.

privacy   Proper handling and use of personal information (PI) throughout its life cycle, consistent with data protection principles and the preferences of the subject.

Registry-style Hub   A CDI architecture style that stores metadata with pointers to data elements in external systems.

reputational risk   Risk to the reputation of the business that arises from errors, delays, omissions, and information security breaches that become public knowledge or directly affect customers.

risk   In general, risk is the probability that a threat agent will be able to exploit a defined vulnerability that would adversely impact the business.

Roles-Based Access Control (RBAC)   The processes and technologies of providing access control based on user credentials and roles.

security   In the context of information security, a set of standards, processes, and technologies that include authentication, authorization, access control, and auditability of user actions in order to protect access to and use of the information resources only by authorized users. Information security goals are to ensure integrity, confidentiality, and availability of information.

separation of concerns   A process of breaking a program or a system into distinct features that overlap in functionality as little as possible.

Service-Oriented Architecture (SOA)   Software design and implementation architecture of loosely coupled, coarse-grained, reusable services, which can be integrated with each other through a wide variety of platform-independent service interfaces.

Single Sign-On (SSO)   The technology that enables users to access multiple computer systems or networks after logging in once with a single set of authentication credentials.

split   An event of creation of two records from a single record when new information becomes available and reveals the existence of two customers mistakenly represented by a single record. Typically this event occurs when two customers have many similar data element values, e.g., father and son living at the same address and having the same name.

spyware   A type of malicious software that installs itself onto a user's computer and sends information from that computer to a third party without the user's permission or knowledge.

transaction risk   Risk that may arise from fraud, error, or the inability to deliver products or services, maintain a competitive position, or manage information.

Transaction-style Hub   A data hub solution that treats the Data Hub as a master system of record for customer data. Other systems receive updates from the Transaction Hub.

visibility   Ability to enforce fine-grained access to and operations on data at the record and/or attribute level based on user entitlements and data usage and access policies.

Web Services   Encapsulated, loosely coupled, coarse-grained, and contracted software objects offered via standard protocols.

Regulations and Compliance Rules Impacting Master Data Management and Customer Data Integration Projects

This appendix contains a representative list of government and industry-specific regulations and compliance rules that impact CDI Data Hubs. This appendix also lists federal agencies involved in enforcement of these regulations.

The impact of the regulations is threefold. First, they require that the information managed inside the MDM-CDI solution is available and protected, and its integrity is not violated. Second, the regulations demand better understanding and an enhanced view of a customer. These regulations are some of the key drivers for CDI projects. Third, they restrict the use of information about customers and therefore they impose constraints on CDI projects and impact the details of architecture, design, and implementation. For instance, regulations limiting information exchange between countries may drive the creation of a compartmentalized Data Hub solution or even an independent but potentially federated Data Hub solution for global projects.

Regulations and Guidelines

Most of the new regulatory requirements deal with acquisition, protection, and understanding of identities, their attributes, and their privacy preferences:

▶ **12 CFR Part 21, Subpart B**   Requirements to Report on Suspicious Activities.

▶ **12 CFR Part 21, Subpart C**   Procedures for Monitoring Bank Secrecy Act Compliance.

▶ **12 CFR Part 573 and SEC Final Rule, Privacy of Consumer Financial Information (Regulation S-P), 17 CFR Part 248 RIN 3235-AH90**   Prohibits a financial institution from disclosing nonpublic personal information about a consumer to nonaffiliated third parties unless the institution satisfies various notice and opt-out requirements and the consumer has not elected to opt out of the disclosure.

▶ **17 CFR Part 210**   Guidelines for records retention.

▶ **Basel II Accord**   Advanced approach to calculating credit risk capital based on internal data and systems, with the focus on the integrity of data and systems used to internally calculate capital under advanced approaches.

▶ **California SB 1386**   Requires control of privacy of individual financial information.

▶ **European Union Data Protection Directive**   Mandates protection of personal data.

► **Federal Trade Commission, 16 CFR Part 314**   Ensures the security and confidentiality of customer records and information; protects against any anticipated threats or hazards to the security or integrity of such records; and protects against unauthorized access to or use of such records or information that could result in substantial harm or inconvenience to any customer.

► **Federal Financial Institutions Examination Council (FFIEC)**   Guidelines for strong authentication require banks and other financial services to assess risk of fraudulent activity and implement an appropriate degree of strong authentication commensurable with the probability of fraud and loss expectancy.

► **Gramm-Leach-Bliley Act (GLBA)**   Mandates strong protection of personal financial information.

► **Health Insurance Portability and Accountability Act (HIPAA)**   Places liability on anyone who fails to properly protect patient health information including bills and health-related financial information.

► **HHS-OIG-Fraud Prevention and Detection**   Guidelines for grants and awards to health care providers.

► **Homeland Security Information Sharing Act (HSISA, H.R. 4598)**   Security Rules and Regulations.

► **ISO 17799**   This standard defines an extensive approach to achieve information security including communications systems requirements for information handling and risk reduction.

► **Japanese Protection for Personal Information Act, Kojin Joho Hogo HouA, May 2003**

► **New York Reg. 173**   Mandates the active encryption of sensitive financial information sent over the Internet.

► **OCC 2001-47**   Rules for third-party data-sharing protection.

► **Sarbanes-Oxley Act (SOX)**   Places strict requirements on company boards and officers to proactively prevent mishandling of information.

► **SEC, NASD, FDA 21 CFR Part 11**   Guidelines for trustworthy electronic records; requires companies to employ procedures and controls designed to ensure the authenticity, integrity, and when appropriate the confidentiality of electronic records, and to ensure that the signer cannot readily repudiate the signed records as not genuine.

Representative Regulatory Bodies

A number of federal and state agencies are involved in enforcing GLBA, SOX, HIPAA, and other regulations:

- ▶ Federal banking agencies:
  - — Board of Governors of the Federal Reserve System
  - — Comptroller of the Currency (OCC)
  - — Federal Deposit Insurance Corporation (FDIC)
  - — Office of Thrift Supervision
  - — Others
- ▶ National Credit Union Administration
- ▶ Secretary of the Treasury
- ▶ Securities and Exchange Commission (SEC)
- ▶ Federal Trade Commission (FTC)
- ▶ National Association of Insurance Commissioners

Index

A

AbiliTec, 362
access control, 204–205
    group-based, 205–207
    role-based, 207–210
access control lists (ACL), 206
accountability, 163
account-centric view, 20, 382
account takeover, 153
account types, 239
accuracy, 301
ACE (Address Correction and Encoding), 358
ACL (access control lists), 206
ACORD, 13, 291
Activity Manager (AM), 351
Acxiom, 107
AddressAbility, 362
Address Correction and Encoding (ACE), 358
addresses, 253, 254
address matching, 12
Address Now, 359
administrative processes, 28–29, 329–330
Advisor Platform, 356
aggregation service, 100–101
AICPA (American Institute of Certified Public Accountants), 143
AJAX, 382
AllFusion ERwin Data Modeler, 357
AM (Activity Manager), 351
American Bar Association, 172
American Institute of Certified Public Accountants (AICPA), 143

AML (Anti-Money Laundering Act), 7, 149
AMQ standard, 291
annualized loss of expectancy, 138
annualized rate of occurrence, 138
Anti-Money Laundering Act (AML), 7, 149
APIs (application programming interfaces), 72
application programming interfaces (APIs), 72
application security, 161, 191
archival component, 317
area number, 304
Ascential Software, 359
asymmetric key, 169–170
asymmetric relationships, 281–282
attribute-level trust, 318
attribute location service, 127
Attribute Locator service, 242
attribute matching, 263–266
attributes, 240–241
    country, 259–260
    discrimination, 256–258
    identity, 254–255
    leading relationship, 260
    party type, 259
    record qualification, 258–260
attrition rates, 25
auditing, 163
auditing tools, 114
authentication, 162
    and access control, 204
    and authorization, 178–179
    definition of, 382

authentication (*Cont.*)
    mechanisms, 175–176
        challenge-response handshakes, 175
        digital certificates, 176
        one-time passwords, 176
        passwords, 175
        personal identification numbers
          (PINs), 175
    multifactor, 176–178
    and privacy, 178
authorization, 162, 382

B

B2B (business-to-business) commerce, 13
backdoor trojans, 186
banking trojans, 186
Basel II Capital Requirements Accord, 53,
    142, 150–151, 390
batch matching, 262
batch processing, 123, 319–322
behavioral biometrics, 177
BGM (bipartite graph matching), 364–365
BI (business intelligence), 42
binary rule, 265–266
biometrics, 177
bipartite graph matching (BGM), 364–365
birthdate, 257
BJ's Wholesale Club, 184
blocked individuals, 54
block-level protection, 194
botnet worms, 185–186
BRE. *See* business rules engines (BRE)
break groups, 268–270
budget, 370
bulk statistical testing, 332–335
Business Event Factory, 357
business intelligence (BI), 42
business metadata, 129
Business Objects, 357–358
business quality assurance, 331–332
business rule, 382
business rule designer/editor, 126
business rule repository, 126

business rules engines (BRE), 125–127
    See also data synchronization
    components of, 126
    definition of, 382
    inference rules, 126
    reaction rules, 126
    rule set, 125
business-to-business (B2B) commerce, 13

C

California Senate Bill 1386, 7, 143, 152, 187
canonical data format, 115, 316
CDI. *See* Customer Data Integration (CDI)
CDI Institute, 23
certificate authority, 176
CFR (Code of Federal Regulations), 187, 390
chaining, 266–268
challenge-response handshakes, 175
change capture, 317
change log, 296
Change Management server, 341
channel role, 208
check digit rules, 303
check sum rules, 303
Children's On-Line Privacy Protection Act
    (COPPA), 187
CIF (Customer Information File), 17, 60–62
citizen master, 36
clustering, 87
CODE-1 Plus, 359
Code of Federal Regulations (CFR), 187, 390
Coexistence Hub, 122, 243–245, 382
combining algorithms, 221
Committee of Sponsoring Organizations
    (COSO), 152
communities of practice, 28
compliance, 7, 41
compliance risk, 137, 188, 382
compression, 194
Computer Associates, 357
Computer Security Institute, 165, 185
confidentiality, 163, 168, 382
consistency, 301

Consumer Proprietary Network Information (CPNI), 55
context handler, 220–221
COPPA (Children's On-Line Privacy Protection Act), 187
COSO (Committee of Sponsoring Organizations), 152
cost reduction, 41
countermeasures, 139
counterparty, 382
country attribute, 259–260
CPNI (Consumer Proprietary Network Information), 55
create, read, update, and delete (CRUD), 93, 206
credit card numbers, 251
CRM. *See* Customer Relationship Management (CRM)
cross-reference record locator, 314, 321
CRUD (create, read, update, and delete), 93, 206
cryptanalysis, 169, 382
cryptography, 169, 382
cryptology, 169
CSIO XML, 291
customer, 382
customer affiliations, 255
customer base, 19
customer centricity, 19–20
    and 360-degree customer view, 43
    business drivers, 41–42
    in CDI Data Hubs, 328–329
    definition of, 383
    senior management's commitment to, 40
    technical challenges in, 47–53
        data integration, 50–52
        data quality, 50–52
        data synchronization, 50–52
        implementation costs, 48–49
        partnership with vendors, 49–50
        regulatory compliance, 52–56
        time-to-market factors, 48–49
    value proposition in, 40

Customer Data Integration (CDI), 13–16
    architecture viewpoints, 69–81
        consumption, 76–78
        data hub styles, 76–78
        reconciliation, 76–78
        reference, 79–81
        services, 70–75
    benefits of, 18–20
    competitive advantages in, 23–29
        administrative processes, 28–29
        customer experience, 24–25
        customer relationships, 25–26
        customer retention, 25
        customer service, 26–27
        information technology, 29
        marketing, 28
    customer centricity in, 44
    and customer relationships, 84–88
    data hub. *See* Data Hubs
    definition of, 6, 14, 60–61, 383
    deployment, 341–342
    drivers of, 41
    ecosystem, 234–235
    and enterprise information security, 219–220
    evolution of, 16–18, 61–65
    geographic views, 37–38
    and identity theft, 154
    implementation of, 232–237
        common trends in, 30–32
        project work streams, 247–248
        scope, 237–241
        senior management concerns in, 233
        workshop agenda, 236
    industry-specific, 32–35
        financial services, 32–34
        gaming, 34
        hospitality, 34
        pharmaceutical, 34–35
        telecommunications, 35
    infrastructure for, 339–341
    key capabilities of, 90–91
    overview of, 368–370

Customer Data Integration (CDI) (*Cont.*)
  party data model, 88–90
  presentation layer, 328–331
    administrative applications,
      329–330
    customer-centric applications,
      328–329
    reporting, 329
  and public sector, 35
  reasons for failure of, 370–373
  regulations and guidelines, 390–391
  requirements, 90–92
  service-oriented architecture platform,
    92–95
  socialization of, 46–47
  stakeholders, 44–45
  technical challenges in, 47–56
    data integration, 50–52
    data quality, 50–52
    implementation costs, 48–49
    regulatory compliance, 52–56
    time-to-market concerns, 48–49
    vendor partnerships, 49–50
  testing, 331–339
  trends and directions, 373–376
customer experience, 24–25
customer fraud, 54
customer groups, 283–284
customer identification, 250–251
  360-degree view, 251–254
  discrimination attributes, 256–258
  false negatives, 253–254
  false positives, 252–253
  fuzzy logic, 270–271
  identity attributes, 254–255
  matching modes, 261–263
  matching rules, 263–266
  minimum data requirements, 261
  record qualification attributes, 258–260
  similarity libraries, 270–271
customer identifiers, 288–289
customer information, 100–101, 311–315
Customer Information File (CIF), 17, 60–62

Customer Relationship Management
  (CRM), 18
  and customer centricity, 42
  definition of, 65, 383
  master data in, 8–9
customer relationships, 25–26
  and customer data integration (CDI),
    84–88
  and hierarchies, 255
  level of, 260
customer retention, 25
customer service, 26–27, 41
customer touch points, 239, 310
customer views, 43

D

data, 190
  integration, 50–52
  length, 302–303
  loading, 121–123
  masking, 338
  modelers, 102–103
  ownership, 111–112
  parsing, 114
  profiling, 301, 383
  protection, 7
  stewardship, 111–112
  strategy, 108–109
  validation, 302–303, 316
  visibility, 214–216
data aggregation, 239–240
data-at-rest, 192
  definition of, 383
  protection of, 193–195
  solutions, 195–196
database protection, 194
database servers, 340
data cleansing tools, 114
data delivery, 127–128
DataDelta, 364
data enrichment, 114
DataFlux, 355–356, 358

data governance, 109–111
    definition of, 383
    and information quality, 297–307
    standards, 292–294
data history, 296
Data Hubs, 115–131
    architecture styles, 241–246
        coexistence hub, 243–245
        identity, 243
        registry-style, 77, 242–243
        transaction, 78, 245–246
    data management in, 115–131
        data delivery, 127–128
        data loading, 121–123
        data synchronization, 123–127
        data zones, 116–121
        enterprise information integration,
            130–131
        metadata, 128–130
    data models, 342
    data transformations in, 321–322
    definition of, 383
    external reference, 77
    key generation and management in,
        102–103
    phased implementation of, 246–247
    products, 350–357
        DataFlux, 355–356
        GoldenSource, 354–355
        IBM WebSphere Customer
            Center, 350–351
        Initiate, 352
        ObjectRiver, 356–357
        Oracle, 353
        Purisma Customer Registry,
            353–354
        SAP, 355
        Siebel, 352
        Siperian Hub XT, 351
        Sun Microsystems, 354
        VisionWare MultiVue, 356
    reconciliation engine, 77–78
    record locator services, 104–105

reference architecture, 79–81, 92
as service platform, 75, 94
visibility and security services, 221–228
data-in-transit, 192–193, 383
data providers, 361–364
    Acxiom, 361–362
    Dun and Bradstreet, 362–363
    Experian, 363–364
data quality (DQ), 112–114
    in Customer Data Integration (CDI),
        50–52, 64
    definition of, 17–18, 383
    processes, 123
    tools and technologies, 114–115
Data Quality module, 352
Data Quality Suite, 360
DataRight, 358
data security, 155–156
    See also information security
    breach, 184–185
    data-in-transit, 192–193
    definition of, 189, 192, 383
    disciplines in, 161
    evolution of, 184–185
    layered security framework, 190–192
    overview of, 189
    risks, 188–189
    threats, 185–187
data synchronization, 123–127
    batch processing, 319–322
    in CDI Data Hub master scenario,
        298–299
    goals of, 310
    identity hub, 311–315
    real-time, 316–319
    transaction hub, 315–319
data warehousing, 297–299, 383
data zones, 116–121
    See also Data Hubs
    enterprise service bus, 121
    ETL/acquisition, 119–120
    hub service, 120
    information consumer, 120–121

data zones (*Cont.*)
loose coupling, 118
separation of concerns, 117
source systems, 118–119
third-party, 119
date validation, 258
decryption, 339
default management, 329
delivery accelerators, 364–366
DataDelta, 364
Exeros, 365–366
Identity Systems, 365
Netrics, 364–365
demilitarized zone (DMZ), 190
denial of service, 173, 180
description orientation, 71
deterministic algorithms, 96
Diffie, Whitfield, 170
digital certificates, 176
digital rights management (DRM), 198
digital signatures, 171–172
direct trust, 168
discrimination attributes, 256–258
distributed query constructor, 314–315, 318
DMZ (demilitarized zone), 190
DNC (Do Not Call) legislation, 55, 143
document authentication, 172
domestic identifiers, 259–260
Do Not Call (DNC) legislation, 55, 143
downloaders, 185–186
DQ. *See* data quality (DQ)
DQXI (IQ8), 358
DRM (digital rights management), 198
DSF², 362
Dun and Bradstreet, 107, 362–363
DWL Customer, 351

E

EAP (Extensible Authentication Protocol), 175
Eastern Europe, 36
EDW (Enterprise Data Warehouse), 17, 63
eEG7 standard, 291
EFS (Encrypted File System), 196

eGate Integrator, 354
EIGG (Enterprise Information Governance Group), 292–296
EII (Enterprise Information Integration), 18, 64, 130–131
eInsight Business Process Manager, 354
Electronic Signatures in Global and National Commerce Act (eSign), 171
e-mail, 193
EMB (Enterprise Message Bus), 313, 340
Encrypted File System (EFS), 196
encryption, 194, 339
encryption algorithm, 169, 383
end-to-end security framework, 161
English, Larry, 297, 300
enrollment, 177
Enterprise Architecture Framework, 66–69, 384
enterprise attribute locator, 314, 318
Enterprise Data Warehouse (EDW), 17, 63
Enterprise Information Governance Group (EIGG), 292–296
Enterprise Information Integration (EII), 18, 64, 130–131
Enterprise Message Bus (EMB), 313, 340
enterprise record locator, 317–318
Enterprise Rights Management (ERM), 196–199
definition of, 384
in health information protection, 201
in HIPAA compliance, 201
and master data management (MDM), 199–202
in regulatory compliance, 200–201
Enterprise Service Bus (ESB), 121, 313, 384
entities, 240–241
entitlements, 384
provisioning, 166–167
and visibility, 214–216
entity-matching server, 340
Entrust, 176
ePortal Composer, 354
ERM. *See* Enterprise Rights Management (ERM)

error processing, 319
ESB (Enterprise Service Bus), 121, 313, 384
eSign (Electronic Signatures in Global and National Commerce Act), 171
ETL. *See* extract, transform, and load (ETL)
European Union Data Protection Directive, 143, 188, 390
eView Studio, 354
eVision Studio, 354
exceptions, 323, 329
Exeros, 365–366
Experian, 363–364
Extensible Access Control Markup Language (XACML), 216–218
Extensible Authentication Protocol (EAP), 175
Extensible Business Reporting Language (XBRL), 291
Extensible Resource Identifier (XRI), 216–218
Extensible Rights Markup Language (XrML), 199–200
external reference data hub, 77
extract, transform, and load (ETL), 17
    acquisition zone, 119–120
    in batch processing, 319–320
    servers, 340
    tools and technologies, 63
    use of, 115

F

Fair Credit Reporting Act (FCRA), 154–155
false negatives, 177
false positives, 177, 252–253
family groups, 282–283
family names, 36–37
FASB (Financial Accounting Standards Board), 143
FBI (Federal Bureau of Investigation), 165, 185
FCRA (Fair Credit Reporting Act), 154–155
federal banking agencies, 147, 392
Federal Bureau of Investigation (FBI), 165, 185

Federal Financial Institutions Examination Council (FFIEC), 53, 143, 147, 151–152, 391
Federal Trade Commission, 143, 147, 391
federated query constructor, 318
FFIEC (Federal Financial Institutions Examination Council), 53, 143, 147, 151–152, 391
field-level protection, 194
file protection, 194
Financial Accounting Standards Board (FASB), 143
Financial Crimes Enforcement Network, 150
Financial Information Markup Language (FixML), 13
Financial Modernization Act of 1999, 54–55
financial privacy rule, 54
Financial Product Markup Language (FpML), 13, 291
financial services industry, 33
FineTune Data, 360
fingerprint scans, 177
firewalls, 160, 172–173
First Logic, 357–358
FixML (Financial Information Markup Language), 13
Forrester Research Inc., 297
FpML (Financial Product Markup Language), 13, 291
fuzzy logic, 270–271

G

gaming industry, 34
garbage in–garbage out, 110
Gartner Group, 185, 357
gender, 257
gibberish generation, 339
GLBA (Gramm-Leach-Bliley Act), 54–55, 142, 146–148, 154–155, 187, 391
golden copy, 261
golden record, 278
GoldenSource, 354–355
government agencies, 35

Gramm-Leach-Bliley Act (GLBA), 54–55, 142, 146–148, 154–155, 187, 391
granularity, 71, 238
group-based access control, 205–207
groupings, 88
groups, 85

H

Health Insurance Portability and Accountability Act (HIPAA), 55–56, 143, 187, 391
Health Level Seven (HL7), 13, 291
Hellman, Martin, 170
hierarchies, 255
Hierarchy Manager (HM), 351
HIPAA (Health Insurance Portability and Accountability Act), 55–56, 143, 187, 391
HL7 (Health Level Seven), 13, 291
HM (Hierarchy Manager), 351
Homeland Security Information Sharing Act (HSISA), 143, 391
hospitality industry, 33
host security, 160–161, 191
households, 282–283
HSISA (Homeland Security Information Sharing Act), 143, 391
HTTP (HyperText Transport Protocol), 174
Hub Service data zone, 120
hub-to-source synchronization, 104–105
hybrid algorithms, 97
HyperText Transport Protocol (HTTP), 174

I

IAA XML (Insurance Application Architecture XML), 291
IBM WebSphere Customer Center, 350–351
identifiers, 51
    customer, 288–289
    identity attributes, 254
    match groups, 287–288
identity attributes, 122
identity grabbers, 186
Identity Hub, 243, 311–315, 384
identity management, 164–166, 205, 384

identity store, 317
Identity Systems, 365
identity theft, 54, 153–155, 165, 185
i/Lytics Data Profiler, 361
i/Lytics Data Quality, 361
i/Lytics GLOBAL, 361
i/Lytics SECURE, 361
implementation costs, 48–49
incorrect data, 51
indicative data, 294
individuals, 85
    direct relationships with, 280–282
    and institutional customers, 284–285
    relationships between, 280–282
inference engines, 126
Informatica, 360
Information Consumer zone, 120–121
information quality, 297–307
    See also data governance
    data validation, 302–303
    deterioration of, 300–302
    and matching process, 299–302
    product vendors, 357–361
        Business Objects, 357–358
        DataFlux, 358
        Group 1 Software, 359
        IBM WebSphere, 359
        Informatica, 360
        Innovative Systems, 361
        Trillium, 358
information security, 158–169
    application security, 161
    data security, 161
    vs. data warehousing, 297–299
    emerging requirements in, 164–169
        identity management, 164–166
        intrusion detection and prevention, 167
        software integrity, 167
        trust, 168–169
        user provisioning, 166–167
    end-to-end security framework, 161
    layered security framework, 159
    network security, 160
    perimeter security, 160

platform security, 160–161
regulatory compliance, 154–155
regulatory requirements, 187–188
risks, 153–154
threats, 185–187
traditional requirements in, 162–164
user security, 161
information technology, costs of, 29
Initiate, 352
Innovative Systems, 361
Instep, 291
institutional customers, 32–33, 284–287
Insurance Application Architecture XML
(IAA XML), 291
integrated risk management, 140–142
integration testing, 331
integrity, 163, 384
International Accounting Standards
Reporting IAS2005, 143
international identifiers, 259–260
intrusion detection, 167, 384
intrusion prevention systems (IPS), 167
IP address spoofing, 173
IPS (intrusion prevention systems), 167
IPSec, 193
IQ8 (DQXI), 358
iris scan, 177
ISO 17799 Standard, 143, 391
Italy, 36

J

JAAS (Java Authentication and
Authorization Service), 161, 384
Japanese Protection for Personal Information
Act, 143, 391
Java Authentication and Authorization
Service (JAAS), 161, 384
Javelin Strategy and Research, 165
just-in-time information, 26–27

K

Kerberos, 176
Key Generation service, 102–103
keyloggers, 186

Key Management service, 102–103
keys, 195
Knowledge Management server, 341
Know Your Customer provision, 7, 53, 149
Korea, 37–38

L

LACS^{Link}, 362
layered security framework, 159, 190–192
LDW (Loss Data Warehouse), 384
legacy systems, 371–372
legal risk, 137
Liberty Alliance, 166
Lifelock.com, 154
linked records, 276
link keys, 98
loading zone, 120
logical view, 70
loose coupling, 118, 385
Loss Data Warehouse (LDW), 384
Lotus, 176
Lowenstein, Michael, 28

M

machine learning algorithms, 97
marketing, 28, 41
Master Customer Index, 353
master data, 8
Master Data Management (MDM), 6–13
benefits of, 18–20
challenges in, 7–11
data quality in, 9–10
data security in, 155–156
definition of, 11–12, 60–61, 385
and identity theft, 154
implementation of, 232–237
project work streams, 247–248
scope, 237–241
senior management concerns
in, 233
workshop agenda, 236
information quality in, 297–299
key capabilities of, 90–91
overview of, 6, 368–370

Master Data Management (MDM) (*Cont.*)
 and reference data, 12–13
 regulations and guidelines, 6–8,
  390–391
 requirements, 90–92
 trends and directions, 373–376
Master Reference Manager (MRM), 351
match engine, 313
match groups, 261–263
 definition of, 385
 identifiers, 287–288
 testing, 336–337
matching, 261–272
 algorithm, 385
 batch, 262, 321
 break groups, 268–270
 chaining, 266–268
 definition of, 385
 fuzzy logic in, 270–271
 information quality, 299–302
 and linking services, 95–100
 modes, 261–263
 probabilistic attribute, 264
 quantification, 264
 record-level, 264–266
 requirements and solutions, 271–272
 rules, 263–266
 similarity libraries, 270–271
match suspect extractor, 313, 317, 321
MCD 7, 357
MDM. *See* Master Data Management
 (MDM)
merge, 276–278, 385
mergers and acquisitions, 33
message orientation, 71
message response assembler, 318
message servers, 340
message validation, 316
metadata, 128–130
Microsoft, 176, 356
Model Compiler, 357
MRM (Master Reference Manager), 351
multifactor authentication, 176–177

N

names, 36–37, 253, 254
National Association of Insurance
 Commissioners, 147
National Change of Address (NCOA), 251,
 271, 362
National Credit Union Administration, 147
National Do Not Call Registry, 155
National Health Index (NHI), 307
National Health Service Number (NHSN),
 306–307
National Institute of Standards and
 Technology (NIST), 271
NCOA (National Change of Address), 251,
 271, 362
NCOA^{Link}, 362
Netrics, 364–365
network orientation, 71
network security, 160
 See also data security; information
  security
 definition of, 385
 goals of, 191
 technologies, 172–175
New York State Identification and
 Intelligence (NYSIIS), 271
next-day settlement (T+1), 12
NHI (National Health Index), 307
NHSN (National Health Service Number),
 306–307
nicknames, 253
NIST (National Institute of Standards and
 Technology), 271
Nokia, 365
nonduplication, 301
nonpublic personal information (NPI), 385
nonrepudiation, 163, 172, 385
NPI (nonpublic personal information), 385
nullification, 338
number variance, 339
NYSIIS (New York State Identification and
 Intelligence), 271

O

OASIS (Organization for the Advancement of Structured Information Standards), 73
ObjectRiver, 356–357
obligations, 221, 385
OCC (Office of the Comptroller of Currency), 148–149, 188
ODS (operational data store), 17, 64
Office of Foreign Asset Control (OFAC), 54, 150
Office of the Comptroller of Currency (OCC), 148–149, 188
one-time passwords, 176
online identity attributes, 255
online matching, 262–263
operational data store (ODS), 17, 62
operational metadata, 129
operational risk, 188
opt-in, 155, 385
optionality, 302
opt-out, 155, 385
Oracle, 352–353
Organization for the Advancement of Structured Information Standards (OASIS), 73
organization role, 207
outdated data, 51
overmatching, 251–252

P

PAP (Policy Administration Point), 219–220
parsers, 114
party, 386
party data model, 88–90
party types, 259
passwords, 175
Patriot Act, 53, 142, 149–150
Payment Card Industry (PCI) Standard, 143
PCI (Payment Card Industry) Standard, 143
PDP. *See* Policy Decision Point (PDP)
PEP (Policy Enforcement Point), 219–221
perimeter security, 160, 172–175, 190, 386
personal identification numbers (PINs), 175

personalization, 178
pharmaceutical industry, 33–34
pharming, 154, 186
phishing, 153–154, 186
phone numbers, 254, 255
physiological biometrics, 177
PINs (personal identification numbers), 175
PKI (public key infrastructure), 160, 169–171
platform-neutral orientation, 71
platform security, 160–161, 191
policy, 386
Policy Administration Point (PAP), 219–220
Policy Decision Point (PDP), 219–228
    components of, 220–221
    decision request in, 221
    visibility and security services, 221–228
Policy Enforcement Point (PEP), 219–221
Ponemon Institute, 184
Postal Service, 362
pretexting provisions, 54
privacy, 7, 155–156, 178, 386
private key, 170
probabilistic algorithms, 96–97
probabilistic attribute match, 264
product matching, 12–13
product types, 239, 255
profiling, 301
project staffing, 373
provisioning, 386
public key infrastructure (PKI), 160, 169–171
public sector, 36
purge component, 317
Purisma Customer Registry, 353–354
Purisma Data Stewardship, 353
Purisma Integration Services, 353

Q

qualitative risk analysis, 138
quality assurance testing, 331–332
quantitative risk analysis, 138
query and reporting component, 126

R

race condition controller, 318
RACF (Resource Access Control Facility), 206
racing conditions, 296
RADIUS (Remote Authentication Dial-In User Service), 176
rational unified process (RUP), 238
RBAC (Roles-Based Access Control), 207–210, 386
RDBMS (relational database management systems), 103
reaction rules engines, 126
real-time input processing, 123
reconciliation engine, 77–78, 122
record-level match, 264–266
Record Locator services, 104–105
record matching, 265–266
record qualification attributes, 258
reference architecture, 79–81
reference codes, 329
reference data, 12–13
referential integrity, 103
Registry-style Hub, 77
    See also Data Hubs
    definition of, 386
    implementation of, 242–243
    loading data into, 122
regulatory compliance, 7–8
    drivers of, 41
    in financial services industry, 33
    regulations, 52–56
    requirements, 142–152
    and risk management, 139–142
relational database management systems (RDBMS), 103
relationships, 85–87
    customer groups, 283–284
    groups, 282–283
    households, 282–283
    individuals, 280–282
    institutional customers, 284–287
Remote Authentication Dial-In User Service (RADIUS), 176

reporting server, 341
reports, 329
reputational risk, 136–137, 188, 386
Research Information Markup Language (RIXML), 291
Resource Access Control Facility (RACF), 206
response assembler, 314
retail banks, 42
risk-based authentication, 151
risks, 136–139
    analysis, 138
    assessment of, 151
    definition of, 137, 386
    information security, 153–155
    and regulatory compliance, 142–152
    types of, 136–137, 188
RIXML (Research Information Markup Language), 291
Roles-Based Access Control (RBAC), 207–210, 386
roles-engineering, 207–209
RosettaNet, 13
Royal Bank, 28
RSA Security, 176
rules engine execution core, 126
rule set, 125
RUP (rational unified process), 238
Russia, 37

S

safeguard rule, 54
sales, 41
SAP, 355
Sarbanes-Oxley Act, 54, 142–146, 152, 187, 391
scenario-based testing, 331–332, 335
SDN (specially designated nationals), 54
secret key, 169
Secure HyperText Transport Protocol (S-HTTP), 174
Secure Sockets Layer (SSL), 174
SecurID cards, 176
Securities and Exchange Commission, 54, 147

security, 386
Security Assertion Markup Language, 216
security management, 163–164
security technologies, 169–178
    digital signatures, 171–172
    encryption, 169
    network, 172–175
segment role, 208
senior management, 40
separation of concerns, 117, 386
serial number, 304
Service-Oriented Architecture (SOA), 66
    See also Customer Data Integration
        (CDI)
    benefits of, 71–72
    in customer data integration (CDI), 31,
        92–95
    definition of, 70–71, 386
    Web services, 72–75
session hijacking, 173
shared key, 169–170
S-HTTP (Secure HyperText Transport
    Protocol), 174
shuffling, 339
Siebel, 352
signature authentication, 172
similarity libraries, 270–271
Similarity Systems, 360
Simple Object Transport Protocol, 180
Single Customer View, 354
single loss expectancy, 138
Single Sign-On (SSO), 178–179, 386
smart cards, 177–178
S/MIME, 193
SOA. *See* Service-Oriented Architecture
    (SOA)
socialization, 46–47
Social Security Administration (SSA), 306
social security number (SSN), 304–306
software integrity, 167
SOUNDEX, 271
source system record locator, 314
source systems zone, 118–119

source-to-hub synchronization, 104–105
Spain, 37
Spanish-speaking countries, 37
spear-phishing, 154
specially designated nationals (SDN), 54
split, 278–279, 386
spyware, 173, 185–186, 387
SSA (Social Security Administration), 306
SSL (Secure Sockets Layer), 174
SSN (social security number), 304–306
SSO (Single Sign-On), 178–179, 386
staging zone, 120
stakeholders, 44–45
standardization, 51
straight through processing (STP), 12
strategic risk, 137
substitution, 339
Sun Microsystems, 354
surnames, 37–38
suspicious activity reporting, 149
symmetric key, 169–170
symmetric relationships, 281
system-level trust, 318
system testing, 331

T

T+1 (next-day settlement), 12
tamper-resistance, 167
team role, 208
technical metadata, 129
technical quality assurance, 331
telecommunications industry, 35
test data, 337–339
Test Management server, 341
Thailand, 37–38
third-party information sharing risk, 188
third-party trust, 168
third-party zone, 119
timeliness, 301
TLS (Transport Layer Security) Protocol, 174
transaction manager, 313–314
transaction risk, 136, 387
transactional risk, 188

Transaction-style Hub, 78
    See also Data Hubs
    definition of, 387
    implementation of, 245–246, 315–319
    loading data into, 122
Transport Layer Security Protocol (TLS), 174
Treadway Commission, 152
Trillium, 358
trojans, 173, 186
trust, 168–169, 318
trusted time source, 163
TS Discovery, 358
TS Quality, 358

U

UAN (Universal Application Network), 352
UK Financial Services Act, 55
Ukraine, 37
uniqueness, 302–303
unit testing, 330–331
Universal Application Network (UAN), 352
Universal Customer Master, 352
USA Patriot Act, 53, 142, 149–150
user adoption, 371
user provisioning, 163, 166–167
user security, 161

V

value proposition, 40
vanity addresses, 253
variance, 339
vendors, 49–50
verification, 163
VeriMove, 360
Verisign, 176
virtual private networks (VPNs), 160,
    173–174
viruses, 173
visibility, 387
VisionWare MultiVue, 356
VPNs (virtual private networks), 160,
    173–174

W

W3C (World Wide Web Consortium), 293
wealth management, 24
Web servers, 341
Web Services, 72–75
    attacks, 180
    authentication, 179
    data integrity and confidentiality,
      179–180
    definition of, 387
    identity management in, 165
    security standard, 180–181
    testing, 335–336
WebSphere Customer Center, 350–351
WebSphere ProfileStage, 350
WebSphere QualityStage, 359
WEP (Wireless Equivalent Privacy), 175
Wi-Fi Protected Access (WPA), 175
Wireless Equivalent Privacy (WEP), 175
Wireless Transport Layer Security
    (WTLS), 175
World Wide Web Consortium (W3C), 293
WPA (Wi-Fi Protected Access), 175
WS-Policy, 216
WS-Security standard, 180–181
WTLS (Wireless Transport Layer
    Security), 175

X

XACML (Extensible Access Control
    Markup Language), 216–218
XBRL (Extensible Business Reporting
    Language), 291
XRI (Extensible Resource Identifier), 216–218
XrML (Extensible Rights Markup
    Language), 199–200

Z

Zachman, John, 67–69
Zachman's Institute for Framework
    Advancement (ZIFA), 68–69